W9-CEW-123

Vietnam's Development Strategies

Taking a developmental approach, this book provides a critical analysis of Vietnam's reform process and shows how the country's reform agenda is still dominated by a 'developmental orthodoxy' inspired by a post-Washington consensus. Masina argues that a wider debate is needed to allow national policy-makers the full spectrum of alternatives with which to make well-informed policy decisions. In particular, the book indicates that two elements central to any analysis of the Vietnamese development reform process are substantially underdeveloped in the current debate: the experience of the East Asian developmental state and the question of socialism within a future market economy.

Vietnam's Development Strategies opens up the debate, to challenge the prevailing orthodoxy and to test possible alternatives for Vietnam. It is a welcome addition to the literature and will appeal to both practitioners working in the field and the academic community in Southeast Asian studies, economics and development.

Pietro P. Masina is Associate Professor of International Political Economy at the University of Naples 'The Oriental' and Secretary of the European Association for Southeast Asian Studies (EuroSEAS). He spent the previous ten years at the Roskilde University, Denmark, where he still maintains affiliation as Associate Professor on-leave. His previous publications include *Rethinking Development in East Asia: From Illusory Miracle to Economic Crisis* (RoutledgeCurzon, 2001).

Routledge Contemporary Southeast Asia Series

1. **Land Tenure, Conservation and Development in Southeast Asia**
   Peter Eaton

2. **The Politics of Indonesia–Malaysia Relations**
   One Kin, Two Nations
   Joseph Chinyong Liow

3. **Governance and Civil Society in Myanmar**
   Education, Health and Environment
   Helen James

4. **Regionalism in Post-Suharto Indonesia**
   Edited by Maribeth Erb, Priyambudi Sulistiyanto and Carole Faucher

5. **Living with Transition in Laos**
   Market Integration in Southeast Asia
   Jonathan Rigg

6. **Christianity, Islam and Nationalism in Indonesia**
   Charles E. Farhadian

7. **Violent Conflicts in Indonesia**
   Analysis, Representation, Resolution
   Edited by Charles A. Coppel

8. **Revolution, Reform and Regionalism in Southeast Asia**
   Cambodia, Laos and Vietnam
   Ronald Bruce St John

9. **The Politics of Tyranny in Singapore and Burma**
   Aristotle and the Rhetoric of Benevolent Despotism
   Stephen McCarthy

10. **Vietnam's Development Strategies**
    Pietro P. Masina

Vietnam's Development Strategies

Pietro P. Masina

LONDON AND NEW YORK

First published 2006
by Routledge
2 Park Square, Milton Park,
Abingdon, Oxon OX14 4RN

Simultaneously published in the USA and Canada
by Routledge
270 Madison Ave, New York, NY 10016

Routledge is an imprint of the Taylor & Francis Group, an informa business

Typeset in Times by Keyword Group Ltd
Printed and bound in Great Britain by TJI Digital, Padstow, Cornwall

British Library Cataloguing in Publication Data
A catalogue record for this book is available from the British Library

Library of Congress Cataloging in Publication Data
Masina, Pietro P.
Vietnam's development strategies / By Pietro P. Masina.
p. cm. – (Routledge contemporary Southeast Asia series ; 10)
Includes bibliographical references and index.
ISBN 0-415-34311-9 (hardback : alk. paper) 1. Vietnam–Economic policy.
2. Vietnam–Economic conditions. I. Title. II. Series.
HC444.M36 2006
338.9597–dc22
2005024435

ISBN10: 0-415-34311-9 (hbk)
ISBN10: 0-203-34130-9 (ebk)

ISBN13: 9-78-0-415-34311-4 (hbk)
ISBN13: 9-78-0-203-34130-8 (ebk)

Contents

Acknowledgements

The usual qualification applies: more people have helped me in this work than those I can name here. I am in debt to the numerous Vietnamese and foreign colleagues who have shared with me their time and their knowledge. My gratitude also goes to the many Vietnamese friends that, over the years, have taught me to love their beautiful country. Although this text reflects the biases and the (often misguided) perceptions of an outsider, I know that without the support of my Vietnamese friends this work would have been even more inadequate. My appreciation goes to (in no specific order): Dinh Thi Ngoc Bich, Dinh Thi Bich Thuy, Dang Dinh Long, Nguyen Thi Nguyet Que, Nguyen Thanh Ha, Nguyen Thanh Tung, Nguyen Quang Sang, Do To Khanh.

A number of research institutions and individual scholars have provided me with invaluable support. I would like to thank in particular: Bui Huy Khoat, Nguyen Quang Thuan, Centre for European Studies; Le Dinh Tien, NISTPASS; Vo Dai Luoc and Le Bo Linh, Institute for World Economy; Vu Cao Dam, Nguyen An Lich, Department of Sociology, Hanoi National University; Nguyen Thu My, Institute of Southeast Asian Studies; Nguyen Thanh Hung, Ministry of Trade; Nguyen Dinh Hoa and Bui Duc Hai, Institute of Social Sciences and Humanities, Ho Chi Minh City; Tran Ngoc Hien, Vietnam Union of Science and Technology Associations; Le Dang Doanh, MPI; Ngo Doan Vinh, Vu Van Hoa, Development Strategy Institute, MPI; Vu Tuan Anh, Vietnam's Socio-Economic Development Review; Dang Ngoc Dinh, Science and Fatherland Journal.

I would also like to acknowledge here my gratitude towards a number of non-Vietnamese scholars and friends who have helped me in various ways: Irene Nørlund, Anders Baltzer Jørgensen, Rolf Hernø, Per Ronnås, Curt Nestor, Laurids Lauridsen, Kristen Nordhaug, Katrine Plesner, Jonathan London, Jakob Lindahl, Helle Buchhave, Morten Larsen, Hanne Mogensen, Sara Rezoagli, Keinichi Ohno, Carlo Batori, Rajneesh Narula, Søren and Mette Davidsen.

A special thought goes to the late professor Enrica Collotti Pischel, whose teaching has always been a unique source of inspiration for me, as it has for several generations of Italian students of Asia.

This research would not have been possible without the moral and material support of the Department of Social Sciences, Roskilde University, which was my academic home for over 10 years. The Nordic Institute of Asian Studies graciously hosted me for 1 year and allowed me to use its excellent library. The European Commission gave me an initial grant through the TMR scheme, making it possible to start this research.

Andrew Crabtree, Mike Parnwell and Jonathan Rigg kindly accepted to be the guinea pigs for different chapters. Not only did they make constructive observations, but they also kindly helped in refining the language. Bruno Amoroso, Chris Dixon, Jaques Hersh and Jesper Jespersen made a number of valuable comments and criticisms of an earlier draft, allowing me to amend and improve the manuscript: I gratefully acknowledge the feedback I received from them. Valuable feedback was also received by two anonymous reviewers, whose detailed comments were a precious support in the final revision.

Stephanie Rogers, Helen Baker and Stephen Thompson at Routledge and Liz Steel at Keyword are kindly acknowledged for making this manuscript turn into a published volume.

My wife Cecilia only had to endure my stress during the last phases of this research, and particularly the final revision. Rather than thanking her for her support, I thank this work for the chance to meet her in Vietnam in the summer of 2002.

The book is dedicated to my parents Clotilde and Ettore Masina, who also share my love for Vietnam. From them I have learned to widen the horizon to the many dramas and the many hopes of the developing word.

Introduction

The research topic

This work is about Vietnam and its future. It is about the prospects for economic development of a large[1] and poor country of Southeast Asia. And it is about the new reality of a region for many years considered as blessed by 'miraculous' economic success and for which the experience of the regional economic crisis in 1997–8 implied a profound rethinking of its development models.

The aim of this study is to review the more controversial issues in the debate about the development strategies for Vietnam and eventually attempt a critical assessment of the *doi moi* (renovation) process. In the following pages we will claim that the function of agenda setting for the reform process is dominated by the international financial institutions along lines inspired by 'development orthodoxy'. The crack in the Washington consensus after the East Asian crisis has compelled a revision of the neoliberal discourse, which is now repackaged in a new version that could be termed a post-Washington consensus. Some policy reviews and an overall amendment to the language may convey the impression that the international financial institutions have now abandoned the development orthodoxy insisted upon in the last 20 years. This study will put in evidence the major issues in policy revision, but will suggest that the basic tenets of the post-Washington consensus are still substantially coherent with those of the previous consensus.

While the revised development orthodoxy occupies centre stage in the public policy debate, there are other two lines of enquiry that are of primary concern for an analysis of the Vietnamese reform process. The first line is represented by the development experience of other Asian countries. After the collapse of the Soviet Union, not only did Vietnam become more economically integrated with the rest of East Asia, but it was also more exposed to the interpretations of the 'East Asian miracle' promoted by Japan (and South Korea). These interpretations argued that economic growth had been achieved through state strategic guidance (the so-called 'East Asian developmental state') and, therefore, suggested a path to industrialization that was at odds with development orthodoxy. However, these strategies were still within the frame of a capitalist logic. There is, therefore, a second line of enquiry that is necessarily important for understanding the economic reforms in a socialist country like Vietnam, especially having in mind the high price that this nation paid for achieving decolonization and implementing a radical programme of political and economic socialist transformation. The question regards the possibility of furthering the socialist transition while embracing market-friendly reforms. Here, the experience from Japan, South Korea and Taiwan has little to offer to Vietnam, given the different purposes that development strategies were serving: economic growth as a modality of capitalist stabilization in Northeast Asia; economic growth as an attempt to consolidate a socialist transition in Vietnam. The main issues where potential contradictions with the proclaimed socialist ideals may emerge regard, on the one hand, how the 'open door' policy will affect the economic sovereignty and which kind of position the country will assume in the international system; on the other hand, they regard the changes within the country in terms of social (class) differentiation.

Although Vietnam is facing quite complex dilemmas in deciding upon its development strategies, the contrast between alternative views is substantially concealed in the current debate. This has also created a major obstacle in conducting our investigation. In order to let the different options emerge, we first had to make an effort in breaking the pervasive dominance of the neoliberal discourse. The following pages have been written with the main objective to claim for the need of a more open debate about the future strategies and about the past achievements of *doi moi*.

This need for a more open debate is confirmed by a certain ideological uniformity in the studies on the Vietnamese reform process. A large part of the international literature has been produced – with some notable exceptions, as we will see further – by a few agencies and a restricted number of scholars, broadly within the cultural paradigm of neoliberal thinking. The dominance of 'orthodoxy' in the studies on contemporary Vietnam would be *per se* an interesting topic to investigate. This is probably a result of the disappointment of many critical scholars with the events subsequent to the Vietnamese victory in the resistance war against the USA (i.e. the invasion of Cambodia, the hard line adopted in managing the reunification, and eventually a perceived betrayal of the socialist ideals through *doi moi*). Disaffection led many scholars to distance themselves from their previous engagement with Vietnam, or even to raise their criticisms openly [as in the well-known case of Gabriel Kolko (1997)]. In general, many of those who had supported Vietnam in the war period remain undecided in their assessment of the reform process inaugurated as *doi moi*: positively impressed by the important economic results achieved, but worried about the possible social implications. A number of scholars continued to produce non-orthodox studies, and a new wave of critical research is emerging as we write these lines. However, it is fair to admit that the scene has been largely occupied by a new generation of Western economists, who (often as consultants for international agencies) took a decisive stance in favour of furthering the transformation of the country into a fully fledged market economy. Thus, much of the literature – including that produced by 'Westernizing' Vietnamese – has the tendency to reproduce the same discourse constantly. At the same time, the Vietnamese authorities have seldom expressed views that were an open challenge to the new established orthodoxy; rather, it has been the implementation of policies to show the extent of dissent in some strategic areas.

Apart from the need not to challenge the views held by the international donors,[2] the Vietnamese leadership has faced two major obstacles in delineating a well-defined national development strategy, as we will discuss further in the following chapters. On the one hand, the reform process has been rather imposed by the events than being freely chosen. The complexity of maintaining a 'socialist orientation' while *de facto* being forced to embark on a transition towards a market economy is evident. The national tradition of reaching decisions by consensus has further complicated the task of the leadership and often led to rather hazy policy declarations. On the other hand, the international organizations [especially the World Bank and the United Nations Development Programme (UNDP)] and a small number of mainstream economists have occupied centre stage in policy research. By virtue of their overwhelming economic and intellectual resources, the international agencies and their advisers have apparently succeeded in exerting a hegemonic guidance even over those Vietnamese institutions charged with strategic planning. National independent research has lost much of its influence and local scholars have been either subsumed in internationally supported research or substantially marginalized.[3]

The national leadership seems to be trapped between the Western and Westernizing modernizers and the representatives of declining economic interests inherited from the central planning era (like many state-owned enterprises (SOEs)). The space for manoeuvre for 'alternative' economic strategies (i.e. the ability to lead the reform process on a path in line with the proclaimed socialist ideals) appears to be rather small.

One should always remember, however, that in a complex country like Vietnam the appearance might not reflect the concrete reality of life. A superficial reading of policy documents may be misleading. The line of resistance of the Vietnamese leadership against the imposition of the international financial institutions is not evident in policy declarations, but in the tough negotiation of concrete measures and a well-defended autonomy in the implementation of reforms.[4]

The dominance of neoliberal thinking in delineating the official reform agenda and the resilience of the Vietnamese leadership in the concrete implementation of reforms makes any assessment of *doi moi* very complex. Mainstream authors interpret the Vietnamese resistance simply as an inability to carry out needed measures. For these authors, the Vietnamese government is constantly responsible for 'delays' and compliance with backward interests. For non-orthodox scholars, instead, these apparent 'delays' may be the symptoms of disagreements about the measures to be taken. But in the absence of an open policy debate the analysis of the contentious issues is not easy. The query is how much the disagreements are based on an alternative vision – not officially stated but clear in the minds of policymakers – and how much they reveal the resistance of stakeholders whose particularistic interests would be adversely hit by the approved policies.

The present research suggests that the Vietnamese decision-making process is multifarious and articulated, and in many instances bottom up rather than top down or, more precisely, a complex web of vertical and horizontal relations. The representatives of different interests – provinces, ministries, and SOEs – have much leverage for influencing the decisions taken by the central administration (and even to resist the adopted decisions). The highest echelons of the party and government have more of a coordinating function than the power to emanate autocratic decisions. This is a further motivation for claiming that the logic of the Vietnamese strategy is better understood *ex post* – based on what is done in concrete terms – rather than by looking at public statements.

The analysis of concrete policy implementation, however, requires a frame for analysis, a frame that allows selection of the data to be collected and to organize the findings in a meaningful way. A frame for analysis able to depart significantly from the conventional wisdom requires that it be grounded in a different paradigm, as will be argued hereafter. We will suggest that the neoliberal paradigm has lost much of its authority owing to its failure in promoting development and economic growth. This failure is now widely recognized as a consequence of theoretical inconsistency. The debate on the East Asian economic crisis has been a major blow to the so-called Washington consensus, i.e. the strategy for economic development based on the neoliberal orthodoxy. From that debate it became evident to many that the neoliberal doctrine had been unable to explain both the long period of economic growth in East Asia and the abrupt crisis of 1997–8. Notwithstanding the hegemonic decline of the neoliberal discourse, its (adjusted) prescriptions still dominate the policy advice enforced by the international financial institutions on developing countries – as we will indicate in the case of Vietnam. A new, alternative, paradigm, able persuasively to replace the failing one, has not yet emerged. We will claim that the 'East Asian developmental state' model has contributed to the crisis of the dominant paradigm by producing evidence that could not be integrated within the existing theoretical foundations. However, that development model is strongly embedded in a particular historical and geographical context and it could not be extended to different contexts without a high level of simplification. Such simplification could lead either to implement import-substitution strategies, like those (not very successfully) applied in Latin America on the advice of structuralist economists, or to be reabsorbed into the existing paradigm (like the so-called 'new growth theory'). An alternative paradigm requires a more radical departure from the prevailing one. A major contender to development orthodoxy has been the neo-Marxist theoretical tradition connected to the 'dependency school'. This contender has been hit and marginalized by the neoliberal counter-revolution of the late 1970s, and further challenged by the collapse of the Soviet Union and the market-friendly reform process in China (and Vietnam). However, the cracking of the Washington consensus is pointing once again at the same issues that the dependency school had identified as an obstacle to economic growth. The widespread criticism of the World Trade Organization, for example, is denouncing the unequal exchange and the risks for developing countries deriving from free trade. Although international trade is widely recognized as an important stimulus for the economy, the impact of rapid trade liberalization on growth and poverty reduction is now a topic at the centre of a wide and heated debate.

Vietnam after the regional crisis

Vietnam was less hit by the regional financial meltdown of 1997–8 than many of its neighbours; but, after 1998 it faced an important deceleration of economic growth. Mainstream (neo-classical) analysts indicated that, after the recovery began in the region, Vietnam risked losing the opportunity for further growth if it did not implement bold and rapid economic reforms: privatizing SOEs, restructuring the financial sector, adopting a 'neutral' trade regime and sustaining the development of the private sector. The 'lesson' from the region was used to support this reform agenda. However, what lessons are to be learned from the regional crisis remains a controversial question. The debate on the crisis did not result in any kind of consensus in interpreting the East Asian development models [see Masina (2002a)].

Vietnam suffered an economic slowdown 1 year before the onset of the regional crisis. This was interpreted by the international financial institutions as a sign that the reform process had lost momentum and, particularly, that the trust from international investors was fading. Therefore, Hanoi was compelled to make the country more attractive to foreign investments in order to benefit from the comparative advantage of a cheap and well-educated labour force. The need for specific reforms was, and still is, undeniable, since Vietnam (like most of its neighbours) is suffering from bureaucratic inefficiencies, red tape, corruption, a faltering legal system, etc. Even more importantly, Vietnam needs reforms to address key issues in terms of policy planning: e.g. identification of priorities in industrial development, growth of a sound financial system able to support strategic investments, etc. But the criticisms directed at Vietnam tend not to give enough attention to the regional dimension. When Vietnam started to suffer from a reduction in the flow of foreign direct investments (FDIs) this was part of a wider regional trend. To place the blame exclusively on national deficiencies risks missing a crucial point. The interpretation presented in this work is that the economic slowdown in Vietnam on the eve of the East Asian crisis had roots in a regional malaise. This interpretation (presented in Chapter 3) has important implications for future development strategies.

The onset of the regional economic crisis has brought to the attention of a wider public the debate on the so-called 'East Asian miracle'. The first chapter of this work supports the view that the concept of 'developmental state' is fundamental for understanding the extraordinary economic trajectories in a number of East Asian countries. Although the experience of the 'developmental state' has been either contested or ignored by the international financial institutions and by mainstream economists, it is quite logical to assume that the Vietnamese authorities have looked at this model as a source for inspiration – and such a model has also been sponsored by Japan, the largest single source of development aid to the country. The view presented in this work is that the debate on the East Asian 'developmental state' represents an important reference for understanding the current directions of *doi moi*. The neoliberal recipes, on the one hand, and the 'developmental state', on the other hand, provide a contrasting range of possibilities and allow the Vietnamese experience to be put into a meaningful comparative perspective.

However, there are at least three major questions to take into consideration in analysing the Vietnamese case against the backdrop of Northeast Asia. First, the 'success stories' of economies like South Korea and Taiwan – with a selective combination of import substitution and export orientation – were supported by a favourable international regime (with the USA interested in promoting economic growth in non-communist East Asia). The recent financial crisis in East Asia was a result of increasing tensions in the international system about the trade regime. Therefore, it will not be easy for a 'new entry' like Vietnam to move in this increasingly hostile environment. An example of these problems is given by the negotiations between Vietnam and the USA on a trade agreement, discussed in Chapter 4.

The second question regards the sustainability of the 'developmental state' strategies. The experience of the other Asian countries has shown a depletion of natural resources and severe damage to the environment, indicating that such a model in a densely populated agricultural country like Vietnam would rapidly cause disastrous effects. Also, in terms of human development, the lessons from the region are controversial. In many areas concerning the experience of the poor, Vietnam has something to teach rather than to learn with respect to its richer neighbours.[5]

The third issue regards state capacity. A 'developmental state' model requires institutions able to carry out complex functions in terms of strategic planning and policy coordination. This has so far been a major obstacle in the attempts to emulate the East Asian models in other contexts. The adoption of a 'developmental state' perspective in Vietnam – notwithstanding a cultural proximity with other regional countries that have built their success story upon such a model – would not be easy either. That would require not only strong political will, but also a great ability in institutional reform (including a change in the mindset of the bureaucracy).

This work makes use of the 'developmental state' model to argue that, even within the prevailing international order, dominated by capitalist forces, alternatives do exist to the development orthodoxy. However, the Vietnamese 'transition' incorporates another fundamental element: an attempt to maintain a socialist aspiration while embarking on market-economy practices. The Vietnamese leadership has been wary of any sophisticated theoretical explanation to delineate how the country can avoid a *de facto* transition towards a fully-fledged capitalist market economy – something that is normally denounced in Vietnam as the danger of a 'peaceful evolution'. An analysis of the reform process must take into account this specific question in the Vietnamese development experience. This work claims that, in order to understand the possible outcomes of this complex transition, we should broaden up the analysis to a set of debates related to Marxist theories, which is officially also the theoretical background of the Vietnamese leadership. The Communist Party of Vietnam (CPV) legitimacy to lead the country rests in its key role in the national liberation movement and in the resistance against foreign aggressions. The success of economic reforms has reduced the risk that younger generations – who do not carry a direct memory of the war period – will challenge the political system until it continues to guarantee a visible improvement in living conditions. Political tension is further defused by a significant transformation in social control, especially in urban areas, giving the new affluent bourgeoisie an increasing freedom to make business, travel, purchase imported goods, consume, and in sum engage in all those activities which are not directly threatening the government and the party. The very success of these economic and social reforms, however, is due to result in new contradictions that the Communist Party will need to address. On the one hand, the new affluent bourgeoisie will eventually ask for more radical changes, including political liberalization. On the other hand, economic inequality will result in class tensions that will challenge the corporatist structure of the Vietnamese political system. These tensions are already emerging, although so far the economic reforms have benefited most of the population, even if some have benefited much more and others have only seen the opening of a window of opportunity rather than a real improvement. Eventually, these tensions will require that the political system becomes more able to handle class-related conflicts and this will require a difficult reform of the Communist Party, if it wants to remain faithful to its ideological roots.

Methodological considerations

Beliefs and valuations

This study criticizes the attempt by the development orthodoxy to impose its own views as objective and based on a superior scientific value. Such an attempt is rather typical of economic and political discourses based on neo-classical economics, whose mathematical-like laws are considered as non-disputable truths. In 1935, for example, in the preface to his *Essay on Nature and Significance of Economic Science*, Lionel Robbins claimed:

> The efforts of economists during the last hundred and fifty years have resulted in the establishment of a body of generalisations whose substantial accuracy and importance are open to question only by the ignorant or the perverse [cited in Easlea (1973: 157)].[6]

Although, as we can see, the current doctrinairism has well-established roots, the neoliberal counter-revolution has been particularly assertive in enforcing a conception of social relations based on the logic of the self-regulated market. As argued by Samir Amin (1998), the ideology of capitalism has always tended to be economic determinist, but the ‘single thought’ endorsed by neoliberalism is exceptionally adamant in relying on ‘pure economics’ as the ultimate yardstick for guiding policy decisions. Contrary to what was done by other civilizations in the past (as indicated by Karl Polanyi), capitalism has attempted to reverse the relation between politics and economics by putting economics in command and politics as a dependent variable.[7] The effort to present policy decisions as dependent on objective scientific laws has the function to conceal the ideological motivations and the interest representation that unavoidably characterize any societal organization. In the over two centuries since the first industrial revolution, this endeavour to subjugate society to the logic of 'pure economics' has been only partially successful, and conflicts (some even resulting in socialist revolutions) have constantly emerged. But since the demise of the long Fordist–Keynesian cycle, the neoliberal counter-revolution has achieved new momentum (and even more so after the collapse of the Soviet Union). We will see in the next chapter how neoliberal thinking, and its related development orthodoxy, has been actually readjusted over time. A basic feature that has not changed was the attempt to disguise the value premises and the ideological foundations of the policies it supported as motivated by objective and scientific laws.

In contesting the logic promoted by the neoliberal forces, this text will not try to oppose a different 'objective' truth. On the contrary, following the lesson of the Swedish economist Gunnar Myrdal, this study rests on the assumption that each scholar (like any other person) is necessarily influenced by 'beliefs' and 'valuations' (Myrdal 1968, 1970). These 'beliefs' and 'valuations'[8] are not only the results of personal choices, but are also influenced by the cultural and social environment in which one is embedded and the interests that one (consciously or not) tends to represent. A scholar should be aware of the ideological and cultural background that will unavoidably affect his/her own research and should not try to conceal his/her own 'beliefs' and 'valuations' in search for an objective scientific investigation. Only an honest reflection on these premises can help the scholar to reduce the risk of being involuntarily biased. Every scientific work is inevitably subjective and partisan; therefore, it is important to make the reader aware of the premises, values and purposes that have guided the scholar in his/her research. For these reasons the following pages will be used to make explicit the beliefs and valuations that are at the root of this work.

My research interest for Vietnam began in the mid 1990s. By that time, the first phase of *doi moi* was completed. Vietnam had already irreversibly moved towards a market-based economy, although the country's leadership proclaimed that this did not imply a desertion of the socialist project. The country was on a path of increasing integration into the world economy, and the political relations at regional and international level had been thoroughly reorganized. My research interest was connected (and still is) to political concerns. Was the Vietnamese transition bound to produce a reversal of the socialist finalities that had inspired its long and costly struggle for liberation and social change? The question was not (is not) 'ideological', i.e. it is not motivated by abstract motivations. On the contrary, this question was (is) very concrete: after the devastating experiences of the 'transition' in the former Soviet Union and in many of its European satellite countries, the possible costs of a similar process in Vietnam could not be ignored. Vietnam, notwithstanding over 30 years of war (and also mistakes in economic management), while still one of the poorest countries in the world, had achieved impressive results in terms of human development: life expectancy, school enrolment, literacy, healthcare services, etc. Were these achievements going to be reversed, as had happened in the former Soviet Union? The case of China indicated a more successful transition to a market economy: economic growth, poverty reduction, generalized improvement in living conditions. As is now evident after many years since the beginning of the reform process, the Vietnamese transition is more closely related to the experience of China than to that of the former Soviet Union. However, the cases of China and Vietnam do also present disquieting questions. Poverty reduction has been coupled with increased economic disparity. Economic restructuring has resulted in redundancy in SOEs at the same time when modernization of agriculture has implied a labour surplus in rural areas. Public services (like schools and healthcare), once free for all, now require the payment of fees (and, often, of even more substantial 'fees' under the table). While the transition process in Vietnam and China is still progressing and open to different possible outcomes, one can even wonder whether these countries will opt for an American *workfare* model rather than a more inclusive Western European-style welfare system. Such an outcome could, after all, be dictated by the increasing economic gaps (even more so in China than in Vietnam) between rich and poor regions and between urban and rural areas. European welfare systems face serious difficulties in managing wealth redistribution within a population whose economic level is extremely homogeneous when compared with that of China and Vietnam.

Gunnar Myrdal did not emphasize the need to clarify 'beliefs' and 'valuations' to suggest that the outcomes of a scientific research are necessarily predetermined by their premises. On the contrary, a critical reflection on these premises is essential for reducing (though obviously not completely removing) involuntary biases. Through this critical self-analysis, a student may even change his/her original beliefs and valuations.

A partial change in my beliefs and valuations did actually occur – or better, what changed was the perspective from which I learned to look at the Vietnamese reform process. This specific research is substantially concerned with the macroeconomic aspects of the reform process. However, it has constantly intertwined with other studies I have participated in, including investigations at grassroots level, about poverty in Vietnam. The findings of these poverty-related investigations are only partially included in this study, but those experiences have transformed my way of thinking.

From the perspective of a European scholar, the long-term implications of the reform process are the major concerns. At stake is the sustainability of the undeniable results in terms of poverty reduction that Vietnam has experienced since the late 1980s. An increase in economic inequality represents a major problem, as it may lead to a transformation in interests' representation in the country and to a departure from the current poverty-reduction drive. From the perspective of the Vietnamese poor, however, short-term achievements have a paramount importance because they represent (often literally) a matter of life or death. A peasant I interviewed in a village of Hung Yen province (Red River Delta) in July 2002 told me that he had accumulated huge debts with moneylenders in order to pay for the treatment of his heart disease. At the time of my interview, his wife was in a hospital in Hanoi to undertake an eye operation, and this was bound to increase the debt burden on the family (which had already forced two of the three children to search for informal jobs in the capital). When I asked if he did not prefer the time when healthcare was free, his answer confused me. He said that at that time healthcare standards were very low and he would have probably died. Better be impoverished by debts than to die. A similar perspective was presented by a widow with three teenage children in the same village. Poverty had forced the two youngest daughters to leave the school and one had become a fruit seller in Hanoi. The work of the two daughters allowed the oldest son to continue education until higher secondary school, and this was regarded by all the family as an investment for the future. The widow explained that, in the past, when schools were free of charge, the quality was low and school enrolment did not guarantee the possibility of finding a good job afterwards. There may be a number of reasons to explain these answers. In any case, they express a point of view that should be taken on board. According to an opinion poll conducted in the winter of 2002, Vietnam is the country in the world in which the population is the most optimistic about the future. My direct investigation has confirmed what is reported by a number of studies (discussed in Chapter 5): that poverty reduction has also been beneficial for many among the poorest and the most vulnerable. For example, I have had it confirmed by a large number of interviews that the living conditions of street children in Hanoi improved substantially during the 1990s (Gallina and Masina 2002).

The fact that the vast majority of the Vietnamese population seems to consider the *doi moi* favourably does not eliminate risks and reasons for concern. There are two major issues that are fundamental for Vietnam and for any other developing country. The first is the social structures and class-related interest composition within that country. A radical process of economic reform like the Vietnamese *doi moi* will obviously affect the national social structures, and this will eventually determine the direction for the furthering of the reform process. The second, related, issue regards the position of the country in the international economic system. These two issues are discussed throughout this research.

Reconnecting to a long tradition of studies inspired by Marx, this work is based on the assumption that the inclusion of developing countries into a global 'world system' (a process in which the current 'globalization' represents only a new phase) has a double (and often contradictory) nature. On the one hand, it tends to destroy traditional productive systems and to enforce a modern (capitalist) mode of production; on the other hand, it tends to establish unequal relations through which the core (the industrialized countries) exploit the periphery (Third World countries) and perpetuate a condition of dependency that can also inhibit the creation of modern capitalist forces. This issue will be discussed further in Chapter 1. Here, it is useful to underline that the integration into the wider economy may imply a significant reduction in Vietnam's economic and political autonomy. This remains a key concern for its national leadership. After the end of the Cold War, Vietnam had no alternative to the furthering of economic and political relations with its Asian neighbours and with the West. But this made more imperative the question of how the country could at the same time exploit the benefits of a wider integration into the world market economy and defend its national interests. This is not a new question, as it has been a paramount concern for economists and political leaders for centuries. This work suggests the need to look at the policies implemented by a number of East Asian countries for analysing this issue. The following chapters will discuss the specific conditions that lead to the adoption of that set of policies that has characterized the so-called East Asian developmental state and the lessons that Vietnam could learn from those experiences. This work holds that the East Asian developmental state has been an instrument of capitalist stabilization in the region and, therefore, could/should not be replicated by Vietnam. However, the 'strategic planning' underpinning that model of economic development represented a successful strategy for breaking the condition of 'dependency' imposed on developing countries and has allowed an impressive catching up. While the East Asian developmental state was successful also because it was coherent with specific geopolitical conditions, it is fair to argue that Vietnam may still benefit from studying those experiences carefully.

Research approach and choice of theories

As already suggested, the beliefs and valuations that underlay the policy advice presented to Vietnam by the international agencies are never explicit. The reform agenda is packaged as merely inspired by 'pure economics' on the one hand, and by comparative experience from development practices in the rest of the world – something on which the international agencies claim unrivalled knowledge – on the other hand. If the conceptual frame defined by this prevailing logic is accepted, then any further research can only respond to problem-solving functions, i.e. can only give answers to questions coherent with the given parameters. As argued by Robert Cox (1995), a critical theory instead has the function to challenge constituted frameworks and to create the conditions for new directions. In this sense, this work is disciplinarily related to political economy, as fittingly defined by Cox:

> Political economy ... is concerned with the historically constituted frameworks or structures within which political and economic activity takes place. It stands back from the apparent fixity of the present to ask how the existing structures came into being and how they may be changing, or how they may be induced to change. In this sense, political economy is critical theory (Cox 1995: 32).

In the following pages, I will present a number of cases in which alternative options in terms of economic policies could be taken, depending on the different models and development theories that one chooses to apply. Each of the policy decisions cannot be understood *per se*, but reflects a wider conceptual frame. While it is possible to verify whether a policy decision is coherent with the theoretical frame in which it is embedded, it is much more complex to define whether it is 'right' or 'wrong' in absolute terms. Specific policy actions, and even specific theories, cannot be understood in isolation: they form part of higher-level theoretical constructions – 'paradigms', as Thomas Kuhn called them in his groundbreaking research. A paradigm consists of a 'strong network of commitments – conceptual, theoretical, instrumental and methodological', thus permitting 'selection, evaluation, and criticism', and that it is 'the source of the methods, problem-field and standards of solution accepted by any mature scientific community at any given time' [Kuhn 1962, cited in Easlea (1973: 11)]. Kuhn confutes the positivist idea for which scientific knowledge development would be a cumulative process resulting from the empirical testing of hypotheses. On the contrary, scientific development is a discontinuous process, where revolutions (paradigm changes) occur when new discoveries cannot be adjusted within the existing paradigm (Blomström and Hettne 1984: 2–3). As long as a paradigm holds, the work of scholars will be 'normal science', which means an incremental process of theory development and a 'strenuous and devoted attempt to force nature into conceptual boxes supplied by the paradigm' [Kuhn 1962, cited in Easlea (1973: 11–12)]. But when the pieces of the jigsaw puzzle fail persistently to fit together in the way they should according to normal sciences, then there is 'paradigm crisis' which opens the way for a scientific revolution and eventually for the rise of a new paradigm.

The explanation of scientific knowledge development provided by Kuhn is obviously contested by those scholars who try to defend the 'objective' value of science and its development as a cumulative process that does not entail revolutions. This is certainly the case of the neoliberal discourse that, in order to maintain its coherence and logical strengths, must reject Kuhn and cling instead to neo-classical economics. Neo-classical economics has two specific characteristics. First, being a positivist offspring, it does not concede space to self-critical analysis and defends its scientific objectivity on the basis of mathematical-like laws. In this sense, neo-classical economics represents the cornerstone of a paradigm, which has inner coherence and strength in interpreting society (other social sciences may be adjusted to operate within this paradigm). Second, neo-classical economics is able to construct meaningful theories by reducing the complexity of society to a few fundamental laws that can then be tested through mathematical models. This simplification (the reduction of man to *homo oeconomicus*) gives explanatory power to the paradigm based on neo-classical economics, but it is an obstacle in reaching an articulated and complex understanding of the real world.

The applicability of Kuhn's theories of scientific discovery to social sciences has been widely discussed and often rejected. On the one hand, society seems to escape from any attempt to constrain its vitality within the straitjackets of universal propositions. On the other hand, differently from natural sciences, in social sciences there is not a marked distinction between the object and the subject of the study, and any investigation of society necessarily also has an impact on the society itself, thus contributing to transform the object of the investigation [see Easlea (1973: 149–154)].

To be sure, an attempt to apply to social sciences a scientific method (inspired by neo-classical economics) has been visible in different fields ranging from sociology to international relations (under the banners of *behaviouralism*). But this attempt has only partially succeeded.

Owing to the differences between social sciences and natural sciences, the rise and the fall of scientific paradigm also tends to operate in a different way. Albert O. Hirschman, for example, pointed out a major difference:

> In the natural sciences, as Thomas Kuhn has shown, the formation of a new paradigm is followed by an extended period in which the paradigm is fully accepted and the labours of 'normal science' are devoted to its verification, application, and further extension. In the social sciences, on the other hand, the enunciation of a new paradigm not only gives rise to similar sympathetic labours, but is often followed almost immediately by a persistent onslaught of qualification, criticism, and outright demolition that is very much part of normal social sciences. This situation explains the distinctive intellectual climate of the social sciences: here the confident belief in a genuine cumulative growth of knowledge, so characteristic of the natural sciences, hardly ever has a chance to arise [Hirschman 1977: 67, cited in Blomström and Hettne (1984: 3–4)].

This excerpt from Hirschman also draws attention to another major difference between natural and social sciences. In natural sciences, the diffusion of a new paradigm implies the dismissal of the previous one. This is not normally the case in social sciences: here, contending paradigms can coexist, although one may maintain for a period of time a hegemonic position. Thus, while the paradigm crisis in natural sciences is the sign of the ascendance of a competing paradigm, in social science the process of formation of new paradigms is less linear.

In a number of studies, however, the emphasis on the difference between social sciences and natural sciences seem to be related to a possible misconception of what a paradigm is, or at least what a paradigm is for Kuhn. A paradigm is neither a theory nor simply a coordinated set of theories. It rests on a *scientific ideal*, a *representation of reality*, and a *research ethic* (Andersen 1994: 21) that are above particular theories. Thus, the dismissal of one theory does not represent necessarily a paradigm crisis.

This work is confronted with three competing paradigms. Although we can claim that each of these paradigms is somehow facing a crisis (but not necessarily a terminal one), they define the field of our investigation because each of them has an influence on some important forces in the Vietnamese transition.

The first of these paradigms is, as already mentioned, the positivist/neo-classical/liberal one. Its representation of reality and its scientific ideal are easily understood from what is presented above. Its research ethic is (allegedly) based on 'pure' science and 'pure' economics. We add 'allegedly' because this paradigm has often been used to cover less 'pure' interests of capitalist forces, although this was theoretically a contradiction of the theory (but was coherent with practical purposes that the development of this paradigm was meant to serve).[9] This paradigm could be defined as an offspring of the fatal encounter between liberalism and positivism.

The second paradigm has its roots in mercantilism and political realism. International economy as an arena of conflict dominates its representation of reality. Its scientific ideal is theories that promote state power and economic development. Its research ethic is political activism to support state-led industrialization.

The set of theories stemming from this paradigm presented in this study belong to a particular subgroup: they are designed by scholars who consider necessary a strong role of the (capitalist) state in promoting industrialization as a condition for escaping underdevelopment. However, these scholars have, in general, no sympathy for the authoritarian regimes that have characterized the application of these economic strategies in East Asia, i.e. the region of more successful application of these strategies. If these scholars can be accused of political ambiguity (a criticism that can be moved also to this work), this reflects the old dilemma between revolutionaries and reformists in the assessment, for example, of the Western European welfare states and Keynesian economic policies. Although a revolutionary can be critical to the role of capitalist stabilization (an intent explicit in Keynes) that these policies obtained, they cannot neglect the improvements in the working classes' living conditions.

The third paradigm is based on Marx and on the scholarly tradition he has inspired. Here, the scientific ideal is theories that can help transforming the world, not only to studying it. Its representation of reality holds that history is shaped by the class struggles determined by the mode of production. When applied to international development studies, a Marxist approach is concerned both with conflicts within the country and between the core and the periphery. The research ethic is critical, based on the analysis of objective and subjective factors, and aiming at transforming reality.

This work mostly deals with those Marxist theories that have analysed the dependent relations existing between so-called developing countries and industrialized countries. Since in the case of East Asia – and, so far, also in the case of the Vietnamese *doi moi* – the result of integration into the world economy has been an impressive catching up rather than underdevelopment, these theories are faced with a formidable challenge. However, this apparent contradiction may be explained as an exception confirming rather than confuting the rule. These theories are important for understanding what the future can hold for the Vietnamese transition.

This work will claim that the Vietnamese reform process has been the result of two factors. One was external: the end of the Cold War compelled a reorganization of economic and political relations and eventually resulted in the 'open door' policy. The other was internal: bottom-up, 'fence-breaking' activities that in the end made the Vietnamese economy 'growing out of the plan' [as in the expression used by Naughton (1995) in his famous study on China]. Like in the case of China, the political sanctioning of the reform process came after a failed attempt of recentralization and revitalization of central planning. Although we found no convincing evidence that the launch of *doi moi* was the result of the ascendance of a national bourgeoisie or the betrayal of socialist idealities by sectors of the party leadership, the reform is bound to produce (as is already happening) a rearticulation of class-relevant dynamics. Marxist theories remain the best tools for investigating this social transformation that, although still at rather an embryonic stage, represents the most important query for the future of Vietnam.

The following chapter will be used to present the theories deriving from these three competing paradigms, and eventually we will present how our eclectic framework has been shaped for conducting this research.

Research strategy

The methodological approach adopted for this investigation reflects, on the one hand, the aims to be achieved and, on the other hand, a number of specific conditions and constraints. Ideally, the methodology is inspired by critical theory, which implies simultaneously analysing the *system,* the *lifeworld,*[10] and their reciprocal relations in shaping social conditions [see Andersen (1994)]. In the context of the present investigation, a critical approach requires not only examining the concrete evidence about the evolution of the Vietnamese reform process, but also the systemic influences that shaped the setting of this process. As in the case of other developing countries, apart from the national preconditions, the space of action for Vietnamese policymaking was influenced from the outside in two ways: in concrete and material terms, via the constraints exerted by the country's growing integration into a wider economy; in a political and theoretical way, via strong conceptual pressure on the process of agenda setting by the international agencies. The first of these two mechanisms of control is quite evident and visible. The second mechanism is subtler and, therefore, less obvious: the strength of neoliberal forces is, in fact, in the ability to present a biased policy advice as neutral. Since the aim of this investigation is not to present problem-solving solutions to specific issues, but to challenge the legitimacy of the prevailing theoretical frameworks, this work was bound to operate simultaneously at the theoretical and empirical levels. Empirical data were collected to demonstrate that, in contentious areas, different options were (are) potentially available, but only one of these options was (is) admitted for discussion by prevailing forces. The selection of data and areas of empirical investigation was guided by clearly stated theoretical questions.

The topic of this research regards the transition from a centrally planned to a market-based economy. Contrary to the experience of other 'transitional' countries, Vietnam (like China) allegedly embarked on this reform process as a way of consolidating the socialist finalities and not departing from them. The first phase of the reform process was substantially completed by the early 1990s and had as its most distinctive feature the redistribution of land from the communes to the private households. From the mid 1990s, a new phase in the Vietnamese transition began and was soon confronted with the problems related to the regional economic crisis. This second phase of *doi moi* is, in many regards, more complex than the previous one because it may lead to a complete systemic change of the socio-economic institutions. At the same time, the geopolitical and geoeconomic context has become more unstable and hardly supportive of the Vietnamese economic development drive. This work is thus dealing with an open process, whose future outcomes cannot be deterministically anticipated, but where it is becoming increasingly visible how key policy decisions may lay the foundation for a radical transformation of the economic, political and social structures. As has been claimed above, this study rests on the assumption that critical knowledge has the task not only to investigate reality *ex post*, but also to create the conditions for a change. While the responsibility for taking policy decisions about the future of Vietnam must rest in the hands of the Vietnamese themselves, a critical study can help in elucidating the different options available. This work tries to contribute to this task by using a comparative approach and presenting how other countries (especially other East Asian countries) have responded to problems similar to those that Vietnam is facing in the second phase of *doi moi*. The major references for this comparison will be: three economies from Northeast Asia (Japan, South Korea and Taiwan), where (capitalist) developmental state strategies were more systematically applied; China, which shares with Vietnam a peculiar transition towards a 'market-oriented economy with socialist characteristics'; and the rest of Southeast Asia (particularly Thailand, Indonesia and Malaysia), where, in comparison with Northeast Asia, the catching-up drive began later and developmental state practices were less systematic.

The first component of the empirical investigation centred on the analysis of official documents approved by the CPV and the Vietnamese Government, reports by the international financial institutions and other major agencies, and statistics. From these official sources it is possible to delineate the questions at the centre of the policy debate within the country and the issues on which the reform agenda promoted by the international financial institutions implies more controversial reforms. This analysis indicates that there is a rather substantial consensus in assessing the past achievements in the reform process, at least until the mid 1990s. Visible differences do exist, instead, on the path and the timing for the following steps. In particular, the international agencies have taken the lead in promoting bold measures towards a reform of the financial sector, privatization of SOEs, trade liberalization, and more space for the private sector in the national economy. From the official sources and the available statistical data it is possible to see how the international financial institutions have used a variety of tools for pushing the country towards the adoption of the measures they supported (alternatively praising and threatening, withholding loans, establishing conditionalities, directing aid to their own targets). In particular, we will show that after the regional crisis the pressure on Vietnam increased through – inconsistent and eventually contested by the events – warnings: Vietnam was going to face a financial crisis within 5 years; Vietnam was not going to recover after the regional crisis; investors were going to abandon Vietnam; etc. In Chapter 3 we will also argue that, on a very sensitive issue (i.e. FDI flows), data were presented in a way that can only be understood as serving specific political purposes.

The reading of official documents and published reports would scarcely allow understanding of the complex policy negotiation within the Vietnamese leadership and between the national leadership and the international agencies. Therefore, the investigation had to rely on a large number of interviews and private conversations with Vietnamese policymakers, officers of international agencies, scholars and colleagues, both Vietnamese and foreigners, that helped in reconstructing some of the different pieces of a difficult jigsaw. This guidance is only occasionally acknowledged in the text; in most cases, formal interviews contributed to an incremental effort in the analysis of information already available through other sources rather than unveiling unknown facts or events. They were, however, crucial in maintaining the chart route of this perilous navigation.

The attempt to put things into a meaningful perspective was also supported by continuous exchanges with Vietnamese and foreign friends, sometimes over a beer or a meal, and often through conversations that were supposedly not related to the themes of this investigation. Through several years of frequent travels to Vietnam, I have been blessed by the friendship of many Vietnamese who gave me the opportunity to see how the reform process was affecting their lives and the lives of the people around them. This contributed to making me keep my feet on the floor while trying to explore the apparently abstract macroeconomic reforms and forced me to reflect on the implications of the different measures for the concrete material life of the Vietnamese people.

Besides the analysis of official documents and formal and informal interviews, the empirical part of this research was also supported by investigations conducted in urban and rural areas, occasional consultancies that gave me access to high echelons of the Vietnamese administration and the donor community, and through my work as coordinator of an EU-financed research project on 'sustainable livelihoods in Southeast Asia'. This research project was based on comparative field studies in Laos, Thailand and Vietnam. In Vietnam, the field study involved communities in Son La (northwest), Hung Yen (Red River Delta), Soc Tran (Mekong Delta) and Tan Trieu (suburban Hanoi). The specific experience of this investigation is discussed in Chapter 5 of this work, which is dedicated to the analysis of poverty dynamics.

The empirical foundation of this work is further supported by a rather large number of secondary sources, both on Vietnam and on the regional economies. In particular, the comparative undertaking is grounded on a bulk of literature concerning the East Asian developmental state. The effort made in feeding the comparative analysis of other countries in the region into the analysis of the Vietnamese reform is quite central to this work and hopefully represents an original contribution.

In presenting this work to the public it is fair to reflect critically on the work done and particularly on the sources used to substantiate the theses supported in the text. With *ex post* wisdom, it is easy to see that many parts of this work could be changed and improved, a couple of chapters added, several parts thoroughly revised – and, of course, even more changes will appear necessary at the time of publication, once new data and analysis will probably have been made available by other authors and institutions. Yet the most serious concern remains the question of the sources. Contrary to the case of other countries, the Vietnamese reform process has scarcely produced an open and public debate, in which the positions of the different national and international agencies would become more easily understandable. Even interviews with policymakers only occasionally revealed a competition between alternative strategies; more often they pointed out questions of timing rather than direction in the reform process, although one could sense that in some areas the magic formula of 'step by step' suggested by the Vietnamese officers implied also a dissent on the path of these steps. A more open debate on the options potentially available for the furthering of the reform process would have certainly made this work easier and probably more accurate. However, the challenge of manoeuvring in these turbid waters also hints at the specific modalities in which policy negotiations are conducted in Vietnam and between this country and the international financial institutions, and it is, as such, an issue to reflect upon.

This work will claim repeatedly that the Vietnamese authorities have chosen to avoid confronting the international financial institutions with strong policy declarations and that their line of resistance could only be detected by looking at how the various measures were implemented. Vietnam, like other developing countries, was not in a position to challenge openly the powerful institutions whose loans were so important. There is, however, something more to it. Historically, the Vietnamese cultural tradition has never been particularly interested in theoretical speculation. Contrary to China, the Vietnamese intellectuals – from Confucianism up to the revolutionary leaders – have been much more concerned with the concrete praxis than with abstract theory. This fundamental pragmatism has also been a significant feature of the Vietnamese revolutionary process [see Chesneaux (1971) and also Masina (1999a)]. The Vietnamese intellectuals have made important contributions to the practical adaptation of theories to the concrete needs of the country, but have avoided engaging in highly theoretical work, both in the Confucian period and later on (Nguyen Khac Vien 1971). This essential pragmatism is something that the same Vietnamese have not only acknowledged, but also emphasized as a positive attitude (also marking their diversity from the Chinese). It is renowned that Ho Chi Minh used to say sarcastically that he had no need for writing much, because Mao Zedong had already written everything that had to be written.

In the articulated Vietnamese decision-making system, national policies are always adjusted and interpreted by the different echelons in the chain of command. Policy decisions have less authority than a foreign observer would be led to believe. In this context, theoretical policy research has a rather low status. Until the 1990s, university lecturers were only meant to teach and not to make research. The research that really matters is conducted by research centres whose prestige is proportional to their proximity to powerful ministers. The substantial policy debate is generally secluded from public scrutiny. Even when one of these scholars/policymakers accepts and gives an interview to a foreign colleague, the outcomes are normally very modest. Scholars who are more remote from the 'sun' may be more open to talk, but not particularly informed. The same difficulty also applies to scientific articles, which are normally written to present a decision already taken rather than to discuss open issues. The real discussions are conducted behind closed doors. And until the late 1990s even the state budget was regarded as a national secret. Paradoxically (or maybe not), I found that there was a more open and interesting debate in local business magazines published in English than in scientific journals published in Vietnamese.

One could mistakenly take the seclusion of the policy debate and the subordinated role of the intellectuals as a result of an authoritarian political regime. Certainly, the political structures of Vietnam are not particularly conducive to open and wide-ranging policy debate (although the role of the parliament has increased substantially since the late 1990s). But, more fundamentally, these conditions reflect centuries of cultural traditions, which have also shaped the forms of modern political structures.

The structure of the work

The interpretations on the rise and the fall of the East Asian miracle offer the opportunity to revise and update a classical debate in the study of political economy. In many regards the present discussion is rooted in the historical opposition between Adam Smith and David Ricardo versus Friedrich List, i.e. the different perspective between economists coming from the first industrial country and economists from a (nineteenth century) 'late developer' like Germany. While the English classical economists could emphasize the virtues of the 'invisible hand' and free trade, the German economist would emphasize the role of the state as the *primum mobile* of socio-economic progress (White and Wade 1988: 1). The famous work of Alexander Gerschenkron (1962) has confirmed that the process of industrialization in Western Europe actually relied on an important role of the state in promoting the development of national industry, including protection of infant industry through import tariffs. Once industrialization had been achieved, however, Western countries returned to the classical theory of free trade. Particularly, it was the USA at the end of World War II that assumed free trade as the cornerstone of its foreign policy and imposed this doctrine on its reluctant allies (Kolko and Kolko 1972).[11] The Bretton Woods agreements, and later on the Marshall Plan, linked American aid for post-war reconstruction to the acceptance of free trade and the close integration of Western European and American economies. Eventually, the same free-trade ideology came to be presented to developing countries as the only path towards industrialization and economic prosperity. Chapter 1 will discuss how, since the late 1970s, the development orthodoxy has been constantly revising and adjusting its discourse constructed around the doctrines of free trade and self-regulated markets – a constant revision that never departed from these ideological tenets.

This work supports the view that economic development in a number of East Asian countries has been achieved through a Listian-type 'developmental state'. In this sense, East Asia has been, until the recent regional economic crisis, an anomaly in the developing world, acting in contradiction to the logic supported by the forces dominating the international regime. The anomaly has been possible for two reasons: first, for a particular system of regional economic integration, based on the developmental experience of Japan; second, for the specific conditions that the Cold War (and the hot wars in Korea and Vietnam) assumed in that part of the world. With the end of Cold War motivations and the rapid growth of a new tier of countries (among which was China), the experience of East Asia was becoming too visible a contradiction within the international regime – and potentially a threat. This consideration led some scholars to argue that, behind the recent regional crisis, there was also an attempt to 'normalize' East Asia and to restore the region within the frame of the orthodox neoliberal practice.

Chapter 1 recalls the key features of the East Asian 'developmental state'. The literature on the East Asian 'developmental state' (the classical studies by Robert Wade, Gordon White, Alice Amsden, Linda Weiss, etc.) offers an important heuristic methodology, which allows analysing not only how a specific country adheres to an abstract model, but also what the country's characteristics and peculiarities are.

The same chapter also introduces the terms of the Vietnamese 'transition' by indicating that the reform process in Vietnam has been rather original – important similarities, though, do exist with the Chinese case, while the path has been substantially different from the experience of Eastern Europe.

Finally, Chapter 1 presents a critical assessment of the key concepts and theories used in this work from a Marxist standpoint.

Chapter 2 reconnects to the question of transition in more empirical terms, by presenting a historical review of the first phase of *doi moi*. Here, particular emphasis is put on the 'double nature' of the reform process in Vietnam: on the one hand, a reform process resulting from changes in policy planning as a result of external and internal constraints; on the other hand, a bottom-up process, in which national authorities have been forced to respond to 'fence-breaking' activities at the grassroots level by eventually incorporating and rationalizing these changes from below into a national frame. The interplay between state policies and 'fence-breaking' activities remains an important feature of the Vietnamese reform process, as will be suggested in the following parts of this work.

Chapter 3 looks at the impact of the regional economic crisis on Vietnam and suggests that the crisis has been used by orthodox scholars and the international financial institutions to increase their leverage on the reform process. A review of the empirical data indicates that such major indicators as the flows of FDI have been interpreted in a rather arbitrary way with the quite evident intent to push Vietnam towards bolder market-oriented reform in a moment in which *doi moi* seemed to have lost its initial thrust.

Chapter 4 brings into the investigation the more controversial issues in the policy reform debate and suggests that, behind the façade of consensus, different views may be supported by the international financial institutions and the Vietnamese authorities. The different options available to Vietnam are also discussed through a comparison with the developmental experience of other East Asian countries.

Chapter 5 tries to address a key question in the assessment of *doi moi*, i.e. the impact in terms of poverty reduction and social differentiation. Here, we will see that the picture is necessarily composite. While the country has achieved major results in terms of poverty reduction, the benefits have not been equally redistributed. Social differentiation is emerging as a major concern for a successful furthering of the economic reforms and potentially even for political stability.

Chapter 6 focuses on the debate on governance – one of the most controversial issues not only in the Vietnamese debate, but also more generally in the post-Washington consensus – and suggests that the East Asian 'developmental states' have relied on a specific fix of government guidance due to particular political contexts. This chapter argues that the question of governance and institutional reform cannot (should not) be separated from an analysis of class-relevant interests and political objectives – contrary to the current attempt to look at governance as a technicality.

1 Reflection on the analytical tools

The purpose of this chapter is to present the main theories and concepts upon which the research has been built. We have already argued that mainstream studies are seldom explicit about their own theoretical foundations – by definition, mainstream views are perceived as based on common sense. A critical research instead must begin with a clarification of the analytical tools in order to make it possible for the reader to understand (and eventually criticize) the logic behind the research process.

We should underline that, in presenting different views regarding the nature of economic development, we should not expect to see a linear process for which new theories incrementally adjust and correct older ones. Recalling again the lesson of Thomas Kuhn, a cumulative process of theory revision and adjustment can only occur within the same paradigm. Theories embedded in different paradigms cannot be confronted or confuted, and not even empirical evidence allows one to ascertain an indisputable truth, because no consensus can be established on the choice of the evidences and on their interpretation. As Kuhn reminded, the transition from a paradigm to another is 'a transition between incommensurables' (Easlea 1973: 15). The effect of trade liberalization on industrialization and economic growth is a classical example of how economists relying on contrasting scientific paradigms cannot find a conclusive agreement, notwithstanding the empirical evidence accumulated in over two centuries.

Four sets of debates are presented in this chapter. The first is the very definition of 'orthodoxy' in development practice and its evolution over time. Since this work aims at breaking the aura of 'superior scientific truth' held by neoliberalism, there is a need to start by looking at the discourse that we intend to challenge. Within the lineage of neoliberal orthodoxy there are important changes that can be traced, reflecting the attempt by the core of neoliberal orthodoxy to maintain hegemony by continuously readjusting its discourse.

Notwithstanding the many attempts to reshuffle and reinvigorate its tenets, the orthodoxy has not been able to come to terms with a key feature of East Asia economic growth: the so-called 'developmental state'. Mainstream academia and the international financial institutions have actually tried (unsuccessfully, in our opinion) to use the Asian economic crisis to rule out the 'developmental state' as a form of undesirable 'crony capitalism' (see Masina 2002a). In contrast with mainstream interpretations, this work holds that the historical experience of economies such as South Korea and Taiwan (experiences that Vietnam has been trying to emulate) cannot be really understood without referring to the 'developmental state' concept. Thus, the second debate presented in the chapter regards the 'developmental state', and in particular its East Asian version.

The third discussion analysed in the following pages focuses on the concept of 'transition'. Although there is a general consensus in defining Vietnam as a country in transition from a centrally planned to market economy, what is precisely meant by such a statement is often unclear. There are reasons to argue that the Vietnamese case is, in many regards, distant from the experience of the former Soviet Union and Eastern Europe, and rather more similar to the Chinese case. This implies that the use of the term 'transition' should be handled with care in order not to generate misunderstandings. This issue is considered theoretically in the following pages, and illustrated on the basis of the concrete Vietnamese historical experience in Chapter 2.

The fourth element in this chapter will be an attempt to reflect critically on the challenge brought by the 'East Asian developmental state' and by the Chinese and Vietnamese transition to the Marxist scholarly tradition. This reflection will allow a deepening of the analysis of the major theories and concepts used in this study.

Orthodoxy and economic development in East Asia

The first element in the theoretical background of this work is a critical review of the so-called 'Washington consensus' or 'orthodoxy' in development thinking. This neoliberal 'consensus' was the result of what John Toye [1993 (1987)] has described as a 'counter-revolution in development theory and practice' interpreted by a group of professional economists during the late 1970s and early 1980s. Within this 'counter-revolutionary' group, differences did exist on certain issues. However:

> they are united in opposition to Keynes and neo-Keynesianism, 'structuralist' theories of development and the use of economic planning for development purposes. On the positive side, they are united by the belief that the problems of economic development can only be solved by an economic system with freely operating markets and a government that undertakes a minimum of functions [Toye 1993 (1987): vii].

This 'counter-revolution' in the development discourse was parallel and connected to the emergence of neoliberal governments (e.g. Thatcher in the UK and Reagan in the USA). The ascendancy of the neoliberal narrative stemmed from the impasse of the previous regime: in the 1970s, economic stagnation, inflation, unemployment, and international financial instability brought to an end a period of growth and prosperity. The first oil shock in 1973 was the event that actually concluded this Golden Age, as the historian Eric Hobsbawm (1994) called it, which had lasted since the end of World War II. The economic crisis resulted in the rise of a new hegemonic thinking. Post-Keynesian economics was overturned by advocates of monetarist policies. Neoliberalism became the doctrine to inspire not only policies in the Western world, but also the development discourse at large.

The paradigm 'shift' was symbolically represented by a change at the helm of the World Bank, the organization which – because of its 'unrivalled budget for research and policy-formulation capacity in comparison to any other development organisation' (Berger and Beeson 1998: 492) – had the largest influence in setting the agenda in the development debate. Berger and Beeson (1998: 490–491) document how the transition from the presidency of McNamara to the presidency of Tom Clausen in 1981 represented a clear shift in the bank's priorities and a 'devout commitment to neoliberalism', which was particularly strong in the new head of the research department, Anne Krueger.[1] This change had immediate implications for the developing world:

> While financial assistance to governments of developing countries had been used in the past as 'a substitute for structural adjustment', it was increasingly used to 'support structural adjustment'. Thus the changing international context allowed the Bank to use structural adjustment loans to lock recipient governments into a particular sort of politico-economic order, one that reflected both interests and assumption of its major sponsors (Berger and Beeson 1998: 489).

The early 1980s was the period when the neoliberal propositions were expressed in the most straightforward manner. Already by the second part of the 1980s the discourse was readjusted in order to reinforce the consensus around the core elements of the orthodoxy. The accent shifted to the need for 'market-friendly' policies, rather than complete *laissez faire*.[2] This shift also implied a reassessment of the role of government in development. The concept of *good governance* was introduced, to replace the less defendable idea of minimum government intervention; however, 'governance', as was confirmed in a 1997 report, was conceived as a technical feature, which concealed the political dimension of state initiatives (Dixon 2002).

The process of continuous readjustment of the neoliberal discourse on development was a direct consequence of the need to defend the orthodoxy from increasing criticisms. The failure of structural adjustment programmes in sub-Saharan Africa, for instance, exposed the World Bank and her 'sister organization' (the IMF) to the accusation of actually having aggravated the economic conditions of those countries (e.g. Mosley *et al.* 1991; George and Sabelli 1994).

The 1990s saw the first wave of neoliberal *cold-warriors* (e.g. Thatcher and Reagan) replaced by a new generation of political leaders (e.g. Clinton, and later on Blair) who attempted to build consensus on a new blend of reformed neoliberal discourse as the core ideology of the post-Cold War age. This was also reflected in the readjustment of the development orthodoxy, as announced in 1991 by a new World Bank president, Lewis Preston. He declared at a World Bank–IMF meeting in Bangkok, that:

> the demise of the Soviet Union Bloc had led to 'the broad convergence of development thinking which has replaced ideological conflict', while a consensus based on the free-market, a balance between the private sector and government and sustainable economic growth was spreading around the globe (Berger and Beeson 1998: 492).

This long experience in remaking the official development narrative, adapting to the changing conditions, also explains the World Bank policy (and the views of some previously 'orthodox' scholars, like Jeffrey Sachs) during and after the East Asian economic crisis. The dramatic events of this crisis exposed, like never before, the 'Washington consensus' to the critical scrutiny of a wide international audience. The failure of the IMF in anticipating the financial meltdown and in responding adequately to the crisis after its outbreak became the symbol of a 'cracking of the Washington consensus' (Bullard 2002). However, the public criticism of the 'Washington consensus' from the same core of its orthodoxy does confirm the traditional attitude to attempt to renovate the neoliberal discourse without a consistent change of paradigm (Masina 2002a).[3] The resignation of the IMF Acting Manager Michel Camdessus – whose unfortunate posture during the signature of a bailout package with the Indonesian President Suharto was interpreted by many Asians as the very symbol of Western arrogance – further supported the idea of an attempt to move towards a new 'consensus' (the so-called 'post-Washington consensus) in development. Probably, the fault of Camdessus had been to have remained the prisoner of superseded doctrinaire positions, thus making his and the IMF position indefensible.

At the core of the neoliberal effort to maintain the orthodoxy in development theory in the midst of the Asian crisis, one central element can be recognized: the attempt to discredit the so-called East Asian 'developmental state' as a viable model for economic growth. Somehow, the 'orthodoxy' has tried to vindicate the failure in incorporating the development experience of countries such as Taiwan and South Korea within the neoliberal explanatory paradigm.[4] Thus, the accusation of 'crony capitalism' was deployed against these countries to indicate that their economic success was impaired by distortions, eventually causing the financial crisis.

The interpretation of economic growth in East Asia had probably already been the most complex battlefield for the development orthodoxy during the 1990s. Since the late 1980s, for example, the World Bank was increasingly under pressure both from Japan and from a group of 'statist'[5] scholars, whose alternative explanation of the development trajectories in East Asian countries had received wide attention. The famous 1993 World Bank study on the 'East Asian Miracle' was requested (and financed) by Japan, which was increasingly assertive in trying to see recognized its own development model as a strategy for the region. This report reached a line of compromise in declaring that a group of high-performing Asian economies had achieved economic growth by 'getting the basics right', i.e. by recognizing the role of government in broader terms while avoiding market distortions by 'getting the price right' (Masina 2002a).

The 1993 World Bank report could not compromise too much with the views articulated by the 'statist' scholars. In fact, these scholars (who were inspired by Keynes, although in a broad sense[6]) presented an explanation of economic growth in East Asia which was an irreducible threat to the neoliberal orthodoxy. In a number of well-documented studies on Japan (Johnson 1982), South Korea (Amsden 1989), Taiwan (Wade 1990), and more widely (White 1988), they emphasized the role of the state in promoting development and governing the market.

The orthodoxy represented by the World Bank had either supported the view that these countries were free from 'distortions' represented by state interventions, or even that state interventions had been used to remove 'distortions', i.e. in order to let the market 'get the prices right' (Berger and Beeson 1998; Dixon 2002). On the other side of the debate, the 'statist' scholars claimed that these countries had achieved industrialization and high growth *because* of selective state interventions, e.g. by channelling financial resources through public banks to strategic industrial sectors.[7] Not only had growth been achieved without 'free-market' policies, but also growth was achieved through policies that intentionally altered the market allocation of resources and supported long-term industrial strategies. To use the famous expression of Alice Amsden (1989: 139–155; 1994: 630–631), these countries succeeded because they 'got the prices wrong' in agency terms (i.e. the World Bank terms).

As is quite clear, this interpretation of economic development in East Asia could not be integrated within any readjustment of the neoliberal orthodoxy. Therefore, the validity of a state-led development model had to be denied. The attempt to confute the 'developmental state' was also visible in Vietnam, where the key international agencies (i.e. the World Bank, IMF, Asian Development Bank and UNDP) carefully presented the experience from the region in terms coherent with the orthodoxy. For instance, in October 1997 (when the region was already in the midst of financial crisis) a World Bank report pointed out to Vietnam good examples from other Southeast Asian countries, which had 'particular relevance given some of the initial similarities between their economies and the Vietnamese economy.' These countries – among which the success story of Indonesia (*sic*!) – were praised because of their emphasis on labour-intensive industry and significant investment in agriculture and rural development:

> This emphasis on agriculture and rural development was important in sustaining the growth outcomes, and also in promoting greater equity with growth. Market friendly policies that removed distortions in the economy, and allowed resources to be allocated more efficiently to high-yielding investments and to activities in which these economies could compete internationally, played a key role in this success (World Bank 1997a: 25).

A few months later, however, the lesson presented to Vietnam had changed. A UNDP Staff Report published in June 1998 specifically to indicate to Vietnam the lesson to be learned from the crisis, insisted on blaming *poor governance* as the culprit, and suggested that market failure was actually produced by *government failure* (UNDP 1998: 2). This apparent schizophrenia is not the result of a substantial disagreement between the two agencies. It revealed the attempt to defend the orthodoxy in an emergency situation. However, it resulted in embarrassing contradictions between the discourses of the different agencies – most visible was the endeavour by the World Bank to distance itself from the hard-core IMF views about the regional crisis (see Bullard (2002)) – or even a turnabout in the declarations of the same agencies.

The East Asian developmental state model

This work is concerned with a specific variant of the 'developmental state', i.e. the complex of growth strategies and institutional arrangements experimented with in East Asia – particularly by Japan first, and by Taiwan and South Korea later on. An 'East Asian developmental state' model can be identified a posteriori by reflecting on the peculiar historical experiences of these countries. The striking economic results achieved in the region make the attempt to investigate the existence of a specific growth model, and to verify the conditions of its replicability within and outside East Asia, an important task in development research.

For the sake of clarity, before entering the discussion about the 'East Asian developmental state' model, it is useful to anticipate two remarks. The first is about the use of the 'developmental state' notion in a wider context, i.e. outside the specific case of East Asia. As noted by Gordon White (1993), the process of state building in the post-war era of decolonization has been intrinsically connected to the notion of development.

'Development' has come to mean a process whereby socio-economic change, rather than evolving through some 'spontaneous' dynamic, can be organized and promoted consciously by some organizing and directing agent; and that agent *par excellence* is the state. The 'developmental state', therefore, is a state which sets out to promote national development by means of an institutionalized pattern of policy intervention guided by some kind of 'plan' or strategic conception, and plays a central role in that process (White 1993: 4).

The label 'developmental state' has been used to refer to a wide variety of cases (especially, but not exclusively, in the developing world) where the role of the state as an agent of economic development was given paramount importance. Notwithstanding their respective differences, these 'developmental states' can be grouped together on the grounds of their divergence not only from traditional liberal *laissez-faire*, but also from the Keynesian managerial state (White 1993: 5).

A very broad and encompassing definition, however, risks making the use of the term 'developmental state' rather ambiguous and useless. On the one hand, the solutions adopted by states in promoting national development have been dissimilar and often divergent. On the other hand, in many cases the rhetoric of development has been used to conceal the support granted to the short-term interests of 'rent-seekers', i.e. a blatant reversal of the 'developmental state' rationale.

The developmental experience of Northeast Asia (and, to a certain degree, also of Southeast Asia) can be contrasted with the experience of other regions like South Asia or Latin America [see Masina (2002a)]. The same issue of corruption, which has occupied a central place in the post-crisis debate, indicates the existence of differences rather than similarities between East Asia and other regions [Putzel (2002), also referring to Mushtaq Khan (2000), introduces a distinction between 'growth enhancing corruption' and 'growth hindering corruption', suggesting that in Northeast Asia a certain level of corruption was functional to accelerated industrialization, while in Southeast Asia corruption also supported rent-seeking behaviours]. This work will not pursue a definition of a general 'developmental state' model, but will search for a much more specific and historically contextual explanation of the 'East Asian developmental state'. Reference to the developmental experiences of other regions, and to their relevant interpretations, will be made only to illustrate specific issues on which comparison can shed more light, either by emphasizing differences or by suggesting similarities.

A second remark should be added when dealing with a socialist country like Vietnam. Within the broad family of 'developmental states' can be distinguished two breeds. Both breeds underline the role of the state in promoting economic growth through planning and government intervention; but one remains within the lineage of the capitalist regime, while the other identifies state guidance as a leverage for socialist transformation. 'State capitalism' and 'state socialism' have long been competing models within East Asia, where China, North Korea and Vietnam have represented examples of socialist 'developmental states' (White 1988, 1993). In the next pages, however, the term developmental state will be used only to identify the specific capitalist variant experimented with in Japan, Taiwan and South Korea (and later, although not always coherently, by some of the Southeast Asian countries). In adopting strategies of radical economic reform, both China and Vietnam have looked for inspiration at the developmental experience of their more economically advanced neighbours. The East Asian developmental state model has been perceived as a solution for reinvigorating the national economy, including granting more autonomy to market institutions, without dismantling state control on the overall direction and finality of societal transformation. By renouncing to key elements of the 'state socialist' model, China and Vietnam have *de facto* moved closer to the developmental trajectory of their neighbours. Nevertheless, the ultimate results of the process of transition in China and Vietnam cannot be easily predicted. The possibility of successfully picking and choosing elements of 'state capitalism' and fitting them within a strategy of 'market socialism' is clearly a complex endeavour, which might lead to an erosion of the socialist aspirations. In the case of Vietnam, although the national authorities firmly reject any hint that the country may gradually be converted into a capitalist state (condemning this outcome as so-called 'peaceful evolution' attempted by inimical Western forces), this work suggests that the experience of East Asian 'state capitalism' seems to exert a strong power of attraction (and this is even more visible in China). Socialist ideals may be replaced by nationalism as a tool for mass-mobilization and for reinforcing a national identity.

Developmental state versus self-regulated market

Research about the East Asian developmental state has its roots grounded in a wider and older scholarly tradition focusing on the role of the state in promoting economic growth (and, hence, also national power). Owing to these explicit linkages, 'statist' scholars (i.e. scholars that put the emphasis on the role of the state) have been defined as 'neo-mercantilist' (or even 'realist', in the language of international relations theorists). For these scholars, international economic relations are essentially a zero-sum game, where national states must guard and defend their interests. Economic power is intended as a condition for state survival, and economic development is a key element in the process of state building.[8] The historical lineage can be traced from contemporary research on Asia to scholars of the nineteenth century whose work was inspired by the need to promote economic development and state power in 'late-comers' such as Germany and the USA. The work of Friedrich List, in particular (with its distinction between 'cosmopolitical political economy' – i.e. based on free trade and reflecting the interests of Great Britain as the first industrial power – versus 'national political economy' – i.e. defending a national economic space where 'late developers' can nurture their infant industry), still exerts a great deal of influence.

Against the backdrop of this wider scholarly tradition, research on East Asia has attained in recent years a high status and autonomy of its own. This was due to the impressive economic performance of a number of East Asian countries, and the appeal that their success exerted on the developing world at large. Thus, the contention about an alleged 'East Asian development model' has achieved a keynote position in recent development economics and political economy research.

At the same time, the growth of a rather autonomous debate on the 'East Asian developmental state' has also reflected a tendency in social sciences to move from a search for universal laws to more contextual analysis. Therefore, the research on the East Asian developmental state has taken into account country- and region-specific conditions in terms of history, international relations, social structures, culture, etc.[9] This attention to the local specific context also advises against any easy generalization on a *regional* 'East Asian' development model.

To a large extent, the study of the so-called East Asian developmental state remains an attempt to analyse how other countries have measured up to the Japanese model. The very special position of Japan in the region should be kept in mind when discussing how the East Asian countries have come to forge their development strategies. First of all, Japan is the only non-Western country so far to succeed in reaching the same economic standing of the most advanced industrial nations.[10] This success has obviously invited emulation by neighbouring countries. Second, as a colonial power, Japan has had a very strong influence in shaping the economic institutions of its former colonies, i.e. South Korea and Taiwan – the two economies which are most similar to the Japanese developmental experience.[11] Third, the economic dominance of Japan on the region has had a major impact on the other countries. The tendency of Japan to organize its productive system in a regional dimension is something that was not halted after the notorious war-period's attempt to establish a so-called 'co-prosperity area'. Rather, in the post-war era the integration of the region within the frame of the characteristic Japanese subcontracting system has increased steadily, with major implications for the industrial development of many Asian countries. FDIs and development aid have been powerful channels for promoting the Japanese developmental model.[12]

It is normal to trace the origin of the East Asian developmental state studies to the pioneering work by Chalmers Johnson (1982) on *MITI and the Japanese Miracle*. Johnson's research suggested that the Japanese system of political economy could be understood not (or at least not simply) in terms of cultural traditions, but more basically by looking at the specific historical events that the country had been facing. The Japanese model of top-down and centrally planned industrialization had developed in order to cope with an international order dominated by Western nations. The experience of war (beginning with the Japanese occupation of Manchuria) had contributed to shape particular political institutions where economic planning was functional to military purposes. Social mobilization through militant nationalism, however, was maintained after World War II, making possible the continuance of centralized bureaucratic control of industrial development. The Ministry of International Trade and Industry could be considered not only as a key institution in this bureaucratic coordination of the industrial building up through aggressive trade policy, but also as a symbol of the Japanese characteristic developmental model.

The volume by Chalmers Johnson had a significant impact, especially in the Anglo-Saxon scientific community: on the one hand, stimulating a new line of research; on the other hand, provoking rejections and attempts to rebuff its core thesis.[13] The fact that many scholars would try to deny that economic success can derive from industrial policy and economic planning is not surprising. Economic 'orthodoxy' has constantly opposed such propositions and even tried to vindicate its shattering wisdom about the Asian experience during the regional crisis (Masina 2002a). Other scholars, however, have built upon Johnson's work, trying to reach a deeper understanding of the developmental model adopted by Japan, and later by South Korea and Taiwan. Among these scholars, probably the most influential has been Robert Wade (1990), with his *Governing the Market*.

While crediting Johnson for his path-setting research, Wade criticizes the failure to elaborate a rigorous theory. According to Wade, the 'picture of centralised state interacting with the private sector from a position of pre-eminence so as to secure development objectives' is not sufficient to delineate a coherent theory:

> Its specification of institutional arrangements is descriptive rather than comparative–analytic, so what the developmental state is contrasted with is not clear. It also says little about the nature of policies and their impact on industrial performance. Indeed, Johnson's institutional arrangements are for the most part as consistent with simulated free market policies as with more directive ones (Wade 1990: 27).

Thus, Wade feels the need to move one step further:

> I now propose a 'governed market' theory which builds on both the idea of the developmental state and on the older development economics' understanding of the nature of the development problem (Wade 1990: 27).

The interpretation supported by Robert Wade focuses on the role of government in guiding the market towards specific purposes, i.e. economic development. This role of the state was made possible by the corporatist and authoritarian regimes existing in East Asia – corporatist and authoritarian regimes that were motivated to discourage rent-seeking activities and to promote economic growth by both national and international constraints [see also Putzel (2002)].

Like other development economists, Wade identifies capital accumulation 'as the principal general force for growth'. But the importance of his *governed market theory* is the emphasis on the specific modalities in which capital accumulation took place in East Asia and was transformed in a powerful engine for growth. The superior performance of East Asian countries is considered as

> the result of a level and composition of investment different from what Free Market and Simulated Free Market theories would have produced, and different, too, from what 'interventionist' economic policies pursued by many other LDCs [least-developed countries] would have produced. Government policies deliberately got some prices 'wrong', so as to change the signals to which decentralised market agents responded, and also used nonprice means to alter the behaviour of market agents. The resulting high level of investment generated fast turnover of machinery, and hence fast transfer of newer technology into actual production (Wade 1990: 29).

The developmental state model suggested by Wade is based on a strong state, with the power and the political autonomy (i.e. insulation from particularistic interests) to enforce national strategies. This 'strong version' of the developmental state is synthesized by Laurids Lauridsen (1995) as a system where the 'visible hand' of the state stimulates and pushes economic development:

- by stimulating very high levels of productive investments, making for fast transfer of newer technology into actual production;
- by directing more investment in certain key industries than would have occurred without state intervention;
- by spreading and socializing investment risks;
- by taming the international market forces to domestic needs;
- by stimulating the 'animal spirits' of investors through 'state created rents';
- by imposing discipline on the private business sector through specified performance requirements;
- and by exposing many industries to international competition in foreign markets if not at home (Lauridsen 1995: 26).[14]

In the same lineage of 'strong' developmental state interpretations can be included another influential author: the MIT professor Alice Amsden. While Wade's *Governing the Market* was based on the study of the Taiwanese experience, Amsden's (1989) *Asia's Next Giant: South Korea and Late Industrialisation* is (as is clear from the title) a study of South Korea (both studies are, however, also rooted in solid comparative analysis). The research by Amsden is, in some ways, an even more ambitious attempt (and, thus, is also more problematic) in so far as it attempts to identify general patterns that could be adapted also to different regions. In Amsden's *Asia's Next Giant* the focus is on the specific characteristics of contemporary late industrialization, which require state interventions different in nature and extension from those of the past:

> The subsidy serves as a symbol of late industrialisation, not just in Korea and Taiwan, but also in Japan, the Latin American countries, and so on. The First Industrial Revolution was built on *laissez-faire*, the Second on infantry industry protection. In late industrialisation, the foundation is the subsidy – which includes both protection and financial incentives. The allocation of subsidies has rendered the government not merely a banker, as Gerschenkron (1962) conceived it, but an entrepreneur, using the subsidy to decide what, when, and whereby relative prices are determined (Amsden 1989: 143–144).

Along the same line of research is also Amsden's more recent work (Amsden 2001), where she defines an analytical framework for understanding the process of industrialization in a wide range of countries: 'the Rest' – distinct from the first group of developers, but also from 'the Other' less-successful developing nations. The focus is on the conditions that made possible this group of successful late developers to build their economic development upon learning from the more industrial advanced countries and to apply this acquired knowledge to their developmental purposes. Amsden identifies these conditions in the existence of an innovative 'control mechanism' able to compensate for the skills deficit:

> A control mechanism is a set of institutions that imposes discipline on economic behaviour. The control mechanism of 'the rest' revolved around the principle of *reciprocity*. Subsidies ('intermediate assets') were allocated to make manufacturing profitable – to facilitate the flow of resources from primary product assets to knowledge-based assets – but did not become give-aways. Recipients of intermediate assets were subjected to *monitorable performance standards that were redistributive in nature and results-oriented*. The reciprocal control mechanism of 'the rest' thus transformed the inefficiency and venality associated with government intervention into collective good, just as the 'invisible hand' of the North Atlantic's market-driven control mechanism transformed the chaos and selfishness of market forces into general well-being [Mandeville 1714 (reprint 1924)]. The reciprocal control mechanism of the North Atlantic minimized market failure. The

> reciprocal control mechanism of 'the rest' minimized government failure (Amsden 2001).[15]

According to these 'strong' interpretations, the East Asian developmental state is based on strategic industrial and trade policies, which can be defined as consisting of four elements, i.e. selectivity, flexibility, coherence and competitive orientation:

> *Selectivity*, in that the state creates progressively shifting competitive advantages instead of just adapting to existing comparative advantages. *Flexibility*, in the sense that adaptation to the shifting international economic conjunctures and the shifting 'windows of opportunity' in the world market requires a high degree of flexibility. *Coherence*, in that the different policies must be part of an overall cumulative and co-ordinated policy. *Competitiveness*, in the sense that policy intervention must be oriented towards development of a competitive production in (predominantly) private enterprises (Lauridsen 1995: 26–27).

These path-setting definitions, based on a binding set of conditions, help in clarifying some aspects of the East Asian developmental model, but necessarily present new questions. And this is even more so when this research tries to verify how the experience of successful neighbours can be a source of inspiration for the Vietnamese development strategy. The first questions regard the nature of the state charged with such formidable tasks. Is the condition of authoritarianism and corporatism a necessity for enforcing a coherent developmental strategy? What about the representation of interests within the country? And how strong (in terms of state capacity) must a government be to carry out these complex developmental tasks? These issues are addressed in the following section (and further in Chapter 5). The second group of questions (discussed in the last section of this part) regard, instead, the viability of developmental state policies in the post-Cold War (and post-East Asian economic crisis) context.

State–business (capital) relations and the role of bureaucracy

The nature of the state (interests' representation, role of bureaucracy, relations between business and government, etc.) has been at the centre of the recent debate on the developmental state model. The question at stake is how the state can maintain a high degree of autonomy (necessary so that it does not succumb to particularistic interests) while having enough connections with the business world to perform well-oriented coordination functions. New studies have emerged that emphasize not the coercive strength of the state authority, but the capacity of bureaucracy to govern the process of economic development through coordination and consensus.

The interest regarding these studies in the framework of the present research is twofold:

- First, the (unquestionable) historical linkage between authoritarianism and developmental state practices in Northeast Asia (Japan, South Korea and Taiwan) (if confirmed as a *conditio sine qua non*) would confine the adoption of such a model to specific geopolitical conditions and to an age already terminated. Nor would this work like to suggest the need to introduce a fascist-like corporatist regime in Vietnam (or elsewhere) in order to achieve economic development.
- Second, a 'strong' state (especially if authoritarianism is ruled out) able to exert its coercive command over business without activating a powerful reaction internally and internationally is something rare in the developing world. Coordination is still a complex task (very complex for a country like Vietnam, as we will discuss in Chapter 5), but somehow more plausible.

Among the scholars that have attempted to reopen a space of action for a 'softer' kind of developmental state, by conjugating state autonomy with embeddedness, are Peter Evans (1989, 1995) and Linda Weiss (1995, 1998, 2000).

Evans has defined this apparently contradictory position of the state versus the business as 'embedded autonomy'. Embedded autonomy operates through a fusion of bureaucratic insulation from particularistic societal pressure and networks of concrete social ties 'that link the state intimately and aggressively to particular social groups with whom the state shares a joint project of transformation' (Evans 1995: 59).

Linda Weiss has embarked on an attempt to define a new theory, which takes the initial steps from Wade's *governed market*, but changes to *governed interdependence*. Looking at Wade's strategic industrial policies, Weiss suggests that:

> what makes the policies so effective is a particular kind of state structure and a particular kind of relationship between state and industry. I call this institutional arrangement 'governed interdependence'. It describes a system of central coordination based on the cooperation of government and industry. Policies for this or that industry, sectors, or technology are not simply imposed by bureaucrats or politicians. They are the results of regular and extensive consultation and coordination with the private sector (Weiss 1995: 594).

'Governed interdependence' rests on a 'distinctive kind of government–business relations' where 'coordination and cooperation go hand in hand'.

> Economic projects are advanced by public–private cooperation, but their adoption and implementation are disciplined and monitored by the state. The claim is not that existing accounts ignore the existence of 'cooperation' in East Asia government–business relations… Rather, the problem is that they are unable to integrate the reality and idea of public–private cooperation into a theory of state capacity… (Weiss 1995: 591).

The stress on state capacity (versus an abstract notion of 'governance') is a very important analytical contribution provided by Linda Weiss. We have already recalled that the concept of governance was developed by the neoliberal orthodoxy when it became evident that there was a need to delineate the functions of the state in regulating the economy, after the ideological contemplation of minimum state intervention. However, the notion of governance is intentionally focusing on efficiency and transparency without any consideration given to the question of *which kinds of institution should be developed in order to accomplish which purposes*. The attempt by Linda Weiss to delineate a theory of state capacity, instead, illustrates how institutions are functional to specific political agendas and, in turn, specific institutions shape particular kinds of economic (and social) development.

By studying the experience of Northeast Asia, Linda Weiss indicates that the capacity of a state to implement policies consistent with developmental and growth-oriented goals depends on a number of conditions, including a competent and committed bureaucracy and insulation against special interest groups.

> Three main features of the East Asian state's internal organisation are relevant in this regard: the quality and prestige of the economic bureaucrats; a strong in-house capacity for information gathering; and the appointment of a key agency charged with the task of policy coordination. These conditions are significant in so far as they contribute to the *insulation* or autonomy of the bureaucracy, thereby preserving policymaking from domination by special interests and other growth-retarding pressures (Weiss 1995: 596).

In Chapter 5 we will return to these three characteristics by discussing the Vietnamese case in view of the developmental experience in the region. Insulation from particularistic interests (especially those represented by the management of the SOEs, who have easy access to the higher echelons of political and administrative power) represents, for Vietnam, a powerful obstacle to any attempt to institute strategic industrial and trade policy.

Developmental state in the post-Cold War era

Among the arguments presented to contrast the 'developmental state' as a model for other countries aiming to follow the path of the first 'Asian tigers', there are two (interrelated) assertions that require some scrutiny. One of these arguments looks at the international conditions for the viability of a developmental state, and the second focuses on the internal conditions.

The first argument is that the scope for state interventions in guiding the development of a national economy is constrained by the growing internationalization of the world economy and by the rules characterizing this process (deregulation, privatization, liberalization, etc.). Explained in different terms, the Cold War regime had been supportive to those state interventions which were functional to

Western geopolitical interests (e.g. the USA supported Taiwan and South Korea building up through economic practices that were at odds with the free-market principles enforced on other, less strategic developing countries). But in the era of globalization there is no space for initiatives that contradict the neoliberal order.

The second argument is that the 'developmental state' can be conceived as a mechanism for promoting a first wave of industrialization, but not for achieving higher levels of economic development. The more an economy (and a society) becomes mature and diversified, the more selective and complex industrial policies become inefficient. This argument has been called 'the irony of state strength' [see Lauridsen (1995: 31)]. That is, an effective developmental state would also create the conditions for its own replacement.

These two arguments contain elements of truth. I have dealt elsewhere with these issues (e.g. Masina 2002a), where I have discussed how the events setting the stage and eventually precipitating the regional economic crisis should be analysed bearing in mind the transformations undergone in the East Asian countries and the changes in the international position of these countries. We recall the main points here briefly.

The end of the Cold War came at a moment when aggressive export from East Asia (and the perspective of China as a new economic giant) had already changed Western perceptions concerning strategic interests. Geoeconomics had already superseded geopolitics in defining Western priorities in Asia (Li *et al.* 2002; Sum 2002). Thus, it should not come as a surprise that the USA, its Western allies and the international financial institutions representing Western interests, tried to dismantle those institutional mechanisms that had supported economic development up to the point that some Asian countries could become dangerous competitors on international markets. This attempt to dismantle the developmental state was already in place before the official end of the Cold War and became even more evident afterwards [e.g. see Li *et al.* (2002) and Dixon (2002)]. The more crucial battleground in this Western crusade regarded the liberalization of Asian financial markets, eventually depriving Asian governments of essential regulatory mechanisms. Financial liberalization, though, was not simply imposed through coercion, but was also embarked upon by the Asian countries as a way to cope with a change in the international position of their countries (Chandrasekhar and Ghosh 2002; Sum 2002). The loss of key regulation tools by states that had previously been ruled by 'strong governments' proved a major factor in setting the stage for the financial crisis. This reading of the Asian crisis does not imply any kind of conspiracy theory – as some authors and politicians have done with their blaming of financial speculators. But it does imply that the Asian crisis can be understood against a background of a mounting clash of strategic interests between Anglo-American capital and Asian national capitals (Amoroso 2002).

While not embarking on a detailed examination of how this strategic clash came about and its concrete implications for Asian countries, we should look here at the theoretical implications of the problem. That is, does the change in the international system mean that the space of action for the 'developmental state' has dissolved? Clearly, this is a question that, if addressed in its general terms, concerns one of the most debated issues in economics and political sciences, i.e. the national state's capacity in the age of globalization. Neoliberal scholars such as Keinichi Ohmae (1990, 1995) have claimed that states have lost power and that this is a positive outcome. At the other end of the spectrum, however, there are a number of people who claim that national institutions still play a strategic role. And this strategic role is not limited to defending national economic space: states intervene by actively internationalizing their economic activities in support of the economic interests they represent. On the resilience of states' strategic functions, authors as diverse as Robert Gilpin (1987, 2001), Susan Strange (1998), Leo Panitch (2000), Jim Glassman (1999), Linda Weiss (1998) and Robert Wade (1996) agree. For these authors, states matter so much that the imperial domain exerted by the institutions of the USA (or those international institutions it controls, like the IMF and the World Bank) is an essential support for the power of American corporations. But state power is not only limited to the rich and powerful nations like the USA: it remains important even in poor and marginal developing countries. In the words of Linda Weiss (1998), the notion of a 'powerless state' is a myth that serves ideological and political purposes. Although the international system does exert constraints over nation states, these international conditions are often exploited by national elites to serve their own agendas. State capacity is limited not so much by external constrictions, but by the will of its own elites, which are often part of international networks that benefit from exploiting the resources of the territory that these elites should represent.[16] National formations characterized by stronger cohesion (as is normally the case in East Asia) do maintain a degree of power in implementing developmental state policies even when they are exposed to strong pressure from outside. For example, Frederic Deyo (2002) suggests that the Thai state may have moved towards a 'developmental state' type of close government–business relationship in support of the national small- and medium-sized enterprises (SMEs) sector after the regional economic crisis, notwithstanding the pressure from the international financial institutions.

Even if we assume that states do maintain power in mediating their integration into the world economy, it should be repeated that the conditions for Vietnam are sensibly different from those in which the developmental experience of Northeast Asia took place. In the case of the latter, heterodox trade practices were accepted by the USA because the economic growth of these countries was functional to Cold War geopolitical considerations. The situation now is completely different, as will be discussed in the following, e.g. by looking at the complex negotiations for a trade agreement between Vietnam and the USA.

The other question to look at is the alleged declining role of the developmental state once a certain degree of economic development has been achieved. Again, the recent experience of the Asian crisis helps in elucidating the issue. The already mentioned financial liberalization, for instance, could not be understood solely as something imposed upon Asian countries. There is some ground in looking at it as something that countries like South Korea and Thailand have also chosen to implement as a means to further their catching-up drive and to diversify their economic basis (Sum 2002; Chandrasekhar and Ghosh 2002; Weiss 1998, 2000). Financial liberalization has reduced the state capability to allocate credit on the basis of strategic planning, thus undermining a key feature of the developmental state. But does this imply that the experience of the East Asian developmental state has come to an end?

An answer to this question depends on the definition adopted to describe the developmental state model. If a hard-core definition is adopted (implying a coercive control on the economic activities by an authoritarian political regime), then it is probably correct to assume that that historical experience was concluded in the late 1980s, when both South Korea and Taiwan achieved a substantial democratization of their political institutions.

But, if the definition applied is more flexible and 'soft' [emphasizing coordination over coercion, as suggested by Linda Weiss (1995, 1998)], then there is no need to rule out that countries may choose to further their developmental experience on the basis of an updated version of the model. The issue was actually so much open to different outcomes that the IMF intervention during the Asian crisis has forcibly attempted the dismantling of the remaining aspects of the developmental state [see Bullard and co-workers (Bullard *et al.* 1998; Bullard 2002)].

It is not possible to conclude such a complex debate on the possible continuation of developmental state practices adequately. It is useful to remember, however, that not only have a number of authors recently confirmed the vitality of such institutional arrangements (e.g. Amsden 2001; Weiss 1998, 2000), but also that some have seen the possibility for the developmental state arrangements facing more subtle and complex tasks once the first stage of industrialization has been achieved. As reminded by Lauridsen:

> The thesis that *more complex economies make industrial policies more inefficient* and that the price mechanisms therefore need to be allowed to work more freely, has been opposed by Amsden and Eoh who argue that industrial policy-making becomes easier as the economy grows more complex, because the number of industries that must be promoted becomes smaller in relation to already existing mature industries that can be left alone (Amsden and Eoh 1993: 380) (Lauridsen 1995: 32).

The Vietnamese 'transition' in comparative perspective

Vietnam at the turn of the millennium is a poor and largely agricultural country in search of a path to rapid industrialization and economic growth. We have suggested that, in the search for this path, Vietnam is somehow inspired by the experience of its neighbouring countries and by the model denominated as the 'East Asian developmental state'. However, Vietnamese economic reform also incorporates another dimension, i.e. a transition from a centrally planned economy to a 'socialist market economy', which makes this country different from most of its neighbours, with the notable exception of China (and Laos). In the terminology developed to delineate the transformations that occurred in Central and Eastern Europe, Vietnam is a 'transitional' economy. A systematic comparison with the historical experience of the European former socialist countries would indicate a number of common features, deriving from the Soviet Union's influence in the setting up of a socialist state in Vietnam (as discussed in Chapter 2). Interesting similarities could also be traced in the attempts of reform towards a so-called 'market socialism' in Central Europe (particularly in Hungary after 1968) and the current reform in Vietnam. However, differences would prove bigger than the similarities, thus making such comparison problematic and complex (and far outside the limits of the present research).[17] The Soviet Union and the socialist European countries were developed industrial countries with a mechanized agriculture. The large majority of the population, both in urban and in rural areas, was employed directly by the state, with a minimal space for 'informal' activities (e.g. petty trade). Vietnam, instead, was and still is essentially a rural-based economy, with a very low percentage of the working force employed by the state.[18] Even in the relatively brief period during which collectivization of agriculture was attempted, families maintained small 'private' lots and the possibility of trading their products. Moreover, both the historical experience which led to the construction of a socialist state in Vietnam and the national and international conditions motivating the beginning of a reform process affected this country in very specific ways, which are rather different from the Eastern European case. In other words, the specific national and international context in which *doi moi* evolved (issues at stake, modalities, timing, external constraints, etc.) brought forth a unique process that does not match up with the explanatory paradigms adopted for the European 'transitional economies'.

Instead, a comparison with the Chinese case proves more useful. Not only has the long-term historical experience of the two countries been closely connected, but important similarities (and important differences) have also characterized the two parallel revolutions and the two parallel processes of economic reform.[19] Both countries have undergone a long revolutionary process where national liberation and socialist transformation have been closely related and interconnected, and where poor peasants have been the leading forces in the revolutionary movement. Both countries embarked on a parallel process of economic reform, with the ruling Communist Parties attempting a transition from central planning to a market economy with 'socialist characteristics'. And while the initial phase of the economic reform was conducted in a condition of hostility between the two countries, relations improved substantially at party and state levels after the collapse of the Soviet Union, thus making the similarities in the two reform processes more openly recognized and in some cases even a result of consultation between the two countries.

The relevant similarities in the historical experience make the study of the differences even more interesting. Two of these differences have a particular importance in the context of this work. The first regards the strengths and political control exerted by the state. Historically, the Chinese State has been stronger than the Vietnamese one. Since the early 1950s the Chinese central authorities have maintained a firm control over the local administrations.[20] Although the economic reform has further enhanced the differences among the various provinces (and the risks of political instability were particularly visible in the mid 1990s), the central government has been able to maintain a firm grip. This was done both by increasing the political representation of the richest regions in the central government and by increasing national control on tax revenues. It should be underlined that the need to find a viable compromise between centrifugal forces existing in several provinces and the attempts to restore a strong national government was paramount in the reform process launched by Deng Xiaoping in the late 1970s. The Chinese leadership accepted the new reform strategy only after a failed attempt to reorganize centralized national planning at the end of the Cultural Revolution (1966–76). The innovative solution promoted by Deng was to use the increased decentralized power as an engine for economic transformation, while reinforcing the modalities of central government coordination and control.

Compared with China, the influence of the Vietnamese central government on the different provinces has always been much weaker. In modern times, the significant decentralization of power was a result of many years of war, when the local administration had to carry out their duties without easy communication with Hanoi. The experience of the war is probably at the root of another evident distinction between China and Vietnam: the need to maintain unity within the ranks of the party, and of society as a whole, has led Vietnam to develop a decision-making process based on consensus. This may explain why Vietnam never experienced such radical political conflicts within the Communist Party as China did during the Great Leap Forward and the Cultural Revolution. The search for consensus still represents a key feature of Vietnamese policymaking, which makes every step in the process of economic reform complex and often cumbersome.

From this difference in the power of the central state may also derive another key difference in the two parallel processes of economic reform in China and Vietnam: reform in China was started when a political faction within the national leadership (i.e. the one led by Deng Xiaoping) gained power indicating the need to improve the economic standing of the country as a necessary means for consolidating the political authority of the party (White 1993). The outset of Chinese economic reform was, to a large extent, a top-down process, and the central government remained the key actor in determining the path of the process (including transient slowdown when the economy was overheated). In the Vietnamese case, instead (as discussed in Chapter 2) bottom-up processes played a more pervasive role. National authorities not only promoted reform strategies to cope with a changing international environment and national economic impasse, but also ratified a posteriori dynamics that had already developed at grassroots level. Both in China and in Vietnam, elements of the 'market' have always coexisted with the plan on a scale incomparable with the experience of Central and Eastern Europe. But in Vietnam the coexistence of market and plan has been more pervasive than in China – especially in the South, where the collectivization of the land was a very short-lived experiment.

The impact of evolving international events was important in shaping the reform process in both countries. Vietnam, however, was clearly more vulnerable and was forced to react fast to the decline, and then to the collapse, of the Soviet Union. This explains why the Vietnamese reform process gained momentum between 1989 and 1991, when it realized a programme of macroeconomic stabilization that has been likened to IMF-induced structural adjustment (see the discussion in Chapter 2). However (and here is a key element and a marked difference with the case of the Soviet Union and Eastern Europe), this macroeconomic stabilization was successful because it did not *start* but rather *concluded* the Vietnamese 'transition'. In the caustic expression coined by Fforde and de Vylder (1996), by that time Vietnam had managed to make 'price matter', even if important distortions in the economy did exist.

Chapter 2 confirms the hypothesis (now acknowledged in Vietnam's studies) that the Vietnamese 'transition' was basically concluded by the early 1990s. By that time, central planning had been replaced by market mechanisms in the allocation of resources and in the organization of production. Once the Vietnamese economy started to operate largely on the basis of market forces, the need to develop a new regulatory framework and a new institutional setting came to occupy central stage in the political debate. While the adoption of a market-based economy was mostly accepted, the specific ways in which this market economy should operate remained a matter of contention throughout the 1990s. The experience of the regional crisis added a new dimension to the debate, which is far from concluded at the time of presenting this work.

Given the still open issues in the process of institutional reform, one might argue that the Vietnamese 'transition' is still not completed. However, it seems useful to stress that the current debate about the development of suitable economic and political institutions and adequate legal and regulatory frameworks has more resemblance with the debate in other poor developing countries than in the industrialized countries of Central and Eastern Europe. Thus, in introducing the debate regarding issues like 'governance' and institutional reform, this work will not deal specifically with the experience of other 'transitional' economies, but will explore the issues more on the basis of a regional and developing-countries' perspective.

Criticism of the analytical tools

We have already argued that the impressive economic growth of a number of East Asian countries since the 1950s can hardly be explained within the frame provided by the neoclassical paradigm. The catching up achieved by these countries confutes both the modernization theories of the post-war period and the new orthodoxy prevailing after the neoliberal counter-revolution of the late 1970s. At the same time, the experience of East Asia also represents a major challenge to dependency theories, including those advanced by neo-Marxist scholars. The dependency school indicated that the Third World suffered for a condition of unequal exchange with the North (industrialized countries) and, therefore, further integration brought underdevelopment rather than the diffusion of a modern productive system. This view was supported by neo-Marxist scholars who argued that dependency reinforced regressive elements in the traditional systems of production – here, they departed from the classical Marxist tradition that had instead emphasized the 'progressive' role of colonialism in promoting a modern (capitalist) mode of production in the South (underdeveloped countries) (Blomström and Hettne 1984). The fact that a number of countries in East Asia (especially in Northeast Asia, but to some extent also in Southeast Asia) not only escaped underdevelopment, but also reached levels of industrialization comparable to those of the North in the span of a few decades can be interpreted as a contradiction for the dependency theories. Further, the rapid economic growth achieved by China and Vietnam after they embarked upon reform processes reintroducing market economy and the simultaneous collapse of state socialism in the Soviet Union were interpreted by conservative scholars as proof of an alleged decline in the explanatory power of the Marxist scholarly tradition. Here, we need to take into consideration some issues stemming from these arguments.

The post-war economic development of East Asia represents in many regards a special case within the Third World. We have already indicated some of its distinctive characteristics. Many of the countries in the region faced national and international conditions that eventually converged in supporting a rapid process of industrialization. This was a region where the process of decolonization was strongly influenced, when not openly directed, by communist forces. China, North Korea and Vietnam (plus Laos since 1975 and Cambodia for a short-lived and tragic phase) indicated the construction of a socialist state as a way to break the colonial dominance. All the other countries of Southeast Asia (Malaysia, Indonesia, Philippines, Thailand and Burma) had at some stage a strong Communist Party and even faced revolutionary insurgency. Although Roosevelt and Truman had given priority to Europe in the post-war reconstruction and they had tried to avoid being caught up in Asian conflicts,[21] it was in this region that the first major military conflict of the Cold War erupted. The Korean War was soon followed by a direct American involvement in Vietnam. The Korean War changed the American perception of Asia. The reliance on ideological motivations (anti-Communist containment) to win isolationist tendency at home and to support an American world leadership (including the Marshall Plan), had made it impossible for the Truman administration to exploit the harsh relations that existed between Moscow and Beijing since the establishment of the People's Republic of China. Until the Korean War, Washington indulged in a rather inconclusive policy: not willing to risk a military involvement in order to prevent the invasion of Taiwan, but unable to come to terms with the new government in Beijing. As soon as the Korean War started, however, the American policy changed and in the American public opinion there emerged the view that China had been 'lost'. This was later a major motivation to justify the intervention in Vietnam: after the loss of China, the USA could not afford losing Asia through a 'domino effect' that would have spread from Vietnam.[22]

Given the specific geopolitical context of East Asia, the USA perceived that the economic development of its regional allies was a necessary instrument of capitalist stabilization (Hersh 1993, 1998). This became the political and economic frame in which Japan was allowed to re-establish a regional productive order, with a triangular relation between the USA, Japan and developing East Asia. The reorganization of a regional system of division of labour was achieved through the extension to the region of the Japanese multilayered subcontracting system, which also activated productive resources available in loco (Arrighi *et al.* 1993), i.e. operating in a way markedly different from the relocation of production to Latin America by American and European companies (Masina 1996).

The specific geopolitical conditions of East Asia can, therefore, explain why this region was in a better condition than others to escape the exploitative nature of the unequal exchange: a condition for which the terms of trade are biased in favour of a country exporting industrially advanced products and against countries exporting raw materials and low value-added products. For many years the USA was willing to maintain a negative trade balance with these countries, whose economic stability was considered strategic. The East Asian US allies were even allowed to manipulate the exchange rates and to introduce selective import tariffs, without facing an American retaliation (e.g. Wade 1990). Obviously, this special relation was bound to come to an end once the East Asian countries had become dangerous competitors for American companies. Eventually, the Japanese-led regional productive order came to conflict with Western geoeconomic interests, and here lay the foundation of the regional economic crisis that unfolded in 1997 (Masina 2002a).

Geopolitical considerations and the inclusion in the Japanese multilayered subcontracting system were decisive factors, but they would not have allowed an impressive catching up if national conditions had not been supportive of a rapid industrialization drive. The East Asian developmental state was the specific device that allowed a selected group of countries to seize the opportunity of industrialization 'by invitation'. We argue here, therefore, that the developmental state played a fundamental role in breaking the dependency and preventing that economic integration with the North would result in underdevelopment.

But why did a small group of East Asian countries succeed in creating conditions for which the state was granted authority over the national capitalist forces in enforcing strategic planning? We will return to this important question in more detail in Chapter 6, where we will also discuss the applicability of a developmental state model to Vietnam. In a few words, we can say that the motivations for this special role of the state bureaucracy were related to the same geopolitical considerations discussed above. East Asia was a region where the conditions for a socialist revolution were very concrete. In the two countries that more systematically implemented a (Japanese inspired) developmental state, i.e. South Korea and Taiwan, the risk of being overthrown by their rivals, i.e. North Korea and China, was extremely high. In such a condition of political risk, similar to the risk that Japan had faced of becoming a colony, the most dynamic sectors of the national capital perceived the need to enforce a process of economic modernization that would serve their aims of political stabilization. Backward capitalist sectors were forced to adjust to this strategy in the name of state survival and capitalist stabilization.

The conditions existing in East Asia in the aftermath of World War II and the Korean War were thus the cause of political and economic strategies that operated simultaneously both at the international/regional and at the national levels. As the conditions were quite special, the policies that resulted from them were also quite special. A number of other factors played a role (culture, the previous experience of Japanese colonization, the existence of an economically dynamic Chinese Diaspora, etc.), but an understanding of the so-called 'East Asian miracle' cannot depart from the nature of the political conflict existing in the region both internationally and in terms of national class struggles. In this sense, the East Asian economic development confirms the validity of the research questions and the analytical approaches that the Marxist tradition has inspired.

The East Asian developmental state was based on a corporatist system that in Chapter 6 we will argue relates to the fascist experience. As with Italian Fascism, the developmental state served purposes of modernization and social transformation, i.e. it was neither a regressive movement nor a movement aiming at maintaining the *status quo*.[23] But the East Asian corporatist state, like the fascist state, conducted the process of modernization with the aim to defend the strategic needs of the capital and to consolidate the prevailing political order. The state guaranteed a certain level of income redistribution, because this was vital to prevent a socialist revolution. But welfare provisions were generally at a low level. Large industrial companies granted some health insurances and pensions to their employees through paternalistic schemes. The economic development of the rural world was partially sustained (e.g. technical and extension services), although in general the national economic policy was biased towards the extraction of resources from agriculture to support industrialization. The precise modalities in which the East Asian developmental state operated obviously varied from country to country, and only in Northeast Asia was the system implemented in a thorough and systematic way. However, the class nature of the developmental state was a common feature across the region. This model was implemented by dictatorships until the late 1980s in Korea and Taiwan; and, notwithstanding the economic success and the partial redistribution of wealth operated through the system, this developmental model has been criticized as a form of 'compressed modernization' (Chang 2002). In Southeast Asia, elements borrowed from the 'developmental state' model were combined with more-traditional forms of capitalist exploitation and also in this case authoritarian political forms prevailed in most countries. A number of authors have underlined the 'uneven' nature of the modernization process in Southeast Asia (e.g. Dixon and Drakakis-Smith 1997; Parnwell 1996; Schmidt *et al.* 1998), indicating how in a context of generalized economic growth that high prices were paid by different sectors of society, not to mention the environment.

In introducing the debate on the East Asian developmental state we do not intend to neglect the dark side of this historical experience. Apologists of the model may rightly argue that the Asian countries that implemented these strategies not only achieved a high level of per capita GDP growth over two or three decades, but even featured lower inequality than other developing countries [see data in World Bank (1993)]. We agree that these results should not be disregarded. Compared with other developing regions, East Asia (some countries more than others) certainly did better in securing an improvement in the living conditions of its population. However, we also agree with the detractors in denouncing the high human, social and environmental costs paid in order to achieve the catching up with industrialized countries.

The experience of the East Asian best economic performers does represent a point of reference in the region. The wish to emulate the prosperity of its richer neighbours is very visible in Vietnam; for example, in the last few years there has been a noticeable admiration for South Korean fashion, cosmetics, mobile telephones and electronics (also due to the images channelled via popular South Korean soap operas).[24] Like it or not, the developmental experience of the region is something that Vietnam needs to come to terms with.

We give large space here to the developmental state because we also explicitly consider that Vietnam *could* and *should* learn a number of lessons from that model. On key issues, the experience of the developmental state as a challenge to the orthodox recipes can present Vietnam with a wide range of possibilities and create the space for independent and conscious strategy decisions. In its transition towards a market-based economy, Vietnam (like China) is dismantling the last leverages of the past central planning. State-led strategic planning may be an appealing formula for allowing the economy to operate on the basis of market laws, but to maintain state guidance in strategic areas. We will discuss later in this text the concrete conditions for the adoption of such policies in Vietnam. From a political perspective, we should not overlook the fact that the technical devices that have been created in order to support capitalist development cannot be neutrally transferred to a country that officially maintains a socialist aspiration. Not only should Vietnam adjust the model on the basis of its own national characteristics and needs, but it should also be able to pick and choose in a way that is coherent with the political (i.e. class-relevant relations within the country) finalities that it intends to promote. The definition of political strategies, and the eventual adoption of selected features of the East Asia developmental state, can be assisted by the research of scholars that in recent years have contributed to a further clarification of the specific variations of the model in the different countries and of their evolution over time. In particular, it is useful to underline that the research of scholars like Linda Weiss has tended to emphasize the coordination (rather than coercion) functions of state strategic planning, thus also suggesting the possibility of integrating these strategies with more democratic and less exploitative political contexts than those of Taiwan and South Korea in the post-war years.

The importance of strategic planning in managing the Vietnamese integration into the world economy is mainly in reducing the risks of dependency. As we will discuss in Chapter 4, for example, the bilateral trade agreement with the USA and entrance into the World Trade Organization (WTO) risks confining Vietnam to the export of raw materials, agricultural commodities, garments and footwear. China, which is experiencing a parallel transition, has the advantage of a much larger internal market and, therefore, is able to impose conditions even on the largest transnational corporations. Vietnam has 80 million people, but it is still a rather small market and it is, therefore, much more vulnerable – we will discuss below that this vulnerability is further enhanced by an industrialization strategy that is highly dependent on FDI.

China has not only succeeded in escaping dependency while re-engaging integration into the world economy, but according to many analysts it is also on course to emerge as the new world hegemonic centre as the USA accentuates its tendency to decline, relying on coercion and military power and proving to be no longer able to guarantee international political and economic stability.

Vietnam has benefited from a number of positive conjunctures in the first phase of *doi moi*, but the post-regional economic crisis is now presenting significant difficulties for the next steps in the reform process.

Vietnam, like China, may succeed in its goals in exploiting a deeper integration into the world economy. Both countries can rely on strong nationalism as a mobilizing factor. This nationalism may significantly influence the national elites and avoid these elites from entering into strategic alliances with other international elites in a joint exploitation of the national resources (this point is developed further in Chapter 6). But nationalism may also lead to a sort of corporatist state, where the national development ideology serves to cover up class-relevant conflicts within the country.

The process of economic reform in Vietnam (like in China) has already produced profound social transformations and a rearticulation of class dynamics. These social changes have so far been mediated by the Communist Party (more in Vietnam than in China), thus preventing a drastic alteration of the political structures. The role of the party in maintaining a guidance role in the midst of such a radical change has been made possible by two factors. First, only 12 per cent of the workforce is employed in industry, while the large majority is engaged in agriculture or in the informal sector (and often in both, with seasonal or temporary fluctuations). Although a rearticulation of class relations is also visible in rural areas, this is not a very pronounced phenomenon yet, especially in the north of the country. The party and some 'mass organizations' operating at grassroots level, like the Women's Union and the Farmers' Association, remain central for the livelihoods of rural communities, and their functions have been scarcely encroached upon by the emergence of a new rural 'gentry'. Second, a rise in inequality (among regions, and especially between rural and urban areas, more than within regions) has been accompanied by such a dramatic poverty reduction to maintain quite a low level of social tension. Compared with China, where poverty has also declined and inequality increased, the Vietnamese case presents less visible signs of distress.[25] In particular, in several industrial areas of China (like the Rusty Belt in the northeast) redundancies have hit workers and exposed them to the loss of social security provisions normally granted by the state companies. In Vietnam, industrial redundancy is a relatively minor problem, while (like in China) the main concern is for the lack of jobs for over 1 million young people that enter the labour market every year. At the current stage, therefore, it is possible to see that a radical transformation is taking place both in terms of production systems and social relations, but it is not possible to draw ultimate conclusions about the impact of these transformations. It is possible to wonder, for example, whether the party will be able (or willing) to intervene for reducing inequality and rebalancing social structures once specific economic targets have been achieved. While it seems reasonable to assume that the Communist Party will remain in control of the political system for many years in the future, it remains to be seen how the party will be able to mediate among different social and economic interests and whether the party will become the political tool of an ascending national bourgeoisie.

Since the judgement on the rearticulation of class-relevant relations is suspended, a precise understanding of the functions of the state (in the present and for the future) is also problematic. In fact, as rightly argued by Schmidt *et al.* (1998: 9), the state cannot be 'fetishized as an autonomous entity'. The state 'should be understood as a social form, that is a form of social relations'. This is true for the 'East Asian developmental state', whose transformative purposes responded to specific political interests. And this is also true for a socialist state like Vietnam in a process of economic transition. Through our investigation we have not found decisive evidence to conclude that the process of economic reform has already involved a transformation of the political agenda for which state apparatuses are now serving finalities in contradiction with the proclaimed socialist aspiration. But we have not found a clear indication of how the national leadership intends to deal with the complex conundrum of promoting a capitalist-style market economy while maintaining a socialist perspective either. The fact that the state sector should maintain a leading role in the economy does not imply *per se* anything about socialism: state-led industrialization with a strong reliance on SOEs was carried out by several capitalist countries. State guidance may lead to socialism only if the interests represented by the state structures are constructed in a way to prevent the tendency of states to respond to the needs of the forces that dominate in the productive process.

While the project of socialist construction in Vietnam appears rather indefinite, the Vietnamese state should be acknowledged for the capable management of the transition in such a way as to reduce the impact of the systemic shock and to shelter the most vulnerable. In particular, a remarkable and positive feature of the Vietnamese transition has been the great attention given to the rural world. Agricultural diversification has been the major contribution to poverty reduction during the 1990s. This has been possible due to a number of state interventions (infrastructure, extension services, stabilization of commodity prices, etc.), which have accompanied the return of market dynamics in agriculture. This is also a crucial area in which the Vietnamese reform has been parallel with the Chinese one. The attempt to reinforce the rural world as a condition for creating a socially broad-based growth, i.e. creating a virtuous and cumulative circle of reciprocally reinforcing causations, reflects the lesson of Gunnar Myrdal and other scholars concerned with the vulnerability of industrialization processes in developing countries [see Fan (1997)].[26]

In this text, agricultural development is rather neglected, because this is an issue on which there is a substantial agreement in the policy debate. But the importance of this sector should not be absolutely overlooked. We should also underline that, for a country that has suffered food shortages as late as in the 1980s, and where a part of the population is still facing malnourishment, if not undernourishment,[27] self-reliance in food production is considered as a key concern. Reinforcing agriculture and the rural world was the first priority established by the Vietnamese Communist Party when the regional economic crisis unfolded in 1997.

The extension of the Vietnamese welfare system is still very limited. Until the Communes were in control of agricultural production they also took responsibility for the provision of basic education and basic health-care system. Today, user fees are charged for most services, and additional payments (under the table) are often requested. The state is able to provide free health-care insurances only to (some of) the poorest. Pensions cover only former state employees. Unemployment benefits exist as temporary measures for workers who have lost the job in SOEs. The creation of a viable system of redistribution should be an indicator to assessing the socialist nature of a state. But also in this case the judgment must be suspended. The state budget cannot really allow a more extended welfare system. There is evidence that a targeted state regional redistribution during the 1990s has played a significant role in supporting poverty reduction in the poorest regions (Beresford 2003). However, the most decisive factor in reducing poverty was the ability of large sectors of the Vietnamese population to seize opportunities created by the reform process and high economic growth – in other words, the benefits of economic growth 'trickled down', to put it in the terms used by mainstream economists. However, poverty reduction apparently proceeded at a less impressive speed in the late 1990s and early 2000s, and concerns do remain for the future. Mainstream economists argue for a further liberalization of the economy, while critical scholars may argue for the reinforcement of formal safety nets so as to create the conditions for a more inclusive growth with equity. While in the short run the scope of action for the Vietnamese state is highly constrained by budget limitations, it remains unclear which kind of welfare model will emerge as the country (hopefully) moves towards higher levels of economic prosperity.

2 The historical background: Vietnam between revolution and economic reform

As is often the case, it is impossible to study the Vietnamese reform process without at least some understanding of the country's recent history. The Vietnamese *doi moi* was launched in a concrete context shaped by decades of war, attempts to create a socialist state in the North and after 1976 in the unified country, and trial-and-error reforms and 'fence-breaking' activities that had already characterized the Vietnamese economy in the 1960s. While this chapter does not have the ambition to present an original and systematic reconstruction of Vietnamese recent history, it will try at least to present key events and issues to help the reader to put the analysis of the recent phases of the reform process into a meaningful perspective.

The making of the socialist state: wars, national reunification and economic policy

At the conclusion of World War II it was evident that in Vietnam, like in other parts of Asia, the colonial era was over. After the 'August Revolution' of 1945, the anticolonial movement, led by Ho Chi Minh and the Communist Party, proclaimed independence. France, however, was not ready to accept this *fait accompli*. The attempt to restate colonial rule on Vietnam (and on the rest of Indochina) resulted in a war, which was terminated only by the French military defeat at Dien Bien Phu (April 1954). The country was temporarily divided into two parts along the seventeenth parallel after the Geneva agreements (July 1954). In theory, the two administrations were supposed to organize elections within 2 years and to prepare for the peaceful reunification of the country. In reality, the conditions for peaceful reunification were very remote, especially for the international constraints.[1] The Democratic Republic of Vietnam (DRV) was established in the North under the leadership of the Communist Party. The Republic of Vietnam, an authoritarian regime increasingly dependent on American support for its very survival, was established in the South. Only in April 1975, after a long and terrible war concluded with the withdrawal of the American army (1973) and the complete collapse of the southern regime, was the country finally reunified.

The next section presents a synthetic introduction to the major policies adopted in North Vietnam for the construction of a socialist state. The following section analyses the process of reunification and the attempt to transfer to the South the economic model adopted in the North. The last section of this part discusses the transitional period, i.e. the period immediately preceding the official adoption of the reform process, and during which a number of policies are anticipated.

From 1954 to the national reunification

The Vietnamese liberation movement against French colonialism eventually succeeded thanks to the support it received from the poor peasants. Thus, land reform was one of the first initiatives that the new DRV government was committed to assume. In many regards the land reform was a success: more than 800,000 ha (2 million acres) of land were distributed and more than 2 million farm families – well over half the total number in the DRV – received at least some land. The reform also had the effect of undermining the historical domination of the landed gentry and supporting the rise of a new village leadership composed of poor and middle peasants (Duiker 1995: 136). Its implementation, however, resulted in abuses and excesses. In order to break the hierarchical structure of the traditional rural world, which could easily have led to a reversion of the reform's results, peasants were invited to criticize the landlords (whose land was confiscated) and lists of 'enemies' were made. The excessive zeal of local officers, combined with the exploitation of the political campaign to regulate private conflicts, led to severe abuses. This reality was acknowledged by the Communist Party in 1956, recognizing that many innocents had been wrongly classified as enemies and thereby deprived of their land. The assumption of responsibility for the errors committed was sanctioned with the removal from office of the party's General Secretary Truong Chinh and several other senior officials who were responsible for carrying out the programme (Duiker 1995: 137).

The next step in the transformation of the rural world was the process of collectivization, which started in 1958. The decision to move towards the collective ownership of land was decided on the basis of the assumption that it would have permitted a more effective use of the land through the consolidation of small farm plots and the introduction of widespread mechanization. The choice to promote collectivization at this early stage of economic development was based more on the contemporary Chinese example than on the Leninist tradition. While Lenin prescribed 'mechanization before collectivization', in 1955 Mao Zedong had reversed this order because he was convinced that industrialization could not be achieved on the foundation of a backward agricultural sector.[2]

The motivation behind collectivization was not merely ideological, but also responded to the need to increase capital accumulation in agriculture while reducing the social costs. In North Vietnam, farm sizes were normally too small to support an efficient production and create surpluses. The price of letting market forces obtain land consolidation would have meant many peasants losing their land and descending into dire poverty due to the lack of alternative job opportunities. Collectivization was, therefore, a meaningful option for giving all farmers (both rich and poor) 'the chance to benefit from capital accumulation in agriculture and to prevent the possibility of peasants losing their land through the bankruptcies which would be the inevitable result of allowing private accumulation and a free market' (Beresford 1988: 59).

The formation of the cooperatives in the North was substantially well received by the peasants. Peasants' support was motivated by the fact that the cooperatives were seen as a way to adapting the traditional forms of corporate solidarity. The cooperatives could fulfil welfare roles, reinforcing the social cohesion between individuals and within the local community. 'They could help families in difficulties, for example, if a parent was dead; they could help the families of men in the army; and they could help finance valuable services such as the rapidly expanding medical and school systems' (Fforde and de Vylder 1996: 57).

By the early 1960s more than 80 per cent of all farm families in the lowland districts had been enrolled in either semi-socialist cooperatives or fully socialist collective organizations (Duiker 1995: 138). A few years after, in 1968, the process of collectivization could be considered as concluded. By that time, 90 per cent of North Vietnamese belonged to the higher-level cooperatives in which all land and means of production were collectively owned and remuneration was awarded according to labour contributed (Beresford 1988: 59). Disappointingly, however, collective ownership did not significantly increase the grain production, in part because mechanization remained low, with less than 7 per cent of the land ploughed by tractor (Duiker 1995: 138). A substantial increase in land productivity would have required a higher capital investment in chemical fertilizers (or livestock to produce organic manure). But this was complicated by the fact that, since 1960, the government priority was the construction of heavy industry, and capital investment was mainly directed to that aim.

To understand the frame in which the Vietnamese leadership made plans for the edification of a socialist state, the particular conditions of the country after the Geneva agreements should be borne in mind. First, North Vietnam was impoverished by years of war and colonial exploitation,[3] and its rudimentary industry and infrastructures were in urgent need of rehabilitation. A well-known Vietnamese scholar reminds, for example, that:

> In 1954, modern industry accounted for only 1.5 per cent of total production, and not a single motor could be found in any village of North Vietnam... One year after the liberation of North Vietnam, annual generation of electricity totaled less than 53 million kWh, and the proportion of modern industry still in full production was around 3.4 per cent (Nguyen Khac Vien 1993: 295).

The other essential factor to remember is that Vietnam was a country at war; therefore, its economy had to be organized in consequence. Huge subsidies to industrial sectors essential for the military needs, for instance, are the rule in each state at war, although they can produce distortions in the economy (Kolko 1997: 20).[4]

The central planning system applied by the Soviet Union and China offered Vietnam a model that seemed to respond to the needs of the country under its particular conditions. This system[5] had a strong emphasis on the need to promote a rapid industrialization through the leading role of SOEs. Like in other socialist countries, the collectivization of agriculture was functional to the accumulation of the capital needed to finance the development of heavy industry. However, the 'DRV model' was also the result of a compromise, adapting the Soviet model to the local conditions existing in the country. The Vietnamese practice differed from the Soviet model in two crucial respects. First, as in China, a large number of state enterprises were managed by provincial or local authorities, with a tendency to decentralization that was greatly accelerated after 1965 in response to US strategic bombing. Second, a large informal economy continued to exist alongside the state-run sector (Irvin 1995: 728).

The working of this central planning system in Vietnam is synthetically described by Fforde and de Vylder in the following terms:

> Capital resources were supplied by the state to SOEs in order to produce a certain product. These resources were essentially supplied free. Each unit was managed by a level of the state bureaucracy (a ministry, if centrally-managed; a provincial or city department, if locally-managed) that allocated labour to it. The unit was then given a regular production target, in quantity terms, and in order for it to meet this target it was provided with levels of current inputs calculated on the basis of simple arithmetic norms. These inputs were supplied directly to the unit by the state, and its output was also supplied directly to the state. The unit was there essentially to produce for the target, and with almost no freedom to chose either what it produced or who it produced for, the unit had little interest in either the value of what it produced or the real costs involved in doing so… (Fforde and de Vylder 1996: 58).

The first Five-Years Plan (1961 to 1965) was successful in developing a modern state industry, showing remarkable rates of growth. This result was also achieved through large supplies of aid coming from China and the Soviet Union. However, as the Five-Years Plan progressed, macroeconomic tension mounted. The tax base did not expand fast enough to cover the expenditure needs and the foreign trade position deteriorated. But the more serious threat to the stability of the system was the poor result in agriculture, leading to an increase in food costs. State employees' real wages fell by around 25 per cent during the first Five-Years Plan and food supplies for non-agricultural workers became more expensive. According to Fforde and de Vylder (1996: 59–60), there were three main reasons to make food supply grow too slowly to meet the increasing demand: '1. Inefficiencies in the cooperatives; 2. Agriculture remained poor of resources; 3. As free market prices rose, cooperators increasingly preferred to work on their so-called private lots'.[6]

From 1965, the paramount concern for North Vietnam became the military effort to support the liberation movement in the South and to resist the intense American bombing in the North. The second Five-Years Plan was postponed and more flexible 1-year programmes were adopted. The country was only able to survive in this emergency situation through substantial foreign aid and credit for otherwise unsustainable imports [see Beresford and Dang (2000)].

Remarkably, North Vietnam not only succeeded in carrying out the military effort, but also achieved important results in socio-economic development (especially healthcare and education). The North Vietnamese performance was notable when compared with the parallel decay of South Vietnam, where the large American military and economic aid could not prevent the progressive collapse of socio-economic institutions. The government of South Vietnam was unable to control large parts of its own territory and to run a viable administration even with the direct support of hundreds of thousands of American soldiers and military and civilian advisers. After the Paris agreements in 1973, and the withdrawal of the American troops, the South Vietnamese regime was clearly not able to survive for long (notwithstanding the ongoing abundant American economic support). Two years after, in April 1975, the North Vietnamese army entered Saigon, putting to an end the war and realizing the reunification of the country. However, the reunification opened a new difficult period in Vietnamese history.

The reunification of the country

When the 'Vietnam war' (or the 'American war' for the Vietnamese) came to an end, the country was finally reunified under a national government for the first time in over a century. The process of reunification and construction of a new state was characterized by severe drawbacks. Many of the problems derived from the way in which the reunification process was handled: the South was integrated into the northern institutions, without an adequate understanding of its social and economic conditions. Party officers from Hanoi, which assumed control of the administration in the South, had often only a limited knowledge of the local situation. The need to rely on cadres from the North was a result of the weak basis available for a new administration. The long clandestine war and specific American covert actions[7] hit the South's intelligentsia very severely. Large numbers of the remaining intelligentsia (including the Chinese ethnic minority) were considered insufficiently trustworthy, because of real or alleged connections with the former regime.[8]

At the time of reunification, the social structures of North and South Vietnam had developed in quite different ways.[9] These differences were the result of the long period of separation after 1954, but also because of longer-term factors connected to the historical heritage of French colonial rule. The clearing and cultivation of new lands in the South had been conducted under French control, and relied more on a system of modern capitalist exploitation than on the traditional organization of the Vietnamese village. As a result, 'private property was established on a more widespread basis in the southern region, whereas in the North and Centre it co-existed with more traditional forms of land ownership' (Beresford 1988: 55). Land ownership in the South at the end of the French colonial period was more polarized than in the North. A process of land reform took place also in the South, although this process was gradual and extended over three decades. The redistribution of land was the combined result of the reforms imposed by the Communist forces on the liberated areas and the several reforms attempted by the regime in the South to consolidate its power. By the time of reunification, the changes that had occurred in land ownership were remarkable:

> Whereas in 1955, the poor peasants had constituted over 70 per cent of the rural population and owned only 14 per cent of the land, by 1978, when the first post-war survey of land tenure in Mekong delta was carried out, they were less than a quarter (and owned 8 per cent of the land). Instead the great bulk of peasants were classified as middle or rich and it was these peasants who produced the large market surplus of the delta (Beresford 1988: 56).

The structure of land tenure in the South explains why the peasants were much less ready to accept collectivization and the creation of cooperatives than those in the North.

In the South, as in the North, the war had an all-encompassing impact in shaping the socio-economic structures. The devastation produced by the war in the rural areas of the South – either because of American bombing or because of Saigon's attempts to cut the connections between the 'Viet Cong' and the peasants – was a major cause behind the rapid urbanization. Large numbers of dislocated villagers were forced to seek shelter in the shantytowns of Saigon and of other major cities. This also led to a number of social problems, such as the spread of drug abuse and prostitution, which were left to the new socialist administration. The urbanization in the South contrasted with the situation in the North, where people sought repair from the American bombing in the countryside (and also some of the industrial plants were relocated in rural areas). In 1975, around 35 per cent of the South Vietnamese population lived in urban areas, while the figure for North Vietnam was only 11 per cent (Beresford 1988: 57). These differences were also visible in the organization of the economy, which in both parts of the country was a 'war economy'. While the 'war economy' in the North emphasized the development of a heavy industry, the industrial basis of the South remained weak (with only 3 per cent of the population employed in the sector, including mining, construction, transport and public utilities). In the South, the service sector, including commerce and administration, accounted for the largest share of GDP (Beresford 1988: 57), and was largely dependent on the circulation of American aid.

The integration of two parts of the country that had experienced such different conditions for decades was not an easy task. The strategy adopted by the national leadership was to accelerate the socialist transformation of the country, through a rapid and radical change in the economic institutions. This decision was announced in December 1976 at the Fourth CPV Congress, and adopted by the party leadership in late 1977. Plans were made to begin the process of socialist transformation in the southern provinces early the following year (Duiker 1995: 146). As in the North, this strategy was based on the creation of joint state–private enterprises in modern industry, the collectivization of agriculture and handicraft industries, and the attempt to bring domestic circulation of goods under state control through the creation of a state trading network and administrative pricing system (Beresford 1988: 63). The decision to abolish private trade and manufacturing was put into practice in March 1978, when all major industrial and commercial enterprises remaining in private hands were suddenly placed under state control and their goods confiscated. Only small firms under family ownership were permitted to remain in private hands. This reform also involved the remaining small private sector in the North, which predominantly consisted of ethnic Chinese merchants and manufacturers (Duiker 1995: 146). The timing and the radicalism of these initiatives were not well received by a large part of the population, especially in the South. The economic outcomes of these changes were rather dismaying.

The collectivization of agriculture achieved different results in the different areas previously controlled by the Saigon regime. Collectivization was successful in the impoverished central regions, and the output recovered and grew rapidly. But in the Mekong Delta the collectivization campaign was a failure: by the mid-1980s only 50 per cent of peasants belonged to cooperatives, and only 36 per cent of the land had been incorporated (Beresford 1988: 63).

The economic and political reforms introduced in the country after reunification had been decided on the basis of optimistic plans concerning the possibility of moving rapidly ahead towards the complete socialist transformation. But this optimism should be understood as 'optimism of will' covering a 'pessimism of reason', i.e. an attempt to inject new energies for coping with a very difficult economic situation.

The war, together with national deficiencies in economic policies, had made North Vietnam exceptionally aid-dependent: 'from 1966 to 1975, foreign grants and loans averaged 63.2 per cent of the non military budget' (Riedel and Turley 1999: 13).

High levels of economic aid were made available to both North and South Vietnam until the war was on. The situation changed dramatically after 1975: the shrinkage of foreign aid and the removal of preferential trade conditions was eventually one of the major factors to force Vietnam to search for a new development strategy. Once the country was unified, the substantial aid that the USA had made available to the South evaporated. As we will see, the relations between China and the unified Vietnam became immediately strained and an increase of foreign aid from the Soviet Union and its satellite European countries could not compensate for the loss of American and Chinese economic support. [For a detailed discussion on this point, see Beresford and Dang (2000).]

By late 1979 the economic difficulties related to the reunification and a severe deterioration of the Vietnamese international relations converged in making the Vietnamese position unsustainable. The event that made Vietnam become an outcast in the international community was the invasion of Cambodia (December 1978), which also produced a Chinese military retaliation (February 1979). At the same time, the poor results of the economic and political measures adopted after the reunification exacerbated the tensions in the country. This, in turn, generated a tragic reaction that further compromised the international standing of Vietnam: several hundred thousand people (mostly ethnic Chinese) flew the country, either moving to China or escaping by sea (thus becoming known to the world as 'boat people'). The drama of the 'boat people', together with the invasion of Cambodia, greatly influenced international public opinion, which had previously expressed sympathy to Vietnam as a victim of American imperialism. This change in its international image had concrete implications for the drying up of economic aid from many countries and movements that had supported Vietnam during the war. Furthermore, poor harvests resulting from bad weather, and also from peasants dragging their feet against the forced collectivization in the South, caused the country to suffer from a severe food shortage, particularly affecting the population of urban areas.

The combination of these negative conditions resulted in 'a systemic crisis' (Fforde and de Vylder 1996: 12). Apart from its transient motivations, and the major challenges created by the international isolation, the crisis also indicated a fundamental weakness in the national economic management. The planning system appeared to be unable to control the allocation of resources adequately. These severe economic difficulties generated a spontaneous process of change, which can be considered as the real starting point of the process then officially adopted as *doi moi*. The 'systemic crisis' deriving from the poor functioning of the centrally planned economy – also a result of higher costs of imported inputs for production (Beresford and Dang 2000; Dang 2004) – led many, including local authorities, to operate outside the plan through a variety of flexible solutions:

> [The 'systemic crisis'] forced economic agents – individuals as well as agricultural cooperatives and state enterprises – to engage in a process of 'reform from below'. 'Fence breaking' [...] became increasingly common, and the authorities had to admit tacitly that the DRV model had (perhaps temporarily) become unsustainable (Fforde and de Vylder 1996: 12–13).

The spontaneous process of 'reform from below' converged with external threats in motivating the Vietnamese leadership in exploring new paths for economic development. As interestingly documented by Dang Phong (2004), in a number of cases it was the local authorities and party leaders experimenting with unorthodox solutions to concrete problems, testing to the limits – and even openly violating – official regulations. 'Fence breaking' from below and from above often also converged in preparing the ground for new policies at the national level. In the words of Dang Phong (2004):

> Fence breaking was not simply a conflict between those who erected the fences and those destroying them. Perhaps initially it was like that, but later on it was often those who had built the fences that began to clear them away... Moreover, once the need for reform was sensed by middle-level leaders..., or directors of key enterprises..., they could use their connections with higher-level leaders who likewise had become open to such ideas, to push reforms through.

It was against this complex background that the Sixth Plenum of the Central Committee in the autumn of 1979 inaugurated a phase of transition in the country.

The transition: from 1979 to 1990

From the Sixth Plenum to the Sixth Congress

The Sixth Plenum was openly confronted with severe economic problems and with the spread of fence-breaking activities across the country. The decisions adopted did not imply a demise of central planning, but they conceded a flexible use of non-orthodox measures in order to reverse the critical economic conditions. Although this flexibility had to be used with the aim of revitalizing the central planning, *de facto* it allowed the development of what Fforde and de Vylder (1996: 126) call the 'transitional model'. In the new environment, farmers were once again authorized to sell their products on open markets, and a limited degree of private commerce and manufacturing was tolerated (Duiker 1995: 148).

In January 1981, Directive 100, popularly known as the 'contract system', was approved, introducing some elements of rural decollectivization. Under this system, tasks (ploughing, irrigating the land, transplanting, etc.) were 'subcontracted' to households. This was a hybrid system, for which peasants were paid by the number of workdays for some activities, while for other activities or for some land they had full responsibility as subcontractors. On the land 'subcontracted', each household was required to provide the state a quota of grain in the form of rent, but any grain produced on the land beyond the established quota could be consumed or sold on the free market (Duiker 1995: 148–149). The cooperative maintained control over supply of inputs and marketing.

State industry was the other main area in which embryonic reforms were experimented, partially in response to 'unplanned' activities, as an attempt to regulate them, and partially in response to economic constraints deriving from changes in the international position of the country and declining foreign aid. The halt of Chinese and Western aid and the higher cost of import from Comecon countries[10] had sharply reduced the volume of supplies coming through the state monopolies. Enterprises were pushed to find alternative sources for obtaining inputs to fulfil their plan obligations. The central planning system created a sub-optimal allocation of productive assets. In particular, the system led to misuse of agricultural resources and to the accumulation of wasteful industrial stocks. Encouraged by the Sixth Plenum, a number of enterprises started to move outside the official rules in order to procure those underutilized resources existing in the economy that could be employed to increase output. Diversification of production was pursued in order to procure cash for acquiring new resources through the market. Goods started to be swapped through direct connections with agricultural collectives or other industries. The availability of more resources gave enterprises the means to increase workers' incentives (bonuses), and so to expand production further.

The diffusion of these activities 'out of the plan' from late 1979 onwards had two major effects. First, it made it possible to make a productive use of underutilized resources existing in the system, and therefore output recovered surprisingly rapidly in some areas. Second, it increased the pressure for change on the subsidized sectors of the economy, because these sectors faced increased competition from market activities (Fforde and de Vylder 1996: 138). These non-orthodox practices were sanctioned by the Communist Party decree number 25 of January 1981, through a new regulation that made it possible for state enterprises to perform additional activities besides those prescribed by the plan. The new 'Three Plan system' (similar to the Chinese dual-pricing system) confirmed that enterprises should give priority to the fulfilment of the plan, using input received from the state and supplying the resulting output to the state at low prices (First Plan). But once having fulfilled this obligation, enterprises were allowed to sell additional output generated by their official productive sector on the market (Second Plan), or to produce and sell the output of their 'minor' products, which were the result of industrial diversification (Third Plan).

These measures regarding agriculture and state industry can be interpreted as the beginning of the official process of reform and the legal basis for the transitional model.

> The plan now had to coexist with the world of autonomous transactions in the hybrid transitional model. Prices, costs, and markets began to play a larger role, and economic agents became used to thinking in more market-oriented terms (Fforde and de Vylder 1996: 13).

The adoption of these initial reforms, however, increased imbalances within the system. Elements of the market economy were sanctioned within a central planning frame, making more visible the conflict between different interest groups. In political terms, the adoption of reforms did not imply the choice to renounce a centrally planned socialist economy. On the contrary, these reforms were accepted only because they were considered useful for making state enterprises more effective in carrying out their plan obligations and for collectives to increase their agricultural output targets. Thus, the adoption of the 'contract system' in agriculture and the 'Three Plan system' in industry was accompanied by restrictions on free trade (Fforde and de Vylder 1996: 141) and an attempt to regain control of the national economy.

The contradictions existing in the system – with part of the economy based on market principles and characterized by staggering prices and the other part of the economy based on a command economy and depending on subsidies – created economic distortions and political tensions. Not only was the national leadership divided on the direction to adopt, but also some forces at the grassroots level pushed for a further liberalization while others (around SOEs dependent on state subsidies) contrasted the diffusion of market-oriented reforms. These contradictions eventually led to a reversal of the positive results achieved in the early 1980s. Output growth started to decline and prices increased from 1983, leading to spiralling inflation. This led to the adoption of the so-called 'Price–Wage–Money–Currency Reform' in 1985, which tried to re-establish macroeconomic stability, through a combination of currency reform, increased state prices and higher wages. However, this reform gave poor results. The rationing of key products did not succeed in arresting the price increases on the free market. With the failure of the 1985 measures, political support for 'hard reform socialism' (i.e. the combination of reforms and re-centralization attempted after the Sixth Plenum) evaporated. This opened the way to new political change, which was also represented by a change in the CPV leadership: after the death of the General Secretary Le Duan (and the temporary replacement by Truong Chinh),[11] the somewhat younger and more liberal Nguyen Van Linh was elected to the helm of the party.

The Sixth CPV Congress and the launch of doi moi

The CPV's Sixth Congress represented a clear shift in the Vietnamese strategy. A line of reform and economic liberalization received strong political backing from the party and its new leadership. Thus (and increasingly from the late 1980s), Vietnam embarked on a number of policy changes, which within a few years transformed international relations, the development strategy and the socio-economic structure of the country.

This fundamental change had two motivations. On the one hand, it reflected the need to address the economic imbalances and shortages produced by the command economy (and aggravated by the persisting war in Cambodia). On the other hand, it derived from the need to cope with the crisis in the Soviet Union, which involved a drying up of economic aid, the loss of the traditional export market, and dangerous isolation in political and military terms.

The emergence of a reformist agenda in 1986 was a direct consequence of the failed re-centralization of controls attempted in 1985. A heterogeneous coalition of local governments and enterprises that had developed a stake in market and off-plan activities converged in pressuring for a new policy.[12] In December 1986, under the slogan of *doi moi* (renovation), the Sixth Party Congress introduced a new strategy of reforms, which reflected the shift in the composition of interest groups dominating the political discourse. The reforms adopted increased autonomy for SOEs, eliminated the state monopoly of foreign trade, and allowed for small-scale private commercial activities. The function of the state came to be described as that of an orchestra director rather than that of a controller of the economic machine (Fforde and de Vylder 1996: 145). The new strategy, however, emphasizing a 'socialist market economy', confirmed the central role of the state in leading the national economy, and ruled out significant reduction of government control over SOEs, dismantling the planning apparatus, or abolition of the dual price system. The adoption of a 'compromising agenda' in the initial phase of *doi moi* leads Riedel and Turley (1999: 20) to interpret the reform as dominated by 'a path of least resistance: rewarding groups that had or could be expected to support a partial marketization and postponing measures that might inflict real pain'.

Notwithstanding, the limitations imposed by this 'compromising agenda', the period following the Sixth Party Congress was characterized by important changes. Reforms were decided and implemented in key areas, including the reorganization (and downsizing) of state bureaucracy and the development of the legal system. Two decrees were approved in 1988 to regulate the 'family economy' (i.e. activities by state or cooperatives' employees undertaken in addition to their main occupation) and the 'private and individual sectors'. The decrees ratified the freedom for any citizen that was not a state employee or a cooperative member to engage in private economic activities. These activities were not regulated by planning, and were understood to be self-managed. Private enterprises had the property of their means of production and were allowed to hire labour and to form joint ventures with state units or cooperatives. Enterprises had to be registered and pay taxes, but local authorities were not allowed to interfere with production or to levy special taxes. Further, private enterprises could receive foreign investments (which were regulated by a specific law), while their exports and imports were to be channelled through state trading organizations.

A new regulation concerning SOEs (decree 217) was introduced in 1987. This made a distinction between enterprises operating in key areas (where the state needed to maintain control over output) and normal enterprises that were only liable to the state for taxes. The regulation was meant to simplify state management and to dismantle the traditional control apparatus, although results of the reform were only partial in this area. Enterprises gained the freedom to recruit workers and to acquire and dispose of resources that were outside the constraints imposed by the plan (although in some areas the Three Plan system was maintained) (Fforde and de Vylder 1996: 158).

Agriculture was the target of another major reform with the aim of increasing output and mobilizing agricultural surpluses through material incentives.

The need to undertake a thorough reform of agriculture had been made visible by a poor harvest in 1987, which resulted in a severe crisis with pockets of famine that lasted into the spring of 1988 (Riedel and Turley 1999: 20)

In April 1988, the party approved a decree, commonly known as the Contract 10 system, which made individual households the base of agricultural production in exchange for the payment of an agricultural tax. Households were awarded land rights for 15 years. At the same time, the decree still restricted the sale, renting and exchange of land except in certain limited situations. The cooperatives retained some duties to support traditional safety nets (e.g. for families of war dead). The decree changed the managerial structure of cooperatives by emphasizing internal democracy and leading to the sacking of incompetent and/or corrupt cadres (eventually this led to the dismissal of 50 per cent of rural cadres). Eventually, the role of the cooperatives was significantly reduced. Cooperatives maintained some administrative functions like tax collection and some residual property rights, but only in some cases did they manage to shift to profitable service functions (Van Arkadie and Mallon 2003: 80).

The decree also prohibited the cooperatives' superior level (the districts) from issuing orders to the cooperatives, and thus 'finally destroyed the rural basis of the command economy' (Fforde and de Vylder 1996: 157). Further, restrictions on grain trade between provinces were removed.

Together with this decree, the government decided to increase investment in agriculture, to reduce the number of intermediaries between the state and producers in supplying agriculture and purchasing from it, and to set up a new Agricultural Development Bank in order to facilitate farmers' access to credit. New measures in 1989 also reduced state involvement in allocation of inputs and in the procurement of outputs at prices below market values. All these reforms contributed to bringing to an end the extraction of surplus from agriculture as a source of capital accumulation for financing the national industrial development. This radical change (also made possible by the end of the armed conflict that had so far absorbed much of the Vietnamese resources) implied a significant reversal of the development strategy. These measures (and further actions through the 1990s, e.g. increased role of extension services and agricultural diversification) contributed to reinforce the livelihoods of the rural areas and brought a remarkable poverty reduction. From provider of subsidized food to urban areas, the rural world evolved into a market for industrial products, thus supporting the industrial production not in terms of low-cost inputs, but in terms of increased demand.

In 1988–9, grain prices doubled in real terms, representing a 'large swing in the domestic terms of trade in agriculture's favour' (Irvin 1995: 730). These measures succeeded in boosting agricultural production, and especially rice output. A record harvest in the 1989–90 crop allowed Vietnam to become the world's third largest rice exporter after Thailand and the USA, reversing a long historical dependency on rice imports.

The policy of *doi moi* had been launched as a strategy for enhancing economic growth. However, the economic results of the first 2 years were dismaying: instability accelerated and the state budget deficit became critical. The pressure of an increasing private sector competition reduced the income of SOEs, which were the main source of support to the state budget. The end of state monopoly on foreign trade and an overvalued exchange rate caused losses to exporters, while undervalued imports increased competition for domestic producers, adding pressure to the state to grant subsidies. Given the difficulty of introducing new forms of taxation, payments of subsidies implied a burgeoning deficit and continuing triple-digit inflation.

Like the poor harvest of 1987 had contributed to promote a more radical reform of agriculture, the critical economic situation of 1987–8 also reinforced the pressure for further steps in the reform process. When the CPV Central Committee met in March 1989 to assess the first 2 years of the implementation of *doi moi*, the commitment to the reform agenda was not only confirmed, but also translated into a bolder plan for macroeconomic stabilization.

Macroeconomic stabilization 1989–90

Counter-inflationary measures were adopted by the government in early 1989 (Table 2.1). Bank interest rates on savings were brought clearly above current inflation, restoring people's trust in the national currency. Positive interest rates motivated people to deposit *dong* with banks and put a sudden halt to the

Table 2.1 Real GDP growth and inflation, 1985–96

	1985	*1986*	*1987*	*1988*	*1989*	*1990*	*1991*	*1992*	*1993*
Real GDP growth	5.7	3.4	3.3	5.1	8.0	5.1	6.0	8.6	8.1
Inflation rate (%)	132	487	317	311	76	67.5	67.6	17.5	5.2

Source: General Statistical Office 1997

hoarding of food and goods. Within a few months the country moved from a shortage economy to a situation where households and enterprises were encouraged to sell their stocks on the market. According to the Vietnamese economist Vo Dai Luoc, the exceptional surplus in rice production of 1989 should also be understood against the background of the situation created by the counter-inflationary measures. In fact, per capita output did not increase sufficiently to justify the abundance of rice on the market (Vo Dai Luoc 1995: 73).

The high interest rates placed strong financial pressure on the SOEs, which found it increasingly difficult to service their debt and were forced to liquidate their inventories in search of liquidity. Eventually the high interest rates and a restrictive money supply policy threatened to lead the country into a severe recession, and consequently these measures were partially relaxed by May 1989. However, these measures were not reversed. At the same time, banks started to lend money to SOEs (charging interest rates higher than inflation), thereby reducing state subsidies to SOEs (Vo Dai Luoc 1995: 75).

Price liberalization for most goods also indirectly contributed to the anti-inflationary policy, reducing the scope for arbitrage and speculation of the price differential between state-fixed prices and market prices. The state retained the function of controlling and stabilizing the prices of key products (e.g. rice and gold), but let most prices fluctuate in line with supply and demand (Fforde and de Vylder 1996: 177; Vo Dai Luoc 1995: 76). The official exchange rates for foreign currencies and precious metals were set at market prices level, thus reducing people's hoarding of gold and hard currencies (Vo Dai Luoc 1995: 76).

Overall, these anti-inflationary measures were quite successful in achieving stabilization, although they did not remove the causes of inflationary tendency and structural instability of the system. On the contrary, these measures made more evident the contradiction represented by the introduction of a market economy without the existence of an effective market for the factors of production: land, labour and capital. Therefore, the reforms of the late 1980s set the agenda for a new phase of the reform process in the early 1990s. At the turn of the decade, however, the Vietnamese 'transition' was substantially over:

> 'as the process continued into the 1990s, Vietnam's development problems would, to an increasing extent, come to resemble those of other low-income developing countries (Fforde and de Vylder 1996: 20).

The adoption by the party of such a bold reform strategy in early 1989 remains one of the most complex puzzles to solve when trying to analyse *doi moi*. The policy of macroeconomic stabilization adopted and implemented between 1989 and 1990 was so severe to be often related to IMF-style structural adjustment. The radicalism of the reforms implemented implies two questions. First, how was it possible to reach a consensus on such a bold reform package? Second, why did Vietnam substantially succeed where most other developing countries adopting IMF-inspired structural adjustment failed? A certain level of consensus exists among scholars in connecting the positive result of the macroeconomic stabilization of the late 1980s in Vietnam – contrary to the case of 'big bang' reforms in other 'transition economies' – to a longer-term process, which had already started to make 'price matter' from the late 1970s. This is the view held by Fforde and de Vylder (1996), now largely accepted in the scholarly community (we will return to this soon). More controversial is the identification of the *primum mobile* behind the reform package adopted in 1989. In particular, it remains unclear what role was played by the IMF and other external actors. Gabriel Kolko (1997), a critic of the *doi moi* process, argued that by that time the Vietnamese leadership was strongly influenced by the IMF, whose line was represented in the country by the influential government adviser Nguyen Xuan Oanh. Mr Oanh was a former IMF officer and a former Acting Premier of South Vietnam. At the conclusion of the war, after a brief house arrest, he became an associate of Vo Van Kiet[13] and from 1983 a government adviser. Although the IMF did not resume lending to Vietnam until the removal of the American embargo in 1994, contacts were also kept between the two sides through regular IMF staff missions, several of which were conducted in the first half of 1989. However, most scholars seem to exclude the possibility that the IMF played a direct role in influencing Vietnamese decision-making. For instance Riedel and Turley (1999: 22), although maintaining that the policy adopted by Hanoi in 1989 resembled 'pure IMF orthodoxy', stress that the IMF had no material leverage over Vietnamese policy, and that the adoption of the macroeconomic stabilization was an autonomous decision by the national leadership. The same conclusion is reached by Ronnås and Sjöberg (1991a,b). These scholars tend to consider the adoption of a bold reform policy as a national decision taken by the Vietnamese leadership in order to cope with a very critical situation.

Reorganizing international relations[14]

The structural transformation of the Vietnamese economy was also a result of a major change in the external relations of the country. Vietnam had to cope with the decline and then the collapse of the Soviet Union, which implied a drying-up of economic aid, the loss of the traditional export market, and a dangerous isolation in political and military terms. Hanoi succeeded in responding to these threats by undertaking an overall reorganization of its international relations, and eventually even improving its international position.

The first contentious area in which Vietnam acted, removing a major obstacle to its international standing, was the question of Cambodia. In September 1989 it withdrew its troops from the neighbouring country and in October 1991 the conflict was definitely concluded with the signature of the Paris agreements. In the few months following the Paris agreements, Hanoi was able to reach a full normalization of diplomatic relations with most Asian countries, including China, with whom Vietnam had a brief but intense armed clash in 1979.

The rapprochement with the nation's Southeast Asian neighbours, already begun in 1992, was successfully concluded by Vietnam's formal admission into ASEAN (July 1995), which also opened the way for participation in ASEAN Free Trade Area (AFTA).

The normalization of relations with the USA was somewhat slower. Washington maintained an embargo on Vietnam until February 1994, but full diplomatic relations were not reinstated until June 1995. Despite this, in July 1993 the American administration removed barriers to multilateral aid, allowing the World Bank to resume lending to the country the following October.

The overall achievement of this global revolution in Vietnamese international relations is remarkable for two reasons. First, this revolution was carefully managed, *improving relations in all directions simultaneously*. While Vietnam proved to have great ability in playing the 'Chinese card' (i.e. letting Southeast Asian countries and the USA understand the importance of a common front with Vietnam) Hanoi was, at the same time, able to obtain a notable improvement in relations with Beijing.

Second, the enhanced international position of Vietnam proved to be a key resource for receiving financial support for economic reforms within the country. From the moment it started to receive official development assistance (ODA) until a few months before the onset of the regional economic crisis, Vietnam seemed to benefit from a kind of preferential treatment that some considered to be connected with its strategic position and its careful foreign policy.[15]

From 1991 to the regional crisis 1997–8[16]

One of the most important results of the first period of reforms was macroeconomic stabilization. Strong revenue improvement (from the larger volume of foreign trade, higher taxation of SOEs and increasing oil production) allowed for the amelioration of the country's fiscal position. The trend was further reinforced by the virtual elimination of direct subsidies to SOEs in 1991. An immediate positive result of this larger state income was the possibility of expanding public spending on health and education from about 7.5 per cent of current expenditure in 1988 to about 18.7 per cent in 1996 (World Bank 1997a: 16).

At the same time, the enhanced fiscal position and the elimination of domestic bank financing allowed greater monetary control and a significant reduction in inflation: after years of hyperinflation, inflation has remained within a single digit range since 1993.

Most importantly, macroeconomic stabilization was achieved together with fast economic growth and poverty reduction (Table 2.2). In the decade 1987–96,

Table 2.2 Selected economic data, 1992–7

	1992	*1993*	*1994*	*1995*	*1996*	*1997*
Population (millions)	68	69.2	70.3	71.5	72.7	73.9
GDP per capita ($)	130	145	186	221	290	339
Real GDP growth rate (%)	8.6	8.1	8.8	9.5	9.3	8.2
Inflation (%)	17.5	5.2	14.4	12.7	4.5	3.6

Source: UNDP Hanoi office homepage

GDP growth was on average 7.3 per cent, increasing to over 9 per cent in 1995 and 1996. Over the decade, this result translated into an annual average per capita real income growth of about 5 per cent, increasing GDP per capita from $100 in 1987 to about $300 in 1996 (World Bank 1997a: 17).

Dialogue with multilateral financial institutions was instrumental to a settlement of Vietnamese external debt, which took place at the end of 1993. Hard-currency debt with bilateral and multilateral creditors was renegotiated through a mixture of rescheduling and an estimated $3.8 billion write-off. In 1998, Vietnam signed an agreement for debt and debt-service reduction with the London Club, which allowed the settlement of all its outstanding private uninsured commercial debt in arrears. Agreements were also reached with former Soviet Union states, allowing Vietnam to convert debt denominated in roubles into hard currency at favourable rates. The last of these agreements was signed with Russia, Vietnam's largest non-convertible creditor, in September 2000.[17]

A World Bank study estimated the Vietnamese convertible debt stock in 1999 to be US$11.14 billion, of which about half was concessional, and the remaining non-concessional debt was mostly linked to foreign investment projects. The same study (presented at the end of 1999 for the annual donors' Consultative Group) considered Vietnamese debt sustainable and foresaw that debt service as a percentage of GDP was due to decline from 7.7 per cent in 1999 to 5.7 per cent in 2002.

In the years before the regional economic crisis, the virtuous circle between macroeconomic stabilization and growth was also a result and a cause of an improved role of the external sector. Foreign trade increased from 46 per cent of GDP in 1989 to 97 per cent in 1996, though imports grew faster than exports, leading to a deterioration of current account balance (Table 2.3). However, export composition improved. Rice and crude oil (the two largest export products) saw their share of total exports declining from 40 per cent in 1990 to 30 per cent in 1996, while there was a rise in manufactured products from barely 2 per cent in 1990 to almost 30 per cent in 1996 (Figure 2.1).

From the early 1990s, FDIs became an important stimulus to growth, accounting for up to 28 per cent of total investment expenditure in the country in 1996. FDI was particularly important in reducing a balance of payments deficit produced by a level of national saving reportedly lower than the rate of national investment (see Chapter 3 for a discussion of FDI flows). It should be noted, however, that the official data on national investments do not properly reflect the real dynamics. Although the data report a remarkable increase in gross investment formation

Table 2.3 External trade, 1992–7

	1992	*1993*	*1994*	*1995*	*1996*	*1997*
Export (million $)	2,581	2,985	4,054	5,449	7,256	9,145
Import (million $)	2,541	3,924	5,826	8,155	11,144	11,622
Current account balance (% of GDP)	−1.3	−10.9	−12.5	−13.1	−10.4	-6.5

Source: UNDP Hanoi office homepage

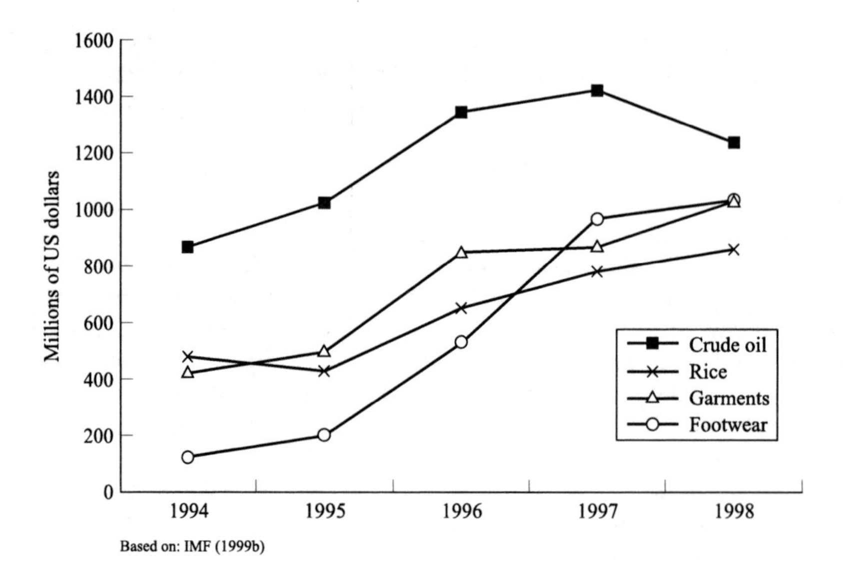

Figure 2.1 Exports: selected commodities

from 14.3 per cent of GDP in 1991 to 25.1 per cent of GDP in 1995, this figure still represents a rather modest rate compared with many other developing countries and well below the investment rates achieved in rapidly growing economies such as China, Thailand, Malaysia and Indonesia (Griffin 1998a: 9). This modest rate of capital accumulation should not have been able to support such rapid economic growth. Therefore, the more likely conclusion is that the level of national investment was actually underestimated (Fforde and de Vylder 1996: 306–307; Griffin 1998a: 9):

> Much may be missed, namely, private investment in urban small and medium enterprises, urban informal sector investments in service activities and workshops, investment by small farmers and land improvements, many investments in small-scale non-agricultural rural activities, and most investments which require an expenditure of labour effort rather than the purchase of equipment and materials… (Griffin 1998a: 10).

Table 2.4 ODA 1991–7 (millions of US dollars)

	1991	*1992*	*1993*	*1994*	*1995*	*1996*	*1997*
Pledges			1,990	1,860	2,000	2,300	2,400
Disbursement	338	356	274	624	611	984	944

UNDP computation, Hanoi office homepage

Table 2.5 Balance of payments (millions of US dollars)

	1993	*1994*	*1995*	*1996*	*1997*
Export	2,985	4,054	5,198	7,330	9,145
Import	–3,532	–5,250	–7,543	–10,483	–10,460
Trade balance	–547	–1,196	–2,345	–3,153	–1,358
Services and transfers	–220	11	417	704	–327
Current account balance	–767	–1,185	–1,928	–2,449	–1,642
Disbursements	54	272	443	772	1,022
Scheduled amortization	–652	–547	–733	–729	–804
Short term loans (net)	–313	124	–184	224	–534
DFI	832	1,048	2,236	1,838	2,003
Capital account balance	–78	897	1,762	2,105	1,688
Errors and omissions	–210	–121	–32	65	–50
Overall balance	–1,056	–409	–199	–278	–4
Financing	1,056	409	199	278	4
Change in NFA (excl. IMF)	477	–292	–439	–441	–265
IMF credit (net)	–39	175	92	178	–54
Debt rescheduling	883	0	0	0	0
Change in arrears	–266	526	546	541	323
Memo item: current account balance/GDP (%)					
Excluding grants	–	–	–10.2	–11.3	–9.7
Including grants	–	–	–9.6	–8.9	–9.9

Based on World Bank (1997a, 1999a)

ODA grew rapidly after the US government removed its opposition towards lending by the international financial institutions. Annual commitments reached US$2.4 billion in 1997. The rate of disbursements remained low, but on the eve of the regional crisis Vietnam improved its ODA absorption capability and implementation speed, allowing the disbursement to grow from US$611 million in 1995 to almost US$1 billion in 1996 and 1997 (Table 2.4).

A large trade deficit (over 10 per cent of GDP since 1993) was balanced by increasing disbursement of FDI and ODA (Table 2.5). However, the trend after 1996 raised concern among national authorities and international organizations.

A decline in FDI commitment posed the risk that the increase in ODA disbursement could not cover the high deficit in the current account, and the government could have been forced to depend on non-concessionary loans for financing the balance of payment. This led Vietnamese authorities to intervene before the regional crisis to curtail the trade deficit with measures directed to curb imports (World Bank 1997a).

As will be discussed in the following chapter, the adoption of drastic measures before the regional crisis in order to contain the trade deficit proved successful. Current account deficit was reduced to 6.5 per cent of GDP in 1997 and 4.2 per cent of GDP in 1998 (UNDP 2000).

Macroeconomic stability was also achieved through a prudent fiscal policy. Budget deficit was at 0.2 per cent of GDP on a cash basis in 1996.

The declining share in SOE contributions to the state revenues reflected both a structural change in the economy and a weakening of their financial performance (Table 2.6; see in the following). Stability was also maintained after the start of the regional crisis, with budget deficits of 1.4 per cent in 1997 and 1.1 per cent in 1998. However, the shrinkage of state revenues (as a percentage of GDP) due to the economic slowdown affected social expenditure, which, after having reached 8.0 per cent of GDP in 1996 (from 4.4 per cent in 1990), declined to 6.3 per cent of GDP in 1999 (World Bank 1999a).

In the years before the onset of the regional crisis, agriculture remained a key sector in the Vietnamese economy, although it represented a declining share of GDP (below 30 per cent from 1993 onwards; Table 2.7). About 70 per cent of Vietnamese workers continued to be employed in agriculture, and about 50 per cent of Vietnamese exports (including forestry and aquatic products) derived from agriculture (Figure 2.2). Between 1991 and 1996 the sector had an average growth of 4.9 per cent (Economist Intelligence Unit 1997: 39).

Table 2.6 Fiscal balance

	1992	*1993*	*1994*	*1995*	*1996*	*1997*
Total Revenues and Grants	19.0	22.5	24.7	23.9	22.9	21.1
Tax revenues	5.0	8.3	9.9	10.5	10.3	9.0
Transfers from SOEs	10.8	11.2	12.1	9.8	9.5	8.8
Other non-tax revenues	2.5	2.2	2.1	2.9	2.5	2.6
Grants	0.8	0.7	0.7	0.7	0.6	0.8
Current expenditure	14.0	18.8	18.3	17.8	16.4	15.7
Capital expenditure	5.8	7.0	6.9	5.4	5.7	6.2
Overall balance (cash basis)	−1.7	−4.6	−1.1	−0.5	−0.2	−1.4
Financing	1.7	4.6	1.1	0.5	0.2	1.4
Foreign loans (net)	2.4	2.7	0.1	−0.7	0.0	0.7
Domestic loans (net)	−0.7	1.8	0.9	1.2	0.2	0.8

Source: World Bank (1999a)

Table 2.7 GDP composition (percentage) by economic sector, 1991–7

	1991	*1992*	*1993*	*1994*	*1995*	*1996*	*1997*
Total	100.0	100.0	100.0	100.0	100.0	100.0	100.0
State	34.1	36.2	40.8	41.3	42.3	–	40.5
Non-state	65.9	63.8	59.2	58.7	57.7	–	59.5
Industry	23.8	27.3	28.9	29.6	30.0	29.7	32.1
State	15.5	17.9	19.0	19.7	–	–	–
Non-state	8.3	9.3	9.9	9.9	–	–	–
Agriculture	40.5	33.9	29.9	28.4	27.2	27.8	25.8
Service	35.7	38.8	41.2	41.6	41.7	42.5	42.2
Transport and communications	3.7	4.2	4.4	4.1	3.9	3.8	4.0
Trade	12.7	13.8	12.8	13.6	13.1	15.9	15.6
Banking	1.4	1.4	1.7	2.0	2.4	1.9	1.7
Public admin., medical, education	8.9	8.8	10.5	10.7	10.2	8.4	8.3
Tourism, NGOs and others	9.0	10.5	11.7	11.3	12.0	12.6	12.5

Based on: World Bank (1997a, 1999a)

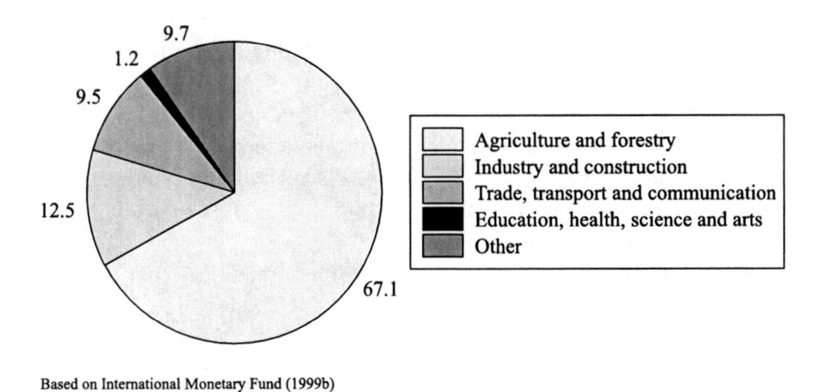

Based on International Monetary Fund (1999b)

Figure 2.2 Employment by sector, 1997

The reforms of agriculture in 1981 and 1988 were further enhanced by a new law approved in July 1993. Households acquired the right to exchange, transfer, rent, inherit, and mortgage land-use rights. The state maintained land ownership, but farmers had long-term contracts, which increased their propensity to invest. After having achieved food self-sufficiency, and actually having reached the status of major rice exporter, Vietnam moved successfully towards product diversification and a larger output of cash crops in the early 1990s. This agricultural diversification resulted in an important contribution to poverty reduction. However, the creation of a decentralized food-processing industry in rural areas, able to employ the labour force laid off as a result of agricultural mechanization, remained a development target that was difficult to achieve because of lack of investments.

Interpretative remarks on the first phase of economic reform

The formative phase of DRV institutions was a crucial period in the shaping of the country's socio-economic dynamics, also preparing the ground and setting the frame for the future economic reforms. In fact, the reaction to the economic problems experienced from the early 1960s onward in North Vietnam was the development of unplanned activities 'from below', often intertwined with experiments and unorthodox *ad hoc* measures 'from above'. This adaptation process included the development of a parallel free-market, which partially eroded the power of state monopolies. Activities outside the plan were even carried out by SOEs, sometimes in order to procure the resources to perform tasks foreseen by the plan. After 1965, with the starting of the American strategic bombing on North Vietnam, and the consequent decentralization of industry, this tendency was further enhanced. The control by central authorities on many areas of the country often became impossible (Kolko 1997).

Fforde and de Vylder (1996) identify these 'fence-breaking' activities of the early 1960s (outside the plan and sometimes in contrast with it) as the first foundation of the Vietnamese reform process. The central thesis of their study is that the reforms inaugurated in the 1980s as *doi moi* were the result of changes already made by society and ratified a posteriori by the national authorities. Thus, they describe the economic and political history of the country as a process in which the Vietnamese leadership tried to accommodate, regulate, or contrast pressures from below, sometimes by supporting a reformist agenda and sometimes by reintroducing a more 'orthodox' strategy.

While not necessarily in contrast with this interpretation, other authors like Melanie Beresford and Dang Phong remind that 'fence-breaking' activities were often promoted by local authorities and SOEs. Rather than implying a 'weakness' of the socialist state, these initiatives indicated a synergic relation between people and political representatives. The reform process was neither 'top down' nor 'bottom up':

> There was a symbiotic relationship between citizens and leaders in which both played an important role (Dang 2004: 20).

Looking at the reform process as the product of forces that from 'above' and from 'below' experimented with new solutions and responded in flexible ways to the economic problems deriving from the war, the changing international environment and shortcomings in the central planning allow one to reach a more nuanced understanding of the Vietnamese experience. On the one hand, these interpretations allow a different measure of the reform by establishing its roots in the early 1960s (and by considering the 'transition' from plan to market already concluded at the end of the 1980s). On the other hand, they offer an explanation of the reform as a 'process'. The definition of the reform as a 'process' means to put in evidence the modality of interaction between the society and the state by confuting a description of the reform as a series of top-down policy decisions and by highlighting the very specific characteristics of the Vietnamese experience.

An issue often debated regards the nature of Vietnam as a 'weak' or a 'strong' state, both in comparison with other socialist states and with other Asian countries. The most common interpretation is the one promoted by Fforde and de Vylder (1996), for which the Vietnamese state was substantially a 'weak state', unable to implement a coherent policy and to implement a full-fledged so-called 'neo-Stalinist' model. This view of Vietnam as a 'weak state' lacking the institutional resources to operate a planning system is confirmed by other authors (e.g. Riedel and Turley 1999: 13). As we have just seen, this view is contrasted by authors like Beresford and Dang Phon, who put the emphasis on the symbiotic relation between state and people. A number of factors may explain the behaviour of the Vietnamese central authorities in responding to pressure from below through fence breaking. First, the different views existing within the Vietnamese leadership, maintained open space for debate and for eclectic experiments.[18] Second, especially under war conditions, the central leadership could not maintain a close control over the activities carried out in the different parts of the country. Local authorities often had a rather free hand in adapting national policies to the local conditions, and at times this adaptation resulted in something very far from the official line. Third, the eclecticism and the pragmatism of the CPV could be understood as a positive resource deriving from the long historical experience of the Vietnamese civilization [see Masina (1999a)]. Pragmatism and ability in learning by doing have certainly characterized the current economic reform process (Griffin 1998a: 13). Finally, the inclination to accommodate pressures coming from outside the state apparatus and its own organization can be understood as a functional specificity of the Vietnamese state (Kerkvliet 1995: 67), and it should be understood as a resource in maintaining a close relation with society rather than as a weakness.

The following chapters will discuss how the reform strategy has been taking shape after the regional economic crisis. Here, we can already formulate some preliminary considerations on the first phase of *doi moi*. The synthetic historical background presented in the previous pages has supported the view that the Vietnamese 'transition', i.e. the transition from a system dominated by central planning to a system where market forces played a decisive role, was already accomplished by the late 1980s. The transition was concluded by the macroeconomic stabilization of the early 1990s, which partially incorporated elements typical of structural adjustment programmes. Using the famous expression coined by Fforde and de Vylder, the rationale of this reform was not much that of 'getting the price right', but rather a question of *making the prices matter* (Fforde and de Vylder 1996: 18).

The achievements of Vietnam during this process of systemic change clearly contrast with the tragic results of many other so-called 'transitional economies', which were inspired by a 'big bang' approach. The gradualist model adopted by Vietnam could rather be compared with the Chinese case, where a longer-term transition allowed the autonomous development of productive forces and capital able to compensate the displacements produced by the reform. Again in the words of Fforde and de Vylder:

> The package of drastic reform did not begin with a severe and unpopular austerity program with layoffs and price increases. Rather, the transitional model had created conditions for both extensive structural changes and commercialisation of the state and cooperative sectors before the final assault on the remnants of the DRV program in 1989 ... By 1989, prices mattered and autonomous capital had been accumulated outside as well as within the state and cooperative structures. This permitted the links between macro policies and micro responses to work reasonably well (Fforde and de Vylder 1996: 19).

The Vietnamese and Chinese cases also differ from the Eastern European and former Soviet Union 'transitions' on another essential point. By promoting a gradual reform, which did not imply the dismantling of key socio-economic institutions, Vietnam and China could make the best use of positive socialist heritage in terms of equality, human capital formation, and good educational and health-care systems. In both China and Vietnam the social institutions were threatened by the 'transition' to an economic system increasingly dominated by market logic, and paid a price in terms of effectiveness of their educational and health-care systems;[19] but neither of the two countries faced a drama comparable to that of the former Soviet Union.

An equitable distribution of land (through land reform, collectivization and de-collectivization) proved to be an important endowment for Vietnam, and a key resource for avoiding increased poverty. In addition:

> Vietnam also inherited from the socialist period a fairly equal distribution of human capital. Literacy was widespread, most people had at least few years of formal education and the great majority of the population had access to health care. As a result, Vietnam possessed at the outset of the reforms a skilled and healthy labour force that was able to respond quickly to economic opportunities (Griffin 1998a: 12–13).

It should be remembered that, notwithstanding its achievements, the process of economic transition in Vietnam was also a painful and dramatic period for a large part of the population. Various sectors of society found ways to cope with the new situation, and often managed to take advantage of the new opportunities. For others, who could not or would not participate in the new 'gold fever' climate, living conditions deteriorated in a period from the late 1980s to the mid 1990s. In particular, state employees, teachers, health-care operators, etc., saw not only their economic conditions, but also their social status undermined. An author very critical of the overall reform process, such as Gabriel Kolko, sees in this mixture of demoralization and economic necessity the dramatic increasing of corruption in the public administration.

> The real income of civil servants dropped by about two-thirds from 1985 to 1991, by which point cadres were compelled to choose between corruption, leaving the state sector, or going hungry, and many chose or were compelled to cheat. In 1993 most civil servants earned between $15 and $20 a month, less than half the wages for skilled workers, and their real incomes have continued to deteriorate since then (Kolko 1997: 75).

Reports denouncing the persisting difficulties for a large part of the population also appear every day in the local Vietnamese media. Although we will see in Chapter 4 that recent studies on poverty have indicated that the number of people living below the poverty line has declined, those studies also underline that many Vietnamese still live only slightly above that line, and need to fight every day to make ends meet. For instance, an article published before the onset of the regional crisis about living conditions in the largest Vietnamese towns stated:

> In the last four years, the price index has risen by 33 per cent while the minimum wage has only increased by 20 per cent. A recent survey on living conditions in Ho Chi Minh City showed that state administrative officers lead difficult lives. The average income in the health care sector is $55 a month, of which 51 per cent come from salary and the rest from other works, and sources such as lunch allowances and bonuses. The education sector is even worse with an average monthly income of $45. The survey found that only 5% of residents have incomes of more than $140 a month, while 15 per cent have incomes of $100–140 per month. About 30 per cent of those surveyed had monthly incomes of between $65 and $100. The survey claimed that, to meet basic needs, a city resident would need at least $65 a month (*Vietnam Economic Times* 1997: 2).

3 Vietnam and the regional economic crisis

Relations between Vietnam and the international financial institutions became critical before the onset of the regional economic crisis. The tension reflected a mood change about Vietnam: the national authorities were blamed for a slowdown in the reform process and the international pressure increased towards bolder steps (as we will see in the following chapter). Before we start discussing the new reform agenda promoted by the international financial institutions, it is useful to examine the arguments used to justify the need and, indeed, the urgency for a change of route. The main claim was that Vietnam, after achieving important results during the first phase of *doi moi*, had entered a period of slower economic growth and was losing the confidence of foreign investors, as witnessed by a shrinkage of FDI flows to the country, which began *before the Asian financial meltdown*. While a limited contraction in the outstanding Vietnamese growth rates was actually true, the change of mood among foreign operators had, in reality, much to do with excessive expectations among foreign operators in the previous years, self-fulfilling predictions (once investors started to foresee an investment shrinkage, they influenced each other to that outcome), and even more with a visible attempt by the international financial institutions to step in with their own reform proposals. Since the 'common wisdom' converged in representing the economic trend as negative and perilous (due to Vietnam's own responsibilities), foreign advice was represented as the only possible salvation.

In the following pages we will argue that this 'common wisdom' was, in reality, not very substantiated. First, the key indicator to prove a future decline of the Vietnamese economy (a contraction in FDI flows) was quite minimal before the regional crisis. Second, the reasons behind the Vietnamese difficulties had at least as much to do with regional and international contingencies as with national problems. With hindsight from the post-crisis period it is easy to see that many of the gloomiest predictions had little substance and probably served only to push Vietnam to abide to the recipes put forward by the international financial institutions.

In the wake of the regional crisis

This section starts by discussing the 'common wisdom' about the lesson that Vietnam should learn from the regional crisis. This common wisdom was based on the mainstream interpretations of the regional crisis: i.e. 'crony capitalism' in East Asia and unstable international financial markets, which eventually made the mixture of unchecked globalization and ill-regulated local institutions collapse into confidence tricks, speculation, and panic.[1] After the crisis, many of the worst hit countries (including Thailand and South Korea) started to implement systemic reforms and, by doing so, succeeded in restoring growth. Therefore, if Vietnam wanted to take advantage of the new regional economic trend, it had to address basic issues which were a hindrance to growth. Vietnam (continuing the mainstream interpretation[2]) had its own form of 'crony capitalism', a 'cosy' relationship between the state and SOEs that resulted in distortions and a sub-optimal allocation of resources (e.g. credit from state banks). The deceleration of economic growth in 1997 (from 9.3 per cent to 8.2 per cent of GDP)[3] had already been considered a result of a slower pace in the reform process by the mid 1990s (World Bank 1997a). The evidence that something was starting to go wrong in the Vietnamese economy was the shrinkage in FDI commitment and disbursement *before the onset of the regional crisis*. A World Bank report indicated that this slowdown was 'unusual, as the pattern in other developing countries is that disbursement continued to grow even after approvals begin to decline, due to a 2–3 years implementation lag'. And this could be linked to the 'cumbersome procedures that still exist for the approval, registration and implementation of foreign-invested projects, and to the perception that the "costs of doing business" in Vietnam are too high' (World Bank 1997a: 3).

After the crisis, a sharp decline in FDI disbursements was again explained as being the result of investors' uncertainty, because investors did not know if 'the government will adopt accelerated reforms'. A World Bank report released in 1999 claimed that investment returned to 'Korea, Malaysia and Thailand but not yet to Vietnam'. It conceded that the 'biggest decline came in FDI from East Asia and Japan, which is not surprising given the crisis in the region', but it immediately reminded its readers that 'declines in FDI commitments had started as early as in 1996' (World Bank 1999a). That is to say, the regional crisis made it more difficult to address problems that already existed for domestic reasons.

It is interesting to note the insistence of the international financial institutions in this explanation of FDI decline. The issue is a very sensitive one in the Vietnamese economic reform debate, given the country's need for investment. This chapter (in contradiction to the wisdom presented above) argues that the supposed causal nexus between a slowing pace in the reform process and shrinkage in FDI flows has probably been largely overestimated. In fact, the empirical analysis of FDI composition can support an interpretation quite different from the one normally accepted.[4]

The first point in our analysis concerns the dynamics of FDI commitments (Table 3.1). The data indicate that FDI commitments to Vietnam increased rapidly during the early 1990s and reached their peak in 1995. As was widely reported, the data for 1996 were inflated by two large real-estate projects approved in December, one of which (it alone accounting for about US$1 billion) was subsequently cancelled in November 1998 (see Freeman and Nestor (2004)).[5] A decline

Table 3.1 Commitments of FDI, 1995–7 (millions of US dollars)

	1995	*1996*	*1997*
Industry	2,467	2,735	1,658
Heavy industry	1,479	1,283	985
Economic processing zone	246	0	218
Light industry	510	862	318
Food	232	590	137
Oil and gas	0	52	51
Construction	686	630	711
Transport and communications	439	688	784
Real estate	2,698	3,300	338
Hotels and tourism	810	–65	112
Office property and apartments	1,888	3,366	225
Agriculture, forestry and fisheries	318	113	589
Services	114	184	324
Total	6,722	7,702	4,456

Source: IMF (1999b)

Table 3.2 FDI commitment, 1995–7 (millions of US dollars)

	1995	*1996*	*1997*
Total	6,722	7,702	4,456
Real estate	2,698	3,300	338
Total *minus* real estate	4,024	4,402	4,118

Source: re-elaborated from IMF (1999b)

in FDI commitments became evident in 1997, marking a worrying change of direction. This decline, however, should be considered while also taking into account the sector composition of commitments. The major factor in the decline was actually real estate, which dropped from 40.1 per cent of the total in 1995 and 42.8 per cent in 1996 to only 7.6 per cent in 1997. Thus, by subtracting the real-estate commitment from the total, one finds that in 1997 there was practically no shrinkage in FDI outside this specific sector. This is especially interesting considering that the regional crisis had already unfolded in the second half of the year (Table 3.2).

Commitment in agriculture, services, construction, transport and telecommunications actually increased. Investment in industry, however, declined in all the sub-sectors.

A drop in real estate in 1997 is consistent with a description of the pre-crisis East Asian economy as being dominated by elements of 'bubble economy' (see Sum (2002) and Chandrasekhar and Ghosh (2002)). The real-estate market in Vietnam was largely speculative in the mid 1990s, as in the rest of the region, and it was dominated by the same East Asian financial groups which defaulted in 1997, thus promptly cancelling former FDI commitments in Vietnam and

Table 3.3 Disbursement of FDI, 1992–8 (millions of US dollars)

	1992	*1995*	*1996*	*1997*	*1998*
Industry	49	737	843	969	330
Heavy industry	20	296	331	422	102
Economic processing zone	3	39	123	75	25
Light industry	10	232	324	365	123
Food	15	171	65	108	80
Oil and gas	73	582	301	1	50
Construction	6	113	274	151	250
Transport and communications	19	159	81	77	15
Real estate	53	433	366	423	113
Hotels and tourism	43	254	219	297	73
Office property and apartments	10	180	146	126	40
Agriculture, forestry and fisheries	12	121	75	285	41
Services	104	115	23	167	2
Total	316	2,260	1,963	2,074	800

Source: IMF (1999b)

elsewhere. The contraction in FDI commitments in industry is something more complex. It could be the result of at least three different factors, or combinations of these. It could derive from a decline in the attractiveness of Vietnam as a productive location – this is the 'official wisdom'. It could derive from a (temporary) decreased propensity to expand production abroad by countries which had traditionally represented a major source of FDI in Vietnam. It could derive from overinvestment in the Vietnamese productive system, beyond the absorption capability of this small economy. In the following pages, this work will claim that all of these three elements played a role, and that it would be erroneous to focus on a single explanation. It is also important to note that a sectoral analysis of FDI commitment reveals that the shrinkage in industry was compensated for by investment in other sectors (notably agriculture), thus redressing a negative tendency rightly criticized by the international donors and the international financial institutions.

The data regarding FDI disbursements too show a picture slightly different from the one described by the international financial institutions (Table 3.3). First of all, the negative trend reported in 1996 was already partially reversed in 1997. But, again, it is the sectoral distribution of FDI that provides the most useful information. The historical series of FDI disbursement is strongly affected by the instability of the oil sector, where (considering the high costs of projects in the field) a single initiative can alter the total significantly for one year. Thus, to study the consistency of trends it could be useful to subtract the disbursement for oil and real-estate projects from the total (Table 3.4).

This simple operation reveals that, before 1998, i.e. before the effects of the Asian crisis became apparent, there was no substantial decrease in FDI in Vietnam. The attempt, therefore, to use an alleged contraction in FDI inflows as an indication of national deficiencies in implementing the necessary reforms proves rather uncorroborated.

Table 3.4 Disbursement of FDI, 1992–8 (millions of US dollars)

	1992	*1995*	*1996*	*1997*	*1998*
Total	316	2,260	1,963	2,074	800
Real estate	53	433	366	423	113
Oil and gas	73	582	301	1	50
Total *minus* real estate & oil	190	1,245	1,296	1,650	637

Source: re-elaborated from IMF (1999b)

Table 3.5 FDI inflows, by selected Asian economies, 1993–8 (billions of US dollars)

	1993	*1994*	*1995*	*1996*	*1997*	*1998*
Hong Kong	3.66	4.13	3.28	5.52	6.00	1.60
India	0.55	0.97	2.14	2.43	3.35	2.26
Indonesia	2.00	2.11	4.35	6.19	4.67	–0.36
South Korea	0.59	0.81	1.78	2.33	2.84	5.14
Philippines	1.24	1.59	1.48	1.52	1.22	1.71
Taiwan	0.92	1.38	1.56	1.86	2.25	0.22
Thailand	1.81	1.36	2.07	2.34	3.73	6.97
Vietnam	1.00	1.50	2.00	2.50	2.95	1.90

Source: UNCTAD (1999)

Further, a point often neglected by most of the literature on Vietnam is that before the regional crisis the country was a host for FDI inflows that were disproportionately high considering the limited dimensions of its national economy. A comparison with other larger Asian economies can be illustrative in this regard (Table 3.5).

Although the data provided by the UNCTAD *World Investment Report* do not concord exactly with the Vietnamese statistics, they enable a rough comparison to be made. Thus, it appears that FDI inflows to Vietnam in 1996 were higher than those to the much larger economies of, for example, India, South Korea, Taiwan and Thailand. This consideration raises the legitimate suspicion that, in the mid 1990s, Vietnam might have been involved in a rush for investments, which might have been above the realistic economic conditions of the country [see Dixon (2000: 284–285) and Freeman and Nestor (2004: 188–190)]. Figure 3.1 shows that FDI inflow to Vietnam in 1996 was higher than the regional average as a percentage of GNP.

A sharp drop in FDI disbursement was visible in 1998. The negative trend was confirmed in 1999, with a further contraction to US$500 million. These data will be discussed in the next section, dealing with the impact of the regional crisis on Vietnam. However, some observations can be added along the same lines. Once again, the reported 'wisdom' that investments were not returning to Vietnam simply because the national authorities were not sending the right signals about

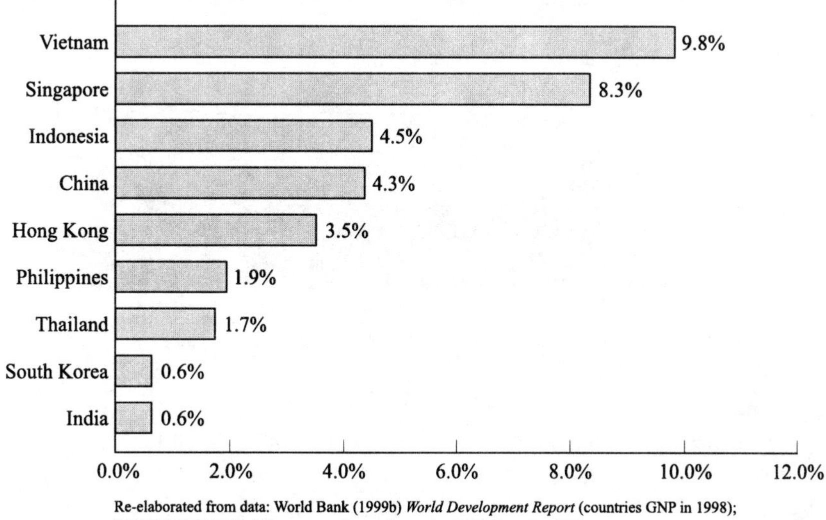

Figure 3.1 FDI as percentage of GNP

their commitment towards enhanced reform requires some qualification. In fact, it can be easily shown that the shrinkage of FDI flows to Vietnam was also connected to a parallel decrease in outward investment from those countries which had represented the dominant source of FDI to Vietnam.

Figure 3.2 shows that over 60 per cent of FDI to Vietnam before the regional financial crisis originated from East Asian countries (in the figure, 'other' also includes China, Thailand and Malaysia). Table 3.6 indicates that these countries had a contraction in their overall investment outflows after the onset of the crisis.

In most of these countries the contraction in FDI outflows between 1997 and 1998 was remarkable. South Korea stands out as being the only exception: in this case there was a slight increase in the global outflow of FDI. However, closer investigation reveals a relocation of investment towards Europe and North America, and a reduction in flows towards Southeast Asia (Table 3.7).

These considerations make it possible to argue that the shrinkage of FDI inflows to Vietnam in 1998 was connected to a general regional trend. This is illustrated by Figure 3.3, where the curves of the FDI outflows from selected Asian countries (in the case of South Korea the data on outflows to Southeast Asia have been used) are compared with the curve represented by FDI inflows to Vietnam. The correlation is clearly visible.

The arguments presented above seem to indicate that the 'official wisdom' had produced an oversimplified explanation of investment flows to Vietnam by neglecting the wider regional economic dynamics. This chapter, however, does not deny that national deficiencies and shortcomings had played a major role in

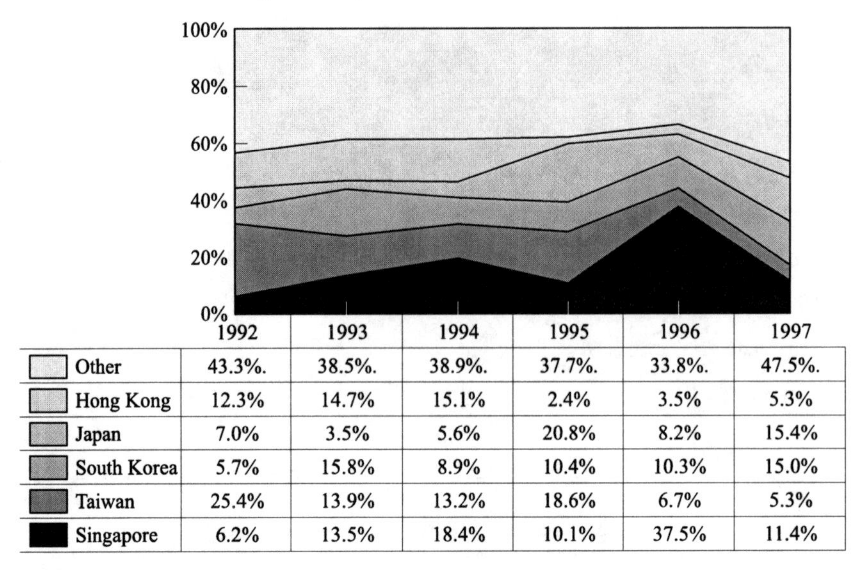

	1992	1993	1994	1995	1996	1997
Other	43.3%.	38.5%.	38.9%.	37.7%.	33.8%.	47.5%.
Hong Kong	12.3%	14.7%	15.1%	2.4%	3.5%	5.3%
Japan	7.0%	3.5%	5.6%	20.8%	8.2%	15.4%
South Korea	5.7%	15.8%	8.9%	10.4%	10.3%	15.0%
Taiwan	25.4%	13.9%	13.2%	18.6%	6.7%	5.3%
Singapore	6.2%	13.5%	18.4%	10.1%	37.5%	11.4%

Source: IMF (1999b)

Figure 3.2 Distribution of FDI commitments by country of origin, 1992–7

Table 3.6 FDI outflows, by selected economies, 1993–8 (millions of US dollars)

	1993	*1994*	*1995*	*1996*	*1997*	*1998*
China	4,400	2,000	2,000	2,114	2,563	1,600
Hong Kong	17,713	21,437	25,000	26,531	24,407	18,762
Japan	13,834	18,521	22,630	23,428	25,993	24,152
South Korea	1,340	2,461	3,552	4,670	4,449	4,756
Malaysia	1,464	2,591	3,091	4,133	3,425	1,921
Singapore	2,152	4,577	6,281	6,274	4,722	3,108
Taiwan	2,611	2,640	2,983	3,843	5,222	3,794
Thailand	232	492	887	931	447	122

Source: UNCTAD (1999)

Table 3.7 FDI outflows from South Korea to Southeast Asia, 1993–8

	1993	*1994*	*1995*	*1996*	*1997*	*1998*
Southeast Asia	486	1,080	1,652	1,625	1,497	1,441
Total	1,262	2,299	3,070	4,233	3,217	3,777

Source: National Statistic Office, Republic of Korea (1999)

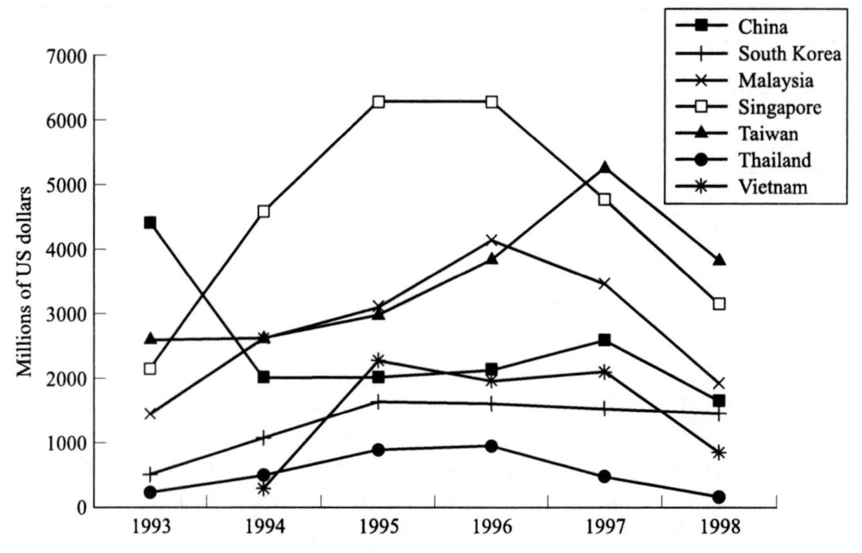

World FDI outflows by China, Malaysia, Singapore, Taiwan and Thailand; FDI flows by South Korea toward Southeast Asia; Total FDI inflow disbursement in Vietnam.
Re-elaborated from: UNCTAD (1999) *World Investment Report*; National Statistic Office, Republic of Korea (1999) *Korea Statistical Yearbook*; IMF (1999b).

Figure 3.3 FDI flows

producing discontent among investors at a critical juncture, i.e. in the wake of a regional economic crisis, when gloomy economic indicators led investors to reassess the rationale for their presence in the region. Once the regional perspectives had become less encouraging, the difficulties of doing business in Vietnam also assumed more visibility as a reason for discontent among foreign investors and entrepreneurs. The Vietnamese authorities came to be blamed for unclear administrative regulations, excessive red tape and corruption. While not contradicting the need to address these national shortcomings adequately (a need that was also recognized by the Vietnamese authorities, as witnessed by a number of reforms introduced during 1999 and 2000), this chapter tries to draw attention to the regional dimension of the crisis, which had been largely neglected.

Our evidence suggests that Vietnam might have been more closely integrated into the regional economic dynamics before the East Asian crisis than previously accepted. This might have resulted in a large flow of FDI to the country – a flow probably exceeding the absorption capability of an as yet small economy with significant infrastructural bottlenecks. In other words, Vietnam might have been affected by the same overinvestment tendencies existing in the region.[6] Part of the FDI flow represented by real estate had a speculative nature, as in the rest of the region. This speculative nature was further suggested by an abnormal share of investment commitments (17.8 per cent of the 1996 total) from an offshore location such as the British Virgin Islands. The contraction in FDI disbursement

Table 3.8 Real GDP growth, percentage

	1996	*1997*	*1998*
China	9.6	8.8	7.8
Indonesia	8.0	4.5	−13.1
South Korea	6.8	5.0	−6.7
Malaysia	10.0	7.3	−7.4
Philippines	5.8	5.2	−0.6
Thailand	5.9	−1.5	−10.8
Vietnam	9.3	8.2	3.5

Source: IMF (2001)

after the onset of the crisis in East Asia was correlated to a regional trend. Further, the fact that investors returned to South Korea and Thailand soon after the crisis is a consideration of no real significance for Vietnam; this trend was clearly connected to the acquisition of local corporations after these countries had been forced to liberalize their markets as a condition for receiving IMF bail-out loans. Nor did Malaysia provide a strong case to support the indications of the international financial institutions; as is well known, Kuala Lumpur actually moved in a rather different direction from the one suggested by Washington (by imposing controls on short-term capital flows) and was, therefore, repeatedly criticized.

Moreover, another consideration could be added to clarify the background for an assessment of Vietnam's economic performance. A comparison with the regional data gives grounds for relating the partial deceleration of the Vietnamese economy in 1997 to a regional trend. In fact, the figures in Table 3.8 show that many other countries in the region (as has been reported in numerous studies) were already facing economic difficulties before the crisis, difficulties that exploded in the form of financial crisis.

The impact of the regional crisis

The interpretation of the data presented above indicates that the association of Vietnam with the regional economy was more pronounced than normally reported. Correctly, two considerations have often been presented to explain why the impact of the crisis on Vietnam had been less severe than on other countries. First, the non-convertibility of the *dong* and the regulation of trade and exchange transactions had partially insulated the country from the vagaries of the financial market and averted speculative attacks. Second, Vietnam was a country where a large part of the economy was still 'informal' and family based. Thus, the protection of traditional safety nets in rural areas and the flexible urban 'informal sector' was able to reduce the negative impact of the crisis on the living conditions of the poorest. This consideration brings us back to one of the key questions in the crisis and post-crisis debate and will be discussed further in Chapter 5.

The first question, i.e. the relative insulation from the regional financial meltdown, is discussed here. The focus we intend to adopt is not an assessment of the short-term impact of the crisis, but an analysis of the medium- and long-term development implications. The questions at stake are the conditions for Vietnam's future economic development and the policies to be implemented in order to achieve the goal of accelerated industrialization. Before the crisis, Vietnam was moving fast along the path taken by other regional 'success stories'. The basic assumption (of national authorities and of foreign investors) was that Vietnam could integrate further into the regional economy and benefit from new rounds of investment from countries whose comparative advantage was shifting towards more technology-intensive and labour-intensive production. Therefore, discussing the impact of the crisis means discussing the way in which this long-term plan has been affected. This chapter will make three basic points:

1 In the short to medium term, the impact on the Vietnamese economy was severe. The crisis implied not only a halt to further productive relocations, but also a reverse trend, with companies retrenching to their original productive bases. The appreciation of the *dong* against most regional currencies partially reduced the attractiveness of the cheap Vietnamese labour force.
2 In the longer term, Vietnam will succeed again in becoming an attractive location for labour-intensive production, especially because of its large population and its well-educated labour force. However, Vietnam faces and will face strong competition from China and other Southeast Asian countries.
3 The broad implications of the crisis should be considered against the background of an increasing political confrontation between Asian economies and Western capital, represented also by multilateral organizations (such as the WTO) and the international financial institutions. Vietnam will come under increasing pressure and will be requested to adopt a 'liberal' economic policy. A number of elements signal that this confrontation between Vietnam and the West has already begun.

The regional crisis and Vietnam's macroeconomic standing

In autumn 1997, when the financial contagion was spreading through the region, Vietnam (which was partially insulated by the fact that its currency was not freely convertible) seemed more concerned with two other internal problems. The first was Typhoon Linda, the worst tropical storm to hit the country in five decades. The second was the tense political situation (with peasant demonstrations and riots against corrupt local officers) in the northern coastal province of Thai Binh. Typhoon Linda devastated central and southern provinces. A few months later, the typhoon was followed by an extended drought that further jeopardized the economy of those areas, affecting cash crops such as coffee in particular. The other 'typhoon', the peasant uprising in Thai Binh, represented a very worrying signal of potential political instability, forcing the leadership to react. The peasant demonstrations received support not only from war veterans and from retired party officers, but also from the army, who clearly resisted the use of force to repress disturbances. Eventually the party leadership intervened, removing controversial local officers, and put a great deal of effort into reopening a political dialogue within the province – the effort included several visits to Thai Binh by top party and government leaders.[7]

During 1998, however, the effects of the regional crisis on the Vietnamese economy became increasingly evident: at the end of the year, all major macroeconomic indicators suggested that the situation was becoming critical. Currency devaluation in many neighbouring countries exposed Vietnam to increased competition at the same time as export markets for its national products, two-thirds of which consisted of East Asian countries, were shrinking. Export growth in 1998 slowed to 0.3 per cent, compared with about 22 per cent in 1997. After a further decline in the first 4 months of 1999, with a 7.5 per cent year-on-year drop, exports recovered appreciably in the second part of the year. The higher price of oil in the international markets and the increased volume of exports in agriculture, garments and footwear resulted in a 23.6 per cent export growth rate in 1999 (UNDP 2000).

To avoid aggravating the trade deficit, which was already considered to be too high before the regional crisis, the government intervened to restrict imports. This resulted in a negative growth in imports in 1998 (1 per cent) and a marginal increase in 1999 (1.1 per cent). The shrinkage in imports brought the trade deficit down to US$2,171 million in 1998 and only US$100 million in 1999. However, although these figures indicated some relief for the national current accounts, the shrinkage of imports also signalled a downturn in productive investment in machinery and capital goods.

Vietnam did not enter a recession, unlike many other countries in the region, but GDP growth declined sharply. During 1998 the government was forced to readjust its expectations downward from the planned 9 per cent to about 6 per cent. The official data indicate that real GDP growth was at 5.8 per cent in 1998 and at 4.7 per cent in 1999.[8] In 1998, in order to regain some competitiveness for its exports, Vietnam devalued the *dong* by about 20 per cent against the US dollar. Notwithstanding this devaluation, in the midst of the regional crisis the Vietnamese currency appreciated consistently against most regional currencies. By the end of 1999 the Vietnamese *dong* had risen by about 20 per cent against the currencies of Thailand, Malaysia and the Philippines and by about 60 per cent against the Indonesian *rupiah*, compared with pre-crisis exchange rates. The Chinese *renminbi* and the Hong Kong dollar remained stable against the US dollar, thus resulting in a *dong* devaluation of about 20 per cent against these two currencies (Table 3.9).

The medium-term implications of these exchange-rate readjustments in the region, which evidently implied a change in comparative advantages, will be discussed further in the next part of this chapter.

In the emergency situation created by the regional crisis, the Vietnamese government proved quite successful in maintaining macroeconomic stability. This was recognized by the international financial institutions, which also admitted that their pessimistic forecasting had been avoided:

Table 3.9 Changes in exchange rates during the financial crisis – December 1999

	Appreciation: national currency versus US$ (%)			*Appreciation: national currency versus VN Dong (%)*		
	Dec 96–Dec 99	*Jul 97–Low*	*Jul 97–Dec 99*	*Dec 96–Dec 99*	*Jul 97–Low*	*Jul 97–Dec 99*
Vietnam	−27	−20	−20	–	–	–
Philippines	−36	−42	−35	−18	−39	−22
Malaysia	−33	−44	−34	−16	−41	−20
Thailand	−34	−53	−35	−16	−50	−22
Indonesia	−67	−85	−66	−59	−84	−60
Hong Kong	−1	0	0	26	5	20
China	0	0	0	27	5	20
Taiwan	−13	−20	−12	10	−4	6
Korea	−26	−49	−22	−6	−47	−6
Japan	13	−22	11	43	−7	33

Source: UNDP (2000)

> In the two years of East Asian recession, Vietnam has followed a cautious economic stance, giving priority to ensuring macroeconomic stability rather than taking risks in order to achieve higher growth. This has led to some successes. Contrary to the fears of eighteen months ago, Vietnam has avoided the serious balance-of-payments, fiscal or banking crises that have been common in the region… (World Bank 1999a).

However, as the same World Bank's report also indicated, the impact of growth contraction had been significant in many regards. A major effect was a fall in investment as a share of GDP: from 29 per cent in 1997 to an estimated 19 per cent in 1999, with half of this decline attributed to the aforementioned shrinkage in foreign investment flows (World Bank 1999a).

Another major implication of the crisis was a slump in government revenues from 23 per cent of GDP in 1996 to 17.8 per cent in 1999 (UNDP 2000). This decrease forced the government to cut expenditure accordingly in order to avoid fiscal instability, thus curtailing resources for an expansionary economic policy (of the kind attempted, instead, by China). However, to reduce the impact of the recession on the population, the government sought to protect social expenditures (World Bank 1999a).

The attempt by the Vietnamese authorities to attract more ODA in order to compensate for the drop in FDI and relieve the balance of payments deficit did not succeed. The regional economic crisis unfolded at the moment in which the dialogue between the Vietnamese government and the international financial institutions was characterized by deep disagreements on the reform agenda and on the timing of its implementation. In 1997, the IMF withheld the sum of roughly US$176 million, which had been agreed in 1994 as the third instalment of a 3-year enhanced structural adjustment facility (ESAF) amounting to US$530 million.

In the midst of the economic difficulties resulting from the regional crisis, the IMF maintained its reluctance to a new ESAF, thus also hampering a fresh World Bank structural adjustment credit. Only in April 2001 (well after the end of the regional crisis and after that the international financial institutions had been the object of severe criticisms for their conduct) did the two Bretton Woods institutions restore concessional lending to Vietnam.

While structural adjustment facilities were withheld, ODA to Vietnam was discussed in Paris in December 1998 by the Consultative Group for Vietnam (CG), the coordination meeting of international donors. The CG pledged US$2.2 billion of development aid to the country, less than the US$2.4 billion committed in 1997. However, the CG offered a further $500 million package during the year in the event of an acceleration of the reform process. In December 1999, the annual CG meeting, held in Hanoi, further increased the share of ODA conditional on acceleration in the reform process. Donors pledged US$2.1 billion, and promised a further US$700 million if the government proceeded in the direction prescribed by the 1999 World Bank-coordinated report *Preparing for Take-off?* In other words, it is quite evident the attempt by the international financial institutions and other Western donors to exploit the economic difficulties of Vietnam during the regional crisis in order to impose their own (neoliberal) prescriptions.

The shrinkage in external trade and FDI, the lower than expected level of ODA, the lack of specific support from the IMF and the World Bank – all of these factors made the country more vulnerable to the risk of running short of foreign exchange in the midst of a regional financial crisis. The national reserves in foreign currencies and gold were put under strong pressure, threatening to make the country unable to repay the short-term debts accumulated by state-owned and private enterprises. However, the measures adopted by the Vietnamese authorities to control import flows and maintain a low trade deficit proved successful in averting the most pessimistic prediction of an impending financial meltdown (UNDP 1998) or high increase in the balance of payments deficit (World Bank 1997a).

The positive results in the macroeconomic position and the improved trade balance did not conceal the negative impact of the crisis. The need to curtail the fiscal deficit and avoid an inflationary upsurge led Vietnamese authorities to adopt a strict monetary policy and renounce anti-cyclical interventions (as done, instead, by China through a large expansion of public spending). This was effective in containing inflation, which, after rising from 3.8 per cent in 1997 to 9.2 per cent in 1998, went down to 0.1 per cent in 1999. The drastic cutback in inflation (to the verge of a deflationary drive) was largely motivated by a drop in food prices (in part as a result of a record rice harvest), which account for the largest portion of a basket of goods and services on which the price index is based. However, it also resulted from a drop in the aggregate demand for investments and national consumption. Reports of stockpiling and of industrial plants producing far below their potential output were recurrent themes in the national and international media throughout 1998 and 1999.

The economic slowdown also had an impact on people's living conditions, though a precise account is limited by the scarcity of data. The official data indicate that urban unemployment rose from 6.85 per cent in 1998 to 7.4 per cent in 1999 (Reuters, 6 October 1999). However, a calculation of unemployment or underemployment in rural areas or in the non-official sectors in urban areas is not available.

Vietnam and the 'flying geese' pattern in the post-crisis environment

In the pre-crisis period, Vietnam successfully increased its integration into the regional productive system. East Asia absorbed about two-thirds of Vietnam's exports and was the origin of over 60 per cent of direct investment in the country. To appreciate the full importance of the association with the region, it should be recalled that Vietnam is a rather outward-oriented economy: in 1996, foreign trade amounted to 89.7 per cent of GDP (Fukase and Martin 1999a: 2). Its exports-to-GDP ratio is higher than that of the other 14 East Asian member countries of the World Bank, including South Korea, Indonesia, Malaysia, Thailand and China (Khan 1998: 23). The high level of integration into the regional economy was inspired by the so-called 'flying geese' pattern, a process whereby Japanese companies (and increasingly those of the Asian newly industrializing economies) relocated labour-intensive production in order to cope with the shifting of their comparative advantages towards more technology-intensive production. We should clarify, however, that the expression 'flying geese' is used here as a short form to indicate an articulated system of regional division of labour which was far from the idyllic cooperation that the 'flying geese' expression is trying to convey. Behind the rhetoric of this image (which Japanese scholars employed to emphasize the role of Japan in leading junior Asian countries towards economic prosperity) lay a reality made of labour exploitation on the one hand and competition among the industrial groups of the different countries on the other hand (e.g. Cumings 1987; Arrighi *et al.* 1993; Masina 1996). The more a number of Asian countries progressed in their effort towards industrialization, the more their companies tried to break the Japanese control and to achieve a world level position on their own (Sum 2002).

Notwithstanding the conflicts that were inherent to the regional division of labour, there is a large consensus in suggesting that the 'flying geese' dynamics have played a key role in promoting economic growth in East Asia since the 1960s. The appreciation of the Japanese yen after the Plaza Accord (1985) forced a new round of FDI to the region, which in turn moved the comparative advantages of economies such as Taiwan and South Korea towards more technological and capital-intensive productions. This compelled a further reorganization of the regional system of division of labour that created new opportunities for a new tier of countries – especially China and Vietnam (Masina 1996; Jomo 2001a). Vietnam tried to benefit from these productive relocations, particularly from South Korea, Taiwan and Singapore, with positive results from 1990 to 1997.

As already anticipated in Chapter 1 and discussed further in Chapters 4 and 6, the first group of Asian industrializers were able to seize the opportunities created by the favourable regional contexts through effective national planning. Probably inspired by the experience of other Asian countries, Vietnam also tried to manage the integration of the country into the regional productive system with state guidance measures that, however, were more closely related to the traditional central planning than to the market governance of Northeast Asian economies (see discussion in Chapter 4).

An analysis of changing comparative advantages in East Asia and the reorganization of regional productive systems in a post-crisis environment would be very beneficial in helping Vietnam in planning medium- and long-term development strategies. But the 'common wisdom' based on neo-classical economics tends to confute the need for such planning, supporting the view that reforms serving further liberalization and a more 'neutral' trade regime would *per se* increase Vietnamese competitiveness. Thus, the international financial institutions, which would have the means for a large-scale investigation, remain silent in providing elements useful in understanding the dynamics characterizing economic restructuring in post-crisis East Asia. This reticence is also evident in the studies produced by mainstream scholars and institutions to assist the Vietnamese authorities in furthering the process of economic reforms.

An investigation of East Asian productive system restructuring during and after the regional crisis is outside the scope of this work. However, the following lines present a sample analysis of a few data with the aim of supporting the need for more exhaustive and systematic research in this direction.

China is generally the first country to be examined in order to understand not only the changes in regional trends, but also more specifically the changing environment for the Vietnamese economy. With its enormous reserve of cheap labour, China is Vietnam's principal competitor as a location for labour-intensive production. China's relatively higher technological level and higher productivity has made production cheaper in many low-range industrial sectors. This has resulted in large-scale smuggling from China to Vietnam (estimated at about 20 per cent of Vietnamese imports).

During the regional crisis, China visibly strengthened its position as a leading force in East Asia. Not only did the country succeed in maintaining growth of over 7 per cent, but it also played a significant role in supporting regional economic stability. China, which had devalued the *renminbi* in 1993, made it very clear during the regional financial meltdown that it would defend the exchange rate of its currency (and that of the Hong Kong dollar) with its large foreign reserves. The stability of the Chinese currency averted a new round of currency depreciation that would have certainly resulted from any *renminbi* devaluation. China's stance was further reinforced by a comparison with the economic and political impasse visible in the other East Asian giant, Japan. In June of 1998, for instance, at a time when the low value of the Japanese yen was putting great pressure on the exports of other Asian nations, China played a major role (behind the scenes) to reverse the trend. The Chinese threat to devalue its currency induced the US administration to dispatch the (then) deputy secretary at the US Treasury, Larry Summers, to Tokyo in order to convince Japan to intervene in defence of the yen.

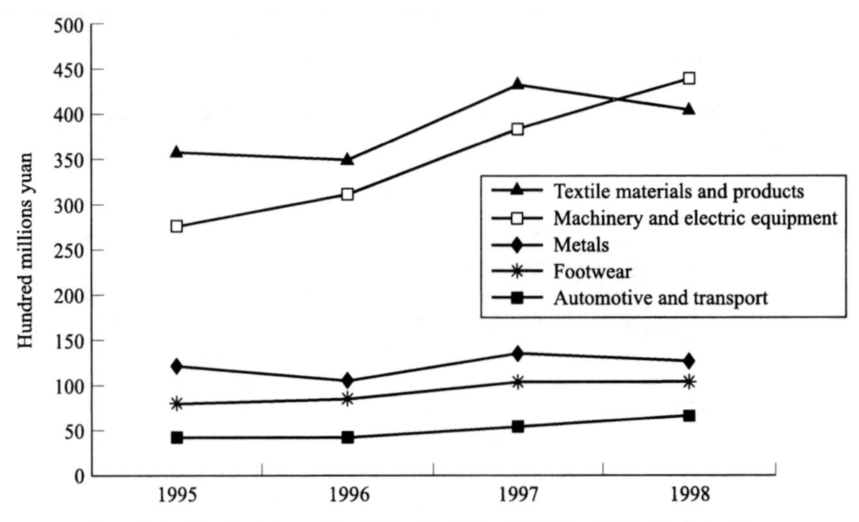

Source: National Statistical Bureau of People's Republic of China (1999) *China Statistical Yearbook n 18*. Beijing: China Statistic Press.

Figure 3.4 Chinese exports: selected commodities

The stability of the *renminbi* during the crisis resulted in a significant appreciation of the Chinese currency against all other major regional currencies. By December 1999 the value of the *renminbi* had increased by over 30 per cent against the currencies of Thailand, Malaysia and the Philippines, 22 per cent against the South Korean *won*, and 12 per cent against the Taiwanese dollar. However, notwithstanding currency appreciation, China avoided a major shrinkage in its exports. The data for 1998 suggest that this was done thanks to *a significant shift in export composition*, moving towards more technology-intensive and higher value-adding production.

An analysis of export composition in the midst of the East Asian crisis indicates that textiles and garments (typical labour-intensive production) suffered the most from currency appreciation. Exports of machinery and electrical equipment, on the other hand, continued to grow, indicating that China is increasingly becoming a big player in a sector long dominated by other East Asian countries. Growth in the export of automotive and transportation equipment was also remarkable, suggesting a successful diversification into more advanced industrial production. Notwithstanding the important diversification in export composition, China did pay a price for the devaluation of other regional currencies: export growth was only 0.5 per cent in 1998 and turned negative in 1999, with a recovery only in 2000 (Figure 3.4).

Thailand is the next country to look at in order to understand how the reorganization of the regional productive system during the regional crisis affected the Vietnamese growth perspectives. In recent years, Thailand has been a competitor to Vietnam, but also a source of foreign investment. Before being hit hard by the

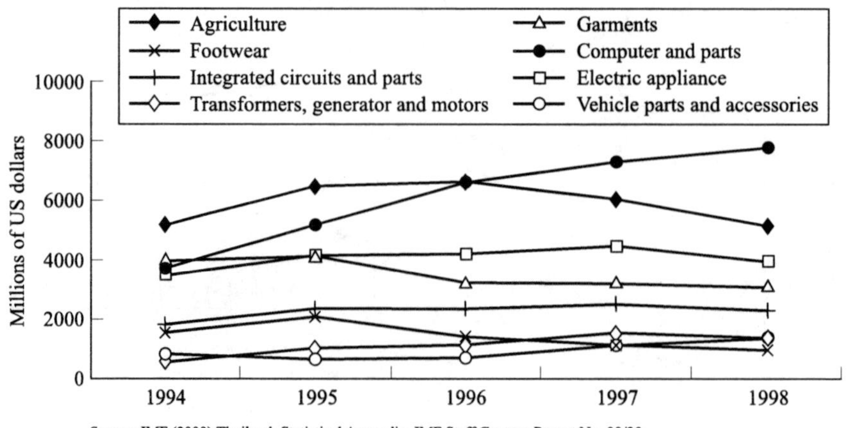

Figure 3.5 Thai exports: selected commodities

regional crisis, Thailand was known as a 'second tier' country (together with Malaysia and Indonesia), one following a path of accelerated industrialization led by the other Asian newly industrializing economies. According to the 'flying geese' model of the regional productive order, Thailand was just one step ahead of Vietnam and China. Thus, the upgrading of Thai production towards more technology-intensive production would leave room for Vietnam in the labour-intensive sector. At the end of 1998, notwithstanding wide currency devaluation, Thai exports were still below pre-crisis levels in US dollar terms. Imports had decreased appreciably, thus allowing a readjustment of the trade balance, but exports apparently failed to take advantage of increased competitiveness in terms of labour costs.[9] A rapid overview of the composition of Thai exports, however, seems to indicate that currency devaluation boosted exports less than might have been expected, because *Thailand did not re-engage in labour-intensive production but carried out further industrial upgrading* (Figure 3.5).

The overview of data contained in an IMF statistical report released in February 2000 indicated that exports in garments, footwear and other labour-intensive production declined in dollar terms in line with a trend started before the regional crisis. Exports in more advanced sectors such as computers and vehicles grew rapidly instead.

As with China, the compositional pattern of Thai exports seems to indicate that the crisis did not undermine and actually probably even extended Vietnam's potential for increasing its market share in the export of labour-intensive production.[10] The data do confirm that this potential was exploited successfully: in 1999 the growth in Vietnam's exports in the garment sector was over 103 per cent, and in footwear it was over 34 per cent (Table 3.10).

The data are also confirmed by a qualitative investigation conducted on behalf of the Norwegian trade unions in the summer of 1999. Using a survey carried out in Ho Chi Minh City and Danang on enterprises engaged in textile, garment and

Table 3.10 Vietnamese export growth, 1995–9

	1995	*1996*	*1997*	*1998*	*1999*
Garments (%)	–9.45	51.04	19.82	10.00	103.61
Footwear (%)	63.93	165.50	81.73	6.94	34.88

Sources: IMF (1999b) and UNDP (2000)

footwear production, the research showed that the crisis did not have a very severe impact on these companies. In particular, foreign-affiliated companies, whose production was mainly directed abroad, could rely on foreign partners in finding new markets. The wage augmentation in dollar terms compared with neighbouring countries was not considered by the managers interviewed as a factor important enough to motivate production relocation out of Vietnam. Although foreign investment in these labour-intensive sectors tended to originate in other East Asian countries, foreign entrepreneurs were acting as middlemen in an international production chain controlled by large Western multinational corporations (e.g. Nike), whose markets were largely located in OECD nations (Nørlund 1999).

The data on Vietnamese export growth in 1999 seem to indicate a favourable trend in the reorganization of regional production systems. This may imply that Vietnam could succeed in further extending its market share in labour-intensive production, benefiting from industrial upgrading in other East Asian countries.

The potential of the Vietnamese economy was indeed soon confirmed not only by a continuing high growth rate (which made Vietnam one of the strongest performers in the region in the late 1990s, contradicting the gloomy predictions of many international financial institutions' economists), but also by a return of a high level of FDI inflows.

Analytical remarks

This chapter has presented the hypothesis that the Vietnamese economy had been more integrated into regional production systems than it is normally suggested. Already in the wake of the regional economic crisis, Vietnam faced a mild deceleration in economic growth and shrinkage in FDI inflows. This was largely a result of the economic imbalances mounting in the region (overproduction, speculative bubbles in the real-estate sector, etc.) which eventually unfolded in the form of financial and economic crisis. The related economic downturn in Vietnam was interpreted by the international financial institutions (and by a number of mainstream analysts) as an indication of national shortcomings in the process of economic reform. Although shortcomings were undeniable – and they may have resulted in discontent among foreign entrepreneurs, thus reducing their propensity to make further investments – the interpretation provided by neoliberal analysts was excessively unilateral, failing to take adequate account of the regional dimension of FDI shrinkage. This unilateral interpretation may be understood as an attempt to push Vietnam towards a more 'orthodox' development strategy.

Contrary to the predictions of the international financial institutions, after the Asian crisis Vietnam was fast in recovering its role as exporter of labour-intensive production (in particular, garments and footwear). However, upgrading its industry towards more value-added forms of production requires industrial strategies that are able to save the country from the tyranny of static comparative advantages. The experience of the region in this regard has also been successful (following what has been described as a 'flying geese' path) due to favourable geopolitical conditions. The reorganization of regional production systems following the East Asian economic crisis will be the decisive factor in determining the conditions for Vietnamese industrial development.

4 The agenda for economic reform

Even before the onset of the regional economic crisis the 'official wisdom' had already converged in identifying four main issues as cornerstones for the enhancement of the economic reform: (1) privatization of SOEs, (2) reform of the financial sector, (3) trade liberalization and (4) development of the private sector. This agenda was confirmed after the crisis by the major international agencies (e.g. World Bank 1999a; IMF 1999a; UNDP 1998). Officially, the Vietnamese authorities subscribed to this agenda; in reality, significant resistance on key aspects of this package did exist. In the words of Tran Xuan Gia, at the time Minister of Planning and Investment at the donors Consultative Group Meeting in December 1999:

> We all agree on *what* reforms need to be done. The discussion is about *how*. We agree that without accelerated reforms we cannot grow rapidly and therefore the question is how best to accelerate the 'doi moi' process (World Bank homepage, emphasis in the original).

The role of 'agenda setting' played by the international financial institutions was implicitly justified against the background of relative impasse within the Vietnamese leadership in promoting a clear-cut reform strategy. Although the state and party leaders maintained a broad commitment to *doi moi*, by the mid 1990s most foreign observers had a sense that the reform process was losing momentum and that the path was becoming uncertain.

There is a wide consensus among analysts in suggesting that the implementation of bold reform measures in the period from 1989 to 1991 was the consequence of the emergency situation deriving from fading Soviet and Eastern European aid. The positive results of these reforms, accompanied after 1992 by increased development assistance from bilateral and multilateral donors and large flows of FDI, decreased the pressure for a furthering of *doi moi* and reduced the leadership's sense of urgency in implementing sensitive measures. By 1994, the positive economic achievements made the Vietnamese government conclude that the systemic crisis was over. This perception led to an attempt to regain control over the foreign-invested sector and to put higher emphasis on self-reliance (Dixon 2000: 284; Dixon and Kilgour 2002: 604–605).

The change of attitude by the national leadership was interpreted by many foreign economists as a risky departure from a sound reform path. Adam Fforde (1998b), for instance, voiced openly the view that too large aid flows to Vietnam would maintain the status quo and delay needed reforms. Ari Kokko described the situation in the following terms:

> Even before the advent of the Asian crisis in July 1997, it had become apparent that it might not be possible to sustain the high growth rate without further reforms. The reason was that serious structural weaknesses had begun to endanger the stability of the economy. The problems included inefficient SOEs and banks, growing current account deficits, and a trade policy bias in favour of import substitution. The development of the private sector was also obstructed by unclear rules, often favouring SOEs, excessive red tape, and corruption (Kokko 1998b: 3).

With the benefit of insight from subsequent events, it is possible to argue that the tone of this quotation proved excessively pessimistic: the problems were real, but Vietnam succeeded in maintaining high growth rates in the aftermath of the regional crisis. It is also possible to argue that the Western scholars and international agencies had been too hard in criticizing the Vietnamese slow implementation of the reform process, which could have been understood as a need to take stock of the results achieved until then before undertaking new controversial measures. While Vietnam was criticized for moving too slowly, it is fair to recall that Vietnam did much better than most other 'transitional economies' exactly because the reform process was gradualist and avoided the uncreative destruction of shock therapies.

As we argued in Chapter 3, foreign enthusiasm in the early 1990s was probably excessive, with investors having unrealistic expectations in terms of short-term profits. This excessive optimism was bound to transform to disillusion within a very few years, as indeed did happen in 1996.[1] Rightly, Gainsborough (2004) argues that this rapid change of mood about the Vietnamese economy was very much a Western construction rather than reflecting concrete facts. The Vietnamese authorities, in reality, never did intend to embark on a wholesale liberalization of the economy in the early 1990s, and while by the mid 1990s *doi moi* may have lost some of its steam, there was no concrete indication that the reform process would be reversed or halted. Rather, the Vietnamese authorities continued on their course of step-by-step reforms, charting their route by trying to maintain a consensus within the party and avoiding an open disagreement with foreign donors.[2]

While it seems undeserved to read the outcomes of the Eighth Party Congress of May 1996 as 'reform immobilism' (Womack 1997), it is fair to argue that the skirmishes between so-called (by Western analysts) 'reformists' and 'conservatives' did not allow the emergence of a clear reform agenda for furthering the *doi moi* (Riedel and Turley 1999: 36–40).[3] As argued by Vasavakul (1997), the party remained split along lines reflecting the representation of different sectoral interests.

No more precise strategy decisions were assumed by the following Ninth Congress of April 2001. The congress was marked by the dramatic dismissal of Secretary-General Le Kha Phieu. This outcome was connected to the accusation that Phieu had abused his power and was not the result of a change in the political balance.[4] The congress appointed as the new party leader Nong Duc Manh, who had emerged as a popular political figure also thanks to his ability in giving a more prominent role to the National Assembly (where he served as chairman) – an institution that had previously been described as a mere rubber-stamp of decisions already taken by the party and the government.[5] The rise to power of Nong Duc Manh was made possible by his talent in mediating among the different interest groups and factions within the party. Although he belonged to a younger generation and was often described as a reformer, his election was not the sign that the party was willing to undertake radical changes.

An attempt to understand the political debate within the Communist Party on the basis of categories like 'reformer' or 'conservative', however, risks oversimplifying reality and even to produce serious misconceptions. As has already been recalled, the Vietnamese leadership tends to act by searching for consensus rather than operating abrupt shifts. This *modus operandi* reflects two essential characteristics of the Vietnamese decision-making process. On the one hand, there is a broad consensus within the core leadership that the reform process is irreversible, but that this should not lead to the dismantling of the core tenet of the Vietnamese revolution. The definition of 'market economy with socialist characteristics' may be scarcely supported by a strong theoretical foundation, but it is in any case rich in political implications, able to coalesce a large part of the current leadership. On the other hand, the interest representation within the various echelons and sectors of the party is much richer than any representation in terms that two competing factions (conservative and reformers) could explain. We will return to the question of interest representation in the last chapter.

The remaining pages of this chapter will try to explore some of the crucial elements of the economic reform process looking at the most contentious issues in the current debate.

After the Asian crisis: the development strategy to 2010

An important set of strategy documents was prepared ahead of the Ninth Party Congress of April 2001. These documents were based on a number of sector studies prepared by the relevant ministries and agencies and involved a rather lengthy and open debate. Eventually, the Ninth Congress approved two key documents: a 10-year *Strategy for Socio-Economic Development, 2001–2010* and a *5-Year Plan for Socio-Economic Development, 2001–2005.* In the process that led to the drafting of these documents, international agencies and Western consultants played an important role; in particular, a joint UNDP–Ministry of Planning and Investment (MPI) exercise for the drafting of background papers for the 10-year strategy was the channel for the involvement of a number of Western scholars. Although the strategy documents approved by the party should obviously be regarded as 'national', it is wise to consider that they also reflect a sort of compromise with the international financial institutions. Once again, the compromise was reached by approving documents that set goals and targets, but fell short of indicating in a precise manner the policies to be implemented for reaching those targets. Only in a few cases did these documents express significant strategy formulations (see the following) – most of the rest consists of a rather boring litany of past achievements and future expectations.

Some light is shed on the more contentious issues by a report coordinated by the World Bank (and prepared in cooperation with the ADB and the UNDP) ahead of the Consultative Group Meeting of December 2000 – *Vietnam 2010, Pillars of Development*. This report was specifically prepared as a commentary on the early drafts of the 10-year strategy papers.

Pillars of Development is also relevant for another important reason: it marks the shift from a superseded structural adjustment approach to a broader-based poverty reduction strategy. In the late 1990s (also thanks to the debate following the Asian crisis),[6] structural adjustment strategies came to be widely acknowledged by public opinion and by the scientific community as a failure, if not a cause of further impoverishment for Third World countries. Although it is open to question whether this debate produced a substantial change in the core tenets of orthodox development practice, the expression 'structural adjustment' was replaced by 'poverty reduction strategies' and the negotiations between the Bretton Woods institutions and local governments were made more open and transparent, also involving representatives of non-governmental organizations (NGOs) and the civil society.

The need of a deeper understanding of poverty dynamics was acknowledged by the World Bank, which in 1999 dedicated its World Development Report to a study of poverty dynamics known as *Attacking Poverty*. This study, however, did not overcome the divide between the World Bank and its critics. In the end, this timid attempt by the World Bank to address one of the issues on which it had been more openly criticized resulted in a major public relations fiasco. Ravi Kanbur, the scholar appointed to direct the drafting of *Attacking Poverty*, resigned because the bank would oppose any significant shift from its development orthodoxy.[7]

An interesting aspect in the preparation of *Attacking Poverty* was a wide investigation on poverty based on participatory and grassroots-informed methodologies. This investigation was inspired by Robert Chambers and his colleagues at the Institute of Development Studies in Brighton, and was financially supported by the British DfID. The wide-ranging exercise had the aim of complementing the traditional quantitative data normally used by governments and international financial institutions in measuring poverty. The results of the investigation were published in three volumes as *Voices of the Poor*. While the findings of *Voices of the Poor* were scarcely reflected in the global *Attacking Poverty*, some of the country studies which formed part of this exercise had a larger impact at national level. Among the countries that benefited the most from this participatory investigation was Vietnam.[8] We will discuss in more detail in the next chapter the findings of the two Vietnam-based studies, *Voices of the Poor* and *Attacking Poverty*, which were released by the World Bank in Hanoi in late 1999. For the moment, it suffices to say that these studies contributed to the understanding that poverty is a complex issue and that poverty reduction strategies must be broad based. New notions (new for the international financial institutions) were finally acknowledged: economic growth is not *per se* a guarantee of poverty reduction if this growth does not translate into more employment and better redistribution of resources; and the poor can be particularly vulnerable if macroeconomic change is not accompanied by measures supportive of their livelihoods.

Pillars of Development was part of this general reassessment of development strategies by the international agencies (and particularly the World Bank) both in Vietnam and internationally. The report took on board the issue of broader-based poverty reduction strategies in a more evident way than in the two strategy documents eventually approved by the Ninth Congress and led to a further round of negotiation. At stake in this negotiation was the future economic assistance to the country by the international financial institutions and by the other multilateral and bilateral donors. This new debate culminated in a *Comprehensive Poverty Reduction and Growth Strategy (CPRGS)* released by the Vietnamese government in May 2002.

Both *Pillars of Development* (World Bank 2000) and the *Comprehensive Poverty Reduction and Growth Strategy (CPRGS)* (Socialist Republic of Vietnam 2002) were built in a way to make poverty reduction emerge as the cornerstone of development strategy. *Pillars of Development* was presented as a set of technical advices aiming at supporting the implementation of the macroeconomic policies decided by the national authorities. The CPRGS was a national document, the drafting of which had been supported by extensive consultations with donors, NGOs, different ministries and agencies, and ultimately approved by the government. However, there is more than one reason to dispute that the content of the CPRGS, although it was 'owned' by the government, necessarily reflected a conceptual frame developed by the international agencies.

A number of recent studies (e.g. Wilks and Lefrançois 2002) have argued that the replacement of structural adjustment policies with poverty reduction strategies has not changed substantially the ways in which the international financial institutions control the process of policy formulation by their client countries. Scholars and policymakers in developing countries often lack information and the technical expertise to challenge views presented as authoritative by the World Bank and its partner institutions. Owing to its large economic and intellectual resources, the World Bank has great leverage in taking the lead in policy formulation, even if the outcomes are presented as national deliberations and as the result of a wide process of consultation. Further, the World Bank's leverage is not only a consequence of its power as a source of intellectual guidance, but also of its role as lender to developing countries. It is fair to underline [as in Wilks and Lefrançois (2002)] that the position of the World Bank is made ambiguous by this double status: on the one hand, an organization which officially aims at empowering developing countries with stronger resources for deciding about their own strategies; on the other hand, a bank which has unbalanced power relationship with its clients and must also guard its own economic interests.

The general pattern in the power relations between the World Bank and developing countries assumes a specific dimension in Vietnam in two contrasting ways.

On the one hand, as we have already suggested, the Vietnamese authorities have constantly avoided proclaiming any long-term strategy that may be at odds with the prescriptions of the international institutions or let emerge in a visible way the nature of disagreements on specific issues. It is no surprise that the documents approved by the Ninth Congress remained vague in indicating the policies to be adopted for reaching the approved economic targets. It is no surprise, either, that the World Bank occupied centre stage with its own prescriptions (*Pillars of Development*) and that this role of guidance also extended to the drafting of the *Comprehensive Poverty Reduction and Growth Strategy (CPRGS).* Quite clearly the World Bank in Vietnam has means for conducting policy research that no other research institution in the country can match.

On the other hand, it should be recalled that, in Vietnam, maybe even more so than elsewhere, the World Bank is not the coherent and orthodox monolith that may appear from many accounts (including this one, which for the sake of brevity may oversimplify the complex interplay between the different actors). Although orthodox economists still play the key role in major decisions, the agency now employs a number of officers and researchers in new fields, ranging from participatory poverty assessment to governance, who tend to be more critical and eclectic in their approach. It should also be recalled that, particularly in Vietnam, the World Bank has been promoting a much softer version of development orthodoxy than the IMF. We have already seen that divergences between the two sister organizations emerged in the late 1990s, when the IMF stopped concessional lending to the country (1997). The same pattern was repeated in the early 2000s. In 2001, the two agencies agreed with Vietnam to resume concessional lending in the frame of the CPRGS, but the IMF had *de facto* already interrupted its lending in 2002, and in April 2004 announced the cancellation of the deal signed in 2001 due to a lack of transparency in the foreign reserves held by the State Bank of Vietnam.[9]

Notwithstanding the tensions with the IMF and the existence of this recent set of policy documents, the debate between the Vietnamese authorities and the international financial institutions risks remaining largely obscure. Some of the aspects of this secluded debate even seem paradoxical. The international financial institutions have often been accused in the past of putting too much emphasis on economic growth and not enough on the way in which this growth was generated or on the impact of growth on poverty, employment, welfare, etc. As we have seen, since the late 1990s the World Bank sees poverty reduction as the centrepiece for development strategies in Vietnam. At the same time, we learn that the inclusion of the term 'growth' in the title of the CPRGS had been made on Vietnamese insistence and against the standard suggested by Washington. *Pillars of Development* (as other previous World Bank reports for Vietnam had also done) openly stated that 'quality' of growth is crucial and a slower rate of economic growth would be preferable if this leads to more job generation and wider poverty reduction. If the core of the 'development orthodoxy' has abandoned the idea that economic growth would 'trickle down' and increase people's welfare, why does Hanoi remain so obsessed with growth? Is this a heritage of the old central planning mindset, or some misperceived ambition by country leaders, or even a disregard for the conditions of the poor? Three hints suggest that the answer may be different from what would appear to be the case. First, the Vietnamese 'obsession' with growth is tacitly supported by Japan and its international cooperation agency (JICA) – if the Vietnamese policymakers may be suspected of being too isolated from the international scientific debate, this is certainly not the case for the Japanese experts. Second, the Vietnamese leadership cannot be easily accused of disregarding the need of the poor: as we will indicate in the next chapter, according to the same World Bank (1999b), *no other country has reduced poverty so much as Vietnam did during the 1990s*. Third, after the collapse of the Soviet Union and the fall of Suharto in Indonesia, the Vietnamese leadership is very much aware that its political survival depends on the economic conditions of the country. High rates of unemployment or inadequate results in poverty reduction could be destabilizing.

These hints suggest that the latent disagreement between the national authorities and the international financial institutions is not about poverty reduction, but *on key elements of the macroeconomic policy*. That is, the accent on growth may indicate that Vietnam identifies an active role of the state in leading the development process (industrial policies, trade policies, control on finance, etc.) as a required factor for securing at the same time economic growth and sustainable poverty reduction. The World Bank uses poverty reduction to justify its claim that Vietnam should not distort the economy with measures that create trade advantages and preferential access to foreign investments for capital-intensive production controlled by SOEs. Market-friendly measures and more encouragement to the private sector would, according to the World Bank, be more effective in creating job opportunities and reducing poverty.

The Vietnamese leadership (in the practical implementation of reforms, if not in policy statements) appears to be scarcely convinced by this interpretation. Rather, Hanoi seems to be looking at the experience of other Asian countries where the state has been the *primus motor* in the economy. Such an interest in practices that we could inscribe within the frame of the 'East Asian developmental state' also justifies the support of Japanese experts for an attitude that is defiant of neoliberal recipes for poverty reduction – Japan is obviously keen on having a new important Asian country following its own path.[10] We argue, however, that while the East Asian developmental experience is regarded as a source of inspiration in resisting the neoliberal prescriptions, the measures adopted so far in the reform process scarcely resemble a coherent developmental state model. At the same time, it is important to underline that the Vietnamese authorities may hold that there is no contradiction between an East Asian developmental-state-type of economic policy and poverty reduction. Successful poverty reduction and low levels of economic inequality have been essential features of the so-called East Asian Miracle, as the 1993 World Bank study recognized. Support to the rural world and corporative systems of economic redistribution have been functional to the implementation of authoritarian developmental states models in Asia [e.g. as illustrated by Wade (1990) and Putzel (2002)]. Corporatist income redistribution was part of a hegemonic discourse that made it possible for the Asian developmental state to mobilize the entire nation through a modernization effort that was perceived as beneficial for all and not only the capitalist groups.

An attempt to disclose the veil of apparent agreement (for which the Vietnamese slow implementation of a number of measures is simply 'delay') reveals that fundamental issues in the reform process are still unresolved. At the centre of this (undercover) debate is once more the interpretation of the developmental experience of East Asia. While the *East Asian Miracle* (World Bank 1993) was a complex and articulated study, its findings are presented by *Pillars of Development* in rather simplistic terms:

> The high performing economies of East Asia (i.e. South Korea, Taiwan–China, Malaysia, Thailand, Indonesia) have demonstrated convincingly the sort of policies that must be implemented to sustain annual per capita growth rates of 5–7 percent over several decades and generate large reductions in poverty. Greater openness to the world, more freedom for the private sector, an effective banking system and macroeconomic and fiscal stability – complemented by superb access to primary education and to infrastructure services – helped these economies to generate high rates of investment, savings, exports, employment and productivity growth (World Bank 2000: 22).[11]

We will see in the next pages that this simplistic interpretation (within the frame of a reformed Washington orthodoxy) is still insisted upon in the most recent documents which aim at inspiring the Vietnamese development strategy after the regional economic crisis. We will investigate the main elements of this debate and try to put in evidence where the line of dissent lies.

Foreign trade

Establishment of a 'neutral' trade regime

Among the policy reforms promoted by the current development agenda, trade liberalization is probably the most controversial. To be sure, the contention on the advantages and disadvantages for a developing country in joining a 'free trade' regime does not regard only Vietnam. The relation between trade liberalization and growth is one of the most debated issues in economic theory and in development studies. However, the international financial institutions and mainstream scholars tend to conceal this debate: their request for trade liberalization in Vietnam is presented as authoritatively based on economic theory and on the empirical experience from developing countries within and outside the region. Mainstream policy advice tends to express the 'orthodox' view in a quite uncompromising way. To give only one example, James Riedel, a well-known Vietnam expert, recently author with William Turley of an interesting OECD-sponsored study (1999), illustrated his view in the following terms:

> In the vast literature on the economic development over the past 100 years, there is no empirical regularity that is more robust across time and countries than the positive relation between openness to trade and economic growth (Riedel 1999: 11).

Such a proposition should probably be understood in its normative value (an attempt to push for specific policy measures in Vietnam) rather than as a contribution to increase the scientific awareness of the problem. But considering the complexity of the debate on the issue, a more cautious approach would be recommended. Most economists would agree that foreign trade is beneficial to economic growth. But the positive virtues of *free trade*, especially for a latecomer, are the object of various degrees of dissent. For instance, a well-known criticism of the neoliberal attempt to impose free trade as orthodoxy in the development discourse is contained in Robert Wade (1990), which also reports a caustic sentence by Dani Rodrik:

> if truth-in-advertising were to apply to policy advice, each prescription for trade liberalisation should be accompanied by a disclaimer: 'Warning! Trade liberalisation cannot be shown on theoretical grounds to enhance technical efficiency; nor has it been empirically demonstrated to do so' (Wade 1990: 20).

It is also important to remember that the current debate about trade liberalization is in many ways paradoxical. While free trade has become a pervasive ideology, the world economy is actually characterized by a revival of protectionism and trade blocs. And this is even more paradoxical, because protectionism is adopted by the same industrialized nations that search to enforce trade liberalization on developing countries. Besides, changes in international trade regulations in the last 20 years have increasingly reflected the interests of industrialized countries and transnational corporations rather than the needs of developing countries. For instance, K.S. Jomo (while suggesting that Southeast Asian nations can still succeed in seizing opportunities offered by the international markets) notes that

> [T]he resurgence of protectionism and the emergence of new international economic governance are creating less favourable circumstances. The extensions of GATT's jurisdiction to foreign investment, the international trade in services and intellectual property rights, as well as the establishment of the World Trade Organization (WTO) have strengthened transnational corporate hegemony and imposed additional costs on new industrialization efforts... (Jomo 2001b: 467–468).

Within this complex environment, Vietnam is engaging in a process of trade liberalization. Although the country has unquestionably benefited from increased international trade during the 1990s, the next steps in this area of the reform process are arduous.

There is a certain level of consensus in reporting that, in spite of the reforms introduced in the past few years, Vietnamese trade policy remains strongly biased in favour of import substitution. This evidence leads the international financial institutions to draw the conclusion that the present trade regime produces a sub-optimal allocation of resources. For instance, a report released by the IMF in 1999 argues:

> Although [trade restrictions are] intended to promote 'strategic' industries, the effect has been to promote inefficient import substitution. Chronic over-capacity, uneconomic production scales, and high costs are common. These problems are not transitory, because the import substituting industries are not competitive and have little prospect of exporting. Such industries impose substantial costs on all sectors of the economy, especially agricultural exports, and contribute little to employment (IMF 1999a: 59).

On the basis of this bleak description the IMF and the World Bank present their normal recipe: *trade liberalization*.[12] Before discussing the current trade regime in Vietnam, it may be useful to restate the goal that this section aims to reach. Although this work does not deny that Vietnam suffers from an inefficient import substitution policy, it tries to illustrate that the *free trade* is only one of the options available for Vietnamese policymakers. Away from the prescriptions provided by the orthodoxy, there are at least two other strategies that have been presented in the debate either on Vietnamese or East Asian development. The first strategy involves export promotion to compensate exporters for the disadvantages produced by the import substitution bias (theory of simulated free market). The second involves a fully-fledged strategic trade policy, with a selective adoption of import substitution and export orientation (as suggested by different authors promoting 'developmental state' policies). While free-trade theory considers state intervention as always counterproductive, the other two theories justify the need (under specific circumstances) for trade policy involving the use of restrictions to imports.

Looking at the concrete Vietnamese case, orthodox scholars consider the existing import substitution bias as a problem that the reform process should seek to remove. Scholars inspired by the developmental state model, instead, try to assess trade policy using as a parameter the efficacy in supporting industrial upgrading and catching-up dynamics. These different views can be traced in the policy bargaining for the definition of a reform agenda for Vietnam. In fact, the Vietnamese authorities, although not openly challenging the rationale of orthodox prescriptions, tend to resist the implementation of downright trade liberalization measures. However, it would be difficult to claim that the trade policy implemented by the Vietnamese authorities reflects a 'developmental state' strategy: it also offers protection to specific interests of powerful actors (e.g. SOEs dominating specific industrial sectors) in areas where these interests are actually not functional to the national catching-up drive.

A precise assessment of the Vietnamese trade policy (strengths, weaknesses and distortions) as conducive to catching up is complicated by the absence of a specific literature. Most literature is, in fact, looking at the present trade regime only to evaluate how much it departs from free-trade orthodoxy and which measures should be taken to redress the import-substitution bias.

In a paper suggesting the adoption of export-supporting measures, to be adopted while gradually moving towards a more liberal trade regime (a position that could be related to the simulated free-trade theory), Ari Kokko has given a description of the Vietnamese import sector that may indicate a catching-up attempt:

> The structure of imports [of Vietnam] is largely what one would expect in a country with an ambitious development program. The bulk of imports is made up of capital goods and raw materials used for investment and production. The most important individual import items are fuel, steel, and fertilisers, but the imports of semi-finished products, such as electronic components and textiles, have also grown rapidly in recent years. Consumer good imports have been remarkably small, representing only around 10 percent of imports in 1996. However, it should be noted that the structure of imports is determined by trade policy rather than pure market forces: import tariffs are higher and license requirements more stringent for consumer goods than for machinery, equipment, and intermediates. In fact, Vietnamese trade policy has explicitly aimed to restrict consumer good imports in order to provide a captive market for local producers (Kokko 1998a: 12).

This description provides an interesting hint about the underlying dynamic in the Vietnamese trade regime. However, this hint does not allow us to distinguish whether these distortions are the result of a rational trade strategy, for which market distortions are functional to an accelerated industrialization drive, or are simply the result of rent-seeking behaviour by leading economic forces.

Vietnam is currently moving towards a less distorted trade regime. With a number of measures adopted since the late 1980s, export quotas have been removed for most export and many import commodities, export duties have been abolished for most products, import duties have been generally reduced and rationalized, and the foreign exchange rate has been unified and substantially led to depend on market forces (Khan 1998; Kokko 1998a; Kokko and Zejan 1996; World Bank 1997, 1999a; IMF 1999a).

The reforms implemented so far, however, have not completely eliminated the distortions existing in the current trade regime. The World Bank indicates that tariffs and quantitative restrictions discourage production in sectors in which the country would have comparative advantages and support production (and attract FDI) in sectors in which Vietnam cannot be competitive (World Bank 2000: 26).

In recent years, Vietnam has signed a number of international agreements and committed itself to further trade liberalization. In particular, it has joined the AFTA, has signed a bilateral trade agreement with the USA (USBTA) and has officially expressed the ambition to join the WTO soon. The commitment to an increasing integration into the global market and trade liberalization has been reiterated by the Ninth Party Congress and has been included in the official development strategy (Socialist Republic of Vietnam 2002: 43). However, the cost for the Vietnamese enterprises risks being very high as a consequence of these international commitments.

In future years it will be possible to see how the Vietnamese authorities will cope with the implementation of these costly measures. It is possible to imagine that some sectors of the Vietnamese intelligentsia see trade liberalization as a way to increase the productivity of the national economic system. However, it seems realistic to assume that the Vietnamese authorities have accepted to play the game of trade liberalization because they perceived that, given the prevailing power structures in the world economy, there were no alternative options. Nonetheless, significant resistance remains. In the next section we will indicate that one of the key trade agreements signed by Vietnam (the bilateral pact with the USA) was the result of a rather painful process and barely reflected a convinced change in the mindset of senior policymakers.

The concrete implications of the agreements subscribed to by Vietnam cannot be easily anticipated. The experience of countries like Japan (but even the USA and the European Union) suggests that it is possible to maintain some discretionary power (e.g. through disguised non-tariff barriers) in protecting national producers even in an officially open trade regime. This may also be done by countries like China and Vietnam, which have a long tradition in resisting external impositions (Perkins 2001: 254).

On the basis of the signed commitments, the Vietnamese authorities agree with the neoclassical recipes; but, on the basis of what concretely has been done until now, this agreement is much less obvious. It is legitimate to assume that there is some line of resistance to complete trade liberalization. Although there is no definite evidence that Vietnam is concretely trying to repeat the lesson coming from high-performing Asian economies (a lesson that is, however, promoted by Japan, the largest source of development aid to the country), it is useful to reiterate here some key aspects of this lesson as interpreted by important 'statist' scholars. The regional experience may help in putting the Vietnamese case into perspective and allow a better appreciation of the issues in the current debate and what are the options open to Vietnam.

'Statist' scholars, reflecting especially on the cases of South Korea and Taiwan, have indicated that these 'latecomers' have succeeded not by adopting free trade, but through the implementation of selective trade policies combining export promotion with import substitution. For instance, Robert Wade (1990) reminds that:

> The evidence suggests that, overall, the policies of import substitution in the 1950s [in Taiwan and South Korea] had a very important role in preparing

> the way for later success. They did so both by channelling resources from agriculture to industry through the exchange rate and domestic terms of trade, and by more direct promotion in certain sectors (Wade 1990: 85).

It is important to underline that the example provided by South Korea and Taiwan (and before them by Japan) did not consist of import-substitution strategies versus export-led growth. Rather, these East Asian countries relied on trade policies combining selective import substitution and export promotion on the basis of national industrial policies. Therefore, industrial sectors which received (temporary) protection from foreign competition were forced to increase their technological skill and their competitiveness (at least on foreign markets) and were not allowed to indulge in rent-seeking behaviour. Even more, the Northeast Asian governments used temporary import restrictions as a source of leverage to impose discipline on industry:

> East Asian governments have generally made protection [against import] conditional, either by specifying limited-duration tariffs and quotas to hasten upgrading and innovation, or by tying protective measures to export obligations. Both Korea and Taiwan pursued such schemes throughout their high-growth era. Japan has also used protection as a creative discipline. In the important electronics industry, companies had to work feverishly to improve productivity and develop technology to meet liberalization schedules. According to JETRO (1993: 139), the government 'always refused to extend liberalization periods, with the specific intention of exhorting domestic manufacturers to pull out all the stops to meet the deadlines' (Weiss 1998: 73–74).

It was the mix of import substitution and export promotion that made possible such diverse interpretations of the Taiwanese and South Korean cases, with scholars emphasizing one aspect or the other of these composite trade policies. The attempt to present the 'miracle' of these two economies as simply based on export-led patterns responds to the neoliberal need to build up consensus on orthodox practices. This attempt, however, does not hold against the evidence coming from the study of the concrete historical development.

> A study of the sources of growth in nine countries from the 1950s to the 1970s concludes that Taiwan and Korea stand out from the others in terms of the contribution of import substitution to the growth of manufactured output (de Melo 1985). They are the only countries in the sample where import substitution contributed as much as one-third of manufactured growth in any sub-period... The overall patterns of manufactured growth with strong import substitution preceding export expansion are observed in virtually all sectors in both countries... Results from the sample are consistent with the proposition that countries which experience fast export-led growth have earlier had a period in which import substitution was a very important component of total growth... (Wade 1990: 84).

The evidence collected by Wade and by the other 'statist' economists is acknowledged by the scholarly community, although with various nuances.[13] Many scholars recognize the importance of selective trade policy (including import substitution) at least in the early stage of the industrialization drive. For instance, one of the most influential economists working on Vietnam, the already mentioned Ari Kokko, who is in general critical of the Vietnamese import-substitution policy, concedes that these policies may have played a positive role in the 1950s and 1960s in Taiwan:

> The Korean experience highlights the danger of selective export promotion, but it would probably be inappropriate to conclude that targeted incentives never work. The Taiwanese experience provides a contrasting example. Taiwanese export promotion policies have targeted specific industries already from the 1960s. The promoted industries included plastic, synthetic fibres, apparel, electronic components, consumer electronics, home appliances, and watches and clocks. Exporters were given access to toll-free import already before a general trade liberalisation was commenced, and low-interest credit was used to subsidise the establishment of new exporter firms (Kokko 1998a: 51).

The distinction made by Kokko between Korea and Taiwan is something we will discuss later on in this chapter. This is very relevant for us because Vietnam has been looking at South Korea for inspiration (especially because of the similarity between the Korean *chaebols* and the Vietnamese SOEs), and after the regional crisis many turned to Taiwan as a better model. We will argue that the insistence on an alleged difference among the development models of the two countries serves specific ideological purposes and it is scarcely supported by the facts.

While the regional experience may provide an important example for Vietnam, there are critical areas in which history cannot be repeated. South Korea and Taiwan were allowed to carry out selective trade policies for a long period of time without facing retaliation because Western countries (especially the USA) were mostly concerned with Cold War geopolitical equilibrium (e.g. Li *et al.* 2002). For a 'late latecomer' like Vietnam (and even more so for a socialist country), no discount can be expected in the post-Cold War environment [see also Perkins (2001: 248)].

The trade agreement with the USA

It may be useful to recall here the contrasted dealings that led to the signature of the bilateral trade agreement between Vietnam and the USA. The story indicates that while the official declarations encourage a rapid liberalization of trade, strong resistance does exist among key political leaders. At the same time, the eventual signature of the deal shows the limited space of manoeuvre for Vietnam, like for other developing countries, in dealing with those countries dominating the international system.

On 25 July 1999, American and Vietnamese negotiators, after 3 years of talks, announced that they had reached an 'agreement in principle' for a trade pact. At stake for Vietnam was the possibility of reaching Normal Trading Relations (formerly Most-Favoured Nation status) with the USA, implying substantial tax reduction for Vietnamese exports (i.e. garments, textiles, shoes and other light industrial products) to the American market.[14] The implications for the Clinton administration, although less dramatic than for the Vietnamese side, were important both in economic and political terms. On the one hand, it included easier economic access to the second most populated Southeast Asian country (and thirteenth worldwide). On the other hand, symbolically, it involved the possibility to heal the wounds of the past, showing that Washington was able to dictate the rules for economic relations with the former enemy and even to acquire leverage on the Vietnamese national economy. As the then US trade representative explained, this agreement was more than a simple trade agreement:

> The provisions of this agreement will go well beyond the bilateral commercial agreements negotiated in the past to end Jackson–Vanik restrictions on other covered economies. When completed, the agreement will set a course toward greater openness, receding government control over the economy, and ultimately greater freedoms for individuals in Vietnam to find jobs and determine their own futures (Irvine 1999).

In other terms, 25 years after the dramatic defeat, the American administration was searching requital by forcing Vietnam to obey the blueprint of capitalist orthodoxy.

After the historical announcement of July 1999, the two sides carried out further talks to define the details of the agreement. The American administration made plans for a signing ceremony early in September, during an Asia-Pacific Economic Cooperation (APEC) summit in New Zealand where both President Clinton and the Prime Minister Phan Van Khai were participating. A few days before that date, however, the Vietnamese government informed the American side not to be ready to sign the agreement.

The reason for the Vietnamese abrupt decision to step back has never been made public. Observers have linked the Vietnamese withdrawal to an unfortunate meeting between the US Secretary of State Madeleine Albright and the CPV Secretary General Le Kha Phieu on the eve of the APEC summit. During that 'less than cordial meeting' Mrs Albright made non-diplomatic comments about Vietnam's poor human rights record (AFP, 17 October 1999) and even stepped outside the agreed agenda by trying to include the issue of democratization (*Los Angeles Times*, 1 November 1999). Journalistic sources also indicate that Vietnam might have decided to await the conclusion of the Chinese agreement with the USA about admission to the WTO before signing its own agreement. This caution could be understood as a way to express 'respect' to the powerful neighbour and with the hope that China (as a more powerful negotiator) could reach a favourable deal with the USA that could eventually be translated to Vietnam (Business Week Online, 15 November 1999; Reuters, 17 November 1999).

Rumours in Hanoi suggest that an incident may have also provoked a Vietnamese reaction. Allegedly, a group of American negotiators made non-respectful comments on the Vietnamese naivety during a private dinner at a restaurant in Hanoi. Their conversation was overheard and reported to the authorities, which formally complained to their American counterpart.[15]

Whatever contingent reasons may have contributed to prevent the signature of the agreement with the USA, it is not difficult to imagine that a major discontent had emerged within the core of the Vietnamese Communist Party about the clauses contained in the draft.

A World Bank research report based on an econometric study, released in November 1999, explained that Vietnam was going to gain important advantages by signing the deal. The findings from this report, authored by Fukase and Martin (1999b), were then often repeated by various sources to highlight the irrationality of the Vietnamese behaviour in withdrawing from such an opportunity. However, two considerations could be made in trying to understand the preoccupation of the Vietnamese side.

The first consideration regards the methodology applied in that study and, therefore, the results achieved. The two authors explained that their study was based on a 'Global Trade Analyses (GTAP) model' which 'is a relatively static multi-sector multi-region Applied General Equilibrium (AGE) model' (Fukase and Martin 1999b: 10). That means that their study was not particularly concerned with the long-term developmental implications of the trade agreement. However, on the basis of their own estimates, Vietnamese output in textiles and clothing would have sensibly increased (respectively by 7 per cent and 31 per cent) as a result of expanded export to the American market, but *output in other more advanced sectors would have decreased* (Fukase and Martin 1999b: 15). Moreover, the trade agreement required Vietnam to liberalize imports and to concede American companies national treatment in such strategic areas as insurance, finance and telecommunications.

A second consideration about the impact of the trade agreement was included as a caveat in the same World Bank study. The export advantages in the key sectors for Vietnam, i.e. textiles and garments, would have been more visible in the first year of implementation; after that period the American administration would have regulated imports through a system of quotas which would have strongly curtailed the Vietnamese export potential. To illustrate the advantages of signing a trade agreement with the USA, the two authors quoted the Cambodian case and concluded with a surprisingly naive remark:

> Unfortunately, the ability of the importing countries to impose quotas has, if anything, been increased by the move from the Multifibre Arrangement (MFA) to the Agreement on Textile and Clothing (ATC). While Article 3 of the MFA required that the exports from an *individual supplier* should be causing market disruption before quotas could be imposed, Article 6 of the ATC allows quotas to be imposed when *total imports* are causing market disruption. For small suppliers such as Cambodia, this change is particularly unfortunate (Fukase and Martin 1999b: 14, emphasis in the original).

Commenting on this same issue, Jonathan Tombes (1999), after reporting a clear warning to Vietnam from a representative of the American Apparel Manufacturers Association, added:

> If Vietnam has not yet learned of the U.S. textile industry's influence in Washington, it will sometime after its woven cotton shirts and similar items reach California ports.

In the months following the failed signature of the bilateral agreement with the USA, Vietnam let emerge its worries about the existing trade regime. Although the country maintained its bid to becoming a member of the WTO, the Vietnamese government openly hailed the failure of the WTO summit in December 1999, defining the collapse of global trade talks in Seattle as a success for developing countries. In a declaration reported by Reuters (9 December 1999) and ABC (10 December 1999), the Minister of Commerce Truong Dinh Tuyen said that rich countries had forced developing nations to accept previous global trade agreements. He also pointed out that rich nations had used technical criteria, such as anti-dumping policies, to build a smoke screen of protection to stop goods from poor countries entering their markets. And he concluded that 'Vietnam needed its own road map for integration into the world economy, something that would have to take into account the country's national independence and sovereignty' (Reuters, 9 December 1999).

After a new round of negotiations, the bilateral trade agreement was eventually signed. The pact was then ratified by the two parliaments and came into force in December 2001. It is difficult to know which kind of progress made the Vietnamese government decide to accept the deal. Possibly, they got some concession in the telecommunications sector. The Vietnamese side insisted on maintaining a national majority ownership on foreign-invested enterprises, both in the production of goods and in the provision of services. However, the deal did not impose regulation on the provision of services across the border, thus creating an opening for foreign companies to sell their services from abroad (e.g. via the Internet) and, therefore, introducing a major factor of liberalization in the economy. The tortuous negotiations and diplomatic accident of the failed signature revealed anxiety about trade liberalization and provided an unusual glimpse of the internal policy discussion within the high echelons of Vietnamese policymaking. Eventually the Vietnamese authorities decided to sign the deal, because probably they felt that the costs for not signing were even higher. While the US government insists on economic liberalization in the developing countries to create a level playing field for both national and foreign companies, the international trade system is certainly not a level playing field: the big players tend to be at the same time those who also decide the rules of the game and those who hire the referees.

The opening of the American market for the Vietnamese export was not the free meal depicted by the *free traders*. During the first 2 years of implementation, Vietnamese exports increased substantially (Table 4.1). Then, as was to be expected, the US government reacted by trying to curb its trade deficit with Vietnam. Using a safeguard clause in the agreement, the American authorities

Table 4.1 Merchandise export to the USA

	1997	*1998*	*1999*	*2000*	*2001*	*2002*	*2003*	*2004*
US$	388,189	553,408	608,953	821,658	1,052,626	2,394,746	4,554,859	5,275,810
Yearly variation (%)		143	110	135	128	228	190	116

Source: US national trade data

accused Vietnam of dumping and imposed trade restrictions. In the well-known case of the catfish quarrel, the American authorities went so far as to declare that the Vietnamese catfish could not be labelled as such, because the only real 'catfish' was the species existing in the USA itself. As a consequence of the American obstructions, export increase to the USA decelerated substantially. This bilateral trade agreement, however, had a lasting influence: it created a precedent for the WTO negotiations. All the concessions made by Vietnam to the USA through the bilateral agreement had now to be extended to all the other trading partners in order to access the WTO on the basis of the Most Favoured Nation rule.

After the enthusiasm of the period immediately preceding the entry into force of the bilateral agreement with the USA (when many companies expected a boom in their exports), the mood in Vietnam became soon quite sober:

> A report from the Trade Policy Department for Americas (TPDA), under the Ministry of Trade (MoT), claimed that the effect from the Bilateral Trade Agreement's tariff reductions, which have been in place for more than three years, has diminished.... 'Two-way trade growth is moving towards a standstill,' said an official from the TPDA... The Vietnam Trade Office (VTO) in the US predicted that garment export revenue is likely to be flat this year at around $2.7 billion, while agricultural export growth will inch ahead at between 0–2 per cent. Export of seafood products to the US decreased substantially by 23 per cent last year to more than $520 million. Likewise, frozen shrimp exports felt dramatically by 43 per cent last year following the anti-dumping penalties imposed on Vietnamese shrimp and catfish producers by the US Government (Vietnam Investment Review, 28 March 2005).

The WTO accession

At the time of writing, the Vietnamese government was in the final phases of negotiations for WTO access. The country had hoped to be admitted in the trade organization by the end of 2004, and it then hoped to achieve this goal by 2005. As we saw from the discussion on the trade agreement with the USA, the Vietnamese government was quite critical about the role played by the WTO. However, joining it was a choice that could not be avoided. Out of the WTO, Vietnamese exports are subjected to discrimination on foreign markets through high import tariffs and quotas. One of the reasons for the difficulties faced by

Vietnamese companies in exporting to the American market, notwithstanding the bilateral trade agreement, was that Vietnam was still competing with exports from other countries that could take advantage of better trade conditions. There were even reported cases in which foreign companies would buy from Vietnam and then re-export to new destinations (e.g. Thailand re-exporting Vietnamese fruit to the USA), making a profit out of the Vietnamese international discrimination. While quotas for exports in garments and textiles had been phased out by 2004 on the basis of WTO regulations, Vietnam would still face these kinds of export restriction for being an outsider. Entry into the WTO was deemed as a needed condition for exploiting Vietnamese export potential.

Accession into the WTO is, however, a delicate and risky matter. Two aspects should be considered here. First, WTO membership implies a commitment to liberalize trade and to reduce protection for national productions. Second, the WTO is not, as often understood, a kind of global free-trade area. The WTO is based on a system of uneven power relations that forces accession countries (typically, developing countries) to accept tougher conditions than the countries that are already members.

We have already discussed in the first part of this section that trade liberalization may have positive and negative effects for a developing country. The positive aspects are represented by easier export to foreign markets and by the removal of distortions in the national economy. While the advantages from easier export are evident to all, *free traders* argue that a country has an advantage to reduce import restrictions even if the other countries do not reciprocate. Reducing import tariffs allows lower prices for imported goods on the national market (thus making cheaper goods available to the poor) and forces the productive system to operate more efficiently in the sectors in which it has comparative advantages. This point is obviously not new: it is based on Ricardo and the tradition of studies that after him had updated and adjusted the theories on comparative advantages. We have already discussed that a simplistic use of these theories to the concrete reality of a world economy dominated by asymmetries in terms of power, access to information, economic development, technological capability, market size, etc., has been contested by a large number of economists, including in recent years the Nobel laureate Joseph Stiglitz and the rising star of international political economy Dani Rodrik. We have also recalled that a tradition of studies reflecting on the East Asia developmental state have indicated that a number of countries succeeded because they were able to defend and promote their infant industry through selective import restrictions. While orthodox scholars claimed that the Asian crisis was the result of distortions produced by the developmental state, we share the view of those arguing that the crisis was rather the result of distortions produced by the financial liberalization during the 1990s, which reduced the leverage of Asian governments in regulating the economy (Masina 2002a).

The experience from the region indicates that trade policy had been a key tool for long-term catching-up strategies. Also, from a shorter-term perspective, however, rapid trade liberalization can present severe risks, especially for the most vulnerable sectors of society. Even assuming that the law of comparative advantages can operate in spite of the many imbalances affecting the existing international markets, the human and social costs can be very severe. Workers in non-competitive sectors cannot always find jobs in competitive sectors, as their age, knowledge, gender or even expectations may not fit with the new job opportunities created in the competitive sectors. For instance, industrial workers cannot easily re-engage agriculture and men cannot find jobs in industries typically employing a female labour force. In neo-classical textbooks these imbalances will eventually be solved through the law of demand and supply, with a perfect allocation of all productive factors. In real life, this 'eventually' involves (at least in the short or medium term) quite a lot of people losing their jobs and diminishing income for families.[16] A similar reasoning can be made when it comes to production. Although their products may not be competitive on a liberalized market, farmers cannot shift to new cultivations or simply abandon agriculture to seek employment in industry from one day to the next. This argument is well known to rich countries (from the USA to Western Europe and Japan) that support their local farmers in many ways by protecting non-competitive production. In a poor developing country like Vietnam, these questions are even more daunting when considering the risks in joining WTO.

Despite all these threats, Vietnam was seeking accession into the WTO in 2005. Like most developing countries, Vietnam was not really free to choose, because being an outsider means being exposed to arbitrary treatment and discrimination by trading partners. But here comes the second issue to examine. The question is not simply whether Vietnam should join the WTO or not. The question is also *under which conditions*. The international financial institutions push Vietnam to implement reforms that create a level playing field and rule of law so as to make competition really fair and effective. The WTO is not enforcing a level playing field or a fair and effective competition. To access the WTO a candidate country must not only accept all the existing agreements, but must also be subjected to lengthy negotiations during which current members can demand extra concessions, with clauses that are more binding and painful than those valid for the countries already members of the organization. If the candidate country does not accept conceding to these 'WTO Plus' requirements, then powerful countries may put a veto on the accession indefinitely.

SOEs

Privatization of SOEs is listed high in the priorities indicated by the international financial institutions for the furthering of the *doi moi* process. The existence of a large state sector is considered as a major burden preventing the country from realizing its economic potential. SOEs, through their connections with political and administrative officers, benefit from explicit forms of state support and unofficial protection in competing with the infant private sector. SOEs drain most of the credit from the still weak banking system, thus depriving the private sector of needed capital. SOEs benefit from formal and informal privileges in international trade (with preferential access to import and export quotas). Furthermore, import-substituting and inefficient SOEs distract most FDI to capital-intensive production, which gives only a modest contribution to employment generation and sustainable industrial development.

This list of complaints is well known to those familiar with the current literature on Vietnam. And we must concede that many of these complaints are correct. However, we may argue that there are different options available for restructuring the SOE sector.

Even during the war and under the centrally planned economic system the state sector never extended as much as in the Soviet Union or in the Eastern European countries, and it declined from around 16 per cent of the labour force to below 9 per cent by the mid 1990s (McCarty 2001: 8–9). Currently, SOEs employ less than 6 per cent of the national labour force. Notwithstanding its limited dimension, the state sector is perceived by the CPV as a key instrument for leading the country towards industrialization and the achievement of its socialist goals. Even more, a leading role for the state sector in the economy appears to be the last ideological stronghold in a context of market liberalization. Socialism is presented as a process of economic development, which is not in contrast with a market economy as long as the state retains the control of strategic industries. This view is confirmed in the list of goals established by the Ten-Year Strategy approved by the party in April 2001:

> 'To continue innovating and developing the State economic sector so as to properly play its leading role in the economy. The State economic sector is an important material force and the instrument for the State's orientation and macro-regulation toward the economy…' (Communist Party of Vietnam, Central Committee 2001: 27).

Officially, the Vietnamese insistence in maintaining the state sector as the leading force in the economy is accepted by the international financial institutions, although it is quite clear that this formal consent hides a substantial disagreement:

> [T]here is no real conflict between the Strategy's emphasis on the state-sector being the 'leading sector' and the effective SOE reform, if such reform is viewed as a prerequisite to being competitive and thus a 'leader' in key sectors. But SOEs may use this emphasis on 'leading', to focus an expanded investment-program without completing reform and seeking protection to avoid losing that investment. Unless SOEs are fully restructured and their management abilities and behaviour altered to compete effectively in the market place, any expanded investment program is likely to repeat many of the experiences of the 1990s, i.e. create few jobs, generate little profit, accumulate high debt and build uncompetitive capital stock (World Bank 2000: 32).

The line of compromise between the Vietnamese authorities and the international financial institutions consists of two elements: divesture and *de facto* privatization of small and non-strategic SOEs, and restructuring of the strategic SOEs. This line of compromise is, however, not easy to implement. Between 1989 and 1991 the number of SOEs was reduced from about 12,000 to about 6,000 through liquidation and mergers of small companies operating under the control of local authorities. These measures were possible because, on the one hand, they were justified by the urgency of macroeconomic stabilization and, on the other hand, they regarded enterprises of relatively low importance in the overall industrial strategy. By the mid 1990s a substantial impasse became apparent. SOEs lost direct subsidies from the state, but they maintained preferential access to credit by state-owned banks and a great deal of leverage in influencing government decisions regarding trade regulation. The attempt to promote the 'equitization' (a more politically correct expression for privatization, with equities sold to employees and managers) of small and medium enterprises fell well behind targets announced by the national authorities and then postponed again and again (World Bank, *Macroeconomic Update*, January 2000: 7; World Bank, *Vietnam Economic Monitor*, Spring 2002: 16–17). A new round of equitization was conducted in 2003 and 2004, with respectively 436 and 657 enterprises transformed (World Bank, *East Asian Update*, April 2005). These changes, however, did not involve large companies, whose transformation was scheduled for the following years. Delays and resistances in the 'equitization' process related to difficulties in raising capital for the purchase of equities and to the managers' and workers' fears of losing the support granted to state enterprises. And an even more substantial obstacle was probably represented by the lack of enthusiasm of government (and local authorities) in giving up control over entities that were perceived as pivotal in maintaining a state-led process of economic development [see Painter (2003)]. In early 2005, a conference held under the chairmanship of the Prime Minister Phan Van Khai posed a new target for equitization during that year (*Asia Pulse*, 25 February 2005). However, international observers remained sceptical about a significant breakthrough in the short run.[17]

For larger enterprises, and for those operating in strategic sectors, the government attempted reorganization with the creation of large industrial conglomerates, merging companies operating in the same sectors or geographical area. This consolidation was conducted ahead of the regional economic crisis and was apparently inspired by the South Korean *chaebols*. The process resulted in the creation of 18 General Corporations and 70 Special Corporations, accounting for an estimated 80 per cent of resources and production capacity of Vietnam's SOEs (Kokko 1998a: 32).

The limited equitization of non-strategic enterprises and the consolidation of the strategic ones into large conglomerates did not solve the problems of inefficiency and rent-seeking behaviour, and the poor performance of large SOEs continued to represent a major challenge for the financial sector reform. Further, the high level of indebtedness of SOEs (in the region of 20 per cent of the aggregate turnover) not only was a threat to the stability of the banking system, but also was a hindrance to the work of those efficient companies in the state sector:

> Loss-making SOEs are also weakening the few efficient firms in the state sector: about a third of the total debt is internal to the SOEs sector. This internal debt alone is nearly seven times larger than the aggregate value of the sector's working capital (Kokko 1998a: 32).

Although the situation improved during the early 2000s, reforming of the state sector continued to pose a major challenge for the furthering of *doi moi*. However, the foundations for a successful reform strategy continued to be vaguely defined. The figures given year after year about the number of SOEs to be equitized, merged or liquidated altogether responded to the development orthodoxy preached by the international financial institutions and foreign donors. However, the government remained adamant on the need to maintain a strong state control on the economy. The national resistance to privatization *tout court* led the World Bank to try to endorse its recipes in a rather conciliatory way.[18] Apparently accepting that Vietnam was determined to maintain a relevant state sector, the accent was put on the conditions for making such a sector viable:

> The evidence of enterprise reform from around the world illustrates that countries that have succeeded in building the best performing state enterprise sectors have done better in implementing comprehensive sector reform programs covering five broad elements: divestiture, competition, hard budget constraints, financial sector reform, and changes in the relationships between governments and SOE managers (World Bank 1997a: 40).

The five elements indicated by the World Bank report can be integrated into quite divergent frames. They may be ingredients of neoliberal recipes synthesized by the slogan of 'putting the price right', i.e. making the state sector operate on the basis of market rules, removing restrictions and distortions. But these five elements (*mutatis mutandi*) could also be integrated within state-led industrialization strategies as done by other countries in the region. Whereas competition was ruled out and credit allocation was regulated by the plan in the centrally planned economy, competition was enforced in industrial catching-up strategies implemented in East Asian developmental states (especially by pushing companies to compete in foreign markets) and credit allocation was based on results. The state sector was forced to reach outcomes that would not have been possible simply by relying on self-regulated market conditions; but rent-seeking behaviours were avoided through strictly enforced performance criteria. Credit allocation was politically directed: it was made available only to those enterprises that could realistically achieve specific targets. The state sector played a major role in this industrialization drive, including in an economy that, after the Asian crisis, was praised in Vietnam as an example of private sector vitality.

> [In Taiwan] in many sectors public enterprises have been used as the chosen instrument for a big push. This is true for the early years of fuels, chemicals,

> mining, metals, fertilisers, and food processing; but even in sectors where public enterprises did not dominate, such as textiles and plastics, the state aggressively led private producers in the early years. Later, during the late 1950s and 1960s, public enterprises accounted for a large part of total investment in synthetic fibres, metals, shipbuilding, and other industries... In advanced electronics, public research organizations and public enterprise spin-offs have been used to acquire and commercialise new technology; and even in the software part of the industry a public enterprise has had a large presence over the 1980s (Wade 1990: 110–111).

Still reflecting on the case of Taiwan, Robert Wade goes on to describe the kind of direct and indirect support that SOEs have received (support that was functional to industrialization strategies established by national authorities):

> Public enterprises are strongly represented in sectors which one would otherwise expect to be dominated by multinational corporations...
>
> Public enterprises have also received preferential investment financing in various forms. These include direct disbursement from the government budget, loans or grants from the two special development funds under the planner's control, foreign loans (all access to which is controlled by the government), and preferential access to longer-term finance through the banking system. They have been able to borrow at concessional rates, but never more than a few percentage points less than the normal rate for secured loans; and when credit is tight the government may – secretly – instruct the banks to make money available for public enterprises before the private ones. Some public enterprises have also been in a monopoly position (Wade 1990: 180).

The Vietnamese consolidation of SOEs into large industrial conglomerates could be understood as an attempt to replicate the developmental experience in the region. It should be underlined that although South Korea is known for its large private *chaebols* and the Taiwanese economy is dominated by small and medium private enterprises, in both cases the post-war industrialization also relied upon large state conglomerates. In Taiwan, for instance, as late as in 1980, the six biggest public enterprises had sales equal to the 50 biggest private industrial concerns (Wade 1990: 178). Similar proportions also existed in South Korea. Large state enterprises played a leading role in a number of heavy industry and chemical sectors, apart from the provision of public utilities. Again, in the words of Robert Wade:

> [State enterprises are important] in sectors where the efficient scale of production is capital-intensive and large relative to both product markets and factor markets, and where linkages to downstream industries are high... The public enterprise sector is also used, whether for military or civilian production, as a substitute for attempts to induce private firms to enter new fields with high entry barriers. The main import-substituting projects of the

> 1970s – petroleum and petrochemicals, steel and other basic metals, ship-building, and nuclear power – were carried out by public enterprises; and major expansion projects in heavy machinery, heavy electrical machinery, trucks, and integrated circuit production have been undertaken by public enterprises (Wade 1990: 178–179).

In the interpretation presented by Robert Wade and other 'statist' scholars, an SOE's leading role in guiding the industrialization process may well be a positive factor. However, the impact of a large state sector in the economy depends on the system of checks and balances established in order to avoid rent-seeking behaviour and to force companies to stick to their targets.

In her famous study on South Korea, Alice Amsden illustrated how the government maintained a tight control even over the largest corporations, both public and private:

> The disciplines exerted by the state, and the rise of big business, were interactive. Big business consolidated its power in response to the government's performance-based incentives. In exchange for stunning performance in the areas of exports, R&D, or new product introduction, leading firms were rewarded with further licenses to expand, thus enlarging the scale of business in general. In exchange for entering especially risky industries, the government rewarded entrants with other industrial licenses in more lucrative sectors, thus furthering the development of the diversified business group in particular (Amsden 1989: 14–15).

In the Vietnamese case, the ability to indicate targets and rigid performance criteria is plainly absent. Not only have state enterprises been habituated to soft budget constraints, but also state support was not dependent on performance (but rather on connections between managers and political apparatuses). Is Vietnam now trying to move towards a more stringent model of industrial policy?

The *Comprehensive Poverty Reduction and Growth Strategy (CPRGS)* approved by the Vietnamese government in May 2002 seems to hint in this direction. It states as an objective to be achieved:

> Issuance of criteria for evaluating business performance and specification of the supervision and sanction mechanisms applicable to different types of SOEs, particularly those that are fully or largely owned by the State and State Corporations, to effectively encourage efficient managers and penalize inefficient ones (Socialist Republic of Vietnam 2002: 35).

But even conceding that the Vietnamese political leadership converges in adopting a strategy that emulates the developmental practices of Northeast Asia, does the country have the resources for implementing this kind of industrial model? One of the very few studies that have tried to give an answer to this question has been published by Dwight Perkins as a chapter in a volume edited by Stiglitz and

Yusuf and published by the World Bank (Jomo 2001b). This study is based on an analysis of the Chinese and the Vietnamese cases in comparison with other East Asian states. In the case of China, Perkins considers that state guidance cannot be conducted on a comparable scale with South Korea and Taiwan due to the size of the Chinese economy and the number of companies operating in its territory. In South Korea in the early 1970s, the largest 47 conglomerates accounted for 37 per cent of industrial production – and, therefore, it was possible for the government to control them. If China tried to create a few hundred conglomerates producing one-third of industrial output, these conglomerates would be 10 to 20 times larger than the South Korean *chaebols* in the 1970s (Perkins 2001: 258). Compared with China, the task to coordinate Vietnamese conglomerates would be a much easier endeavour:

> The state share of gross industrial output in 1992 was 71 per cent, and this share rose during the reform period of the 1990s... The Vietnamese central government, therefore, had direct control of most industrial output even after a decade of reform. By controlling a few hundred enterprises, the government policymakers in Hanoi could, in principle, direct and supervise most of the industrial production that mattered (Perkins 2001: 259).

Political will is, however, another proposition over and above having the capacity to carry out complex and delicate functions of industrial coordination. We will return to this issue in more precise terms in Chapter 6. However, we should underline here that the historical development of Vietnamese institutions and an industrial culture still rooted in a centrally planned economy mindset might be a formidable obstacle.

Looking at the experience in the region, a number of authors have pointed out that state coordination was conducted through a mixture of 'embedded autonomy' (Evans 1992, 1995) and 'government interdependence' (Weiss 1998), where the state bureaucracy retained functions of strategic planning but did not interfere with the management of individual companies. The Vietnamese (and Chinese) institutional and industrial frame, combined with political and cultural traditions, may result in a major constraint. On the one hand, Vietnam does not have an efficient bureaucracy insulated from particularistic pressures coming from politicians and individual enterprises. This is a significant difference compared with Japan and South Korea, and also with other Southeast Asian countries where at least some agencies maintain a large autonomy and prestige. On the other hand, in Vietnam, like in China, the legacy of the past is still very present, and strategic planning may easily be interpreted as a revival of command central planning:

> The economic bureaucracy in both countries was built and trained to carry out a Soviet-style system of central planning, not the kind of strategic planning that existed in Korea and Japan... The latter system relied on guidance while the Soviet-style system relies on orders... It is likely that the decision to create a Korean or Japanese-style strategic planning system would become

> an excuse to retain as much of the old planning bureaucracy as possible. Some of these people could be retrained for the new approach, but many would stick as well as they could to the old ways they know best (Perkins 2001: 260).

Vietnamese policymakers are now confronted with a difficult dilemma. They have decided to move out from the command planned economy and have indicated that the adoption of a market-based economy is permanent. They are pressured from several quarters towards the adoption of a more market-friendly economic policy. At the same time, they seem to perceive that replicating the successful catching-up results in industrial development of other Asian countries requires complex institutional changes, which may be beyond the existing institutional resources and most probably beyond the ruling political balance.

A further issue should be considered in order to verify the replicability of the developmental state-type of industrial policy in Vietnam. The Asian countries that adopted a state-led model of industrial development did so through a political compromise between the state apparatus and the national bourgeoisie. For these countries, significant results in economic development was a *conditio sine qua non* for state survival against powerful threats – in Japan from colonial dominance and in Taiwan and South Korea from Communist contenders. A strong role of the state in promoting industrialization, even against the will of particularistic and backward factions among capitalist forces, was imposed on the basis of an ideology and an institutional practice that is closely reminiscent of European fascist regimes. A corporatist state was functional to a historical function of modernization, which went well ahead of the most regressive aspects of political repression and class exploitation (we will return to this interpretation inspired by Antonio Gramsci in Chapter 6). The existence of powerful threats made the local capitalist forces willing to accept limitations to their autonomy and allow the state to perform strong guidance functions [see Masina (2002a)]. This special linkage between state apparatuses and capitalist forces was a result (but also a condition for a further development) of a cohesive national bourgeoisie, which maintained its national roots during successive waves of economic internationalization. The existence of a rather cohesive national bourgeoisie can be understood as a powerful resource in the development of East Asia – note, incidentally, that nationalism has become the main leverage that China is using to mobilize its national forces and the Chinese communities overseas.

Even in those countries in which the national roots of the local bourgeoisie are more pronounced, however, elites have a tendency to become internationalized and to enter into strategic alliances with other international capitalist forces [see Yeung (2002) and Plesner (2002) for South Korea]. Not only do national elites have a tendency to become internationalized, but they also try to use state resources ('internationalizing' the state) for achieving their own purposes (Glassman 1999).

Contrary to the experience of other countries in the region, Vietnam is largely dependent on FDI for its industrialization drive. This flow of investment, linking foreign corporations to powerful sectors of the national bourgeoisie via the SOEs, is due to have major implications for the political balance of the country. An interesting definition of SOEs as a site of alliances of insider and outsider groups is provided by Adam Fforde:

> Nominally, SOEs produce around 1/3 of GDP and possess a very high share of Vietnam's modern economic assets. They employ around 2 million people in a population of around 75 million. Yet, what are they? What are Vietnamese SOEs and how does this reality fit with the policy dialogue and real political processes? The basic argument made is that they are, in practice, sites of de facto joint ventures between various 'insiders' groups. It is the complexity and incoherence of these alliances that gives the political economy its stability, as it permits for adjustments as and when resources availability shifts: insiders can co-opt outsiders (such as sources of FDI), when they wish (Fforde 1998a: 6).

Here, a major question is open to further analysis. Are these insider groups going to retain their national rooting and are they willing to accept state coordination of their economic activities? Or are they using their political clout to mobilize state resources in order to achieve the status of internationalized elites in a system of alliances with foreign elites? For Taiwan and South Korea the challenge to state-led development practices produced by increasingly internationalized elites came at a stage when the aspiration to close the gap with the West in terms of industrial development had been substantially achieved. For Vietnam, the possibility that its national elites may be co-opted into international capitalist networks is a concrete risk at a stage in which the country is still struggling to achieve basic levels of industrial development. Although the leadership is concerned with a possible destabilizing role of a burgeoning private sector, an even more powerful challenge to state guidance towards socialist goals may come from the SOEs through their alliances with foreign capitalist forces via FDI.

Financial sector

The restructuring of the financial sector is not only a pivotal issue in the Vietnamese reform process, but also one of the most complex. In this field we can see the convergence of many dilemmas affecting the transition from central planning to a market-oriented economy. Vietnam must cope at the same time with a large level of non-performing loans (especially to SOEs), which would suggest financial restraint, and with the need to increase capital mobilization rapidly for industrial development.

A major reform in the financial sector was undertaken in the late 1980s with the shift from a mono-bank system to a two-tier system. The functions of the central bank, i.e. the State Bank of Vietnam, came to be separated from those of four state-owned commercial banks (SOCBs). Through the 1990s the commercial leg of the two-tier system was further extended with the advent of new actors: joint-stock banks, joint venture banks and representative offices and branches of foreign banks. Although the banking system became more articulated after the early 1990s, the four SOCBs maintained a clear dominance. By 1998 these four SOCBs accounted for 82 per cent of total bank assets and 80 per cent of loans and deposits (IMF 1999a: 27). In early 2005, the largest four state-owned banks still controlled 70 per cent of mobilized funds and outstanding loans of the national banking system (Le Xuan Nghia 2005: 3).

The need to cope with a faltering supervisory framework, unclear regulatory standards and imprudent lending motivated a number of reforms in the late 1990s and early 2000s, and in particular compelled the merger or liquidation of a number of joint-stock banks that were undercapitalized and suffered from serious governance problems. However, the high level of non-performing loans was not only the result of unskilled or imprudent behaviour by bank managers, but was also the result of political interference. Lending to SOEs was often conducted on the basis of political decisions, with which even the four large SOCBs were forced to comply. At the same time, banks had limited tools for evaluating the feasibility of projects presented by small and medium enterprises, which often maintained only rudimentary accounting systems, or to assess effectively the collateral offered as a guarantee for loans. Overall, in the early 2000s the banking system remained strained and in a fragile condition, although it became increasingly able to support the expansion of the private sector, whose development was boosted by the approval of a new Enterprise Law in 2000 (see next paragraph).

In 2000, when Le Duc Thuy was appointed as the new Governor of State Bank of Vietnam, the central bank made public an estimate for which the non-performing loans (NPLs) represented 14.5 per cent of total lending. In the same period, another state publication reported an estimate for which NPLs could be as high as 28 per cent (World Bank, *Macroeconomic Update*, January 2000: 4). The fragility of the system was denounced in January 2000 by the international credit rating agency Standard and Poor stating that, owing to poor disclosure and under-developed risk management, systems 'the Vietnamese system is likely to remain at the highest end of the global industry [risk] spectrum' (*Agence France Press*, 24 January 2000). The concerns related to the excessive exposure to NPLs that motivated a state intervention through an injection of fresh capital, which by 2003 allowed the resolving of nearly 60 per cent of NPLs identified in 2000 (World Bank, *Country Updates*, 20 April 2004). This state intervention did not resolve completely the underlying issues in the banking system's fragility, and NPLs from state-owned banks to SOEs remained difficult to assess. However, from the early 2000s the banking system became able to mobilize increasing amounts of credit. This credit expansion was largely directed to the needs of the fast-growing private sector, which by 2003 accounted for over 60 per cent of all bank credit extended (World Bank, *Country Updates*, 20 April 2004).

The improvements in the banking system operation did not remove the need for a radical reform of the financial sector. The shortcomings existing in the system were openly recognized in the strategy documents approved by the government and by the Communist Party ahead of the Ninth Party Congress. Like in the case of the reform of the trade system and the restructuring of SOEs, the long-term perspective and the ultimate aims of the financial sector reform also remained unclear. Once again, contrasting models can be examined to understand the alternatives available for the Vietnamese reform process.

In the post-regional-crisis environment there is little doubt about the need to enhance the governance of the financial sector. Improving the regulatory and surveillance systems is rightly the objective of a number of projects supported by bilateral and multilateral agencies. Nonetheless, it should be kept in mind that the so-called economic *miracle* attained by other Asian countries was the result of credit practices that clearly departed from Western orthodoxy (e.g. Wade and Veneroso 1998). One of the key tenets of the East Asian developmental state practices was the ability to channel investment to strategic sectors, where market forces would not have supported new initiatives without a strong guidance from the state. Not only were the state-controlled financial institutions able to mobilize national savings, but the state also intervened in directing credit to activities that would accelerate economic development.

> [The North East Asia developmental states] played an active role in creating market institutions such as long-term development banks and capital markets to trade bonds and equities, and in establishing an institutional infrastructure that enabled markets to work more effectively. These institutions and markets helped insure that the high volume of savings was invested efficiently. Governments also used their control of financial markets to help direct resources in ways that stimulated economic growth... [Stiglitz 1996: 173, quoted from Booth (2001: 35)].

Much of the credit allocation behind the extraordinary industrial development of South Korea and Taiwan was the result of state-led policy lending rather than commercial lending motivated by the invisible hand of the market. However, the same caveats already discussed for the reform of the SOEs also apply to the financial sector. In Northeast Asia, policy lending was motivated by strategic planning and operated on the basis of reasonable industrial plans. Credit was allocated to those enterprises that had a realistic chance of succeeding and performance criteria were rigidly defined. Companies operated on the basis of hard budget constrains. The support provided by the government was 'political', in the sense that it responded to policy strategies but did not depend on particularistic demands coming from local or national policymakers. Although enterprises had very high debt/equity ratios this was functional to a successful industrialization drive and not to rent seeking. State control was essential in maintaining the coherence of the system and in averting free riders. And obviously, a system constructed on a special relation between (public) banks, enterprises and governments was due to encounter a systemic crisis once financial liberalization was enforced (as happened in East Asia in the 1990s) and private enterprises could borrow freely on international markets in defiance of national regulatory discipline.

Where does Vietnam stand in this attempt to reform its financial sector? Once again, the reforms introduced so far do not allow the drawing of definite conclusions about the directions for the future. Policy declarations and the reforms implemented until the early 2000s seem to indicate that the country is struggling to put some order in its ailing financial sector, taking the advice of the international financial institutions. For example, in 1999 the government apparently conceded to the need of separating policy lending from commercial lending, also through the institution at the end of 1999 of a National Development Assistance Fund supporting policy-based lending, i.e. making more transparent the relation between SOCBs and SOEs (World Bank, *Macroeconomic Update*, January 2000: 6).

However, 2 years later, in the Ten-Year strategy, the Communist Party felt the need to reiterate the need to separate policy lending from commercial lending, hinting that not so much has been achieved in this direction. The long list of objectives stated in the Ten-Year strategy is too vague and inclusive to give any sense of priorities or political commitment. Most of the prescriptions are reasonable whatever development model is selected. Only a few lines of this document could be interpreted as a hint of an attempt to move towards forms of strategic planning, although these prescriptions could also be coherent with more orthodox strategies:

> To ensure finances for the strategy-prioritised tasks. To realise policies encouraging development of key economic areas while reserving more investments for difficulty-stricken areas. To continue innovating policies subsidising for generation employment, restructuring of State enterprises, and helping to develop small and medium sized enterprises; to press ahead with popularisation of the public service delivery sector, at the same time ensuring for the poor access to basic social benefits (Communist Party of Vietnam, Central Committee 2001: 20).

As in the case of the SOEs and trade reforms, here we want to underline that, in the current critical stage of post-regional-crisis rethinking of development strategies, contrasting options are opened to Vietnam. Given the condition of the financial sector in the country, a number of the transparency and regulatory measures indicated by the international financial institutions are badly needed. However, in redefining the overall rationale of financial sector reform, a distinction between what can be done under self-regulated market orthodoxy and what can be done on the basis of a more activist state-led industrialization model should be kept in mind. To be sure, we must underline once more that strategic planning is substantially different from an allocation of resources ruled by central planning, although policymakers may be tempted to justify the old habits from the command economy period in terms of strategy planning.

Role of the private sector

Trade, SOEs and the financial sector have been key issues in the negotiations between the Vietnamese government and the international financial institutions for a long time. In the post-Washington consensus a new theme assumed increasing prominence: the role of the private sector as a resource for poverty reduction. The reasons for this increased attention have already been anticipated earlier in this chapter. Agriculture cannot provide jobs for the around one million young people that every year enter the labour market. The agricultural sector is actually already overcrowded, with high levels of underemployment, and incipient mechanization is due to increase redundancy drastically.[19] Nor are SOEs able to absorb more labour. Through the 1990s, SOEs also struggled to increase their competitiveness by increasing efficiency and by curtailing prior overstaffing. An attempt to accelerate the industrialization process and to make the country present in new strategic sectors made SOEs prioritize foreign investments in areas that were capital intensive and labour saving. This trend raises concerns about the possibility of generating new employment opportunities. For example, between 1990 and 1995 the manufacturing state sector almost doubled production at constant prices, but employment declined by about 13 per cent (Ronnås and Ramamurthy 2000: 16). Given the limited ability for agriculture and state enterprises to generate new jobs, it is quite understandable that the private sector is considered as the only viable alternative.

In the command centrally planned economy the private sector was first strongly constrained, if not suppressed altogether; then, since the early 1980s, it has been alternatively tolerated or frowned upon. With the advent of *doi moi* the country was admittedly moving towards a system where the state sector would maintain the lead, but where the private sector was also officially encouraged to develop. However, regulations and restrictions inherited from the previous era made the growth of the private sector difficult, while the development of a capitalist private sector (i.e. medium and large private enterprises) was still regarded with apprehension.

The economic slowdown produced by the regional economic crisis was the final push for making the government decide on more decisive action in support of the private sector. A new Enterprise Law was eventually approved, with validity from 1 January 2000. The immediate effect of this law was impressive: in 2 years, 36,000 new private SMEs were licensed, against 6,000 in the 2 years ahead of the new law (World Bank, *Vietnam Economic Monitor*, Spring 2002: 16). Part of this imposing result may be tentatively explained by the fact that a number of SMEs had previously operated without official approval – once again, it might have been the emergence of 'fence-breaking' activities (as discussed in Chapter 2) which motivated the government to recognize *ex post* a change already undertaken in society. In any case, it is apparent that the approval of the new law, and a number of related policy decisions in the following period (among which was the removal of the incompatibility between membership in the Communist Party and ownership of private enterprises), created a climate more favourable to the development of this sector. By the mid 2000s the private sector emerged as a major force in the Vietnamese economy, with large numbers of companies created every year. For example, 35,000 private enterprises were registered in 2004, representing a year-on-year increase of 26 per cent in number and 24 per cent in registered capital (World Bank, *East Asia Update*, April 2005).

Despite all these changes since the early 2000s, the international financial institutions argued that more had to be done to make the private sector develop its potentiality as a driving force in the Vietnamese economy and to generate more employment. This view was officially recognized by the Communist Party, which in effect seemed to have moved towards a more conciliatory position with regard to private economic activities. The Ten-Year strategy approved by the Ninth Congress in 2001 stated as an important objective:

> To renew and complete the legal framework, dismantle all obstacles in terms of mechanisms, policy and administrative procedure with a view to maximising all resources, generating a new impetus for the development of production and business by all economic sectors with different forms of ownership. All enterprises and citizens are entitled to invest in businesses in the forms stipulated by laws and to be protected by the law. All business organizations in different or mixed forms of ownership are encouraged to develop on a long-term basis, co-operate and compete equally, and constitute an important integral part of the socialist-oriented market economy (Communist Party of Vietnam, Central Committee 2001: 16–17).

Notwithstanding this official sanction, we saw already that, in crucial areas like access to credit, private SMEs faced a *de facto* discrimination in that the country's scarce financial resources were more easily available for SOEs. However, by the mid 2000s, private enterprises accounted for about 60 per cent of capital lent through the banking system. In other words, the conditions in which the private sector operated had improved substantially, but the situation was far from an 'equal competition' among the different sectors of the economy, as stated in the official documents.

Some reluctance towards an unrestrained development of the private sector among the Vietnamese leadership may be related to three major reservations. First, the private sector may be considered unable to play a major role in strategic sectors, where there is the need to mobilize huge amounts of capital for long periods of time. The private sector may accentuate a dependency of the country on labour intensive and low-tech export sectors such as garments and footwear. Second, the private sector may be considered as a vehicle for foreign capital domination – national producers may be trapped into commodity chains in which foreign transnational corporations control prices, outlet markets and labour division. Third, the emergence of a capitalist private sector may be perceived as a challenge to the state's authority and ultimately as a factor of political destabilization.

These fears are quite reasonable for a poor developing country, and especially for one that has committed to a market-oriented economy but which officially has not abandoned the aspiration to socialism. There are a number of considerations that may help in putting these issues in a wider perspective. These considerations regard the modality of integration into the wider economy and the relations with foreign capital, the leverages available to the state for promoting industrial development, and the class-relevant structures within the country.

Vietnam is an economy in which not only foreign trade represents a very high proportion of GDP, but also where FDI is expected to play a much greater role in promoting industrialization than was historically the case in other East Asian countries at the same level of economic development. Given the overwhelming control on FDI by SOEs, the perception that the private sector may become a vehicle of foreign dominance may be misplaced: there is no reason to guarantee that SOEs will not become the real Trojan horse for foreign corporations. In theory, state control over SOEs may provide a stringent adherence to national objectives. In reality, large SOEs tend to act quite independently, and the availability of large economic resources may even result in a strong influence over the state apparatus. The role performed by managers of large enterprises does not depend so much on the fact that these enterprises are private or state owned. Their position in relation to national and foreign forces depends on the question of whether these managers have developed a sense of national rooting and loyalty to national development objectives or they have been socialized to the logic of international capitalist elites. The power of attraction (money, connections, status, power) of international capitalist forces is not only limited to national representatives of foreign corporations, but also can easily extend over state managers and even administrative and political elites.

The modalities in which the elites and even the upper strata of the bourgeoisie in Third World countries are normally engulfed into the logics and interests of international capital are well-known phenomena. East Asian countries have often been pointed out as notable exceptions to this general trend. However, the resilience of the East Asian national bourgeoisie against the inducements coming from foreign capitalist forces was not (or not only) the result of strong SOEs, but of a wider socialization of national leaderships towards national development objectives. Thanks to this strong consensus, the state was able to extend its functions of strategic planning over the private sector.

Particularly in the case of Northeast Asia (Japan, South Korea and Taiwan), the state exerted (and still exerts) a role of guidance and coordination over the private sector: channelling investments, encouraging industrial upgrading, avoiding waste of resources through unregulated competition, supporting export, etc. Quoting once again the classic study by Robert Wade on Taiwan:

> To say that public enterprises [in Taiwan] have often played a central role in creating new capacities is not to say that private firms have been left alone. Incentives and pressure are brought to bear on them through such devices such as import controls and tariffs, entry requirements domestic content requirements, fiscal investment incentives, and concessional credit… And large-scale private firms are often exposed to more discretionary government influence, taking the form of what in Japan is called 'administrative guidance' (Wade 1990: 111).

The experience of Northeast Asian countries indicates that the question for a country that wants to achieve rapid industrialization is not so much public versus private, but which kind of state guidance over both the state and the private sectors. Of course (as we will discuss in Chapter 6) guidance requires particular administrative structures and particular skills. Vietnam in this sense is a *weak* state, i.e. it has limited capacity in performing complex guidance functions. This should not be confused with the strength to impose, through coercion, rules and regulations that can prevent the development of the private sector but cannot use its resources for achieving national development objectives.

The private sector is suspected to be a factor in social diversification, which may even challenge the country's political system. Also in this case some qualifications are needed. Since the beginning of *doi moi* the country has witnessed an increasing gap between rural and urban areas and between the richer and poorer strata of the population, although in a general frame of significant poverty reduction. A new class of affluent bourgeoisie is visible in the major cities (and on a smaller scale in rural areas). However, this affluent bourgeoisie does not derive its wealth only from private enterprises, but also from its ability to exploit for its own benefit the complex web of relations linking state officers, managers of SOEs and private entrepreneurs. The rent positions deriving from personal connections are a general phenomenon that goes well beyond the even high level of abuse and corruption. In a country where the largest part of the population is made up of poor peasants it is quite obvious that the well-connected urban bourgeoisie will exploit its resources to acquire wealth and extend its dominance.

Social diversification is undoubtedly due to emerge as a major challenge to a political system officially inspired by socialist finalities. On the one hand, there is the risk that the national bourgeoisie (alone or in alliance with international elites) may exploit the authoritarian state forms to serve its class purposes. That is, the national bourgeoisies may hijack the socialist state apparatus for anti-socialist purposes. On the other hand, there is the possibility of what the party leadership calls the 'peaceful evolution', i.e. social changes leading to a Western-style capitalist democracy. In this case also the national bourgeoisie (in close association with international elites) would seize power, leading to a reversal of the socialist national ideals.

Embarking on a process of radical reforms, including the transition towards a market-oriented economy, as Vietnam has done with the adoption of *doi moi*, is something that necessarily compels a change in the class-related structures. This is something that cannot be overlooked by a national leadership that is officially inspired by a Marxist dialectic. The development of an industrial private sector is part of this process of social transformation, but it is only one aspect of this process, together with other major changes such as the *de facto* privatization of land and a free labour market. The development of the private sector may lead to the creation of a competing leadership, challenging the Communist Party – but this is not the only contradiction that the Vietnamese political system is confronted with. To cope with a more fragmented society in terms of class structures the Communist Party may be forced to allow a more dialectic representation of class interests, e.g. like allowing a more independent role for trade unions. This is already partially happening, and in a more consistent way than in China – the

Vietnamese official trade unions have apparently found new vitality in dealing with private entrepreneurs, both national and foreigners (Chan and Nørlund 1999). Signs of an increasing awareness of the importance to create channels for interest representation are also visible in the dynamism of the National Assembly, where the debate about new laws is now open and meaningful and where ministers are confronted by assertive deputies in televised public hearings.

In sum, the political implications of the debate about the private sector relate to a much broader set of issues. The need to cope with an emergent private sector may become an important factor for a decisive revival of the Vietnamese political institutions, although it is too early to predict towards which ends.

Readjusting the common wisdom: the myth of Taiwan

There is a taste of irony in reassessing some of the writings published in the months immediately following the regional crisis. We have already seen that a number of authors and institutions have tried to use the crisis to deny the validity of 'developmental state' practices [see Masina (2002a)]. This was also done in the debate relative to Vietnam, with an explicit attempt to portray an alleged Taiwanese model as an alternative to the South Korean one. The fact that Taiwan was substantially resilient to the regional crisis was taken as a demonstration that market-friendly practices were more successful and desirable. The difficulties that South Korea was facing were instead emphasized to show that state-led industrialization, based on large conglomerates (*chaebols*, but read Vietnamese SOEs) was necessarily entailing economic failure.

The taste of irony is also due to the fact that only a few years after it was the turn of Taiwan in facing severe problems, due to a global economy deceleration that curtailed opportunities for the Taiwanese companies in exporting to Western markets. Taiwan and Singapore had appeared to be insulated by the crisis of 1997–8, but their dependence on exports to the USA made them face economic disarray at a time when the rest of the region (including South Korea) was starting to recover from the regional crisis.

Notwithstanding the impasse in the early 2000s, Taiwan represents an outstanding example of successful industrialization and its experience remains an important case study for Vietnamese analysts. Thus, it may be useful to dedicate a few lines to discuss how the Taiwanese and the South Korean models have been presented to Vietnam; these interpretations are still circulating in the country, although they may have lost much of their vim and vigour.

The following two quotations illustrate the ideological attempt to construct a reading of the Asian crisis in order to prevent Vietnam from adopting a state-led industrialization process. The quotations are from the contributions of two respected scholars in a volume published in 1999 and reflect views widely present in Vietnam's study circles at the time.

> The resilience of the Taiwanese economy to the financial crisis in the region, and the vulnerability of the Korean economy, attests to the superiority of

> implementing an export-oriented industrial strategy that is free from special incentive schemes to promote selected industries. In other words, the Asian crisis has not diminished the validity of export-oriented industrialisation per se as a development strategy, but it has conclusively demonstrated the unworkability of 'picking winners' in the implementation of this strategy (Leung 1999: 6).
>
> The fundamental issues are crystallised most vividly in the contest between the 'Korean model' and the 'Taiwan model' of export-oriented industrialisation. The Korean model, whose most prominent features are a high degree of economic concentration in the family-run *chaebol* (business conglomerates) and a heavy-handed industrial policy of picking and promoting 'winners', was a natural favourite of many in the Vietnamese government. Certainly it offers an approach with more of a socialist orientation than the Taiwan model, which features intricate networks of small and medium-sized private companies, and thus a low level of economic concentration and much less government guidance or support for industrial development. The Korean model was therefore seen as a way to have it both ways: a capitalist system, but with government in command (Riedel 1999: 26).

Riedel's remark that the Korean model was considered as appealing by the Vietnamese policymakers because it allowed the government to remain in command even in a market-based economy is certainly correct. We have already insisted on the need to make a clear distinction between a command economy and strategic planning. The Vietnamese policymakers would be deceived if they misunderstood this essential difference. However, the fact that the 'Taiwanese model' was substantially different from the 'South Korean' model when it comes to the importance of the state in leading the industrialization process can be contested.

The government's active role in leading state and private enterprises (the large Japanese *keiretsu* or South Korean *chaebols*, as well as the Taiwanese SMEs) towards industrial upgrading was part of a general model adopted by the different economies in Northeast Asia. If differences undoubtedly existed in the different national cases – notoriously the South Korean economy is dominated by large industrial conglomerates, while Taiwan has a much wider presence of small and medium enterprises – there is no consensus on the fact that the Taiwanese state played a less active role in strategic guidance than the South Korean one. Actually, Linda Weiss claimed that the Taiwanese resilience to the regional financial meltdown could rather be understood as a result of higher levels of state intervention than in South Korea.

> The state centred on Taipei has held fast to a transformative project (... the strong push for industrial upgrading) and institutionalised that project in dedicated agencies and programmes. In short, its regime goals and institutional arrangements were largely intact when it set about regulatory reform in the late 1980s and 1990s. Because of this, the Taiwanese approached liberalisation quite differently from Korean authorities. Korea perceived and

> used liberalisation in a way that complemented the larger goal of *dismantling* the structure of credit activism and industrial policy. In Taiwan, however, the process of liberalising capital inflows involved reregulation to *enhance* existing capabilities (Weiss 2000: 31).

In this context, we cannot enter the discussion about the liberalization processes in South Korea and Taiwan in the 1990s. But we must remember that the assertion for which Taiwan in the earlier stages of its industrial development did not 'pick the winners' (as instead South Korea did) is at least controversial. The pioneering study by Robert Wade (1990) presents solid evidence that 'picking the winners' was systematically done by Taiwanese authorities every time they identified new priorities in industrial upgrading, either by pushing national companies towards production in new sectors or increasing competitiveness on international markets. Incentives and support, but also penalties on poor performers, were constantly applied, up to selecting specific firms for specific tasks.

Interestingly, this strong state activism in Taiwan is confirmed by recent studies, although in new forms that respond to the changing national and international conditions.

> Some ten years on [after the publication of Wade's *Governing the Market*], in spite of the rise of democratic politics and neoliberal reformers convinced of the benefits of financial liberalisation, the government's commitment to economic transformation remains firm, at least for now. The emphasis, however, has shifted: away from promoting capital accumulation and towards the constant shift of industrial structure and accelerated upgrading of technology. Indeed, Taiwan boasts one of the most comprehensive programmes for upgrading skills and technology in the industrialized world [Chu and Weiss 1999, cited in Weiss (2000: 28)].

The recent difficulties in the Taiwanese economy may even lead to a further enhancement of state guidance. The depression of traditional Western export markets and the increasing role of China as the regional growth engine is comporting a reorientation of the Taiwanese productive system, with a closer integration with the Chinese mainland economy. This process, although it may be regarded as unavoidable, is obviously highly sensitive in political terms and may result in an active role of the government in coordinating key issues such as technology transfer.

For the purposes of our investigation, it is enough to indicate that an alleged Taiwanese model, as distinct from and contrasting with the South Korean one, is an ephemeral ideological construction, meant to put pressure on the Vietnamese policymakers in the aftermath of the regional economic crisis. Although important differences exist, the role of market guidance played by the state presents common features in both countries.

5 Poverty reduction, inequality and social differentiation

After 15 years of very successful poverty reduction, Vietnam remains a very poor country. However, living conditions have improved substantially for the largest part of the population, both in urban and rural areas. By the mid 2000s there was a widespread optimism (shared by the government and the donors' community that Vietnam would be able to 'graduate' from the status of LDC by 2010 and would be able to meet the UN Millennium Development Goals (MDG) ahead of schedule in several areas. The impressive results achieved since the late 1980s were due to a sustained period of economic growth, which (contrary to the experience of many other developing countries) effectively managed to 'trickle down'. The Vietnamese experience was so remarkable that the country came to be considered a model for other developing countries in the region and beyond. The interpretation of this success, however, was open to alternative readings. Until the late 1990s the international financial institutions continued to warn on the need for bolder measures in liberalizing the economy if growth and poverty reduction targets had to be met. The government did continue to reform the economy, but the steps were certainly less daring and less rapid than those suggested by the international agencies. Was the Vietnamese success a result of the advice received from the international financial institutions? Or was success the result of the Vietnamese careful and gradual implementation of the reform process?

Notwithstanding the important achievements, continuing on a path of poverty reduction remains a daunting objective for the Vietnamese leadership. Even a temporary setback in the efforts to improve people's livelihoods could have a devastating impact in political terms. After the regional crisis, the ghost of Suharto's Indonesia is hanging over Vietnam. Discontent of people who feel excluded from the benefits produced by the reform process is a matter of major concern, especially considering that the Vietnamese leadership bases its legitimacy on socialist ideals of justice and shared prosperity.[1] This concern is neither remote nor abstract. There is no doubt that the Vietnamese virtuous circle of economic growth and poverty reduction had a dark side: inequality increased, leading to new forms of exclusion and vulnerability. Starting from a rather equalitarian structure, Vietnam at the turn of the century emerged as a country with significant social differentiation. The general perception, though, is that as long as the majority of the population experiences a substantial improvement in living conditions inequality will be accepted as a transitory evil. However, the signals that inequality is creating new tensions at the grassroots level are already visible.

Social differentiation also implies an increased diversification of class interests and, therefore, a need to revise the instruments for interests' representation through the political system. On the one hand, the political system needs to represent and support the poor and marginal, and of those who face modern forms of exploitation in the liberalized labour market. On the other hand, the government does not want to create straitjackets for those who are gaining the most from the reform process and whose increasing wealth is considered as a resource for the country's further development. Although there is a clear understanding of the potential conflicts that too large an inequality can ignite, it is not easy to balance the different interests.

Conventional economic theory suggests that, in the early stages of economic growth, a developing country will see a worsening in income distribution. The so-called 'inverted U' Kuznet curve shows that, in a first phase, an increase in average GDP per capita corresponds to a more unequal distribution of wealth, while in a second phase inequality is reversed. This theory, based on statistical evidence from Western countries that have achieved industrialization in the past, indicates that the transition from a traditional and rural-based economy to a modern and industrial-based economy involves a costly structural change. This structural change will see people moving from a traditional and backward sector to a modern industrial sector. This will create two kinds of economic gap: one between the modern sector and the traditional sector; the other within the modern sector, in which inequality will initially be higher than in the traditional sector. This theory seems to describe well the current trends in Vietnam, where some parts of the population, especially those living close to the two growth poles of Ho Chi Minh City and Hanoi, can exploit new opportunities created by the market economy. Others, those living in marginal areas (like the mountainous regions) and especially the members of ethnic minorities, remain confined in a poor traditional sector, while being exposed to the challenges produced by the modern economy. The Vietnamese trend, however, is not necessarily set to confirm a Kuznet curve prediction. Notwithstanding an increase in inequality since the socialist past, Vietnam maintains a rather equal distribution of income when compared with other developing countries in Asia and (much more so) in Africa and Latin America (see Table 5.2). Possibly, the Vietnamese development could repeat the experience of other East Asian countries in which poverty reduction became a resource for economic growth rather than an outcome of growth (World Bank 1993). The catching-up drive of the high-performing East Asian economies integrated strategic planning in the industrial sector with policies directed to support the rural population so as to expand the national market. The East Asian case seems to confirm the model promoted by Gunnar Myrdal, who suggested that the creation of a national virtuous circle through the creation of a national market for local producers was a necessary condition for escaping dependency and succeeding in economic development.[2] While many developing countries in other regions have empirically demonstrated the dynamics described by the first part of the Kuznet curve, i.e. increased inequality through integration into a modern market economy, very few have been able to climb on the second part of the curve through a successive better income redistribution. The international experience, therefore, signifies that 'growth with equity' and 'through equity' is the best strategy to achieve long-term and sustainable results in terms of growth and poverty reduction.

Economic growth, poverty reduction and inequality

At the end of 1999 two major studies about poverty were presented to the Consultative Group Meeting for Vietnam. These studies were part of the global reassessment of poverty dynamics discussed above, which culminated in the troubled publication of the World Bank's *World Development Report 2000: Attacking Poverty*. While the resignation of Ravi Kanbur indicated a lack of international consensus on poverty-reduction strategies, in the case of Vietnam these two reports did represent a bold step forward for the understanding of the multidimensional aspects of poverty.

The first of the two studies (World Bank 1999c) was called *Vietnam: Voices of the Poor* and was part of a worldwide exercise managed by the World Bank with the financial support of the British development agency (DfID). The Vietnamese report was based on four participatory poverty assessments conducted by different NGOs in four provinces: Lao Cai (Northern Uplands), Ha Tinh (North Central Coast), Tra Vinh (Mekong Delta) and Ho Chi Minh City (South East, the largest town in the country). The rationale of these investigations was to convey a grassroots-informed understanding of poverty and wellbeing in terms of both economic and non-economic conditions (social capital, harmony, participation in community activities, etc.). The study also focused on the vulnerability context (shocks, like floods or ill health, and stresses, like declining price of rice or coffee), the resilience of traditional safety nets, and the strengths of coping mechanisms in allowing communities to react.

The second study (World Bank 1999b) was called *Attacking Poverty (Vietnam)* and was the offspring of a Poverty Working Group formed by the government, donors and NGOs. This study combined the findings of *Voices of the Poor* with statistical data, and especially the results of two living-standards surveys conducted by the General Statistical Office in 1993 and 1998. By integrating different sources, based on qualitative and quantitative investigations, *Attacking Poverty* was able to provide a multifaceted interpretation of poverty dynamics.

The picture that emerged from these two studies was that, although Vietnam remained a very poor country by any international standard, poverty reduction in the 1990s had been outstanding.

> It is estimated that in the mid-1980's, seven out of every ten Vietnamese were living in poverty. A little more than a decade later – a decade of rapid

> economic growth – the incidence of poverty has halved. There have been very striking reductions of poverty in Vietnam… (World Bank 1999b: ii).

Data from the two living-standards surveys showed that the number of people living below the national poverty line had declined from 58% in 1993 to 37% in 1998. All the indicators presented in the two studies converged in confirming a substantial reduction in poverty. Even those living below the poverty line improved their condition during the 1990s because the depth of poverty decreased.

Importantly, the improvement was established not only by statistical data, but also by people's perceptions of increased wellbeing reported in the participatory exercises. However, vulnerability remained very high not only for the many who live slightly above the poverty line, but even for the more well-off strata of the population. The weakness of formal safety nets made households very vulnerable to shocks, e.g. the illness of a family member could rapidly drive a household with sustainable incomes into poverty traps (e.g. through debts).

Another investigation conducted by a team of European and Vietnamese researchers[3] indicated that informal safety nets were not able to compensate for the loss of the 'iron pot' that, at the time of socialist cooperatives, sheltered orphans, widows or other vulnerable groups. In many communities the coverage of informal safety nets (especially in the North) became stronger when more resources became available in the late 1990s. However, these safety nets were most effective for extended family or clan members and, in some cases, neighbours, while members of different ethnic groups and migrants tended to be much less integrated, if not totally excluded.

Notwithstanding the weakness of formal and informal safety nets, the investigation confirmed an improvement of living conditions even for many vulnerable groups, sometimes benefiting from new services provided by the market. For instance, migrants and marginal people (like street children) could find shelter in Hanoi by renting a room for 2,000 dong per night, thus at least escaping the hardship of sleeping rough – something that would have been impossible until the early 1990s (Gallina and Masina 2002). Seasonal or temporary migration to a major city (in our investigation from Hung Yen in the Red River Delta to Hanoi) could allow households to survive in their village, and in some cases to accumulate savings to invest in agricultural diversification or in off-farming activities.[4]

Two new living-standards surveys were conducted in 2002 and 2004 (Figure 5.1). Data from 2002 indicated that poverty reduction had progressed further during the period 1998–2002, although at a slower pace than in the previous 5 years.

Preliminary analysis of data from 2004 survey, however, suggested that the progress had been wider than the one reported by the 2002 survey, possibly because the panel selected in 2002 was not consistent with those of 1993 and 1998. While statistical calculations remain very complex in a country where a large part of the economy is informal and both income and consumption are only partially reflected in monetary transactions, the general consensus is that Vietnam also continued to succeed in a fast poverty reduction after 1998.

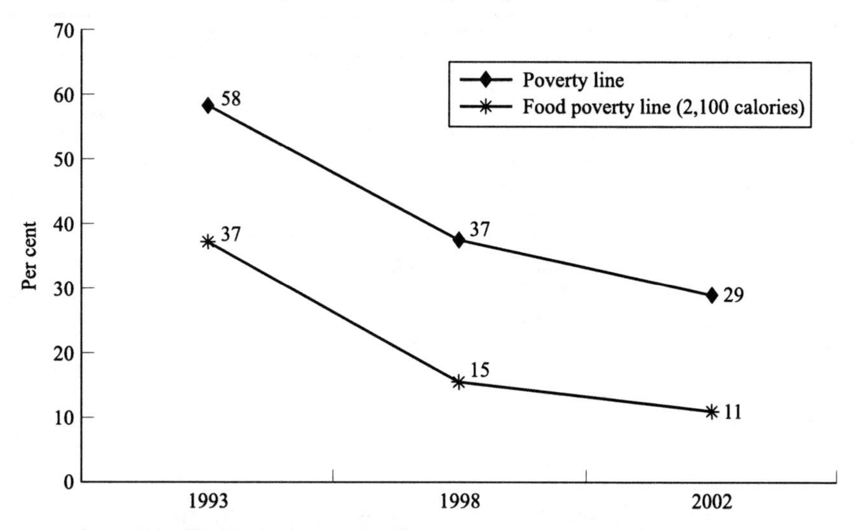

Figure 5.1 Poverty incidence, 1993–2002

> The resulting improvement in living conditions has been widespread, and preliminary figures from the Vietnam Household Living Standards Survey (VHLSS) 2004 indicate a substantial decline in the poverty headcount since 2002, the year of the last survey. While it is still too early to report a poverty rate with confidence, there is a clear expectation to see sustained progress towards the attainment of the Vietnam Development Goals (VDGs) and other key development outcomes (World Bank, *East Asian Update*, April 2005).

The set of living standard surveys, participatory poverty assessments conducted in the frame of the CPRGS, and an increasing number of studies by independent researchers on poverty, vulnerability and inequality have created a good basis for a nuanced analysis of the relations between economic growth and poverty reduction in Vietnam.

Agricultural diversification was identified by *Attacking Poverty Vietnam* (World Bank 1999a) as the driving force in poverty reduction. Table 5.1 shows that agricultural incomes have increased by 60.6 per cent over the period 1993–8, raising the importance of agriculture as a share of income for rural households.

Attacking Poverty also reported that inequality had slightly increased over the same period. For example, the ratio of the richest to the poorest quintile went up from 4.9 in 1993 to 5.5. However, by international standards Vietnam remained a moderately equal society and the levels of inequality were comparable to those of South Asian countries and were lower than those of other Southeast Asian countries (World Bank 1999b: 69). In Table 5.2, based on comparative data provided by the UNDP *Human Development Report 2004*, we selected a number of Asian

Table 5.1 Sources of agricultural incomes in rural Vietnam, 1993–8

	Average household income (Constant 1998 '000 VND)		*Growth over 5 years, 1993–8 (%)*	*Share of household income*	
Source of income	*1993*	*1998*		*1993*	*1998*
Agriculture	2,867	4,606	60.6	37.2	46.8
Non-farm enterprises	1,443	1,884	30.5	18.7	19.2
Wage income	1,687	1,685	–0.1	21.9	17.1
Other income	1,710	1,663	–2.8	22.2	16.9
Total	7,707	9,838	27.6	100.0	100.0

Source: World Bank (1999b: 51)

and Latin American countries to compare with the Vietnamese data, while we kept out of the table African countries that normally have a very high level of income polarization. As was to be expected, Vietnam performed much better than Latin American countries. But Vietnamese data also show less inequality than most Asian countries – particularly relevant and worrying is the comparison with China, whose high level of inequality appears as a serious warning for Vietnam given the similarity in the two reform processes. In the selected panel, only South Korea and Indonesia in East Asia and Bangladesh and Sri Lanka in South Asia demonstrate a more egalitarian social structure than Vietnam.

An important aspect of the moderate increase in income inequality in Vietnam is that this was the result of a growing gap between urban and rural areas, but there were 'almost no changes in inequality within rural areas' (World Bank 1999b: 70). While the increasing gap between rural and urban areas (as visible in Figure 5.2) compels serious concern, the low level of inequality within rural areas (where most of the population still lives) is somehow a positive factor, as we will discuss further in the next section.

While there is a unanimous consensus in acknowledging the Vietnamese success, the debate is open about the future strategies. This debate presents aspects that are apparently paradoxical – but document well the ongoing shift in development wisdom worldwide. A non-orthodox reader from the 1980s would have hardly believed that the following quotation could ever appear in an official World Bank publication.

> Although rapid growth will be central to reducing poverty in the coming decade, the *quality and pattern* of growth will also be important. This is because better quality of growth, in the sense of more evenly distributed growth across the population, will reduce poverty more even with a lower growth rate. A lower growth rate that is accompanied by sufficient higher employment-creation with a larger share of manufacturing jobs created in rural areas, where most of the poor live, is likely to be more poverty-reducing

Table 5.2 Comparative perspective of Vietnamese inequality

			Share of income or consumption (%)				*Inequality measures*		
HDI rank	*Country*	*Survey year*	*Poorest 10%*	*Poorest 20%*	*Richest 20%*	*Richest 10%*	*Richest 10% to poorest 10%*	*Richest 20% to poorest 20%*	*GINI index*
28	Korea, Republic of	1998	2.9	7.9	37.5	22.5	7.8	4.7	31.6
138	Bangladesh	2000	3.9	9	41.3	26.7	6.8	4.6	31.8
111	Indonesia	2002	3.6	8.4	43.3	28.5	7.8	5.2	34.3
96	Sri Lanka	1995	3.5	8	42.8	28	7.9	5.3	34.4
112	Vietnam	1998	3.6	8	44.5	29.9	8.4	5.6	36.1
130	Cambodia	1997	2.9	6.9	47.6	33.8	11.6	6.9	40.4
25	Singapore	1998	1.9	5	49	32.8	17.7	9.7	42.5
76	Thailand	2000	2.5	6.1	50	33.8	13.4	8.3	43.2
23	Hong Kong	1996	2	5.3	50.7	34.9	17.8	9.7	43.4
94	China	2001	1.8	4.7	50	33.1	18.4	10.7	44.7
83	Philippines	2000	2.2	5.4	52.3	36.3	16.5	9.7	46.1
45	Costa Rica	2000	1.4	4.2	51.5	34.8	25.1	12.3	46.5
59	Malaysia	1997	1.7	4.4	54.3	38.4	22.1	12.4	49.2
43	Chile	2000	1.2	3.3	62.2	47	40.6	18.7	57.1
72	Brazil	1998	0.5	2	64.4	46.7	85	31.5	59.1

Source: UNDP, *Human Development Report 2004*. Table reorganized by author

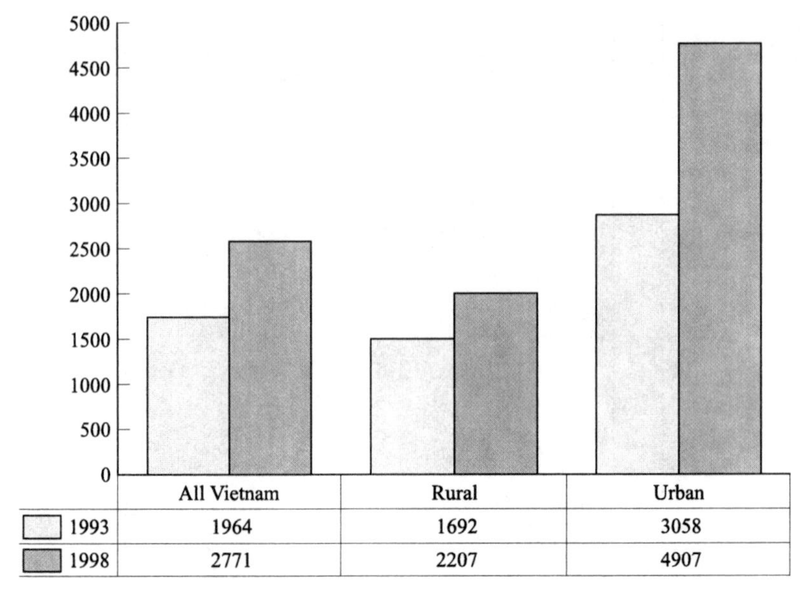

Figure 5.2 Growth in real GDP per capita expenditure by rural–urban, 1993–8

> than a higher growth rate that is less employment-creating or more urban-biased. It is therefore important for Vietnam not only to ensure a high rate of growth but also to promote a better quality and pattern of growth (World Bank 2000: 2).

For years the World Bank, together with her sister institution the IMF and a large part of development orthodoxy, had been criticized for supporting an approach for which the benefits of growth would naturally 'trickle down' to the population. After the Asian regional crisis and the demise of the Washington consensus the tone of the debate has changed substantially. Although we challenge the view that the agency embarked on a significant paradigm shift, certainly the World Bank in Vietnam has been at the front line in exploring new directions. However, reading between the lines of the World Bank documents it becomes clear that the emphasis on the quality of growth serves the aim to justify the continuation of traditional approaches to development. Quality of growth is to be obtained through a more significant role of the private sector in the economy, which can be achieved by liberalizing, privatizing, etc. That is, the key tenets of the old orthodoxy are justified with an apparent change in perspectives that, in reality, conceals a substantial continuity of purposes.

Relying on the positive correlation between economic growth and poverty reduction experienced by the country since the early 1990s, the Vietnamese authorities seem to be scarcely convinced by the argument of 'quality of growth' versus 'quantity of growth'. Rather, the 'quality of growth' they are interested in is the possibility for Vietnam to achieve an equal footing in international economic relations by developing a modern industry in strategic sectors. The experience of many years of war should be taken into account for understanding this attitude. The controversial examples from the region also point in the same direction – although Vietnam should not neglect that the successful poverty reduction in East Asia was accompanied by regressive and authoritarian political practices aimed at consolidating the capitalist regime. In the East Asian fast developers the role of the state in promoting poverty reduction was not much in redistribution, but in creating the preconditions and enabling opportunities to allow a large part of the population to lift itself out of poverty.

Although since the launch of *doi moi* the Vietnamese policymakers have been more concerned with growth than with redistribution, the country has been able to take advantage of the positive legacy of the socialist period. This legacy has been a decisive factor in enabling a large part of the population in seizing the new opportunities created by the reform. The comparatively well developed educational and health-care systems (considering the country GDP per capita), the relatively equal redistribution of land, and large investments in modern infrastructures have been the building blocks for successful poverty reduction. Although challenges in terms of equality and vulnerability remain immense, by the mid 2000s Vietnam had achieved very remarkable results. It had enabled a virtuous circle in the economy for which the different regions of the country (with the exception of the mountainous regions inhabited by ethnic minorities) moved in the same direction, if at a different speed, and where the national economy became more integrated through the creation of a national market for both agricultural and industrial products. At the same time, the country integrated with the international market, with a realistic perspective to escape the damnation of static comparative advantages and to climb to more value-adding productions.

Social differentiation, inequality and vulnerability: challenges to poverty reduction achievements

While poverty reduction must be acknowledged as successful overall, and indeed remarkable by international standards, social differentiation has emerged as a significant dark side and potentially as a major threat for the future. Social differentiation is largely related to differences in the ability and conditions for seizing the opportunities created by economic liberalization, and these differences account for the increasing economic gap between urban and rural areas, and among the various rural regions. When market-oriented reforms were unleashed, key urban areas, special economic zones and rural areas in the two deltas were in a better position to benefit from it. People living in more marginal areas had fewer opportunities, while facing new threats related to the dismantling of the socialist redistributive system.[5]

One could argue that the regional variation in the impact of economic reform had repeated in Vietnam what had already been experienced by many other developing countries. Therefore, one could wonder why the Vietnamese authorities did not do more to mitigate the tendency towards social differentiation. Like for the Chinese reform process, during the implementation of *doi moi* it was accepted that some regions and some sectors of the economy would grow faster than others. The hope was that, once the economy was set in motion the richest regions would act as engines of growth, pulling the rest of the country towards prosperity. Given the results of similar strategies in other developing countries, the Vietnamese choice to move along this path could appear surprising, especially considering that, for the government in Hanoi, economic inequality remains an evil to be contrasted.

Three factors should be kept in mind in trying to interpret the Vietnamese policymaking, explaining at least in part the conditions behind the adoption of critical measures in the *doi moi* process. First, the decision to dismantle many features of the command economy, including agricultural cooperatives and the free and universal access to public health care and primary education was not as much a government choice as a need imposed by severe economic constraints. Second, the government maintained a strong commitment to redistributive policies, although the resources at its disposal were obviously not adequate to the aim. Third, and related, as the economic conditions in the country began to improve sensibly, the government became more confident that, with a strong commitment, it could succeed in reducing the gap among regions through state interventions in terms of infrastructures, safety nets for the poorest, and support to economic initiatives (i.e. SOEs) across the country.

We have already discussed in previous chapters how the launch of *doi moi* was largely the result of a systemic crisis due to a variety of international and national causes, which eventually motivated the adoption of a new course in economic policy (building upon experiments conducted since the 1970s). After reunification, the party and government indicated universal and free access to basic education and health services as rights of citizenship. Each commune was meant to host not only a primary school but also a commune health centre (CHC) to handle basic health-care needs. Financing of this extended network of schools and health centres depended on the state central budget and on the communes themselves through resources generated by the production cooperatives. As documented by Jonathan London (2004), the increasing economic shortage during the 1980s made the central government unable to meet its commitment, leading to a decline in the quality of services. The situation became even more critical with the dismissal of agricultural cooperatives: basic education and community health centres 'become increasingly dependent on local finance precisely as the state's local capabilities began to collapse' (London 2004: 130). The introduction of 'cost recovery' schemes, i.e. user fees, was a way to guarantee a resumption of services in a situation of severe limitations in the state budget. The reliance on 'cost recovery' schemes, however, was also maintained after the economic situation had substantially improved and the state was, therefore, able to channel more resources to education and health-care services. A combination of larger state investments in the social sector and household contributions through user fees allowed a major improvement in the quality of services through the 1990s.

Enrolment in primary and secondary education increased dramatically (London 2004: 135). Although the cost for user fees became a major burden for many households, the improvement in quality made the investment worth the cost; this explains why school enrolment expanded at the same time in which the cost of education increased faster than household incomes.[6] In the same way, the decline of the commune health centre, which had played a paramount role in the provision of health-care services in the past, should be considered against the backdrop of a major change in the quality of demand. In the case of problems more serious than flu, families tend now to go directly to district or provincial hospitals, if not private health-care centres, because commune-level structures are not (and cannot be) staffed with fully trained medical doctors nor are they equipped with modern technologies.

The increased demand in terms of quality creates a new pressure on state finance and explains the continued reliance on user fees. Even more substantial user fees are required 'under the table' by health and educational officers to compensate for low wages. Only a limited number of poor households are covered by free health insurances (which, however, are associated with a negative bias because they are discriminated against compared with patients able to pay cash). Primary education is officially exempted from user fees, but local authorities normally charge construction fees or other contributions from parents, and also in this case informal contributions are often paid to ensure that pupils are properly taken care of by underpaid teachers. Thus, if the quality of service provision has improved substantially since the early 1990s, in line with the general increase in the country's wealth, then health care and education have become sensitive areas for enhanced inequality (Gabriele *forthcoming*; London 2004). In the case of health care there is a growing amount of evidence that the poor have been negatively affected by the cost of user fees and by the spread of private health-care institutions. Although the problem has been identified by the government and is at the centre of policy dialogue with donors, the state budget for health care remains low as a percentage of GDP by international standards (Gabriele *forthcoming*). By the late 1990s, inequality in the access to social services had also become a major obstacle in further extending the poverty reduction effort.

As we noted above, state policies are inspired by the idea that the key answer to poverty remains the effort to enable the conditions that allow people to support themselves. The state budget allocation contains important redistributive mechanisms, transferring resources from richer to poorer provinces, continuing practices inherited from the socialist planning period (Beresford 2003). These redistributive policies also include rudimentary safety nets, like the mentioned health insurances for the poorest and exemption from (formal) school fees for poor children. However, the real core of redistribution is in infrastructures and income-generating initiatives, including land allocation. Successful poverty reduction initiatives like 'Programme 135' and the 'Hunger Eradication and Poverty Reduction' have at their core this kind of perspective, whether they target ethnic minorities or Kinh people. However, after many years of impressive results in poverty reduction, there is a growing concern that the next targets will be difficult to reach even if the country should continue to sustain strong economic growth for a number of years. Ethnic minorities (living in mountainous regions) and other marginal groups are less likely to be able to benefit from new opportunities exactly because of their marginality. As the World Bank representative Klaus Rohland commented in a press conference presenting a report monitoring the MDG progress:

> There are ... sub-groups of the population that growth will not automatically lift out of poverty: ethnic minorities, people dependent on fragile forest lands for a living and, possibly, the growing numbers of rural landless households in certain parts of the country. [And some groups] see their vulnerabilities increase as the growth process intensifies. These vulnerable groups include migrants to urban areas, employees of private firms without trade unions, farmers losing land to developers and young people infected by HIV/AIDS (*Agence France Press*, 13 April 2005).

Inequality and vulnerability are themes that are bound to become more central in the Vietnamese policy debate once the fulfilment for remarkable results in poverty reduction leaves space for new demands from society. While in the current political debate poverty is associated with backwardness, there are aspects of poverty and vulnerability that are in fact a result of modernization and integration into the wider economy.

6 Interests representation, role of bureaucracy and governance

Previous chapters suggested that the rationale behind the reform agenda supported by the international financial institutions is inspired by neoliberal orthodoxy, although repackaged as a post-Washington consensus that blends the old paradigm with poverty-oriented measures and more open debate on policies. In order to challenge the neoliberal discourse, Chapter 4 relied on the experience of the region interpreted along the lines of a 'statist' tradition. By contrasting competing approaches with development, this work tries to contribute to a wider framework for analysis of the current debate in Vietnam at a very critical stage in the reform process. Chapter 6 will proceed in the same direction. Chapter 4 claimed that, behind the appearance of general consensus on the direction of the reform process, the Vietnamese administration is looking at different experiences for inspiration and a conspicuous interest in the models adopted by other East Asian nations is visible. At the same time, Vietnam is under a strong pressure to implement governance models that are more compatible with liberal market mechanisms than with state-led industrialization attempts. While there are significant hints that Vietnam is adopting some of the institutional arrangements of a 'statist' tradition, the official debate is, as usual, largely dominated by the discourse promoted by the international agencies. The aim of this chapter is to look at how these competing models are influencing Vietnamese policymaking and to delineate the inherent incompatibility among governance models based on contrasting views on the role that the state and economic institutions should play in order to promote sustainable economic development.

This chapter will only touch upon selected aspects of governance, and particularly economic governance, as relevant for our purposes. We are aware that this selective approach will leave out from the discussion a number of key issues that are very important for Vietnam, but which would force us to depart from the line of argumentation we have adopted.[1]

State functions and the role of bureaucracy

One of the most distinctive features of the East Asian developmental state has often been reported to be the very special way in which national bureaucracies have exerted a role of guidance (in hard authoritarian or soft corporatist manners) over the different economic actors, including powerful capitalist forces. Before presenting the modalities in which this state guidance was implemented, we should briefly explore the political setting that made it possible for the national bureaucracy to perform such an extraordinary task without generating the opposition of capitalist groups.

We will argue in the following pages that state guidance was possible because key state agencies were insulated from the particularistic demands of specific companies and industrial sectors, and strategies were designed on the basis of higher national imperatives of economic development. This understanding of the *modus operandi* of East Asian states follows the pioneering work of Chalmers Johnson (1982), where the American scholar developed the idea that, in Japan, politicians do not rule, but 'reign'. That is, politicians fulfil the function of mediating among different social groups and creating a political consensus, but the role of designing and implementing economic strategies is left entirely to a capable bureaucracy insulated from political interference.

This dichotomy between bureaucracy and politics has been subsequently contested by a number of authors. On the one hand, for example, Moon and Prasad (1994: 364) dispute the argument on the grounds that not only Park Chung Hee in South Korea, but also a number of powerful prime ministers in Japan have both reigned and ruled. On the other hand, a number of authors (see below) have revealed that the role of the bureaucracy is far from *super partes*, and strong direct linkages do exist between the bureaucracy and capital. The key question, however, remains unanswered: why in some Asian countries did states have such power in exerting guidance through strategic planning over capitalist forces and this interference was not opposed? The analysis provided by one of the most original Marxist thinkers, Antonio Gramsci, may helps to elucidate the question.

For Gramsci, the interplay between the bourgeoisie and the state is never deterministic. The bourgeoisie uses the state apparatus for their own purposes, but the way in which the state operates must reflect the concrete historical conditions and the composition of class forces. In order to maintain their power, the dominant groups may be forced to implement a 'passive revolution', i.e. to carry out a process of restoration-revolution in which the demands of the oppressed classes are partially and gradually answered. This 'passive revolution' operates through concessions from above, reduces the strength of the working class in challenging the prevailing order, and thereby consolidates the political power of the bourgeoisie. This intuition allows Gramsci to understand not only the regressive, authoritarian nature of Italian Fascism, but also its historical function in the modernization of the country. In a passage referring to the fascist Italy corporatist experience, but which could be easily translated to the context of Northeast Asia, Gramsci writes:

> The ideological hypothesis could be presented in these terms: a passive revolution would be expressed by the fact that, through legislative intervention by the state and through corporatist organization, more or less deep modifications in the country's economic structure would be introduced in order

> to reinforce the element of the 'production plan'; that is, socialization of and cooperation of production would be reinforced without affecting (or only regulating and controlling) profit appropriation by individuals and groups. In the concrete frame of Italian social relations, this could be the only viable solution for developing the industrial productive forces under the direction of the traditional ruling classes, in competition with the most advanced industrial formations of countries that monopolize raw materials and have accumulated immense capital (Gramsci 1977: 1228, my translation).[2]

The mandate to state institutions for taking the lead in modernizing the productive structures comes from the most advanced sectors of the bourgeoisie. The state apparatus may rely on strong political backing even in undertaking measures that hit back at regressive capitalist interests, if the defence of backward interests endangers more advanced ones. But what can produce such a dramatic need for change, up to making capitalist forces willing to give up part of their autonomy and to operate a passive revolution instead of simply repressing working-class demands? Why, for example, did Northeast Asia not follow the same path of many Latin American countries?

Fascist Italy, Japan since the Meiji restoration, and post-war Taiwan and South Korea shared some similar features. In all these cases modernization was a condition for survival. Italy was close to a socialist revolution before the advent of fascism. Japan was at risk of becoming a colony. South Korea and Taiwan had to cope with powerful external and internal threats. In all these cases, the survival of traditional and backward economic interests could not be guaranteed, and the state was compelled to lead a process of modernization in the collective interests of the bourgeoisie. This state intervention temporarily reduced the autonomy of capitalist forces, but it had the function of allowing traditional ruling classes to defend and consolidate their strategic economic interests. We should add that corporatist policies were more coherently implemented in Northeast Asia because, in reality, fascist Italy always remained uncertain between a state-led modernization drive and a more traditional authoritarian regime. Two tendencies competed within the Fascist Party, with the more regressive and traditional factions eventually prevailing as the regime consolidated its power.

The very strong political mandate to state institutions in Northeast Asian countries allows an understanding of the unique nature of the institutional arrangements. We may agree that, in some regards, even in Northeast Asia the dichotomy between politics and bureaucracy was often more theoretical than real, with money politics always playing an important role. However, three considerations can be advanced. First, politics became more corrupted and seized by particularistic demands when the threat of state survival became less urgent. For a long time, corruption was integrated into a framework of state guidance and was not in contradiction to it. Second, powerful and competent agencies within the state bureaucracy did exist and were able to operate with an autonomy that has no equal in other regions. Third, if it is true that the bureaucracy (even the most insulated agencies) had strong linkages with capital, then the mandate the bureaucrats received was to make these agencies provide services to the advanced capitalist sector as a whole more than to a specific interest group.

Peter Evans (1989) has coined the expression 'embedded autonomy' to describe the situation where key state agencies maintain strong linkages with the business world, but also maintain significant autonomy in transforming the inputs received through these linkages into policies. Confirming the strategic function played by a capable and meritocratic bureaucracy as suggested by Chalmers Johnson, Evans writes:

> The efficacy of the developmental state depends on a meritocratic bureaucracy with a strong sense of corporate identity and a dense set of institutionalized links to private elites… Embedded autonomy depends on the existence of a project shared by a highly developed bureaucratic apparatus with interventive capacity built on historical experience and a relatively organised set of private actors who can provide useful intelligence and a possibility of decentralised implementation (Evans 1989: 561, 575).

Scholars inspired by a 'developmental state' approach have underlined the function of strategic guidance exerted by a highly competent bureaucracy over market forces. However, the modalities of this function of strategic guidance have been conceptualized in different ways (for a good review of the debate see Lauridsen 1995). A first group of authors (Chalmers Johnson, Alice Amsden, Robert Wade, etc.), as we have already discussed in Chapter 1, acted as 'icebreakers' in challenging the development orthodoxy by emphasizing how *strength* and *authority* had allowed a group of East Asian governments to guide the process of accelerated industrialization. A second wave of authors, such as Peter Evans and Linda Weiss, has been confronted with a different task. Both South Korea and Taiwan (two major examples of 'developmental states') progressively dismantled the authoritarian features of their political systems during the 1980s. These scholars, therefore, had to investigate the conditions for state guidance on the basis of *coordination* rather than *coercion*. The question at stake was to explore whether a 'developmental state' practice could be compatible with democratization and wider integration into the world economy.

Evans and Weiss provided two (complementary) explanations of the mechanisms through which state guidance is implemented. Evans emphasizes 'embedded autonomy', i.e. state agencies well informed and connected with the business world, but autonomous in the decision-making. Weiss developed a theory of 'governed interdependence', where strategic planning is exerted through coordination with market forces, and where the state can preserve effectiveness and autonomy in dealing with a strong capital. For Linda Weiss, coordination has the power to interpret the experience of East Asia better than other theories (like Wade's 'governed market') and also offers a framework that maintains its validity for the present:

> In contrast to existing approaches, GI [Governed Interdependence] theory rejects the notion that the state's ability to 'impose' its decision is central to its

> transformative capacity. Unilateralism is more likely to be a developmental minus than a plus. It implies the capacity to act, but not necessarily to act effectively. Of central importance is the state's ability to use its autonomy to consult and to elicit consensus and cooperation from the private sector... Through its linkages with key economic groupings, the state can extract and exchange vital information with producers, stimulate private-sector participation in key policy areas, and mobilize a greater level of industry collaboration in advancing national strategy (Weiss 1998: 39).

In discussing the current debate on the developmental state as relevant for the Vietnamese reform process, there are two issues that have particular importance. The first is the question of 'insulation' or 'embedded autonomy'. In a developmental state framework, 'insulation' is something completely different from that available in authoritarian command economies and also from the institutional autonomy (e.g. of central banks) prescribed by neoliberal *governance* recipes (see below). The second issue regards the interaction between state agencies and business organizations (or, in general, interests' organizations, including the trade unions).

Historically, both authoritarian guidance and coordination have existed in East Asian developmental states. The case of Park Chung Hee's Korea, for example, was an extreme case of centralized decision-making:

> [In the 1970s in South Korea] the president's office designed how the entire heavy industry sector was to be developed, down to and including the scale of individual factories. The president's office then negotiated with the leaders of the *chaebol* to determine who would carry out the government's plans. In this manner, the Korean president, working with a committee of a few dozen specialists, was able to provide hands-on direction to the development of what soon accounted for more than half of all Korean manufacturing output and a comparable share of exports (Perkins 2001: 258).

However, such extreme cases of centralized decision-making do not represent a typical feature of the model. Northeast Asian countries that experienced the more coherent developmental state practices relied on specialized agencies (MITI in Japan, the Economic Planning Board in Korea, the Council for Economic Planning and Development in Taiwan) that were able to engage in policy coordination benefiting from both (a) high-quality information about business needs (embedding) and (b) seclusion from direct contacts with special economic constituencies (autonomy); see Weiss (1998: 52).

This seclusion was functional to catching-up dynamics, whose political rationale was shared by both capital and state bureaucracy. 'Embedded autonomy' and 'governed interdependence' were instruments of guidance over the market in order to achieve specific purposes. Therefore, seclusion was *not* (as in much of the current governance debate) a technical fix to determine which independent institutions should preside over the regulatory frameworks meant to guarantee the optimal functioning of the free market [see Jayasuriya (2001), and below].

Anne Booth (2001) has argued that Southeast Asia also experienced some cases of 'insulated bureaucracy', like the Bank of Thailand and the Ministry of Finance in Thailand, Indonesia and Malaysia. But, in Southeast Asia, more than in Northeast Asia, policymakers have always been more ready to listen to influential business lobbies. Interventions in both capital and labour markets were crucial and often carried through at the instigation of, and with the full cooperation of, powerful industrial groups (Booth 2001: 45). Quoting MacIntyre (1994), Anne Booth suggests that Southeast Asian countries are somewhere between the strong developmental states of Northeast Asia and the kleptocratic regimes of many African countries:

> Their governments [Thailand, Malaysia and Indonesia] are not hopelessly captured and corrupt but, on the other hand, they are frequently beholden to sectional interest groups, and tainted by nepotism and cronyism. Nevertheless, the Malaysian, Thai and Indonesian governments have been capable of coherent policy formulation and implementation in the face of external shocks, and have thus been able to maintain the momentum of growth over several decades. In this, they resemble Taiwan and South Korea to a greater extent than regimes in other parts of the developing world (Booth 2001: 45).

The functioning of this very special institutional arrangement, especially in Northeast Asia, was guaranteed by the mutual recognition by governments and business forces of the advantages provided by cooperation. Although key agencies were sheltered from particularistic influences, they nonetheless maintained strong institutional linkages with the private (and public) sector.

> In so far as public and private decision-makers get together to exchange information and to coordinate actions, information gaps are minimized and each generally ends up making better decisions than if trapped in isolation. Rather than engaging in purely top-down decision-making, abstracted from the real conditions of production, the economic bureaucracy therefore has a vital mechanism for acquiring production-related information and for coordinating agreement with the private sector in order to design and implement policies better. Moreover, institutional linkages, the forums of negotiation between government and business, make industrial policy decisions more open to public scrutiny… thus reducing the risks of corruption or political favouritism (Weiss 1998: 58–59).

The possibility for key state agencies to act in coordination with business interests without being trapped into corrupt relations with the particularistic interests of specific companies was provided by the encompassing nature of business representation. Quoting Linda Weiss once more: 'Industry or trade associations tend to be highly centralized and increasingly active in the design and implementation of policy' (Weiss 1998: 60). The encompassing nature of business representation and the importance of a 'vast substratum of intermediate organizations [with] a dense and multiple network of affiliation' are also confirmed by Moon and Prasad (1994: 372–373) as key resources in shaping industrial policies.

How does Vietnam fit into this model of state–business relations? Behind the appearance of a top-down dirigisme reminiscent of the past command economy, in reality, institutional settings and forms of policy negotiation since the early 1990s have become quite convergent with the East Asian experience. In a recent study on business association and policymaking Jonathan Stromseth (2003) reveals that, through the 1990s, Vietnamese authorities have supported the transformation of a number of business associations into bodies able to offer both to channel reliable information to state agencies and to facilitate a coordinated implementation of policies. The nature and the role of these business associations are taking a shape akin to those of Northeast Asian developmental states.

> As the political leadership in Vietnam has sought to pull officially-sponsored business associations into corporatist forms of policy-making and interest representation, some of these associations have responded by articulating strong demands on their constituents' behalf. The intensity of this response appears to suggest that bottom-up pressures are reinforcing the evolving pattern of increased representation, with the associations being pushed to assume stronger advocacy roles by their constituencies in Vietnamese society (Stromseth 2003: 64).

The important role of these business associations in facilitating coordination between government agencies and enterprises was officially acknowledged and also supported in strategic government documents in the early 2000s. The CPRGS indicates as one of the government priorities the strengthening of representative business associations:

> Enhancement of the business association's roles in providing business development services for their members, linkage between Government and enterprises, export and trade promotion, right protection of their members (Socialist Republic of Vietnam 2002: 36).

Among these business associations, a paramount role is played by the Vietnam Chamber of Commerce and Industry (VCCI). This association was created in North Vietnam in 1963 in a centrally planned economy context as a *de facto* government agency. With *doi moi* the function of this association changed: on the one hand, becoming more representative of its own constituency and much less an instrument of top-down directives; on the other hand, by virtue of its ability to represent the business world, it came to be associated with government policymaking with important consultative functions (Stromseth 2003). The consultative function of the VCCI and other major business associations seems to be a clear indication of a policymaking system that, in moving out from a command economy tradition, is taking the direction of government coordination with modalities reminiscent of those of other Asian countries. The evolution in the role of these business associations in their function of corporatist representation and their growing importance in the coordination with state agencies is confirmed by the expansion of their voluntary membership. Again, the most significant is the case of the VCCI, which grew from 93 members in 1963, to 700 in 1992, 1,600 in 1995, and 6,700 in 2002. Notably, as noted by Stromseth (2003: 66), more than half of these member enterprises are private companies. The representative role of the VCCI is further enhanced, as 'membership also includes other Vietnamese business associations – 101 at present count – many of which possess substantial memberships themselves' (Stromseth 2003: 66).

As we can see, since the early stages of the reform process, Vietnam has tried to create corporatist forms of state–business relations, which are quite reminiscent of the relations existing between other East Asian countries and their business world. Although Vietnam certainly has several channels to exert guidance over the business sector, the question that remains to be answered is whether Vietnam has or can achieve the *capacity* to implement such complex and sophisticated functions as are needed for successful strategic planning. As we discussed in Chapter 4 in the section on SOEs, in a comparative study on China and Vietnam, Perkins (2001) suggests that, in principle, Vietnam could be able to exert coordination over its state sector – current state-owned conglomerates control a large share of the Vietnamese industrial production, but their dimensions are still manageable for state apparatuses. Strategic planning requires a clear departure from the consolidated practice of the command economy, but this would require a change in the mindset of many state officers. The question, therefore, is how to reach the kind of capacity building and institutional change that could enable the Vietnamese bureaucracy to support a modern form of state-led industrialization. As we will see in the next section, this is not the direction in which the Western tradition of *governance* is leading Vietnam.

State capacity and modern governance

Institutional change and capacity building are not new concepts for Vietnam (nor for other developing countries). Programmes supporting modern *governance* are currently implemented in Vietnam with the support of a large number of donors and with the UNDP, the World Bank and the Asian Development Bank in the frontline. While aspects of this governance debate are rather uncontroversial, we would like to discuss here the rationale of these programmes and the kinds of capacity building and institutional reforms that they promote from our perspective inspired by the regional experience.

The reading of the reports drafted by the various international agencies indicates that there is a concrete effort to help Vietnam improve the work of the state administration in a number of key areas. Increasing transparency and fighting corruption are obviously important aims. *Governance* is presented in Vietnam along the same lines as the international agencies have recently done throughout the developing world: transparency, accountability, human development and salary reforms, rule of law, etc. The recipes include strengthening the quality of administrative staff. The state should be encouraged to focus on more-capable and better-paid civil servants, and this notion is normally associated with the recommendation to reduce the number of employees in the public administration. As usual, in the case of Vietnam the recommendations are packaged in a clever and careful way. For instance, in the *Vietnam Development Report 2002*, the World Bank is suggesting that the 'downsizing' of public administration (needed to allow better wages) should be implemented carefully, considering the negative experiences in many other countries (World Bank 2001: 58). A more recent report published by the World Bank (2005) is even more cautious in supporting downsizing. Much would seem to have changed from the time when the hard-core development orthodoxy of the first period of the Washington consensus identified the state as an obstacle for the optimal operation of market forces and economic development. Thus, do the governance reforms suggested to Vietnam represent neutral and benevolent proposals?

Here, we intend to argue that, although individual measures can be useful and beneficial, the rationale of this modern governance embedded in a new 'post-Washington consensus' is only a partial deviation from the old orthodoxy. The new attention to the role of the state (hence the importance of governance) does not imply a departure from the policies associated with the Washington consensus, but simply an attempt to create a new political consensus for a continuation of the same long-term strategies. The post-Washington consensus (PWC) concedes that states have an important role to play and that the economy cannot be left alone to the vagaries of the self-regulated market. The new governance programmes intervene in reinforcing the regulative functions of the state – but in technical forms that conceal the political implications of institutional changes. In this sense, 'strong states' and institutional 'insulation' are part of the conceptual background of neoliberal governance, although with aims that contrast with the transformative functions supported by a developmental state framework.

> One of the key differences between the governance programs advocated within the framework of the Washington consensus and the Post Washington consensus [is that] in the former, governance connoted the effective implementation of policies of economic liberalisation while in the latter, there is greater emphasis on governance as an instrument to promote the regulative capacity of the state... Indeed, the recent emphasis on governance is reflected in the increasing attention given to the provision of regulatory frameworks in previously deregulated sectors of the economy. And this is where the PWC can be clearly distinguished from the Washington consensus: it envisages a strong state – albeit restructured – in a more regulatory direction as a precondition for liberal markets (Jayasuriya 2001: 2–3).

Central to this new conception of state functions is the emphasis on the 'rule of law', i.e. the creation of a level playing field for market forces which is *per se* opposite to state intervention in the economy in terms of strategic planning in defence, for example, of national industry. The 'rule of law' within the country may become an ally of powerful economic forces, including transnational corporations, in the same way as the supranational 'rule of law' enforced by the WTO.

Rightly, Painter (2005: 263–264) suggests that the post-Washington consensus approach to governance is not unwelcome for many Vietnamese policymakers, as they see it as compatible with managerial functions of the state, through a selective mix of a 'statist' and neoliberal recipes, in pursuing industrialization strategies typical of a latecomer economy. Also referring to Jayasuriya (2002), Painter (2005) sees a line of convergence between the statist approach and the neoliberal vision of governance contained in the post-Washington consensus in a technocratic and managerial conception of society. This analysis touches upon a central feature of modern neoliberal governance. In reinventing the role of the state, the post-Washington consensus (notwithstanding its claim to wider consultation with stakeholders and participatory processes) promotes the development of technocratic institutions that mediate social and economic interests not on the basis of an open democratic process, but through decision-making justified on the basis of technical expertise and managerial capacity. In this inherent corporatist and indeed authoritarian form (even if in velvet gloves), the statist tradition and modern neoliberalism have a point of convergence that may be of interest for sectors of the Vietnamese leadership as a possible fix for maintaining a state control on the economic development process. Here, however, we want to emphasize the differences between modern neoliberal governance and statism, which are even more important than the similarities. These differences are deep in terms of both policy functions and institutional arrangements.

In a modern governance approach, policy aims are implicit and not part of an open political negotiation. At the very bottom of this neoliberal governance vision there is the belief that viable institutions are needed conditions for allowing the free market to operate on the basis of an optimal allocation of resources. Institutions have the role of creating a level playing field for economic development by removing possible causes of market failures. The functions of a state institution in a statist tradition are instead very different. The basic assumption is that catching up cannot be achieved through a normal allocation of resources on the basis of a self-regulated market. The state has the function of creating selective distortions so as to maximize results. Institutions are not simply charged with technical regulatory functions, but with a clear and open policy mandate. Thus, the institutional settings in these two approaches are quite divergent. In a post-Washington consensus modality, the emphasis is on a central bank independent from government, on a ministry of finance promoting financial restraint (keeping inflation low) rather than looking to policy outcomes (employment, growth, etc.), and on an overarching rule of law (including legal requirements from international treaties, like those deriving from WTO membership) which predominates over the rule of the parliaments. In a statist tradition, the emphasis is on institutions able to carry out strategic planning, with catching-up outcomes as keystone and the rule of law as dependent variable. In the case of Vietnam, one view sees progressive liberalization and the creation of skilled technocratic elites as the condition for making the national economic forces fully able to exploit existing resources. The other view sees a transformation of planning institutions (e.g. the MPI) into an agency for strategic planning as the condition needed to enable a successful industrialization process, removing the constraints posed by a condition of dependency and taking advantage of opportunities available for latecomers.

State functions and interests representation

The political dimension of the East Asian developmental state (at least as experienced in Japan, South Korea and Taiwan) should not be ignored. The ultimate end of state strategic planning was to promote economic growth and modernization of productive structures as a necessary tool for preserving the political dominance of the ruling classes. The leading role played by a capable and meritocratic bureaucracy is highly coherent with the interests of national capitalist forces. Both Peter Evans and Linda Weiss confirm that state capacity in promoting transformative policies does not depend on the weakness or fragmentation of dominant groups. On the contrary, 'encompassing organisation of industrial interests makes effective policy-making more likely' (Weiss 1998: 34). Ollman (2001), for example, has interestingly investigated the complex linkages between the state bureaucracy and Japanese *keiretsu*: although state officers are insulated from direct interference in promoting strategic planning, they belong to the same capitalist economic elites managing private corporations – whose ranks they will eventually join upon their early retirement from public offices.

As noted by Dixon (2000), the process of industrialization in the first generation of East Asian countries was closely associated with the support of capitalist interests *vis-à-vis* those of labour, and this class dimension was also exploited to attract foreign investments.

> In all cases, [the expansion of the foreign sector] necessitated the undermining of the power of organised labour (Amsden 1994; Dragsbaek Schmid 1997). Indeed, Amsden (1994: 632) concluded that the 'market friendly approach' that the World Bank attributed to the Highly Performing East Asian Economies amounted to 'not so friendly to labour' (Dixon 2000: 283).

For a market-oriented economy 'with socialist characteristics' the experience of the region is rather problematic. Although Vietnam may be tempted to emulate the successful economic trajectory of other Asian countries, the Communist Party may obviously want to avoid moving towards a situation in which strategic planning responds to the needs of a national capitalist bourgeoisie.

Here, two important questions can be raised (without being able to find conclusive answers to either). The first is what are the underlying dynamics in the *doi moi* process in terms of class reorganization? The second is how can a political mandate for modernization and rationalization of the productive system through strategic planning be obtained in Vietnam on the basis of a political balance more favourable to the working class?

The class-relevant implications of *doi moi* may be less obvious than they appear. Some authors, like Kolko (1997), have been fast (probably too fast) in concluding that the market-oriented reforms implemented since the late 1980s correspond to a selling out of the socialist revolution. For Kolko, Vietnam has 'lost the peace' and its leadership has sold out the country to its former enemies.

The concrete dimension of class-relevant dynamics remains barely explored by the current literature on the Vietnamese reform process. In rural areas (where most Vietnamese live and work), *doi moi* has implied a redistribution of land to households, including the rights to rent, mortgage or inheritance. Officially, land cannot be sold, because it remains the property of the communes. In reality, use rights are understood as property and a market for land has developed. In particular, in the South there are increasing indications that poor peasants may be forced to sell their land because of debts, and in some cases they may migrate to urban areas in search of new opportunities. However, as indicated in the previous chapter, inequality within rural areas remains rather low by international standards. Migration from and within rural areas is mainly the result of a very limited amount of land available to each household and a lack of off-farm activities able to absorb the redundant labour force. Although inequality is increasing, there is only limited evidence of the emergence of a new landed gentry, with distinct or opposite interests compared with those of the average peasant. The grassroots representative system is normally able to reflect the needs of the majority of the population and is only occasionally being encroached upon by the local bourgeoisie to serve its own particularistic interests.

A national bourgeoisie is clearly emerging in cities and in major rural centres. In part, this new affluent bourgeoisie is taking advantage of the opportunities created by opening of the market through a myriad of very small and household enterprises. At the same time, this new bourgeoisie is benefiting from a rent derived by its strategic position in the intermediation between the state administration, SOEs, market forces, and also a growing foreign sector. This role of intermediation (and particularly the leverage represented by SOEs in the system) has been explored by a number of studies (e.g. Fforde 1998a; Gainsborough 2004; Painter 2005). The liberalization measures introduced with *doi moi*, and in particular the ability of SOEs to eat into financing opportunities represented by FDI, allowed the creation of a 'state–business bloc', i.e. the intertwining of public and private interests along blurred lines between legitimate and less-legitimate business relations.

> Many factions emerged within this broad 'state–business bloc': local governments and branches of central ministries used their new freedoms as SOE owners to generate 'off-budget' income, and managers of SOEs used them to accumulate profits and appropriate wealth. Among these 'bureaucrat businessmen', varying interests and circumstances created conflicting perspectives on the daily practices of party control and administrative enforcement. A set of state–business relations evolved that was closely inter-connected with existing party and state patronage systems (Painter 2005: 268).

The creation of a 'state–business bloc' can have either a regressive or a progressive nature, and current evidence from Vietnam points in both directions. The regressive nature is represented by the possibility that strong economic groups (clustered around powerful SOEs in the Vietnamese case) may choose to use the rent provided by their political connections to prevent a genuine development of national economic forces. Integration into the wider economy may even reinforce the ability of powerful groups to benefit from their rent position through the creation of strategic alliances with foreign partners to the aim of a joint exploitation of national resources.[3] The progressive role, instead, may be guaranteed by a strong national commitment of dominant groups, which may derive not only from ideological motivations, but also from the perception that the independent modernization of economic forces may result in wider advantages. In this second case, a 'business–state bloc' may play a decisive role in underpinning strategic planning functions by the state, as long as these planning functions are coherent with its economic interests.

At the turn of the century Vietnam presented hints of both tendencies. Rent-seeking behaviours are widespread not only among state officers with linkages to powerful SOEs, but also among those who are in a position to benefit from the insecure regulatory frame in which the private sector operates.

> Where business comes into direct contact with state organs (regulation, taxation, registration and licensing, loans from state banks and so on), the gaps in administrative infrastructure (for example in the tax collection bureaucracy) not only make it difficult to achieve consistency and regularity of enforcement, but also at the same time encourage 'rent-seeking' behaviour (Painter 2005: 269).

These regressive tendencies are undeniable, and they represent a major threat for Vietnamese political stability. In particular, there is a concrete risk that economic interests crystallized around major SOEs may erode from within the political system, undermining the ability of the Communist Party to mediate among different interests and to promote a development strategy that conjugates economic growth with equity. These risks are well understood by the Vietnamese leadership, and it seems that by the mid 2000s a certain ability to balance the different interests prevailed.

Two major factors play a role in preventing the state from falling into the hands of regressive economic elites. First, the party maintains strong roots in Vietnamese society, and also through the vital role played by mass organizations such as the Women's Union or the Farmers' Association. These roots give the party the mandate to represent the interests of a broad spectrum of social forces.[4] This is also witnessed, for instance, by the ability to rejuvenate key organizations like the trade unions, which in the new economic environment are due to play a much more active role than during the central planning era. A number of studies indicate that with *doi moi* the Vietnamese trade unions have succeeded in improving their ability to defend workers rights, especially in relations with foreign companies (Nørlund 1999; Chan and Nørlund 1999; Dixon 2000):

> [In Vietnam] trade unions are deeply embedded in the party and government structures, and protection of the working conditions and wage levels is both expected by workers and remain central to official policy (Dixon 2000: 283).

The second major factor in leading to the creation of a national bourgeoisie rather than a *burguesía compradora* is the strong role played by the national identity in East Asia, and in Vietnam in a very special way. Nationalism is emerging as the glue that keeps the country together in a process of deep social and economic transformation. It is important to note that, like in other Asian countries, the strong national commitment of the ruling classes is not only ideological, but also reflects concrete economic interests. Like in other East Asian countries, the national bourgeoisie could have more advantages in creating national virtuous circles (the creation of a national market through significant poverty reduction) than by entering in a dependent relation with international capitalist forces. Although the Vietnamese reform process is far from linear and contradictions are clearly visible, it is reasonable to assume that a national option has more appeal for leading forces, also because current trends justify a certain level of optimism.

Conclusions. Transition: where to?

This work has explored the rationale of the new reform agenda in Vietnam as it has emerged in the period following the regional economic crisis. The aim of this study was to help in delineating a framework for analysis that could help with looking at things from a different perspective than the pervasive discourse established by the international financial institutions that, we have claimed, have a great influence in setting the path for the current reform process. As a tool for expanding the scope for policy debate and to explore possible alternatives, we have referred to the experience from the region as interpreted according to a 'developmental state' approach.

Our study indicates that the development strategy supported by the international financial institutions is largely inspired by a so-called post-Washington consensus. Such a new (neoliberal) consensus incorporates many of the fundamental tenets of the previous consensus. However, there are some new features, which are particularly visible in the policy negotiation for Vietnam. Poverty reduction has assumed centre stage in the policy debate – albeit that this is used to reintroduce the usual refrain of liberalization, privatization and competition. Differences do exist between the different agencies and within them. Thus, it is quite common to find documents by international financial institutions that depart from the prevailing logic. However, as a result of the major cracks in the Washington consensus that have been produced by the East Asian regional crisis, most mainstream positions are now often concealed behind more presentable packaging.

The debate on governance signalled a major change in the foundation of the new consensus: the regulatory functions of the state are now emphasized after two decades of deregulation. However, governance is interpreted as the creation of efficient institutions removed from political influence (but obviously very accessible to the big capital[1] that rule in the name of their technical expertise rather than on the basis of a political mandate. This new approach to governance is not specific to Vietnam; it is also visible in the industrialized Western world. However, in the case of a poor developing country, such a regulatory and institutional frame may further expose the country to a dependent relation with powerful (foreign) capitalist forces.

The first phase of *doi moi* has been characterized by impressive economic results and by substantial poverty reduction. After the regional economic crisis, many East Asian countries (with Vietnam among them) have resumed fast economic growth. However, the future for a market economy with socialist characteristics is uncertain, because the ideological rationale that supports the reform process is very ambiguous. The identification of a guiding role for the state sector of the economy *per se* is neither a guarantee that the state will be able to exert control on the national economy nor that socialist objectives can be maintained. A more clear definition of aims, power structures, social and institutional actors and policies would be required, although this clarification may be hampered by the CPV tradition to move along a consensual decision-making process and to avoid confrontation with the international financial institutions.

Hints do exist that the Vietnamese leadership is looking to the developmental experience of other countries in the region and that a model of state-led industrialization is considered as the most appropriate for Vietnam. In our work, however, we have recalled two major issues that seem not to be clearly addressed in official documents profiling future developing strategies.

First, 'developmental state' strategies in Asia were based on strategic planning – something very different from the kind of command central planning which the Vietnamese bureaucracy is used to. A change towards strategic planning practices would require capacity building and institutional reforms along lines contrasting with the so-called 'modern governance' promoted by the international agencies.

Second, the political mandate for the implementation of such extraordinary state functions in market guidance was a result of the need by capitalist forces to protect their long-term interests in a situation of crisis (through a 'passive revolution'). The political mandate for state-led industrialization along a 'developmental state' model in Vietnam would require a different kind of political consensus – something that is currently barely visible in the country. Central to the possibility of implementing a 'developmental state' kind of economic policy will be dependence on the role of the national elites, i.e. on the choice to act as a national bourgeoisie or to pursue integration into a transnational alliance of capitalist forces. The experience of East Asia has normally indicated that the national bourgeoisie tends to maintain strong roots (and to be sensitive to nationalist calls), but examples of 'comprador bourgeoisie' are also visible.

In conclusion, this work indicates that, in this crucial stage of the Vietnamese reform process, many of the elements of the debate tend to be concealed behind a fictive generalized consensus. This work has sought to disarticulate some aspects of this neoliberal consensus and to suggest a number of areas in which alternative strategies should be more openly discussed.

Notes

Introduction

1. Contrary to the perception of most Westerners, Vietnam is a large country. With more than 80 million inhabitants it ranks thirteenth in the world and second in Southeast Asia (after Indonesia) for population. This misperception regarding the country's populace is symptomatic of the substantial lack of information in the West about Vietnam. The 'Vietnam war' remains the most popular genre in American fiction literature, but general understanding about the country is scanty and dismaying. As we will see, the number of scientific studies about Vietnam is also rather limited.
2. The need for a developing country in search of concessional loans from the international financial institutions and preferential access to Western markets not to challenge openly 'orthodox' thinking is a general condition. This has also been experienced by other East Asian countries, such as South Korea and Taiwan, at an earlier stage of their industrialization drive, when they made an effort to conceal characteristic features of their development strategies and officially bowed to Western prescriptions; see White and Wade (1988: 7–8) and Dixon (2002).
3. International agencies have an irresistible power in co-opting local scholars, in a process that risks undermining the scope for critical and independent research. By participating in foreign-sponsored research, local scholars not only receive allowances many times higher than their normal salaries, but also get access to professional training, travel grants, new career opportunities, etc. Thus, owing to their intellectual dominance and their economic means, the international organizations have great leverage in promoting conformist and opportunistic behaviours among local scholars (as well as among international scholars highly paid for their consultancy jobs). International cooperation in policy research, which is often intended to promote capacity building and institutional strengthening, risks achieving dismaying results even when it is carried out with the best intentions.
4. We will see in Chapter 4, for example, that substantial disagreements have emerged since 1996 in the negotiation for structural adjustment loans, up to the point that the IMF suspended the third instalment of a loan already approved. We will also see that Vietnam forced the USA to reopen negotiation for a bilateral trade agreement, when Washington was already preparing for the signature.
5. A number of recent studies (see in the following) have indicated that Vietnam can be taken as a model for its impressive results in terms of poverty reduction and for its ability to reach the target provided by the Millennium round.
6. Incidentally, we may recall that Robbins' neo-classical tenets were soon to be contested successfully by such an 'ignorant' and 'perverse' economist as Keynes (and the same Robbins was led to modify his views).
7. Polanyi shows, however, that society eventually reacted and succeeded in bringing the market under political and social control [see Cox (1995: 39)].

8. 'The beliefs express our ideas about what reality actually is, or was, while valuations express our ideas of how it ought to be, or ought to have been' (Myrdal 1970: 15).
9. This apparent contradiction is well elucidated in Amin (1998).
10. The concepts of *system* and *lifeworld* are defined by Jürgen Habermas is his *The Theory of Communicative Action*.
11. In a longer term, world-system analysis perspective, Immanuel Wallerstein [1997 (1983)] motivated that hegemonic countries promote free trade when they are at the apex of their power, but start to violate free-trade norms once their hegemony declines.

1 Reflection on the analytical tools

1. Berger and Beeson remind that the 'intolerance of dissent' maintained by Anne Krueger was not necessarily shared by other World Bank officers and those policies always coherently implemented by the different departments. This was possible because, under President Clausen, the bank lost the monolithic structure that she had under the McNamara administration – for a critical and vivid description of the McNamara presidency see George and Sabelli (1994).

   In 2001, Anne Krueger was appointed as Chief Economist of the International Monetary Fund (IMF) by the administration of George W. Bush.
2. The 1991 World Development Report conceded that 'market-friendly policies – neither complete laissez faire nor interventionism – are optimal for growth and income distribution' (Berger and Beeson 1998: 491).
3. Rightly, a reviewer of my edited volume on *Rethinking Development in East Asia*, in whose Introduction I have already reported this interpretation, reminded me that as an Italian I should quote *Il Gattopardo* by Tomaso di Lampedusa, i.e. the strategy to change everything in order not to change anything. We may wonder if the recent views of the former World Bank Chief Economist (and Nobel laureate) Joseph Stiglitz are part of this paradigm readjustment or represent a real conversion on the road to Damascus.
4. Toye, for instance, recalls that Francis Fukuyama, in his *The End of History*, failed in giving an explanation of the success story of these countries (although acknowledging their high economic growth) and confused their cases with the 'genuinely free-market' (and less successful) case of 'the Chicagoan experiment in Pinochet's Chile' [Toye 1993 (1987): 12].
5. In this work 'statist' is used to indicate a group of scholars who emphasize the role of the state in promoting economic development, and could be loosely referred to as supporting a so-called 'developmental state' approach. These scholars should not be confused with those supporting centrally planned economies.
6. According to Toye, these scholars were inspired by Keynes, as 'an advocate of reform capitalism, in which the state plays a supplementary and co-ordinating role in a basically market economy'. However, in more precise terms, the strategy adopted by East Asian countries relied on 'long-term industrial policies, rather than the short-term demand management policies which are the hall-mark of Keynesianism in its narrow (too narrow) sense' [Toye 1993 (1987): 13–14].
7. The specification of *selective* state interventions should be noted. Here lies a key element in the discussion regarding the Vietnamese case. Obviously, not all forms of state intervention are beneficial.
8. For a more detailed analysis of neo-mercantilism and the other historical traditions in international political economy, a key reference remains the volume by Robert Gilpin (1987). Björn Hettne (1993) provides a very interesting discussion of neo-mercantilism and its developmental implications.
9. This search for more contextual analysis is, in itself, a reason of conflict with more 'orthodox' (i.e. neoclassical) studies, especially with those economists or institutions

that have attempted to interpret reality in terms of universalistic mathematical models. It is well known that the World Bank and the IMF have often (and rightly) been accused of trying to impose the same prescriptions throughout the developing world without any consideration for the specific national contexts.

10. In the language of the world-system scholars, Japan is the only country that has moved from the 'periphery' to the 'core'. The special status of Japan is also well illustrated by the definition of 'Triadic globalization', i.e. a world economy dominated by a 'triad' of which Japan represents one vertex.
11. See Bruce Cumings (1999) and Robert Wade (1990) for a discussion of this crucial issue. Concerning the present work, it is useful to contrast the Japanese promotion of heavy industry in Korea and of modern agriculture in Taiwan with the French more short-term predatory attitude in Vietnam. In colonial Vietnam, only some small-scale light industry was developed, to serve the needs of the French local residents and of the colonial elite.
12. A well-known account of the role of Japan in shaping a regional productive system is provided by Bruce Cumings (1987) [we have dealt with this issue in Masina (1996)]. For an analysis of the complex web of economic relations between Japan and the other Asian countries before and during the Asian economic crisis, see Sum (2002) and Masina (2002a).

    Japan has quite openly attempted the promotion of its own developmental strategy as a model for the region with the aim to reassert its hegemony. As discussed in Masina (2002a), this attempt has produced tensions within the international financial institutions, which have perceived the Japanese initiatives as a challenge to the 'orthodoxy'.
13. For a review of the debate motivated by Chalmers Johnson's work, see the volume edited by Meredith Woo-Cumings (1999).
14. In his review of the main literature analysing the East Asian developmental state model, Laurids Lauridsen defines as a 'strong version' the interpretation inspired by Wade, but also by other authors such as Alice Amsden (1989), apart from Chalmers Johnson (1982).
15. Amsden's *The Rise of 'the Rest'* is a very stimulating contribution. But the attempt to pull together a rather heterogeneous group of countries, including some whose economic performance has been substantially dismaying, within a single explanatory frame risks making the whole construction problematic.
16. For an interesting reappraisal of this point, which relates to the classical 'dependent development' debate, see Glassman (1999).
17. It is useful to recall that the ultimate aim of the reforms introduced in Hungary in 1968 and in other countries belonging to the Soviet bloc was to 'rationalize' central planning, not to replace central planning with market mechanisms. Both in the Chinese and Vietnamese reforms there is, instead, a clear acceptance of the need to supersede central planning, while maintaining state guidance in economic development. See Naughton (1995) on this point in relation to China.
18. The state sector in Vietnam never did employ more than 16 per cent of the workforce, and the percentage declined sharply in the first phase of the reform process: it was about 10 per cent in 1991 and below 9 per cent by the mid 1990s. Employment in the SOEs accounted for only 9.7 per cent of the workforce at the launch of *doi moi*, and it was down to 6.2 per cent in 1991 (McCarty 2001: 8–9).
19. Notwithstanding the obvious relevance of this comparative analysis, the number of studies dedicated to the two countries is surprisingly limited. A remarkable exception is the volume edited by Chan *et al.* (1999).
20. The major threat to the central authority was represented by the so-called Gao Gang affair in the early 1950s. The leader of Manchuria (a key industrial region) was suspected of challenging the authority of Beijing (probably with Soviet support). Gao Gang eventually committed suicide in 1954.

21. Still, in January 1950, Truman and the State Secretary Acheson had confirmed that Taiwan and South Korea were outside the defence perimeter guaranteed by the USA. And the State Department had clearly indicated the intention to not be involved in the Chinese civil war in defence of Chiang Kai-shek.
22. For an historical reconstruction of the American 'China policy' in the period 1947–71, see Masina (1993).
23. In Chapter 6 we will rely on the analysis of Fascism by Antonio Gramsci to make this point.
24. This process of identification with the Asian models was also visible on the occasion of the 2002 World Football Championship – a quite annoying experience for this writer, who unfortunately watched the match between Italy and South Korea in Hanoi!
25. Regional inequality was already remarkable before the start of *doi moi*, and it was further increased by the different ways in which regions were able to cope with the new opportunities and threats created by the reform process; for a more detailed account, see Beresford (2003).
26. A direct influence of Myrdal's ideas on Vietnamese policymakers remains difficult to verify. The long-term cooperation with the Swedish Development Agency (SIDA) may have contributed to making the lesson of the Nobel Prize economist known in Vietnam, or at least indirectly received through the work of the Swedish experts. I acknowledge the comments on this point received by colleagues in the Vietnam Studies Group mailing list, and particularly the hints by Oscar Salemink and Shawn McHale on the role of SIDA.
27. Rice and vegetables, with very little intake of proteins, still constitute the diet of many poor peasants.

2 The historical background: Vietnam between revolution and economic reform

1. Two main factors, at least, should be recalled: first, the increasing American involvement in South Vietnam, which in a few years led to a direct military intervention; second, the ambiguous role of China, successively denounced by the Vietnamese Communist Party. During and after the Geneva agreements, the Chinese government was not too keen in promoting the reunification of Vietnam, which was considered as a potential contender in the Southeast Asian geopolitical equilibrium. A Vietnam divided and dependent on Chinese support was a more appealing option for Beijing.
2. The need for Mao to accelerate the process of industrialization in China – culminating in the dramatic Great Leap Forward – was also motivated by the underlying conflict with Soviet Union. This conflict became openly visible in 1957, and led to a complete rupture in the 1960s.
3. An assessment of the long-term development implications deriving from the French colonial rule remains a controversial issue. On the one hand, France certainly subjected the country to a regime of harsh economic exploitation (e.g. Marr 1981); on the other hand, France also contributed to the development of a consumer-goods-related light industry (Nørlund 1989). However, contrary to the experience of the Japanese colonization in Manchuria, Korea and Taiwan, France did not support Vietnam in the development of a heavy industry. The differences between the Japanese colonization of Taiwan and the French colonization of Vietnam are well discussed by Bruce Cumings (1999): Japan financed physical infrastructures (roads, railways, harbours and irrigation), but also promoted agricultural extension, technical schools, peasants associations, etc. Nothing of this kind was realized by France. The question of the reforms introduced by Japan remains a sensitive one, because it risks

being confused with a justification of the Japanese colonial rule [see also discussion in Wade (1990)].

4. Gabriel Kolko (1997: 21), recalling the war experience in other countries such as Germany, Britain and the USA, concludes that: 'Few, if any, of Communist Vietnam's economic policies from 1955 to 1975 differed in principle from what states normally do during wars'.
5. Important differences existed between the Chinese and the Soviet models, and in both countries the 'models' changed over time. However, the Chinese system during the First Five-Years Plan (1953–8) was also strongly influenced by the Soviet example.
6. Even in the full 'socialist collectives' peasants were allowed to maintain private plots, corresponding to 5 per cent of the collective land. The products from these plots could be sold on local markets. In many areas peasants tended to dedicate more energy to these lands than to the collective farming; and in some cases the dimensions of private plots were increased with the consent of local authorities.
7. For instance, the notorious CIA-led Operation Phoenix was directed to the systematic murder of those democratic activists, who were considered sympathetic with the Communist forces.
8. The Vietnamese historian Nguyen Khac Vien (1993: 390) criticizes the 'atmosphere of political suspicion [toward] those who had worked in the Saigon Administration'. This led to the dismissal of thousands of former officers from all levels of the new administration, even in technical services. Also, errors were made in sending to 're-education camps' officers whose association with the previous regime had not been marked by criminal behaviours.
9. For the sake of simplicity in this text, the conventional dichotomy North/South is employed. However, at least five geographical areas could be distinguished with different socio-economic characteristics. Traditionally, the country is considered as consisting of the North (Bach Bo), the Centre (Trung Bo) and the South (Nam Bo). This distinction relies on historical and natural differences (reflected in the French colonial organization), and still plays an important role. [For a critical assessment of the three regions in the revolutionary movement, see Chesneaux (1972).] At the time of reunification, the part of centre below the seventeenth parallel was more easily integrated into the new socialist system than the rest of the 'south', exactly for this long historical heritage (Beresford 1988: 63).
10. After Vietnam became a full member of Comecon (1978), it lost the right to the preferential treatment it had received due to war reasons. The price for many imported commodities increased 2.5–3 times (Dang 2004: 25).
11. Truong Chinh, former general secretary of the party and pre-eminent ideologue, had been a supporter of accelerated socialist transformation in the south in the 1970s. However, from 1984 he became convinced of the need to implement a reformist agenda. He, together with other senior leaders, initiated preparing the ground for the subsequent major change (Riedel and Turley 1999: 18).
12. This coalition is described by Fforde and de Vylder (1996: 143) as resulting from the convergence of three groups:

    1 technocrats and pro-markets reformists, pushing for a total dismantling of the DRV model;
    2 rising commercial interests within the state sector in search of better economic benefits;
    3 southern liberals who wished to see a return to the pre-1975 system.

13. Party leader in Ho Chi Minh City and later prime minister.
14. This section is based on Masina (2002b).
15. This interpretation has been confirmed by officers of the UN system in Hanoi, during informal talks in the spring of 1998.

16. Parts of this and following sections are based on Masina (2002b).
17. This deal fixed the amount of the debt at US$1.7 billion (Russia had initially claimed 11 billion) to be repaid in 23 years, with 10 per cent to be paid in cash and the rest through commodities and export opportunities (*Far Eastern Economic Review*, 9 November 2000).
18. In this sense, Vietnam (like China) was never 'Stalinist' or 'neo-Stalinist'. A wide debate within the leadership has always existed (and still exists) without the prevailing group eliminating the other and without the formation of permanent factions. The stress within the CPV has been on collegiality of the decisions, and the party has maintained its unity even in the face of the devastating split between China and the Soviet Union (Vietnam even attempted a mediation between the two). A comparison between Vietnam and China [see Chan *et al.* (1999: 9)] suggests that not only was the political conflict within the Communist Party in Vietnam less harsh than in China, but also class warfare within society was less violent.
19. For Vietnam, e.g. see World Bank (1998).

3 Vietnam and the regional economic crisis

1. For a critical review of the different interpretations, see Masina (2002a) and the other contributions in the same volume.
2. It should be noted that there are only a very limited number of international analysts working on independent interpretations of Vietnam's current economic development. This makes it possible for a small group of scholars and international financial institutions' officers to lay down an interpretative frame that is constantly repeated in reports, media, studies, etc. This is what can be schematically defined as 'common wisdom'. Within this general 'common wisdom', however, significant differences exist in the interpretation of specific issues.
3. In March 1999, the General Statistical Office of Vietnam revised the historical series of economic data for the country. The real GDP growth rate for 1997 was reported at 8.8 per cent in the old series and at 8.2 per cent in the new series (IMF 1999b).
4. Here, and in the following, the FDI data are those reported by IMF sources. The choice of the source responds to the aims of this chapter, i.e. to show that even on the basis of these figures the account provided by the international financial institutions is rather inconsistent. For a detailed discussion on the complexity of assessing FDI data in Vietnam, see Freeman and Nestor (2004).
5. I wish to thank Curt Nestor for his comments on this point, and more generally on FDI to Vietnam.
6. In pre-crisis East Asia there was an overinvestment tendency, visible in key industrial sectors and motivated by a strong 'catching up' drive [see the discussion presented by the different contributions contained in Masina (2002a)].
7. In an interview with a high official in the Ministry of Foreign Affairs in October 1997, I was told that the management of the Thai Binh disturbances showed that the Vietnamese political system was functioning well, the state being able to react and respond to the people's demands.
8. The international financial institutions have suggested on several occasions that these figures should be revised downwards. They have estimated growth at about 3 or 4 per cent in 1997 and about 2 or 3 per cent in 1999. Vietnamese authorities might have tried to adjust figures upwards for political purposes. The international financial institutions, instead, might have presented a bleak scenario in order to push the government to accept their prescriptions. The fear expressed by the World Bank (1999a) in December 1999 that 'Vietnam now faces the possibility of becoming one of the slower performers in the region' was not confirmed by the data.
9. The data on the composition of exports contained in the Statistical Annex of an IMF Staff Report published in February 2000, cover the period until 1998. In that year, the

Thai economy had a contraction of about 10.4 per cent. GDP growth turned positive only in 1999.

10. This is also confirmed by analysis of the export composition of another important 'crisis' country, such as Korea. Not even in 1998, with an economic contraction of 5.8 per cent, huge devaluation and shrinking exports, did South Korea see a growth in export performance of its light industry. (See data contained in the IMF Staff Country Report No. 10/00, *South Korea: Statistical Annex.*) At the end of 1999, Indonesia, the largest Southeast Asian country, was still in the midst of economic recession and political instability, which reduced its ability to compete in international markets.

4 The agenda for economic reform

1. This sense of frustration was similar to the one registered among foreign investors by the mid 1980s. The head of the Beijing office of one of the largest European industrial groups told us in 1986 how his group 'had' to be there in the hope of future opportunities, but for the moment it was wasting money and resources. The rush to invest in China came at the moment in which the Chinese market was still smaller than that of a medium-size European country, and this often resulted in frustration among investors.
2. In a round of interviews conducted in the summer 2003 with numerous high-ranking representatives of Vietnamese research institutes and policy think-tank in Hanoi, 'step-by-step' was constantly repeated as the 'magic formula' for successful reforms.
3. 'The Congress documents were significant not as guidelines for policy but as snapshots of the contested ground, over which bickering and bargaining would continue once the Congress was over' (Riedel and Turley 1999: 39).
4. Le Kha Phieu had apparently used his connections with the army for spying on his fellow party leaders. Such unacceptable behaviour led the three elder 'Senior Advisers' to the Central Committee – Do Muoi, Le Duc Anh and Vo Van Kiet – to let it be known that Phieu had lost their support, thus making it impossible for him to be re-elected.
5. It is often reported that the popularity of Nong Duc Manh is also due to the rumour that he was a natural son of the late President Ho Chi Minh. When confronted with a direct question on this issue, Mr Manh always replied that 'in Vietnam we are all Ho Chi Minh's children'.
6. E.g. see Masina (2002a) and the other contributions collected in the same volume.
7. The World Bank and the US Treasury, in particular, would insist on a hard-line message regarding free trade. See Kanbur (2001) for an account of the current disagreements in development policies; this account, however, is shy in reporting the reasons that forced its author to resign from his important job. For more detailed information about the resignation of Kanbur (and Stiglitz's resignation as World Bank Chief Economist), see Wade (2001).
8. The Vietnamese *Attacking Poverty* and *Voices of the Poor* are actually considered as the most successful among these studies. This seems at least to be the view among international experts, as it was confirmed during a private conversation with a representative in the Poverty Working Group of the OECD's Development Assistance Committee.
9. The IMF argues that in the early 2000s the problem was only technical (i.e. a lack of direct information on the Vietnamese foreign reserve) and did not imply a disagreement in the terms of policies.
10. I rely for this point regarding the views of the Japanese experts (and before the Asian crisis also of South Korean advisers) on private conversations with scholars (Vietnamese, Japanese, but also Western) and with officers of international agencies. The research directed by Professor Keinichi Ohno in cooperation with the Vietnamese

National Economic University has also indicated the need for industrial policies that related more with the experience of Japan and other Asian countries than with the neoliberal orthodoxy.

11. Once again we must note how the World Bank's regime of truth is constructed by simply ignoring the wide scientific debate. The publication of the *East Asian Miracle* has resulted in a wide debate, which became particularly vibrant with the unfolding of the regional economic crisis. For an agency with so large a responsibility in assisting developing countries in shaping their own developing strategies is quite unfortunate to simply deny this debate. The review of existing literature can easily show that there is rather little general consensus on what has been 'convincingly demonstrated' about the developmental experience of the high performing East Asian countries.
12. As usual, differences do exist between these two *sister institutions*. While the IMF is asking for a neutral trade regime, the World Bank is somehow more nuanced in arguing for trade liberalization.
13. We have already seen that even the World Bank's *East Asian Miracle* of 1993 had to concede that growth in these countries was a result of something more than 'getting the price right'. The importance of state-led development strategies has been even more openly recognized in the more recent studies of one of the key authors of the *East Asian Miracle*, i.e. Joseph Stiglitz (2001).
14. Vietnam was one of the few countries in the world not to have normal trade relations with the USA, together with North Korea, Laos, Cuba and Iraq.
15. These rumours were reported to me by a well-informed foreign expert, but neither I nor my informant had the possibility to verify their reliability.
16. The mutual misunderstanding between those looking at different time perspectives in addressing economic development and poverty reduction is aptly analysed by Ravi Kanbur (2001).
17. This scepticism was confirmed by interviews with representatives of key international organizations in April 2005.
18. Once again, it should be underlined that World Bank officers in Vietnam have proven to be quite able in mediating between Washington doctrinaire views and the concrete conditions in the field.
19. Although Vietnam relies on intensive agriculture (e.g. rice transplanting), in densely populated rural areas there is an oversupply of labour. For example, for an average family in the Red River delta with around 6 or 7 *sao* of land (one *sao* is about one-third of a hectare) farming cannot absorb more than two people; all the other members of the family must find occupations in off-farm activities (which are scarcely available) or migrate. In an investigation conducted in two villages of two different districts in Hung Yen province (Red River delta) in July 2002, it emerged that almost every family had at least one member working in Hanoi either as seasonal or long-term migrants. Of these migrant workers only a very tiny number could find occupations in industry, while the vast majority would work in informal occupations (especially selling fruit or tea, and shoe shining) or in services (night guards in shops, care for elderly people or children, etc.). This investigation was conducted by the author with a team of European and Vietnamese scholars in the frame of an EU INCO-Dev project on 'Sustainable livelihoods in Southeast Asia'.

5 Poverty reduction, inequality and social differentiation

1. This point was stressed repeatedly during interviews with Vietnamese scholars and policymakers.
2. The author of the *Asian Drama* would have been glad to see that many Asian countries escaped poverty through policies that are often reminiscent of his teaching.

3. This comparative investigation was coordinated by the author and conducted by a network of European and Asian scholars in the frame of an EU INCO-Dev project on 'Sustainable livelihoods in Southeast Asia'. Fieldwork in Vietnam was carried out in Soc Trang (Mekong Delta), Hung Yen (Red River Delta), Tan Trieu (Hanoi), Hanoi City and Son La. The team working in Vietnam was coordinated by Bui Huy Khoat, Dinh Thi Ngoc Bich and Irene Nørlund.
4. For the field study reports and a list of publications also involving a comparative study in Laos and Thailand, see: www.ssc.ruc.dk/inco.
5. This issue is discussed in more detail by the different contributions contained in Taylor (2004).
6. The propensity of households to invest in health care and schooling was confirmed by a number of interviews conducted by the INCO-Dev research team in several locations of the country. Interviewees reported that improvement in quality compared with the 1990s justified, in many cases, getting into debt to pay for emergency costs. Interestingly, in the Red River Delta there is evidence of households mortgaging or selling their land to support university education for their youngsters – which demonstrates the perception of investment in education as a valuable investment (information kindly provided by Do Ta Khanh).

6 Interests representation, role of bureaucracy and governance

1. Two of these key issues are the process of decentralization and grassroots democracy on the one hand, and the question of corruption on the other hand. These issues are dealt with by the *Vietnam Development Report 2005* (World Bank 2005) for the Consultative Group Meeting of December 2004. This report has a rather balanced position, and the part on corruption is very refreshing, as it allows one to look deeper than the usual stereotypes.
2. L'ipotesi ideologica potrebbe essere presentata in questi termini: si avrebbe una rivoluzione passiva nel fatto che per l'intervento legislativo dello Stato e attraverso l'organizzazione corporativa, nella struttura economica del paese verrebbero introdotte modificazioni più o meno profonde per accentuare l'elemento di «piano di produzione», verrebbe accentuata cioè la socializzazione e cooperazione della produzione senza per ciò toccare (o limitandosi solo a regolare e controllare) l'appropriazione individuale e di gruppo del profitto. Nel quadro concreto dei rapporti sociali italiani questa potrebbe essere l'unica soluzione per sviluppare le forze produttive dell'industria sotto la direzione delle classi dirigenti tradizionali, in concorrenza con le più avanzate formazioni industriali di paesi che monopolizzano le materie prime e hanno accumulato capitali imponenti.
3. This is what has historically been done by Latin American dominant groups, which came to be known as *burguesía compradora.*
4. It should be noted that while the political system is often criticized for the high level of corruption, few people challenge the legitimacy of the party to rule the country.

Conclusions. Transition: where to?

1. For big capital we mean large companies like the Transnational Corporations (in the case of Vietnam, also large SOEs), major international or national banks, and more broadly powerful economic lobbies whose interests may differ from those of the country and in some instances even from those of the medium-level bourgeoisie.

Bibliography

Amin, Samir (1998) *Spectres of Capitalism: a Critique of Current Intellectual Fashions*. New York: Monthly Review Press.

Amoroso, Bruno (2002) 'Economy and Politics in the East Asian Crisis', in P. P. Masina (ed.), *Rethinking Development in East Asia: From Illusory Miracle to Economic Crisis*. Richmond: Curzon Press.

——— and Jin, Ye (2002) 'Vietnam in the Cyclone of Globalisation', in B. Amoroso and A. Gallina (eds), *Essays on Regional Integration and Globalisation*. Roskilde: Federico Caffè Centre.

Amsden, Alice H. (1989) *Asia's Next Giant: South Korea and Late Industrialisation*. Oxford: Oxford University Press.

——— (1994) 'Why isn't the Whole World Experimenting the East Asian Model of Development: Review of the East Asian Miracle', *World Development*, 22, pp. 627–633.

——— (2001) *The Rise of 'the Rest': Late Industrialization Outside the North Atlantic Economies*. New York: Oxford University Press.

———, Eoh, Yoon and Dae Euh (1993) 'South Korea's 1980s Financial Reforms: Good-bye Financial Repression (Maybe), Hello New Institutional Restraints', *World Development*, 21(3), pp. 379–390.

Andersen, Heini (1994) 'Kritisk Teori', in H. Andersen (ed.) *Videnskabsteori og Metodelære*. Frederiksberg: Samfundslitteratur.

Arrighi, Giovanni, Ikeda, S. and Irwan, A. (1993) 'The Rise of East Asia: One Miracle or Many?', in R. A. Palat (ed.), *Pacific-Asia and the Future of the World System*. Westport (CT): Greenword Press.

Bell, Peter F. (1996) 'Development or Maldevelopment? The Contradictions of Thailand's Economic Growth', in Michael J.G. Parnwell (ed.) *Uneven Development in Thailand*. Aldershot: Avebury, pp. 49–62.

Beresford, Melanie (1988) *Vietnam: Politics, Economics and Society*. London and New York: Pinter.

——— (2003) 'Economic Transition, Uneven Development, and the Impact of Reform on Regional Inequality', in Hy V. Luong (ed.) *Postwar Vietnam*. Lanham (MA): Rowman & Littlefield Publishers.

——— (2004) 'Lessons from the Asian Crisis for the Sustainability of Vietnamese Economic Development', in Melanie Beresford and Tran Ngoc Angie (eds), *Reaching for the Dream*. Copenhagen: NIAS Press.

——— and Dang Phong (2000) *Economic Transition in Vietnam: Trade and Aid in the Demise of a Centrally Planned Economy*. Cheltenham: Edward Elgar.

Beresford, Melanie and Tran Ngoc Angie (eds) (2004) *Reaching for the Dream*. Copenhagen: NIAS Press.

Berger, Mark T. and Beeson, Mark (1998) 'Lineages of Liberalism and Miracles of Modernisation: The World Bank, the East Asian Trajectory and the International Development Debate', *Third World Quarterly*, 19(3), pp. 487–504.

Blomström, Magnus and Hettne, Björn (eds) (1984) *Development Theory in Transition*. London: Zed Books.

Booth, Anne (2001) 'Initial Conditions and Miraculous Growth: Why is Southeast Asia Different from Taiwan and South Korea?', in K. S. Jomo (ed.) *Southeast Asia's Industrialization*. Basingstoke: Palgrave.

Bullard, Nicola (2002) 'Taming the IMF: How the Asian Crisis Cracked the Washington Consensus', in P. P. Masina (ed.), *Rethinking Development in East Asia: From Illusory Miracle to Economic Crisis*. Richmond: Curzon Press.

———, Walden Bello and Kamal Malhotra (1998) 'Taming the Tigers: the IMF and the Asian Crisis', in K. S. Jomo (ed.) *Tigers in Trouble: Financial Governance, Liberalization and Crises in East Asia*. London: Zed Books.

Chan, Anita and Nørlund, Irene (1999) 'Vietnamese and Chinese Labour Regimes: On the Road to Divergence', in A. Chan, B. J. T. Kerkvliet and J. Unger (eds) *Transforming Asian Socialism: China and Vietnam Compared*. St Leonard (Australia): Allen & Unwin.

———, Kerkvliet, Benedict J. Tria and Unger, Jonathan (eds) (1999) *Transforming Asian Socialism: China and Vietnam Compared*. St Leonard (Australia): Allen & Unwin.

Chandrasekhar, C. P. and Ghosh, Jayati (2002) 'Finance and the Elusive Recovery: Lessons for Emerging Markets from South Korea and Thailand', in P. P. Masina (ed.), *Rethinking Development in East Asia: From Illusory Miracle to Economic Crisis*. Richmond: Curzon Press.

Chang, Kyung-Sup (2002) 'South Korean Society in the IMF Era: Compressed Capitalist Development and Social Sustainability Crisis', in P. P. Masina (ed.), *Rethinking Development in East Asia: From Illusory Miracle to Economic Crisis*. Richmond: Curzon Press.

Chesneaux, Jean (1971) 'Le Communisme vietnamienne', in Jean Chesneaux, Georges Boudarel and Daniel Hemery (eds) *Tradition et Révolution au Vietnam*. Paris: Editions Anthropos.

——— (1972) *Le Vietnam: Études de Politique et d'Histoire*. Paris: Maspero.

———, Boudarel, Georges and Hemery, Daniel (eds) (1971) *Tradition et Révolution au Vietnam*. Paris: Editions Anthropos.

Chu, Wan-wen and Weiss, Linda (1999) 'Taiwan's Developmentalism before and after the Financial Crisis', Department of Government, University of Sydney, unpublished paper.

Communist Party of Vietnam, Central Committee (2001) *Strategy for Socio-Economic Development, 2001–2010*. Approved by the Ninth Party Congress in April 2001.

Cox, Robert (1995) 'Critical Political Economy', in Björn Hettne (ed.) *International Political Economy: Understanding Global Disorder*. London: Zed Books.

Cumings, Bruce (1987) 'The Origin and Development of the Northeast Asian Political Economy: Industrial Sectors, Product Cycles, and Political Consequences', in F. C. Deyo (ed.) *The Political Economy of the New Asian Industrialism*. Ithaca: Cornell University Press.

——— (1999) *Parallax Visions: Making Sense of American–East Asian Relations*. Durham & London: Duke University Press.

Dang Phong (2004) 'Stages on the Road to Renovation of the Vietnamese Economy: a Historical Perspective', in Melanie Beresford and Tran Ngoc Angie (eds) *Reaching for the Dream*. Copenhagen: NIAS Press.

Dapice, David O. (2003) Viet Nam's Economy: Success Story or Weird Dualism? A SWOT Analysis', A Special Report Prepared for United Nations Development Programme & Prime Minister's Research Commission, Hanoi, June 2003.

De Melo, J. (1985) 'Sources of Growth and Structural Change in the Republics of Korea and Taiwan: Some Comparisons', in V. Corbo, A. Krueger and F. Ossa (eds), *Export-Oriented Development Strategies: The Success of Five Newly Industrializing Countries.* Boulder: Westview.

Deyo, Frederic C. (ed.) (1987) *The Political Economy of the New Asian Industrialism.* Ithaca (NY): Cornell University Press.

——— (2002) 'The "New Developmentalism" in Post-Crisis Asia: The Case of Thailand's SME Sector', in Yue-Man Yeung (ed.), *New Challenges for Development and Modernization.* Hong Kong: The Chinese University Press.

Dixon, Chris (2000) 'State versus Capital: the Regulation of the Vietnamese Foreign Sector', *Singapore Journal of Tropical Geography*, 21(3), pp. 279–294.

——— (2002) 'The Developmental Implications of the Pacific Asian Crisis', in P. P. Masina (ed.), *Rethinking Development in East Asia: From Illusory Miracle to Economic Crisis.* Richmond: Curzon Press.

——— and Drakakis-Smith, D. (eds) (1997) *Uneven Development in South East Asia.* Aldershot: Ashgate.

——— and Kilgour, A. (2002) 'State, Capital and Resistance to Globalisation in the Vietnamese Transitional Economy', *Environment and Planning A*, 34, pp. 599–618.

Dragsbaek Schmid, Johannes (1997) 'The Challenge from Southeast Asia: Social Forces between Equity and Growth', in C. Dixon and D. Drakakis-Smith (eds) *Uneven Development in South East Asia.* Aldershot: Ashgate.

———, Hersh, Jacques and Fold Niels (1998) *Social Change in Southeast Asia.* Harlow: Longman.

Duiker, William J. (1995) *Vietnam: Revolution in Transition.* Boulder (CO): Westview Press.

Easlea, Brian (1973) *Liberation and the Aims of Science: an Essay on Obstacles to the Building of a Beautiful World.* London: Chatto & Windus 1973.

Economic Intelligence Unit (1997) *Vietnam: Country Profile*, various issues. The Economist Group.

Evans, Peter B. (1987) 'Class, State, and Dependence in East Asia: Lessons for Latin Americanists', in F. C. Deyo (ed.) *The Political Economy of the New Asian Industrialism.* Ithaca (NY): Cornell University Press.

——— (1989) 'Predatory, Developmental and Other Apparatuses: a Comparative Political Economy Perspective on the Third World State', *Sociological Forum*, 4, pp. 233–246.

——— (1992) 'The State as Problem and Solution: Predation, Embedded Autonomy, and Structural Change', in S. Haggard and R. R. Kaufman (eds) *The Politics of Economic Adjustment.* Princeton (NJ): Princeton University Press.

——— (1995) *Embedded Autonomy: States and Industrial Transformation.* Princeton (NJ): Princeton University Press.

Fan, Cindy Chi-fun (1997) 'Uneven Development and Beyond: Regional Development Theory in Post-Mao China', *International Journal of Urban and Regional Research*, 21(4), pp. 620–639.

Fforde, Adam (1998a) 'Strategic Issues in Vietnamese Development Policy: State Owned Enterprises (SOE)s, Agricultural Cooperatives and Public Administration Reform (PAR)'. Seminar Paper – Political and Social Change, RSPAS, ANU.

——— (1998b) 'Handouts Won't Help Vietnam', *Wall Street Journal*, September 16.

Fforde, Adam and de Vylder, Stefan (1996) *From Plan to Market: The Economic Transition in Vietnam*. Boulder (CO): Westview Press.

Freeman, Nick and Nestor, Curt (2004) 'Rethinking Foreign Investment in Vietnam: Fuzzy Figures and Sentiment Swings', in D. McCargo (ed.) *Rethinking Vietnam*. London: RoutledgeCurzon.

Fritzeen, Scott (2002) 'Growth, Inequality and the Future of Poverty Reduction in Vietnam', *Journal of Asian Economics*, 13, pp. 635–657.

Fukase, Emiko and Martin, Will (1999a) *A Quantitative Evaluation of Vietnam's Accession to the ASEAN Free Trade Area (AFTA)*. Washington: Development Research Group, World Bank.

——— (1999b) *The Effects of the United States' Granting Most Favoured Nation Status to Vietnam*. Washington: Development Research Group, World Bank.

Gabriele, Alberto (forthcoming) 'Social Services Policies in a Developing Market Economy Oriented Towards Socialism: the Case of Health System Reforms in Vietnam', *Review of International Political Economy*.

Gainsborough, Martin (2004) 'Key Issues in the Political Economy of post-*Doi Moi* Vietnam', in Duncan McCargo (ed.) *Rethinking Vietnam*. London: RoutledgeCurzon.

Gallina, Andrea and Masina, Pietro P. (2002) *Street Children in Vietnam: An Inquire into the Roots of Poverty and Survival Livelihoods Strategies*. Federico Caffè Centre Research Report No. 3 2002, Roskilde University.

General Statistical Office (1997) *Social Indicators in Vietnam, 1990–95*. Statistical Publishing House.

George, Susan and Sabelli, Fabrizio (1994) *Faith and Credit: The World Bank's Secular Empire*. Harmondsworth: Penguin.

Gerschenkron, A. (1962) *Economic Backwardness in Historical Perspective, A Book of Essays*. Cambridge: Belknap Press of Harvard University Press.

Gilpin, Robert (1987) *The Political Economy of International Relations*. Princeton: Princeton University Press.

——— (2001) *Global Political Economy*. Princeton: Princeton University Press.

Glassman, Jim (1999) 'State Power Beyond the "Territorial Trap": the Internationalization of the State', *Political Geography*, 18, pp. 669–696.

Gramsci, Antonio (1977) *I Quaderni del Carcere*. Edizione critica dell'Istituto Gramsci a cura di Valentino Gerratana. Torino: Einaudi.

Griffin, Keith (1998a) 'Restructuring and Economic Reforms', in K. Griffin (ed.) *Economic Reform in Vietnam*. Basingstoke: Macmillan.

——— (1998b) 'The Role of the State in the New Economy', in K. Griffin (ed.) *Economic Reform in Vietnam*. Basingstoke: Macmillan.

Hersh, Jacques (1993) *The USA and the Rise of East Asia*. Basingstoke: Macmillan; New York: St Martin Press.

——— (1998) 'The Impact of US Strategy: Making South East Asia Safe for Capitalism', in J. D. Schmidt, J. Hersh and N. Fold (eds) *Social Change in Southeast Asia*. Harlow: Addison Wesley Longman.

Hettne, Björn (1993) 'Neo-Mercantilism: What's in a Word?, in J. Martinussen (ed.) *New Institutional Economics and Development Theory*. Occasional Paper No. 6, International Development Studies, Roskilde University.

——— (ed.) (1995) *International Political Economy: Understanding Global Disorder*. London: Zed Books.

Hirschman, Albert O. (1977) *The Passions and the Interests: Political Arguments for Capitalism before its Triumph*. Princeton, NJ: Princeton University Press.
Hobsbawm, Eric J. (1994) *Age of Extremes – The Short Twentieth Century 1914–1991*. London: Pantheon Books.
IMF (1999a) *Vietnam: Selected Issues*. IMF Staff Country Report No. 99/55.
——— (1999b) *Vietnam: Statistical Appendix*. IMF Staff Country Report No. 99/56.
——— (2000) *Thailand: Statistical Appendix*. IMF Staff Country Report No. 00/20.
——— (2001) *The World Economic Outlook (WEO) Database May 2001*. Washington: IMF.
Irvin, George (1995) 'Vietnam: Assessing the Achievement of *Doi Moi*', *Journal of Development Studies*, 31(5), pp. 725–750.
Irvine, Reed (1999) 'A Special Report on the U.S.–Vietnam Trade Agreement', *Vietnam Business Journal*, 7(4).
Jayasuriya, Kanishka (2001) 'Governance, Post Washington Consensus and the New Anti Politics', Working Papers Series, No. 2, April 2001, Southeast Asia Research Centre, City University of Hong Kong.
——— (2002) 'Globalisation, International Standards and The Rule of Law: A New Symbolic Politics', Working Papers Series, No. 24, March, Southeast Asia Research Centre, City University of Hong Kong.
Jerneck, Anne (1995) *Adjusting State and Market in Vietnam*. Lund: Department of Economic History, Lund University.
Johnson, Chalmers (1982) *MITI and the Japanese Miracle: The Growth of Industrial Policy, 1925–1975*. Stanford: Stanford University Press.
Jomo K. S. (ed.) (1998) *Tigers in Trouble. Financial Governance, Liberalisation and Crises in East Asia*. London: Zed Books.
——— (2001a) 'Introduction: Growth and Structural Change in the Second-tier Southeast Asian NICs', in Jomo K. S. (ed.) *Southeast Asia's Industrialization*. Basingstoke: Palgrave.
——— (2001b) 'Rethinking the Role of Government Policy in Southeast Asia', in J. E. Stiglitz and S. Yusuf (eds) *Rethinking The East Asian Miracle*. Washington: The World Bank and Oxford University Press.
Kanbur, Ravi (2001) 'Economic Policy, Distribution and Poverty: The Nature of Disagreements', *World Development*, 29(6), pp. 1083–1094.
Kerkvliet, Benedict J. T. (1995) ' Rural Society and State Relations', in B. J. T. Kerkvliet and D. J. Porter (eds) *Vietnam's Rural Transformation*. Boulder (CO): Westview Press.
——— and Porter, Doug. J. (1995) 'Rural Vietnam in Rural Asia', in B. J. T. Kerkvliet and D. J. Porter (eds) *Vietnam's Rural Transformation*. Boulder (CO): Westview Press.
Khan, Azizur Rahman (1998) 'Integration into the Global Economy', in K. Griffin (ed.) *Economic Reform in Vietnam*. Basingstoke: Macmillan.
Khan, Musthaq (2000) 'Rents, Efficiency and Growth' and 'Rent-seeking as Process', in M. Khan and Jomo K. S. (eds) *Rents and Rent-Seeking*. Cambridge: Cambridge University Press.
Kilgour, Andrea and Drakakis-Smith, David (2002) 'The Changing Economic and Urban Situation in Vietnam', in P. P. Masina (ed.), *Rethinking Development in East Asia: From Illusory Miracle to Economic Crisis*. Richmond: Curzon Press.
Kokko, Ari (1998a) *Managing the Transition to Free Trade: Vietnamese Trade Policy for the 21st Century*. Policy Discussion Paper No. 98/05, Centre for International Economic Studies, University of Adelaide.

——— (1998b) *Vietnam – Ready for Doi Moi II?* SSE/EFI Working Paper Series in Economics and Finance No. 286. December 1998.

Kokko, Ari and Zejan, Marion (1996) 'Vietnam 1996: Approaching the Next Stage of Reforms', *Macroeconomic Reports* 1996:9, Swedish International Development Cooperation Agency, Stockholm.

Kolko, Gabriel (1986) *Vietnam: Anatomy of a War 1940–1975*. London & Sydney: Allen & Unwin.

——— (1997) *Vietnam: Anatomy of a Peace*. New York and London: Routledge.

Kolko, Joyce and Kolko, Gabriel (1972) *The Limits of Power: The World and United States Foreign Policy, 1945–1954*. New York: Harper & Row.

Kuhn, Thomas (1962) *The Structure of Scientific Revolutions*. Chicago: University of Chicago Press.

Lauridsen, Laurids S. (1995) 'The Developmental State and the Asian Miracle: an Introduction to the Debate', in L. S. Lauridsen (ed.) *Institutions and Industrial Development: Asian Experiences*, Occasional Paper No. 16, International Development Studies, Roskilde University.

Le Thanh Khoi (1978) *Socialisme et Développement au Vietnam*. Paris: Presse Universitaire de France.

Le Xuan Nghia (2005) 'Orientation of the Banking Sector Development Strategy Towards International Integration', in *Workshop on 'The 2006–10 Socio-Economic Developed Plan (SEDP) for the Banking Sector'* sponsored by the State Bank of Vietnam, the International Monetary Fund and the Danish Government, 18 January 2005.

Leproux, Vittorio and Brooks, Douglas H. (2004) 'Viet Nam: Foreign Direct Investment and Postcrisis Regional Integration', ERD Working Paper, No. 56.

Leung, Suivah (ed.) (1999) *Vietnam and the East Asian Crisis*. Northampton: Edward Elgar.

Li, Xing. Hersh, Jacques and Johannes Dragsbaek Schmidt (2002) 'The New "Asian Drama": Catching Up at the Crossroads of Neoliberalism', in P. P. Masina (ed.), *Rethinking Development in East Asia: From Illusory Miracle to Economic Crisis*. Richmond: Curzon Press.

Liljeström, Rita, Lindskog, Eva, Nguyen Van Ang and Vuong Xuan Tinh (1998) *Profit and Poverty in Rural Vietnam: Winners and Losers of a Dismantled Revolution*. Richmond: Curzon Press.

London, Jonathan (2004) 'Rethinking Vietnam's Mass Education and Health Systems', in Duncan McCargo (ed.) *Rethinking Vietnam*. London: RoutledgeCurzon.

McCargo, Duncan (ed.) (2004) *Rethinking Vietnam*. London: RoutledgeCurzon.

McCarty, Adam (2001) 'Governance institutions and incentive structures in Vietnam'. Paper presented to the conference *Building Institutional Capacity in Asia (BICA)*. Jakarta, 12 March 2001.

MacIntyre, Andrew (1994) 'Business, Government and Development: East and Southeast Asian Comparisons', in A. MacIntyre (ed.) *Business and Government in Industrialising Asia*. Ithaca: Cornell University Press and Sydney: Allen & Unwin.

Mandeville, B. (1714 [repr. 1924]) *The Fable of Bees: or, Private Vices, Public Benefits*. London: Oxford University Press.

Marr, David G. (1981) *Vietnamese Tradition on Trial, 1920–1945*. Berkeley: University of California Press.

Masina, Pietro P. (1993) *Le Nazioni Unite e la questione della rappresentanza della Cina*. Masters thesis. Università di Roma 'La Sapienza'. Mimeo.

——— (1996) *Regional and International Dynamics in the Development of East Asia: The Case of Foreign Direct Investment.* Federico Caffè Centre Research Report n.1 1996, Roskilde University.

Masina, Pietro P. (1999a) *Vietnamese Development Strategies between Tradition and Modernity.* Federico Caffè Centre Research Report n.5 1999, Roskilde University.

——— (1999b) *Vietnam and the Regional Economic Crisis.* Federico Caffè Centre Research Report n.8 1999, Roskilde University.

——— (2002a) 'Introduction', in P. P. Masina (ed.), *Rethinking Development in East Asia: From Illusory Miracle to Economic Crisis.* Richmond: Curzon Press.

——— (2002b) 'Dealing with the crisis in Vietnam: the rethinking of development strategies', in P. P. Masina (ed.), *Rethinking Development in East Asia: From Illusory Miracle to Economic Crisis.* Richmond: Curzon Press.

——— (2002c) 'Vietnam and the regional crisis: the case of a "late late-comer"', *European Journal of East Asian Studies*, 1(2).

Moon Chung-In and Prasad, Rashemi (1994) 'Beyond the Developmental State: Networks, Politics, and Institutions', *Governance: An International Journal of Policy and Administration*, 7(4), pp. 360–386.

Mosley, P., Harrigan, J. and Toye, J. (1991) *Aid and Power: The World Bank and Policy-based Lending*, vols 1 and 2. Routledge: London.

Myrdal, Gunnar (1968 [1959]) *Value in Social Theory: A Selection of Essays on Methodology.* Edited by Paul Streeten. London: Routledge.

——— (1970 [1958]) *Objectivity in Social Research.* London: Gerald Duckworth.

National Statistic Office, Republic of Korea (1999) *Korea Statistical Yearbook.*

National Statistical Bureau of People's Republic of China (1999) *China Statistical Yearbook* no. 18. Beijing: China Statistic Press.

Naughton, Barry (1995) *Growing out of the Plan: Chinese Economic Reform, 1978–1993.* New York: Cambridge University Press.

Nguyen Khac Vien (1971) 'Confucianism et Marxism au Vietnam' in Chesnaux, Jean – Boudarel, Georges – Hemery, Daniel (eds) *Tradition et Révolution au Vietnam.* Paris: Édition Anthropos.

——— (1975) *Tradition and Revolution in Vietnam.* Berkeley: Berkeley University Press.

——— (1993) *Vietnam: A Long History.* Hanoi: The Gioi.

Nguyen T. Trien (2003) 'Trade Policy Under Globalization and Regionalization', in Binh Tran-Nam and Chi Do Pham (eds) *The Vietnamese Economy: Awakening the Dormant Dragon.* London: RoutledgeCurzon.

Nørlund, Irene (1989) *The French Empire, the Colonial State in Vietnam and the Economic Policy, 1885–1940.* Copenhagen Discussion Papers No. 9, Center for East and Southeast Asian Studies, University of Copenhagen.

——— (1999) 'What's the Impact of the Asian Crisis? Economy and Living Conditions in Joint Ventures in the Ho Chi Minh Region and Da Nang'. Passau: Universität Passau. Paper presented at the Fourth Euroviet Conference, 16–18 September 1999.

———, Gates, C. L. and Vu Cao Dam (eds) (1995) *Vietnam in a Changing World.* Richmond: Curzon.

Ohmae, Kenichi (1990) *The Borderless World: Power and Strategy in the Interlocked Economy.* London: Harper Collins.

——— (1995) *The End of the Nation-state: The Rise of Regional Economies.* London: Harper Collins.

Ollman, Bertell (2001) 'Why Does the Emperor Need the Yakuza? Prolegomenon to a Marxist Theory of the Japanese State', *New Left Review*, (8), pp. 73–98.

Painter, Martin (2003) 'The Politics of Economic Restructuring in Vietnam: the Case of State-owned Enterprise "Reform"', *Contemporary Southeast Asia*, 25(1), pp. 20–43.

——— (2005) 'The Politics of State Sector Reforms in Vietnam: Contested Agendas and Uncertain Trajectories', *Journal of Development Studies*, 41(2), pp. 261–283.

Panitch, Leo (2000) 'The New Imperial State', *New Left Review*, (2), pp. 5–20.

Parnwell, Michael J. G. (ed.) (1996) *Uneven Development in Thailand*. Aldershot: Avebury.

Perkins, Dwight H. (2001) 'Industrial and Financial Policy in China and Vietnam: a New Model or a Reply of the East Asian Experience', in J. E. Stiglitz and S. Yusuf (eds) *Rethinking the East Asian Miracle*. Washington: World Bank.

Plesner, Katrine (2002) *Globalisering og den Sydkoreanske Stat: Hvilken Rolle Spiller States I Sydkoreansk Økonomi I 1990erne?* MA Thesis, Roskilde University. Mimeo.

Putzel, James (2002) 'Developmental States and Crony Capitalists', in P. P. Masina (ed.) *Rethinking Development in East Asia: From Illusory Miracle to Economic Crisis*. Richmond: Curzon Press.

Riedel, James (1999) 'Needed: A Strategic Vision for Setting Reform Priorities in Vietnam', in Suivah Leung (ed.) *Vietnam and the East Asian Crisis*. Northampton: Edward Elgar.

——— and Turley, Williams S. (1999) *The Politics and Economics of Transition to an Open Market Economy in Vietnam*. OECD Development Centre, Technical Papers No. 152.

Rigg, Jonathan (1997) *Southeast Asia: The Human Landscape of Modernization and Development*. London: Routledge.

Ronnås, Per and Örijan, Sjöberg (eds) (1991a) *Socio-economic Development in Vietnam*. Stockholm: Sida.

——— (1991b) 'Dismantling the Centrally Planned Economy', *The Journal of Communist Studies*, 7(1), pp. 7–19.

Ronnås, Per and Ramamurthy, Bhargavi (eds) (2000) *Entrepreneurship in Vietnam: Transformation and Dynamics*. Copenhagen: NIAS Press.

Schmidt, J. D., Hersh, J. and Fold, N. (1998) *Social Change in Southeast Asia*. Harlow: Longman.

Socialist Republic of Vietnam (2002) *The Comprehensive Poverty Reduction and Growth Strategy (CPRGS)*. Hanoi.

Stiglitz, Joseph E. (1996) 'Some Lessons from the East Asian Miracle', *World Bank Research Observer*, 11(2), 151–178.

——— (2001) 'From Miracle to Crisis to Recovery: Lessons from Four Decades of East Asian Experience', in J. E. Stiglitz and S. Yusuf (eds) *Rethinking the East Asian Miracle*. Washington: World Bank.

Strange, Susan (1988) *States and Markets*. London: Pinter Publishers.

Stromseth, Jonathan R. (2003) 'Business Associations and Policy-Making in Vietnam', in B. J. T. Kerkvliet, R. H. K. Heng and D. W. H. Koh (eds) *Getting Organized in Vietnam: Moving in and Around the Socialist State*. Singapore: Institute of Southeast Asian Studies.

Sum, Ngai-Ling (2002) 'The Material, Strategic and Discursive Dimensions of the "Asian Crisis" and Subsequent Developments, in P. P. Masina (ed.) *Rethinking Development in East Asia: From Illusory Miracle to Economic Crisis*. Richmond: Curzon Press.

Taylor, Philip (ed.) (2004) *Social Inequality in Vietnam and the Challenges to Reform*. Singapore: ISEAS.

Tombes, Jonathan (1999) 'Market Access. The Question is, "When"', *Vietnam Business Journal*, 8(4).

Toye, John (1993 [1987]) *Dilemmas in Development: Reflections on the Counter Revolution in Development Theory and Policy*. Oxford: Basil Blackwell.

UNDP (1995) *Vietnam: Report on Poverty*. Hanoi: UNDP.

——— (1998) 'East Asia: from Miracle to Crisis. Lessons for Vietnam', UNDP Staff Paper. Hanoi: UNDP.

UNDP (2000) 'Socio-Economic Bulletin (Vietnam)' (2000). Web site of the UNDP in Vietnam: http://www.undp.org.vn/economics/bulletin, accessed 30 January 2006.

Unger, Jonathan and Chan, Anita (1996) 'Corporatism in China: A Developmental State in an East Asian Context', in B. L. McCormick and J. Unger (eds) *China After Socialism: In the Footsteps of Eastern Europe or East Asia.* New York: M. E. Sharp.

UNCTAD (1999) *World Investment Report.* Geneva: UNCTAD.

Van Arkadie, Brian and Mallon, Raymond (2003) *Viet Nam: a Transition Tiger?* Canberra: Asia Pacific Press.

Vasavakul, Thaveeporn (1997) 'Sectoral Politics and Strategies for State and Party Building from VII and VIII Congress of the Vietnamese Communist Party (1991–1996), in A. Fforde (ed.) *Doi Moi: Ten Years after the 1986 Party Congress*, Political and Social Change Monograph No. 24, Australian National University.

——— (2002) 'Rebuilding Authority Relations: Public Administration Reform in the Era of *Doi Moi*'. Report commissioned by the Asian Development Bank. Ho Chi Minh City: Adam Fforde and Associates.

——— (2003) 'From Fence-breaking to Networking: Interests, Popular Organizations, and Policy Influences in Post-socialist Vietnam', in B. J. T. Kerkvliet, R. H. K. Heng and D. W. H. Koh (eds) *Getting Organized in Vietnam: Moving in and Around the Socialist State*. Singapore: Institute of Southeast Asian Studies.

Vietnam Economic Times (1997), October issue.

Vo Dai Luoc (1995) 'Monetary Stabilization: The Vietnamese Experience', in Irene Nørlund, Carolyn L. Gates and Vu Cao Dam (eds), *Vietnam in a Changing World.* Richmond, Surrey: Curzon Press.

Wade, Robert (1990) *Governing the Market. Economic Theory and the Role of Government in East Asian Industrialization.* Princeton (NJ): Princeton University Press, 1990.

——— (1996) 'Japan. The World Bank, and the Art of Paradigm Maintenance: *The East Asian Miracle* in political perspective', *New Left Review*, (217), pp. 3–36.

——— (2001) 'Showdown at the World Bank', *New Left Review*, (2001/7), pp. 124–137.

——— and Veneroso, Frank (1998) 'The Asian Crisis: the High Debt Model versus the Wall Street–Treasury–IMF Complex', *New Left Review*, (228), pp. 3–23.

Wallerstein, Immanuel (1997 [1983]) 'The Three Instances of Hegemony in the History of the Capitalist World-economy', in G. T. Crane and A. Amawi (eds) *The Theoretical Evolution of International Political Economy: A Reader*. Oxford: Oxford University Press, pp. 244–252.

Weiss, Linda (1995) 'Governed Interdependence: Rethinking the Government–Business Relationship in East Asia', *Pacific Review*, 8(4), pp. 589–616.

——— (1998) *The Myth of the Powerless State: Governing the Economy in a Global Era.* Cambridge: Polity Press.

——— (2000) 'Developmental State in Transition: Adapting, Dismantling, Innovating, not "Normalising"', *Pacific Review,* 13(1), pp. 21–55.

White, Gordon (ed.) (1988) *The Developmental State*. Basingstoke: Macmillan.

——— (1993) *Riding the Tiger: The Politics of Reform in Post–Mao China*. Basingstoke: Macmillan.

White, G. and Wade, R. (1988) 'Developmental States and Markets in East Asia: an Introduction', in G. White (ed.), *The Developmental State*. Basingstoke: Macmillan, pp. 1–29.

Wilks, Alex and Lefrançois, Fabien (2002) *Blinding with Science or Encouraging Debate? How World Bank Analysis Determines PRSP Policies.* Bretton Woods Project and World Vision.

Womack, B. (1997) 'Vietnam in 1996: Reform Immobilism', *Asian Survey*, 37(1), pp. 79–87.

Woo-Cumings, Meredith (1999) 'Introduction: Chalmers Johnson and the Politics of Nationalism and Development', in M. Woo-Cumings (ed.), *The Developmental State*. Ithaca, NY: Cornell University Press.

World Bank (1993) *The East Asian Miracle: Economic Growth and Public Policy*, Oxford: Oxford University Press.

——— (1997a) *Vietnam: Deepening Reforms for Growth.* Hanoi: World Bank.

——— (1997b) *World Development Report: The State in a Changing World.* New York: Oxford University Press.

——— (1998) *Poverty, Social Services, and Safety Nets in Vietnam.* Washington, DC: World Bank.

——— (1999a) *Vietnam: Preparing for Take-off?* Hanoi: World Bank.

——— (1999b) *Vietnam Development Report 2000: Attacking Poverty.* Hanoi: World Bank.

——— (1999c) *Vietnam Voices of the Poor in Vietnam: Synthesis Report of Participatory Poverty Assessments.* Hanoi: World Bank.

——— (2000) *Vietnam Development Report 2001: Vietnam 2010 – Pillars of Development.* Hanoi: World Bank.

——— (2001) *Vietnam Development Report 2002: Implementing Reforms for Faster Growth and Poverty Reduction.* Hanoi: World Bank.

——— (2005) *Vietnam Development Report 2005: Governance.* Hanoi: World Bank.

Yeung, Henry Wai-Chung (2002) 'Business as Usual? Changing Business Networks in Pacific Asia in a Globalizing Era', in Yue-Man Yeung (ed.) *New Challenges for Development and Modernization.* Hong Kong: The Chinese University Press.

Index

EVENING THE SCORE

Further Titles by Deborah Nicholson from Severn House

HOUSE REPORT

EVENING THE SCORE

Deborah Nicholson

This first world edition published in Great Britain 2004 by
SEVERN HOUSE PUBLISHERS LTD of
9–15 High Street, Sutton, Surrey SM1 1DF.
This first world edition published in the USA 2004 by
SEVERN HOUSE PUBLISHERS INC of
595 Madison Avenue, New York, N.Y. 10022.

British Library Cataloguing in Publication Data

Nicholson, Deborah
Evening the score
1. Women theatrical managers - Alberta - Calgary - Fiction
2. Murder - Investigation - Alberta - Calgary - Fiction
3. Detective and mystery stories
I. Title
813.6 [F]

ISBN 0-7278-6137-9

Typeset by Palimpsest Book Production Ltd.,
Polmont, Stirlingshire, Scotland.
Printed and bound in Great Britain by
MPG Books Ltd., Bodmin, Cornwall.

For Patrick, Bonnie and Shelby,
because family is everything.

For Sandy Stockton,
my partner in crime.

And for Theatre Calgary and the Calgary
Philharmonic Orchestra.
Hug a musician; they never get to dance.

Prologue

The rain was pounding down harder than she had ever seen before. Thunder and lightning were crashing directly overhead, making the ground shake. She pulled her car into the nearest space to the door, turned off the lights and ignition and made a mad dash for it. She was soaked by the time she let herself in. She looked down at her dripping clothes and laughed. It didn't matter. She was on her way to see her boyfriend with the best news of her life. And in another month, if everything went according to plan, he would be her husband. She had missed him so much while she'd been gone and could hardly wait to see him again, to give him the good news. She dropped her hand protectively over her stomach and smiled. She knew a baby would bring them closer together, would cement their relationship and convince him that it was time to settle down. This might have been a little sooner than he had planned, but she knew he would be thrilled and would realize that it was all meant to be. She would have to drop out of college, but, being married to a famous conductor, she wouldn't need a college degree. She could just stay home and raise their house full of children.

She got out of the elevator and ran down the hall with all the exuberance her twenty-year-old legs could manage. She let herself in and was surprised to find the apartment in darkness.

'*Chéri!*' she called, but got no answer. He must be out.

She pushed her way into the bedroom, dropped her dripping coat on to the rack and turned on the light. In that moment, her life changed for ever. There he was, in bed, naked, with another woman.

'*Mon Dieu . . .*' He stood up and came over to her.

She turned and ran out the door before he could touch her,

passing by the elevator and running down the stairwell. She thought she might be sick as her world swayed around her and she tried not to faint.

She didn't notice the rain as she got back into her car, not stopping to turn on the lights or fasten her seat belt. She sped out of the parking space and into the traffic. The cars she cut off blasted their horns but she didn't hear them. She couldn't see or think of anything except the sight of him in bed, naked, on top of that woman. She didn't see the red light, or the other car veering to try to avoid her, or even the windshield as she started to fly through it. And then she didn't see anything for several days, until she woke up in a hospital bed. And when they told her she should be fine, with months of therapy, but that she had lost the baby and any chance to have other babies, she didn't see or hear anything for several months.

Monday October 20

Musicals. I have a love/hate relationship with them. They bring in the crowds, almost without fail, but after hearing the same songs for four weeks straight – twice a day when there is a matinee – well, you get a little tired of them. And when I find myself humming those songs in the grocery store, then I know it's time to move on.

My name is Kate Carpenter. I am thirty-three years old, blonde (still, thanks to Clairol), with blue eyes and the first smattering of wrinkles framing them when I smile. I work for Calgary's largest theatre company, Foothills Stage Network, as the front-of-house manager. I know it sounds exciting, but the glorified job description entails hiring and supervising ushers and bartenders, dealing with audience complaints (trust me, they rarely compliment and mostly complain), and working almost every night and weekend. In reality I spend most of my time counting cash floats for the sales tables and adding up how many T-shirts we have sold after the show has ended and the actors have gone home. I also get to count liquor inventories for the bars twice a night (four times when we have matinees) as well as trying to keep our audience happy while they pay $5.95 each for watered-down, non-premium drinks. What a life. But for some reason, I love it. Working nights and weekends suits me, as I am not known as a morning person. I get to drink all the coffee I can swallow and I supervise a smart-ass staff that seems to have little respect for me. Despite that we are a happy little band and we manage to get through eight shows a week.

I live in a cute but tiny loft with my boyfriend Cam. He works at the Plex too, in the maintenance department. He has his HVAC ticket, which I think means that he does heating and air conditioning. I don't really care about that, but I do love the fact that everything in my place works since I started dating him. He is a great handyman who actually fixes broken things instead of just talking about fixing them. He is also incredibly good-looking and a fitness nut, which I'm learning to live with. Cam always thought he could convert me, but after the first time he took me for a run, he pretty much gave up on that idea. So now, while I sleep in, he gets up bright and early and goes jogging. A great compromise as far as I'm concerned.

Cam moved into my life about two years ago and my apartment about two months ago. We had a murder in the theatre lobby during *Much Ado About Nothing* and I somehow got involved in it. Cam was my knight in shining armour, moving in to protect me. Luckily he did a good job of it, or I would be just another greasy spot on the stage by now. I'm glad that's all behind us and we can get on with the business of settling in together.

I don't have a great track record with relationships, and Cam is divorced, but we are struggling through. I thought, when he first moved in, that it would only be temporary, but when the danger had passed and it was time to move him out, I couldn't make myself do it. It seems I've gotten used to having him around. And I always say that Cam's greatest attribute is that no matter how hard I push him away, he keeps coming back.

Cam and I had just returned from a mini vacation on Vancouver Island, tanned and relaxed. One of my favourite places in the world is Long Beach in the Pacific Rim National Park. When I was little we used to camp right on the beach, surrounded by hippies and other assorted dropouts from society. The first year we got washed away at high tide, but Mom dried out the tent, Dad dried out the engine of the car and we survived and learned and kept going back for more. Now, as grown-ups, we stayed in a hotel, but it was right across the road from the beach. When life gets me down, I love to lie on the beach with a book, pretend to read and let the crashing Pacific surf cleanse my mind. Cam and I walked for miles and miles when the tide was out. Plus, we were lucky enough to catch the tail end of the grey whale migration. Nothing like sitting on the patio of a great seafood restaurant, watching a grey whale breach in the harbour. Cam had never been there before and he is already talking about planning our summer vacation there next year. Luckily, camping is no longer allowed on the beach, as I'm much more of a room service type of girl these days.

But for now, it's back to reality. Home, my tiny loft and work tomorrow. It will be the first preview for the new show, but for today I have ten days' worth of laundry to get through. I couldn't even guilt-trip Cam into doing it for me, as he has been busy in the kitchen, defrosting the fridge and spraying some disgusting stuff into the oven to try to get my five years of grease off the racks. Personally, I would have happily stopped using the oven once the smoke alarm started going off and ordered takeout instead for the rest of my life. Cam loves to cook, though, and he has insisted on getting the kitchen back into shape. He has scrubbed the floor and cleaned out some sort of trap in the dishwasher that I never even knew existed. At least the dishwasher doesn't flood the kitchen anymore. So now I can use real dishes and wash them in the dishwasher instead of eating out of takeout cartons. Cam once said something about being able to wash the dishes in the sink if the dishwasher was broken, but I just laughed. He knows me better than that, but I guess you can't blame the guy for trying.

I had almost finished folding the last load of laundry, desperately trying to think of a reason to go to the theatre before Cam could make me dust or start vacuuming. Graham, my eighteen-year-old assistant, called me yesterday to tell me that something exciting was happening at the theatre and left instructions for me to call him as soon as we got back into town. I think Cam had had enough excitement for a lifetime because he threatened to cut the phone cord if I even thought about calling Graham before tomorrow. Everyone still thinks we're out of town and Cam likes it that way.

I carried the laundry basket up the cute spiral staircase to the bedroom. Cam has started moving some of his stuff in and it's getting a little crowded up there. I know I could probably put half my stuff in storage but I've been avoiding that. I set the laundry on the bed and sat down beside it. The bookcases would be a good place to start, I thought. Crammed with years and years of music and textbooks from university, most of which I haven't cracked open since my last final, I'm sure I wouldn't miss half of them if I packed them up. Yet I have been a little scared to do it. If I let Cam start to put his stuff on my shelves it'll mean he's here for good – something I haven't really admitted to myself yet.

I stood up and grabbed his underwear and socks from the basket. I've rearranged my drawers and Cam now claimed half of them. I don't really miss the space, like I said; it's just that the idea of the whole commitment thing is a little hard for me. My closet has one of those modular units, with everything from a jewellery drawer to a scarf rack, and everything is arranged by size, style, and colour. I have too many clothes and accessories, but by rearranging everything slightly, I had freed up space for Cam without crowding myself too much. Maybe it would stop me from buying clothes for a while . . . or maybe I'd just keep more of them in my office at the theatre.

'Are you finished down there yet?' I called over the loft rail to Cam.

'Not quite,' he answered. I could hear him scrubbing something.

'I need coffee, Cam. When am I going to be able to get into the kitchen?'

I leaned on the railing and propped my chin in my hands. Cam really is a good-looking man and he looked especially good from this vantage point. I love to watch him work. Actually, I love to watch anyone work, as long as it isn't me.

'Katie.' He is the only person who can get away with calling me Katie. 'You really won't die if you don't have a coffee for five minutes.'

'You know, it's a lot easier just to buy new rings for the burners,' I offered.

'I'm almost finished.'

'I could walk down to Gus's and pick up a cappuccino for us,' I suggested, hoping he'd give me one of his automatic yeses.

Gus owns the coffee shop located at one end of the Plex. I go there so often that Gus jokes that if I ever quit my job at the theatre, he will go out of business.

'Sure, and sneak into the theatre while you're there?' Cam asked. 'I don't think so.'

'Can I have a cigarette then?' I asked. I'm quitting, but that only seems to mean I don't buy my own and only smoke Cam's – or anyone else's that I can beg. 'I thought you really were quitting this time,' he said.

'I am, just not today.'

'Did you finish the laundry?' he asked, changing the subject.

'Are you going to give me a cigarette or not?' I was determined.

'All right.' He took a cigarette out of his pack and set it on the counter.

I came downstairs and picked up the smoke. 'Can I have a light?'

Cam took his head out of the oven and rinsed his hands in the sink.

'No,' he said, smiling at me. 'You do realize that smoking is really bad for you.'

'Please?'

'No, we both decided we were quitting,' he repeated. 'Besides, you know what they say about kissing someone who smokes.'

'No, I don't, and I wouldn't say it if you ever hope to kiss me again,' I threatened.

'OK, but we did promise each other we were going to quit, Katie.'

'Then why do you have this in your pocket?' I asked, holding up the cigarette.

'Because I knew that if I threw them out here, you would scavenge them from the garbage, hide them somewhere and smoke them when you were alone.'

I put the cigarette in my shirt pocket and wrapped my arms around Cam's neck, pulling him away from the sink.

'Katie, I have to finish the oven before we pass out from the smell,' he protested, but I felt his arms encircle me.

As I kissed him, my hands wandered down his back, stopping when I reached his back pocket. I found his lighter, removed it, and pulled away from him.

'Sucker,' I teased.

He grabbed the lighter out of my hand and put it on top of

the kitchen cupboards, where he knew I couldn't reach it.

'Now let's see you get it,' he said, turning back to the sink and rinsing out his cloth. 'And perhaps if you finish your share of the chores, I'll get it down for you.'

'I'm living with my mother!' I pouted, climbing back up the stairs.

I finished putting the clothes away, hoping I wasn't actually supposed to iron anything. Maybe he wouldn't notice. I straightened out the bed, swiped at some dust on the bedside table, and looked through the CDs on the rack. I picked out a new Train CD that I had just bought and put it on, cranking up the volume. This and my piano are the two reasons I live in a concrete building. I can play my music as loud as I want and the neighbours rarely hear a thing.

I heard Cam humming away downstairs. It's nice living with someone with the same taste in music. We hardly ever disagree about what to listen to, unlike trying to pick a movie to watch. That is something we can never agree on. When Cam picks, he tries to educate me in the classics, like the Three Stooges, or Laurel and Hardy, while I prefer more modern fare like a good Bruce Willis action movie or maybe a classic like Indiana Jones or *Star Wars*. We are both convinced that we will eventually turn each other on to our tastes in movies, but so far neither of us has been successful. Not like we need anything else to argue about. That is something we do really well.

I heard the coffee pot beeping and poked my head over the rail again.

'Coffee?' I asked, feeling my mouth water at the thought of a nice strong cup of the African blend I had picked up last week. Cam had come through for me again.

'And a cigarette,' he said, waving his lighter.

I bounded down the stairs like a child on Christmas morning and sat at the little wicker table I have set up in the kitchen. I noticed my plants were wilting and decided I had better water them before the day was over.

Cam poured me a coffee and lit my cigarette for me. I hadn't smoked for twenty-four hours and it tasted great. I seem to be a born smoker, which is why I am having such a hard time quitting. At least that is my theory. Cam lit a cigarette and sat down across from me with a beer for himself.

'Well, the place is looking good,' he said.

'Are we going to have to do this cleaning thing all the time?' I asked.

'Katie, I promised you I would cook every meal as long as we're together, but I am not the maid. We are going to split the chores.'

'What about hiring a cleaning service?'

'I think we can manage this once a week or so, don't you?' he asked. 'Besides, if we keep it up, it won't be so bad. This place has been suffering from a few years of neglect.'

'God, your room-mate must have been glad to see you go,' I said. 'Did you try to run his life, too?'

'I have certain standards, Katie, like not being able to write my name in the dust on the coffee table.'

'I think you're exaggerating slightly,' I protested. 'I've never been able to write my name in the dust on the coffee table. Now, the TV screen is a whole different story.'

'Well, they're both clean now,' he said proudly.

'You're one in a million,' I said, taking another cigarette from his pack. While I didn't really appreciate the abuse I was taking, I loved the way the apartment was beginning to look and I didn't want to derail his enthusiasm.

'You have absolutely no will power, do you?'

'Very little. How do you think Graham's doing?' I asked to change the subject.

Graham had also been involved in the murder during the previous show, and had the injuries to prove it. He was sporting a brace on his right leg, had some new front teeth, and a few assorted bruises. I hadn't fared too well either, I thought, looking down at the cast that was to stay on my arm for at least another week.

'I'm sure he's fine,' Cam said. 'We would have heard if he wasn't. And he didn't sound too sick when he left the message on the answering machine.'

'I suppose.'

'It's just killing you, isn't it?' he asked. 'Being away from the theatre for ten days. I would have thought that after the last month you spent there, you would never want to go back.'

'It was kind of exciting, Cam.'

'Getting thrown down a flight of stairs was exciting?' he asked. 'That kind of excitement I can do without.'

'Well, Sam and Ryan thought it was exciting.'

My best friend and her husband had just returned from a vacation the night after the murderer had been apprehended, and Cam and I had gone out for coffee with them, regaling them with tales of murder and intrigue. It was a story from which I intended to get plenty of mileage.

'We should give them a call and see if they want to do a movie tonight,' Cam suggested.

Just then, the phone rang. I turned to answer it but Cam put a hand on my arm, holding me down.

'Don't even think about answering that,' he warned me.

I listened to my message play, heard the beep, and waited anxiously to hear who was calling.

'Hello, Katherine? Are you there? Pick up, darling, it's Mother.'

I looked at Cam. 'Oh God, my mother!'

The machine continued recording. 'Katherine, I'm coming into town tomorrow and I just wanted to let you know. My plane won't get in until seven, so I'll take a taxi to the theatre and meet you there. I can only stay for two or three weeks but I'll tell you all about it when I get there. Bye for now.'

'I finally get to meet your mom,' Cam said.

'I was hoping you wouldn't have to so soon. I thought we would wait until we'd been married for ten years or so,' I said.

'Katie, seriously, I can hardly wait to meet her,' he said. 'Where does she stay when she's in town?'

'On the couch.'

'For three weeks?' he asked. 'Isn't it going to get a little crowded here?'

'Not after you move out,' I said.

'What?'

'I haven't even told her I've been seeing you,' I said. 'She's going to die if she finds out you're living here.'

'Well, you'd better come up with something.' He smiled. 'I've already given notice at my old place, remember?'

'Shit, my mother and you together in this apartment for

three weeks? Maybe I'll just get struck by lightning right now and won't have to live through it.'

He ruffled my hair, laughing at me. 'You know you never have that kind of good luck.'

'Well, my bad luck is your bad luck,' I said. 'You're looking at enforced celibacy until my mother leaves.'

'What are you talking about?'

'Take advantage tonight, Cam, it may be your last chance for a while,' I teased him.

'Forget the movie then,' he said. 'We're not leaving the house tonight.'

I stood up and ran over to the phone, dialling Sam's number.

'Too late,' I told him. 'I think a movie would be fun tonight. Maybe dinner afterwards, a late night and then straight home for a good night's sleep.'

'You can be cruel,' he said. 'After all I've done for your kitchen.'

'Hi, Sam, it's Kate,' I said into her machine. 'Book the nanny for the night and let's go to a movie. It's my last free night before the show starts. Call me as soon as you get in.'

I hung up and turned to find Cam standing right beside me.

'You're just joking about your mother staying here, right?' he asked as he kissed me.

'No,' I said, kissing him back, letting my hands work their way up under his sweater and trace the outline of his spine. 'I wasn't joking about any of it.'

'Then I think you'd better accompany me upstairs before Sam calls you back,' he said, grabbing my hand and pulling me towards the stairs.

Sam called back an hour later and we arranged to go to an early show. She and Ryan like Arnold Schwarzenegger as much as I do and we agreed that *someone* had to see *Terminator 3* so it might as well be us. Between our house-cleaning and frolicking, Cam and I both needed a shower. He wanted me to come and wash his back but I knew we'd never be ready on time if I did, so I sat on the couch, leafing through a magazine, waiting for my turn in the bathroom – something else that was new to me. I looked around the apartment, glad Cam had bullied me into cleaning the place up now that I knew my mother was coming to stay. I don't think she's ever seen it this clean or organized before and I hoped she would be impressed by it. My mother hadn't even arrived yet and I was already worried about getting her approval. It's amazing how I become a child again the second she appears in my life.

It was after five and I was sure everybody at the theatre would have gone home for the day, so I called the box office number and left a message to say that I would need a ticket for Mom the next night. I thought she'd have a much better time watching the show than sitting around the lobby watching me. I heard Cam come out of the bathroom so I got up to go take my shower. He stood in front of the bathroom door, wrapping a towel around his waist, and for a moment I thought about cancelling our movie date and staying in for the night, after all.

He gave me a quick kiss on the cheek and headed upstairs to get dressed. I love the way he smells fresh from the shower. I took a deep cleansing breath to clear out those thoughts, and then I jumped in the shower and washed my hair.

'We're going to be late,' Cam said, poking his head into the bathroom.

'It's not my fault,' I said.

'Well, hurry up in there or I'm coming in after you.'

I stuck my head around the shower door. 'Better get your hormones in check there, boy. We're about to have a house guest.'

'I think that's what did it for me,' he said, wiping the steam off the mirror and pulling out his razor. 'I was looking forward to us living together peacefully and not being in the middle of a murder investigation, but we don't seem to be having much luck with the peacefully part. Is life always going to be this much of an adventure with you?'

'You ain't seen nothing yet,' I joked, rinsing the shampoo out and then turning off the water.

'We could always move,' he suggested.

'By tomorrow?'

'It could be done,' he said.

'Well, as much as I'd like to avoid a three-week visit with my mom, I don't think running away would be the adult thing to do.'

'Well, the offer stands if you change your mind.'

'Don't hold your breath.' I wrapped a towel around my hair and pulled another one around my shoulders. 'I'll be dressed in a minute.'

'OK. I'm almost finished here,' he said.

He was standing at the bottom of the stairs, waiting with my coat and bag, when I came back down. He helped me slip my jacket on and I threw my bag over my shoulder.

'The place looks good,' I said, taking one last look before he opened the door for me. 'I think you're going to be a good influence on me.'

'It's a tough job, but somebody has to do it.' He shepherded me out the door and secured our new double locks, another souvenir from our little adventure last month. I don't like the fact that I have two dead bolts on my apartment door, but I was even less pleased by the fact that someone had managed to break into my place twice in the past month. *Our* place, I thought – I have to remember that I'm not a solo act any more.

The movie lived up to everything the critics had said and less. We all decided we needed a drink to mourn the passing of Arnie's career. I suggested Vaudeville's, at the Plex, but three no votes led us to Kensington, another trendy, overpriced section of town. The boys had their beer and Sam and I had our drink of the month. We're on Cosmopolitans this month. It makes us feel classy, and it's what the girls from *Sex and the City* drink.

'So, are you ready to get back to work?' Ryan asked.

'I've had to hide her keys to keep her away,' Cam replied.

'Same old Kate,' Sam said.

'Well, I had some good news today,' I offered, changing the subject.

'What?' Sam's eyes lit up.

'Mother's coming tomorrow.'

Sam almost spat a mouthful of Cosmopolitan across the table and Ryan laughed into his hand.

'Wasn't she just here?' Sam asked.

'Seems like it, but it was well over a year ago.'

'You guys shouldn't be talking about the woman like that. I've never met her and you're giving me a very bad impression,' Cam put in.

'You won't need us to do that,' Sam said.

'That's right,' I agreed. 'She'll do that herself. Probably while she's doing a white-glove inspection of your dusting.'

'Well, Kate, if he's been dusting there's bound to be an improvement over when she was here last and you were in charge of cleaning,' Sam teased.

'No, the place looked great that time. She hired a cleaning service, remember?' Ryan said.

'I wanted to do that again, but slave-master here wouldn't hear of it,' I complained. 'It's that sick "no pain no gain" attitude of his.'

'I think he is having a positive influence on you, though,' Sam said.

'Thank you,' Cam said. 'I wondered when someone would come to my defence.'

'Don't get too used to it,' Sam said. 'By the way, I got some news today, too.'

'Oh, what?'

'I'm catering your preview tomorrow night.'

'What?' I asked. 'I thought the Plex was catering it themselves.'

'I don't know what happened. It was very last-minute; they just called.'

'I wonder what's up,' I thought out loud.

'I don't know,' Sam said. 'But for a preview, they sure want some fancy stuff. And the budget has gone way up, too.'

'OK, you two, no more theatre gossip. You'll find out what's going on tomorrow,' Cam reminded me. 'Tonight I'd like to stay off that topic and talk about anything else.'

'Can we at least talk about the menu?' I asked.

'No!' Cam and Ryan both piped up.

'OK, OK.' I surrendered.

'Maybe we should call it a night,' Cam suggested.

'No way,' I said. 'I told you I wanted a late night and then straight home to bed for a good night's sleep.'

'That's not going to happen, babe,' Cam laughed.

'You two really need to get over this new lovers living together phase. All these sexual innuendoes are starting to get really boring.'

'You're just jealous,' I said.

‘Jealous? We put our daughter to bed at seven every night and have the house to ourselves. You’re the ones that live in a small loft and have your mother moving in for the next three weeks.’

‘But we can still do it on the kitchen table,’ I said.

‘Trust me, you’ll get over that; the bed is so much softer,’ Ryan said.

‘That’s enough,’ Cam interrupted. ‘I give in, we can talk about the theatre.’

Tuesday October 21

I had set the alarm for ten o'clock and it started buzzing right on schedule. I waited for Cam to reach over and shut it off – his job because he is the morning person. If it were left up to me, I would just push the snooze button twelve or fifteen times. Why do they bother putting snooze buttons on alarm clocks if you're not supposed to use them? When nothing happened, and the damn thing kept buzzing, I opened my eyes and turned my head to look at Cam's side of the bed. I knew we must be back to normal because Cam was not in bed; he was probably out jogging. I rolled over and reached for the clock, hitting the top of it violently but missing the off button. I was finally forced to sit up, focus my eyes, and turn it off. I contemplated going back to sleep, knowing Cam would wake me when he got back, but thought better of it. I smelled coffee coming from the kitchen and decided a cup or two would help.

I stumbled down the stairs, searched three cupboards looking for a mug, remembering Cam was reorganizing my kitchen before he started on the rest of my life, and poured myself a cup of coffee. I sat on down in the breakfast nook, opened the newspaper and sipped my coffee gratefully. Cam always starts the coffee before he goes out running and I think that's one of the most caring things he does for me. In fact it's probably his self-preservation instinct. I am a much more civilized person if I've had several cups of coffee before he gets back from his run. I heard the front door open and close, then Cam poked his head around the corner and saw me reading the paper.

'Well, look at you. Managed to get out of bed all by yourself this morning?' he asked.

'I used to manage just fine on my own,' I told him.

'Well, it's too bad you're up, I had planned a really special way to wake you up this morning.'

'It's not too late,' I said. 'I can run back upstairs.'

'No, the moment has passed. Besides, there is one reason and only one reason that you are up and cheerful this morning.'

'And what is that, Mr Know It All?'

'You can hardly wait to go to the theatre.'

'I really hate it when you act like you think you know me so well.'

'But am I right?'

'I hate it even more when you're right.'

I sat at my desk, anxiously awaiting Graham's arrival. It was the first time I had been back in the theatre since the last play. I don't remember much about the play, but I sure remember the murder that we opened with and the swan dive I took off the forty-foot high fly towers to close it with. I knew that the murderer had been caught and was safely behind bars awaiting trial, and I knew that I had survived the fall, thanks to Scott, our theatre's assistant stage carpenter, and his amazingly strong abdominal and shoulder muscles, but I still felt a little uncomfortable being back there. It's funny how a noise that I wouldn't even have noticed two months ago suddenly made me jump. Every time the radiator creaked or a door slammed, the hair on the back of my neck would stand straight and the goose-flesh would rise. I guess I'll just have to work at getting comfortable here again, and try to believe that no one else wants to kill me. I mean, I know I can be annoying sometimes, but I really don't think they are lined up out there to do me in.

I had called Graham around noon and left a message saying that I was imposing some mandatory overtime and I wanted to see him in the office at two o'clock. I couldn't stand the thought of waiting until four o'clock or later to find out what his message had been all about. I made some coffee and did a little general tidying up. My office looked like it had been occupied by an eighteen-year-old for the last ten days and I was working on slowly reclaiming it while I waited for Graham to appear. I heard the fire door at the end of the corridor open, so I quickly scooted behind my desk with my coffee and lit a cigarette, not wanting to appear too anxious. I shouldn't have worried; Graham looked excited enough for both of us as he came through the door.

Graham is very young, just about to turn nineteen and he wants to be an actor more than anything else in the world. He has worked for me as an usher throughout his high-school years. Graham believes that being in the theatre is an education for him, whether he is seating people, hanging up coats or serving drinks, he just wants to be here. He is tall, blond, and quite well built for someone his age. He looks vaguely like a young Kenneth Branagh and he is convinced that's who he is going to be when he grows up. He is pretty good, too. I've been dragged to all of his productions since he first started working for me and I've been impressed. He sings, he dances, he acts, and he dreams of seeing his name up in lights. When he graduated and my former assistant quit, I decided to take him on full-time. He might be a little star-struck, but he works harder than anyone else I have ever hired. That helps me put up with his smart mouth and a bit of attitude.

'I have been dying to talk to you,' he said, dumping his backpack and coat in the middle of the floor. 'Why didn't you call me sooner?'

'We just got back,' I lied. 'Now tell me what is going on.'

'We're famous!' he cried, flinging his arms into the air. 'We are about to make it on to the map. The world is going to be watching us.'

'Enough clichés, what are you talking about?'

'We've got the piano competition!' he exclaimed.

I sat back in my chair and gave him a dirty look. All of this build-up and he was just going to tease me.

'Right,' I said. 'Now tell me another one.'

'Seriously, Kate, we have got the piano competition. Starting Friday, the world will be watching the Centenary Theatre.'

'Graham, the piano competition is at the Concert Hall. It has been scheduled for over a year. Now quit fooling around.'

'Well, life is just full of these wonderful little mishaps,' he said a little too cheerfully. 'And sometimes the lucky few – us in this case – benefit from it. The Concert Hall is flooded.'

'Flooded?' I still wasn't following his story.

'In a glorious act of God, some huge pipe somewhere burst,

spewing millions of gallons of sewer water all over the stage of the Concert Hall. If I'd planned it myself it couldn't have been more perfect. It happened very late one night last week, and I know because the Spaz called me at three o'clock in the morning, trying to track you down. They wanted to set up a contingency plan in case they couldn't get it cleaned up in time. And apparently, they couldn't! It's ours.'

'I still don't understand,' I said.

'Kate, the Concert Hall is out of commission for at least two more weeks. It reeks of sewage, half the electrics have shorted out, the floor won't hold a music stand, let alone a grand piano, and the sound system is history. There is no way they can hold the piano competition or anything else there for at least two weeks. We're the next biggest theatre in town that could take them, since the Jubilee is half torn apart for renovations. I found out the next afternoon that they had officially moved the piano competition to our theatre! And then I started trying to call you.'

'Oh my God! I can't believe this. This competition is world famous. There was a huge competition just to get it here. This is better than landing the Olympics!'

'It *is* the Olympics, at least in the concert world.'

'We're never going to be ready in time,' I said. 'I've got scheduling, cleaning, ordering, panicking; I don't know what to do first.'

'And we've got previews starting for our own play tonight,' Graham said. 'Ulcer City, here we come.'

'Does everyone else know?' I asked.

'They announced it to me, and the technical staff, last week – under strict orders to keep it quiet – and they've been absolutely panic-struck that I couldn't find you. So all the techies know and the admin staff know.'

'How about the public?' I asked.

'Lots of enquiring calls from the papers wondering what's going to happen, but nothing official until the big announcement tonight, onstage, before the play begins. I guess they're inviting all the press and making the big announcement. That's really going to suck for the press to be here for the first preview though. I don't think the director is very happy about all this.'

'What they are planning on doing is making Foothills Stage Network sound like we're saving the day, stepping in at the last minute, reorganizing cast and crew so the competition can go on. Those poor actors could blow every line, but the public sympathy should be running high, so only good can come of this. And after a murder in the lobby last month, I suppose we need this kind of good publicity.'

'Do you know who is going to be in town for the competition?' Graham seemed to be floating off the ground he was so excited.

'No, I don't. But I bet you do.'

'You're right. A fledgling actor has to keep on top of celebrities that are in town. Never know when you might get discovered.'

'Well, you can tell me later because I need to go to the green room right now. I have to see if there's an updated performance schedule posted and say hi to the guys.'

'OK, what should I do while you're gone?' he asked.

'Try to get your feet back on the ground.'

'Seriously,' he said.

'I was serious. But you can also go up to the admin tower and pick up our cash from the safe and empty my message box for me. Time to start counting money again.'

'On my way,' he said. 'Don't you be too long.'

'I'll do my best, Graham, now get out of here!'

Graham took off, not at his normal pace, but still pulling off a fast limp, the brace not slowing him too much. He started singing 'If They Could See Me Now' at the top of his lungs. Graham is always singing, dancing, and hamming it up. He thinks any time could be audition time. He works in the theatre, after all, and he always hopes someone might overhear him and he'll be discovered. He already knows every word to every show tune ever written – he has to become a star.

'If they could see you now they'd say you weren't working hard enough,' I shouted after him. Happy to have had the last word for a change, I grabbed my keys. All our doors lock automatically and security has had to let me in so many times, after I had forgotten my keys, that they swear they're going to start charging me for the service. I don't really want to find out if they're serious or not. I headed out through the main lobby, and into the backstage right hall, past the dressing rooms and on to the green room. I saw the door was open and the lights were on, so somebody must be home. I rounded the corner and saw Trevor, Scott and Dwayne sitting around the coffee table over a set of blueprints.

These three guys are the resident technicians in the theatre. They pride themselves on the fact that they have over fifty years' experience in the theatre between them. And they have appointed themselves my big brothers, watching and critiquing every move I make.

'It's the Three Stooges live and in person,' I greeted them.

'Management in the house,' Scott yelled. 'Hide the beer.'

I would never admit it, but Scott is my favourite. I'm sure it has something to do with his washboard abdominal muscles and the fact that he had saved my life. Not that I'm shallow or anything.

'Hide it or share it,' I joked. 'Better yet, offer me a coffee.'

'You're going to need it,' Trevor said, getting up to pour me a cup. 'I don't think any of us is going to be getting much sleep for the next two weeks.'

Trevor is our technical director and the oldest of the three. He hails from California but pretends to be from somewhere in the south. He always tries to be so serious about the theatre, and he has the cutest little stomach that peeks out of his shirt like Winnie the Pooh's.

'Don't we sound excited about the piano competition?' I asked sarcastically, leaning against the fridge, too wired to sit, and accepted the mug that Trevor held out for me.

'Do you know what this means?' he asked.

'According to Graham it means that we're all going to be famous,' I said as I sipped my coffee.

'That junior butthead doesn't know anything,' Trevor said.

'Well, according to Trevor it means the biggest headache we've ever seen around here,' Dwayne informed me.

Dwayne rounds out the threesome. He is tall, thin, with skin the colour of café au lait and a slight trace of an exotic accent. I can never decide whether the accent is real or if he just wants us to think he's from some far-off Caribbean island.

'How come?' I asked, leaning forward and checking out

the blueprints, not that they actually meant anything to me.

Trevor picked up a pencil and used it for a pointer. 'Try to follow this, Kate. This is the set for *Rock and Roll*. This is the doorway into the workshop. This is the empty stage that is required for the piano competition. This means that every night, as soon as the theatre is empty, we have to take the *Rock and Roll* set down and hang the curtains for the piano competition. Then, every afternoon, at four o'clock, when the piano competition is over for the day, we have to move the *Rock and Roll* set from the shop and back into the theatre.'

'Gross,' I said. 'And the three of you are going to be able to do this?'

'No, we're going to have to use the running crew from our show. That makes five more guys plus the techies from the Concert Hall, because they don't have anything better to do right now. Still, this is not my favourite way to run a show,' he complained.

'Well, you won't be alone,' I said. 'I haven't seen any actual paperwork yet, but I can imagine we'll be doing almost exactly the same thing in the lobby every day.'

'Oh, the glamorous world of the theatre,' Scott laughed. 'And to think, I could be pumping gas for a living.'

'Yeah, pays lousy but the hours suck,' Dwayne said.

'Well, I was in a good mood until I talked to you guys. I think I need to go find Graham again. At least he's excited.'

'I told you; the junior butthead doesn't know anything. Wait until he's had a couple of days of this under his belt and then see how excited he is.'

'I don't know, Trevor, there are going to be movie stars here. I think Graham's going to really enjoy this.'

'Movie stars?' Scott asked. 'Lord help us.'

'Oh God.' I set my coffee down on the table.

'What's the matter?' Scott asked.

'I just remembered. My mother's coming tonight. She's staying with me for the next three weeks. I must have done something very bad in a past life to deserve all this happening at once.'

'Look on the bright side; you'll never have to see her. You'll be here eighteen hours a day.'

I stood up and rinsed out my coffee cup in the sink. 'I've

got to get to work. If my life is about to fall apart, I'd at least like it to be in an organized manner.'

I hurried back through the lobby and up the stairs towards my office. Graham and I had some work to do.

'Graham, I've just been talking to the guys . . .' I started to say as I came through the office door. Graham was standing in the doorway talking to someone and I pushed him out of the way so I could begin to sort through everything that had to be done in the next three days. 'And you won't believe—' I stopped dead when I saw who was in the office with Graham.

'Katie?'

There was that pet name, but it wasn't Cam using it.

'Katie, is that you?' He sounded as surprised as I felt.

I looked up into those familiar blue eyes and had to reach for the door handle to steady myself. His hand reached out to catch me and I felt a tingle rush up and down my arm where he touched me. I felt a catch in my throat and the air leave my lungs. It wasn't possible. He was not supposed to be here. He was from the past.

'Stephan?' I squeaked, breathless. I moved from the door to my desk, my feet taking care of themselves, as my brain was still not functioning properly. I held on to the back of my chair, as my knees felt suddenly weak and I was still having problems catching my breath.

'Katie?' he asked again, a smile beginning to show on his face, and one growing on mine to mirror it.

'Stephan Bouchard?' I asked again, unable to come up with anything else to say to him, overwhelmed by his presence in my office.

'Katie, it is you! What on earth are you doing here?'

His eyes lit up and that smile broke wide across his face. Suddenly it was ten years ago and I was that young girl sitting in her first university lecture, staring dreamily across the lecture hall at him. I was almost dizzy from the historical whiplash.

His French accent, jet-black hair, and sky-blue eyes still made my knees go weak, I thought, amazed at my reaction. He had a little more grey in his hair than the last time I had seen him, a few more wrinkles around his eyes and his smile, but don't we all. He wore a thick cable-knit sweater, black Armani dress pants and there was a distressed black leather coat tossed over the back of one of my chairs. Stephan hadn't changed much; he still took my breath away just by standing in the same room as me.

'Stephan?' I repeated for good measure, just to make sure I really had the right person. 'What are you doing here?'

'I'm here for the piano competition. I've come to meet with the house manager.'

'I'm the house manager.' I looked at him again, shaking my head in disbelief. 'It's like seeing a ghost from my past.'

'I'm a little bit shocked as well.'

He came closer and wrapped his arms around me, pulling me close to him with an old familiarity. He felt so strong, so warm, so French. The familiar aroma of his cologne filled my nostrils and my brain filled with memories that I had spent so many years trying to forget. He kissed both my cheeks and then pulled back a step, not letting me go just yet, but looking me over.

'You look beautiful,' he finally pronounced.

'Hardly, but thanks.' I blushed, realizing I was still in his arms but not really wanting to pull away. I felt a strong urge to fuss with my hair and put on lipstick. 'You, on the other hand, look wonderful.'

'I can't believe you're the house manager here. I haven't heard anything from you in years. I had no idea you were involved in the theatre again.'

Graham cleared his throat, suddenly making his presence an uncomfortable reality. 'I take it you two know each other.'

'Uh, yes, we're old friends,' I said, slightly embarrassed, trying to gently pull away and knowing Graham was never going to buy that explanation.

Stephan wasn't embarrassed, though, and didn't release me.

'I'm so happy you're back in the theatre,' he said, staring deep into my eyes. 'Even though it's only in an administrative capacity. Katie, when are you going to tire of this menial work and get back to your music?'

'Excuse me?' Graham asked. 'What's this about your music?'

'You are looking at one of the most gifted pianists that never made it to the concert stage,' he explained.

'And this is one of the greatest French bullshit artists you will ever meet,' I replied. 'Graham, why don't you go start the liquor inventory and let me get caught up with my friend?'

'I can take a hint,' Graham said, picking up some forms from the desk and heading for the door.

'I'm sorry, I didn't think I was being subtle,' I called after him as he walked down the hall.

'Katie, this must be fate,' he said. 'I can't believe I've run into you like this after all these years. What do you think it means for us?'

'Stephan.' I finally pulled away from him, though reluctantly and slowly. 'Let's quit talking about how many years have passed or about what fate has in store. There isn't an "us" any more. And I still prefer to pretend I'm young. Do you want a coffee?'

Making coffee for him would keep my shaking hands busy for a few minutes – maybe long enough that they wouldn't betray my nervousness.

'Yes please. Black, with—'

'Two sugars,' I finished. 'I still remember.'

'So you have thought of me over the years,' he stated, rather than asked, raising a perfectly arched eyebrow.

'You were my first love and my first big heartbreak, not to mention the greatest teacher and inspiration I've ever had. Hard to forget something like that, you know.' I was blushing slightly, glad my back was to him, having a hard time opening the sugar packets.

'And you gave me hope when I thought I had none,' he said, smiling at me.

'How is your wife?' I asked, trying to splash a little cold water on this gradually overheating scene. I was also trying to remember that Cam was somewhere in the building and could very well turn up at any moment.

'She is very well, thank you. She will be here later in the week, for the competition.'

'And what exactly are you doing here with the competition?'

'Official conductor of the Symphony,' he said. 'I have accepted the post with the Symphony for the next three years and my debut will be during the piano competition. By the way, it hasn't been announced yet, so I would appreciate you keeping it quiet until the press conference.'

'Not a problem,' I said. 'I'm getting very good at lying. Congratulations, Maestro.'

'Thank you. I guess this means we'll be seeing a lot of each other.' He smiled, our hands touching as I handed him his coffee cup.

I pulled away and quickly turned to fix one for myself as I felt the colour rising in my cheeks again.

'I guess it does.' I couldn't decide if that was a good thing or a bad thing. 'And you'll get to meet my new boyfriend. He works here, too.' More cold water splashed on the conversation. And yet, it didn't seem to slow Stephan down one bit.

'A musician?' he asked hopefully.

'No, a little more blue-collar than that.'

'Katie, I can't believe that you've thrown your entire creative life away like this.'

I had colour in my cheeks again, but this time from a twinge of anger at his summation of my life. Especially since he hadn't been in it for the past ten years. I turned around, coffee in hand, and perched on the edge of my desk.

'Stephan, I know you will never understand, but I am happy. I have found a really good balance. I still have music in my life, just not as the focal point of it. Besides, I was never half as good as you seem to remember. I was pretty much a hack with one or two stock concertos under my belt. Anyone can play Tchaikovsky and sound good, but now I can spell it, too.'

He laughed, as he always had at my jokes. I sat down behind my desk, liking the separation it gave me from him as he sat across from me, sipping his coffee.

Stephan Bouchard. I couldn't believe he was sitting there – a chapter from my past opening up before my eyes, that beautiful angular face that I hadn't seen up close for so long, staring across my desk at me. What I found hardest to believe was how strong my feelings still were for him.

'Nicole will be here next week, too,' he said, breaking the silence and my stare. I'm sure he was used to it, though; being who he was, he elicited a lot of silent stares from the girls.

'Nicole?' I asked. 'God, I haven't seen her since she was nine or ten. She must be all grown up now.'

'She is; she's twenty and one of the competitors.'

'Little Colie has become a concert pianist?' I asked. 'I guess you finally found someone to focus your musical obsession on after I left.'

'No, actually I quit trying to make stars after I failed so miserably with you.' He laughed. 'I never taught Colie; I always turned her over to others. I knew that if I taught her I would destroy any chance we had of having a father/daughter relationship. She wanted to become a pianist all on her own. You should remember her dedication, you taught her for a year.'

I couldn't even sit there and talk to him without a flush coming to my cheeks. I tried to concentrate on what he was saying and come up with an appropriate answer.

'God, she was better than I was when she was nine years old,' I said.

'You've grown your nails,' he observed, looking at my hand holding the coffee cup. 'Long nails, poor technique.'

'I don't need good technique any more,' I said, feeling my ire starting to rise again. 'Remember?'

'You had wonderful technique.'

'But I had no heart.'

'Perhaps a little true, but your touch could bring tears to my eyes.' He smiled at me again.

'That's only because you made me play scales for six hours a day. Do you know I haven't played a scale since the last time I saw you?'

'You hated them that much?' he asked.

'No, playing them reminded me too much of you.' And those eyes that I kept falling into. 'I had to get over that.'

'And what is this cast on your arm?' he asked.

'Little accident last month. It'll be off soon.'

'Permanent damage?'

'No, I will live to type another day. Can't keep a good administrator down.'

'It's a waste, Katie, such a waste.' He sighed. He glanced at the clock over the doorway. '*Merde*, I have run out of time; I have another meeting to get to. May I come back later and discuss the competition with you?'

'I'll be here all night,' I promised.

'Well, I'll be back for the announcement before your little play tonight. Perhaps we can talk then?'

'Of course,' I said, wondering how I was going to fit him, my mother, opening night, Cam, and organizing the competition all into one night. My head hurt just thinking about it. With any luck, this pain in my head might be an aneurysm and then Graham could deal with everything.

Stephan stood up and so did I. He came around the desk and wrapped me in his arms again, kissing me on the lips this time. I knew I should push him away, and I tried, but I couldn't really make my arms work. A knock on the door finally made me pull away from him. I looked over Stephan's shoulder and saw Cam standing in the doorway. My heart fell into my stomach, which had fallen to somewhere below my knees.

'Cam!' I said, a little too enthusiastically. 'Stephan, this is the man I was just telling you about.'

I slipped under Stephan's arm, broke from his embrace and pulled Cam into my office, which was starting to feel very small and very crowded.

'Cam, this is Stephan Bouchard.' I looped my arm through Cam's, pulling him towards Stephan. 'I knew him while I was at university. Stephan, this is my boyfriend, Cam.'

I waited for a little male bonding to happen but all I got was tension you could cut with a knife. Stephan was the first to move, finally holding out his hand. After what seemed like an eternity, Cam accepted it.

'Lovely to meet you,' Stephan said. I guess Europeans are much better at dealing with ex-lovers' lovers than we are. Cam remained silent. Stephan turned back to me and kissed my cheek. 'I will see you later, Katie.'

And then he was off down the corridor, leaving my life in ruins, just as he had the last time he had left it. Cam watched Stephan walk down the hall and then finally turned back to me.

'He calls you Katie?'

I glanced up at my clock, realizing I was rapidly running out of time, but I felt like I had a big fire to put out.

'Let's talk,' I suggested.

'Good idea,' he agreed. 'You start.'

'Not here,' I said. 'Let's go to Grounds Zero and sit in a corner booth. This is pretty personal and I'd rather not discuss it in my office.' I felt my pocket to make sure I had my keys, still trying to be the responsible house manager.

'Fine,' he said icily, kicking the doorstop out from my door and holding it open for me to pass through.

'I've just got to run down and let Graham know where I'm going,' I said. 'I'll meet you down there.'

'It's OK, I'll come with you. Obviously it's still not safe to leave you alone in this theatre. I guess not all the crazies are behind bars yet.'

'Cam.' I was beginning to feel exasperated. 'There is a perfectly logical explanation for what you saw.'

'Which I can hardly wait to hear.'

We walked silently down the hall, down the stairs and into the lobby. Graham was behind the Broadway Bar, stocking beer in one of the fridges.

'Hey, boss,' he called. 'Where are you off to?'

'Cam and I are just going to Grounds Zero,' I explained. 'We have to talk.'

'I bet you do.' Graham laughed.

'I'll be back as quick as I can. Are you OK here?'

'I'll be fine. We'll be ready for tonight by the time you're back,' he promised.

'Thanks.'

Grounds Zero is one of those great places that you can smell before you can actually see. They roast their own coffee beans and there is always a smoky, aromatic haze hanging over the restaurant. It's a little place, located just down the block from my office, on the corner of the Plex, basically under what is the orchestra stage of the Concert Hall. I hoped Gus was open and not flooded out too.

We walked into Gus's little restaurant and I breathed a sigh of relief to find it both open and empty. We sat in a booth in the furthest corner from the counter. Gus has big ears and likes to know what's going on, but I was hoping to keep this part of my life private. Gus came over to the table with an order pad in his hand.

'Hi, kids, what can I get you and why aren't you sitting at the counter?' he asked.

'We just need a little privacy, Gus,' I said. 'Don't take it personally.'

'Most people come back relaxed and happy from a holiday,

Kate. Or maybe your problem is you just haven't had enough caffeine today.' Gus can be almost as sarcastic as me at times.

'She's just caught up in a little game of truth or dare right now,' Cam said, smiling a little too sweetly at me.

'I think this is more than even I want to know. Same old thing for you, Kate?' he asked.

'Yes, please.'

'I'll have a regular coffee,' Cam said.

'I hear there's an old flame of yours in town, Kate,' Gus said, waiting for me to tell him more.

'God, how do you know this stuff?' I asked.

'It's an art.' He laughed as he headed back toward the counter to fetch our order.

Gus always seems to know what's going on before anyone else does. He's somewhere around sixty years old, a retired oilman who hadn't enjoyed retirement a lot. Gus had always liked to drink coffee and eat, so Grounds Zero was a natural extension of those habits. He also likes to snoop and gossip. The restaurant business is a perfect fit for him.

I pulled a packet of sugar out of the dish and began playing with it. I was nervous and didn't have a cigarette with me, so this was the next best thing.

'Well, I guess I know how you felt when you were forced to tell me about your ex-wife,' I said, trying for a little empathy from him. 'Stephan is a chapter from my past that I wasn't ready to confess to you yet.'

Cam went through a very nasty divorce, which had unfortunately made him a suspect in last month's murder investigation. Which had also led him to confess all to me before he was really ready to talk about it. Which had also led me to doubt him for the first time in our relationship and we were still trying to rebuild from there. This was really not a good time for Stephan to reappear in my life.

'It's not like my ex-wife,' he said. 'She's in my past. I walked into your office and found you kissing him.'

'He was kissing me,' I argued, clinging to the technicality. 'But I get your point.'

Gus set our drinks down in front of us and waited for a comment but he hurried back to the counter when neither of us said anything.

'I thought you didn't like anyone to call you Katie,' Cam said, looking decidedly hurt. He meant he thought he was the only special one in my life. Would I be able to convince him that he was?

'Cam, it was such a long time ago. You are the only one in my life right now.'

And then it all came flooding back.

I was twenty-one years old when I met Stephan Bouchard. I was young for my age, and green. I had never been away from home and I had never had a serious boyfriend. And I had certainly never had anyone tell me I was as beautiful or talented as Stephan did. I was a music major at the University of Calgary, dreaming of a career playing the great concert halls of the world with the most renowned conductors and orchestras. I had dedicated my life to studying music, which would explain the lack of boyfriends. Then one day I looked up from my piano and saw this beautiful man standing over me. He had jet-black hair and brilliant blue eyes. He was tall and muscular and spoke with an enchanting French accent, but the thing I found most attractive about him was his musical genius. The fact that he thought I was brilliant didn't hurt, either.

Stephan was a visiting lecturer that semester and came back as a professor the next year. He was trying to make his mark on the world as well. He dreamed of being a world-famous conductor, being invited to lead orchestras all around the world. And he thought that if he could find a talented young student while he taught for a couple of years, and if he could turn that student into a concert-class musician, then he would be taking his first steps towards building his reputation as well. He chose me. Stephan tutored me privately and was convinced that I was going to become the next star of the concert world, whether I liked it or not. Of course, at that time I not only liked it, I believed it. I fell head over heels in love with him and we had the most heated, passionate love affair ever imagined – our little secret, which I never shared with anyone except my mother. It ended after I had known him for a year and a half. That was when his wife had moved to Calgary to join him. His wife and his young daughter, Nicole – quite a surprise to me. Being French, Stephan seemed surprised that

I was upset; apparently wives and mistresses were commonplace in his world, but they were not in my innocent little life.

I spent the entire summer crying in my room, thinking my heart would never mend. In September, reality set in and I realized that I had to go back and finish my degree, with Professor Bouchard supervising my progress. Somehow, it all became very civilized. He and I found a way to be friends; I worked as his teaching assistant and gave his daughter piano lessons. When I realized his daughter had more musical potential at nine than I did at twenty-one, reality set into my musical world as well.

I finished university and got my degree, found a more skilled teacher for Nicole, and took a clerical job in a library. I grew my nails, stopped practicing scales and started playing just for myself.

I can still play Tchaikovsky's Piano Concerto No. 1, but that's my secret. It makes me feel good to know I can still do it. I still have good technique, even though I don't practice on a regular basis. That is what I'm a natural at and something I know I'll never lose.

Stephan and his family left Calgary that year as well. He had taken a position as conductor with some European symphony and, in the years that followed, had worked his way through several world-class orchestras. I know because I followed his career closely and still have a box of his newspaper clippings somewhere. It was quite a coup for the city and our symphony that he had accepted this position in Calgary.

I still have a very special place in my heart for Stephan; I just wasn't sure exactly where it was, or even what he meant to me anymore.

'But I am totally in love with you, Cam,' I finished, having poured my heart out to him. 'If I'd had any idea at all that he was coming to Calgary, or to the Plex, I would have told you everything about him. The last thing I wanted was for you to walk in on something like that. Please tell me you understand.'

Cam took another sip of his coffee before answering me. 'I'm sorry I reacted that way,' he said, just not quite as warmly as I had hoped.

'Hey, we're even now. Two weeks ago I thought you were trying to murder me.' I tried a smile out on him.

He laughed. 'I can't compete with someone like him, Katie. He's everything I'm not.'

'No, Cam, you're everything he's not. I was twenty-one years old and at that age I couldn't help but fall in love with someone like him. Now I know what I want and what I don't want. As exciting or intriguing as Stephan and his lifestyle may seem, he's not what I want now that I've grown up.'

'You looked like you enjoyed seeing him.'

'I did, surprisingly so. He was a very important figure in my life. And I adored his daughter,' I said. 'I really would like it if we could all get together and spend some time catching up.'

'I think I might be able to manage that, given a little time to get used to all this,' Cam said. 'What about his wife?'

'She never knew about us, as far as I know,' I said. 'I thought about telling her, when I first broke up with Stephan, but then I thought better of it. No point ruining everyone's lives.'

'I really want to hear you play something. I never knew you played seriously. I've only ever heard you fool around on the piano. I had no idea.'

'When I get my cast off and get my fingers moving again, I promise I'll play for you. I think I'm ready to start sharing some of my secrets with you.'

'Good.'

'Cam, I really have to go back to work. I have so much to get done that if I don't get started now . . .'

'It's OK,' he said. 'I promise my fragile male ego is secure once again.'

I leaned over the table, kissed him, and then pulled away to leave. He stood up and pulled me back to him.

'I'm going home to shower and change for tonight,' he said, holding me very close. 'I'll be at the theatre by seven, OK?'

'I'll be waiting.'

'But I want to make sure you miss me,' he said as he leaned down and kissed me. I felt my toes curl.

'I'll definitely miss you,' I promised, feeling slightly breathless, and separated myself very reluctantly from him. 'By the way, Stephan could never kiss like that.'

‘Glad to hear it.’ He laughed as he headed out the door and along the street.

I headed outside and turned down the street toward my theatre. The Centenary Theatre had been dedicated in honour of Calgary’s hundredth birthday, hence the creative name. But, creative or not, federal, provincial and local grants for that celebratory year had got this theatre built and saved the entire Plex from going another ten million dollars over budget. The Plex had been created to house all of Calgary’s arts organizations under one roof. It comprises theatres, concert halls, rehearsal studios, recording studios, restaurants and shops and, most importantly to me, Gus’s little coffee shop. Grounds Zero is on one corner of the block that was the Calgary Arts Complex and my theatre, the Centenary, is at the other. In between us, rising over ten storeys, are the offices and studios of every major arts organization in the city. Money-wise, it had been a wise decision to house them all together and divvy up the theatre space into shared allotments. However, from the personality perspective, I’m not always sure it was the right thing to do. Some days, when walking down the halls of the admin tower, you would swear World War Three was going on. Not everyone likes to share, apparently.

I used my key to let myself in the front door. Magnetic locks control our theatre, so you can only open the main entrance by calling security. But there is a side door, in the public corridor, which has key access. You can get out of this building fairly easily, but you have a really hard time getting in. All the locks are coded alphanumerically, and it is engraved on the lock. My theatre and its environs are C for Centenary. The lock I let myself through was C1, as in the main lock. This way, I can give the bar staff keys for just their areas (C6 if you must know) and the same with the ushering staff. I have a master key to all C areas, as well as some other shared rehearsal areas and the administration offices. I’m not really sure if this was done for security reasons – after all, what would someone steal? A piece of scenery? It was done more for protection. This building is a vast warren of nooks, crannies, dead ends, basements and sub-basements, and getting lost is something most people do on a regular basis for their first six months or so working in the Plex. There are rumours that a construction worker still wanders the basement corridors, trying to get out. And construction ended over ten years ago.

I climbed the first set of the thousand or so stairs I would climb tonight. You enter the theatre at ground level but have to walk up a total of 144 stairs to get from the main lobby to the second balcony. I really should be the fittest and slimmest woman on the planet for the amount of stairs I climb every day, but then if I stopped smoking and eating junk food, perhaps I might notice a bit more of a difference.

When I crossed the main lobby, I saw that Graham had been true to his word and all the tables were set up, merchandise out for sale and fridges stocked. He must have really hustled to have this done for me. I continued on up the next flight of stairs and down to my office. Graham was sitting on the desk, talking on the phone, which he hung up quickly as soon as he saw me.

'Who was that?' I asked him, slightly surprised at his reaction.

'Mandi,' he replied, blushing.

Shit, I thought, someone else I had to put on the list to invite to Graham's birthday party, a small thing I was supposed to be planning that I had totally forgotten about. Like I really needed one more thing happening in my life right now, I thought, and then felt an immediate pang of guilt at this self-centred attitude of mine.

'That little nurse from the hospital? Are you still seeing her?' I asked.

'We've gone out a couple of times.'

'This is a record for you, Graham. What's it been? Two weeks now?'

'And aren't you a fine one to talk,' he said. 'Who is this French Lothario from your past? You were practically drooling.'

'I most certainly was not!'

'Jeez, Kate, I thought your eyes would pop out of your head when you first saw him. Is he an old flame?'

'What he is is private and off-limits. I would prefer not to hear any rumours about us floating around this building and if I do, I am going to know who it was that started them. I will hunt you down like the dog that you are and flay you. Do I make myself understood?'

'Definitely.'

'Great job in the lobby by the way,' I said, lightening up. 'Thanks for getting all that done.'

'Shucks, it was nothing,' he said. 'I also took the liberty of sorting through this junk that was in your message box. Lots of phone messages, none that urgently need to be returned. Here's the new performance schedule for the next two weeks, including all the piano competition stuff, staff requirements, etcetera, etcetera, etcetera.'

'*The King and I*,' I said.

'What?'

'Yul Brynner in *The King and I*. He used to say "etcetera, etcetera, etcetera".'

Graham and I both consider ourselves to be the trivia masters when it comes to Broadway musicals and we often throw out a phrase or song and try and stump the other with a game of name-that-show. I had thought that was what Graham was doing now.

'I wasn't doing show tunes, Kate; I was referring to this mound of competition stuff. They've given you press clippings, historical data and a list of competitors, judges and celebrities, with a memo asking you to read through it all so you will sound fairly intelligent should anyone ask you a question about it.'

'I don't have to read it.' I winked at him. 'I have you to do that.'

'Sorry, Kate, but you're the musical genius here, or so I've heard. I really think you should be in charge of this stuff now.'

'All right, all right. I'll become the piano competition expert if you just shut up about me being a musical genius. Which, by the way, I can assure you I'm not.'

'Fine.' He turned his attention back to the mound of papers he was piling in front of me. 'OK, next is a cleaning schedule. They are actually going to clean and paint this place over the next couple of nights, spruce it up a bit. Lots of memos, most of which you can probably toss, a few volunteer applications that need your approval – and look here, a note that Maestro

Stephan Bouchard is coming up here this afternoon to meet with you.' Graham laughed.

'A little late on that one,' I said, crushing the note into a ball and tossing it toward the garbage can, missing as always.

Graham bent over and picked the paper up, tossing it into the can for me.

'Two points!' he exclaimed.

I pulled all the papers he had placed in front of me into a nice tidy little pile and shoved them all away in my top drawer, except for the performance schedules. 'Can you pull some blank calendars from the file cabinet for me?' I asked him.

He found some and gave me a handful. 'Are we going to have enough staff for this?' he asked.

'Not even close. Besides, our staff are working a lot on *Rock and Roll*. I'm not going to force anyone to work twelve-hour shifts.'

'So what are we going to do? Use volunteers?'

'For the competition? I don't think so. Besides, we seem to have a massive budget for staff here and I intend to spend every penny of it. I'll hang these up tonight and our ushers can have first crack at signing up, then we'll open it up to the Concert Hall staff. I mean, they're not doing much right now, while they're waiting for their stage to dry out. Hey, can you make a note that we'll have to check the uniforms for dry-cleaning. We're going to need about fifteen staff a day for the next two weeks, so we best be prepared.'

'Got it,' Graham said, pinning the note up on my bulletin board.

I heard the door open at the other end of the corridor and looked up to see Leonard Lovelace, one of our ushers, ambling down the hall towards the office.

'Oh man, is it that time already?' I asked, seeing it was almost six o'clock.

'Yes it is,' Leonard said, dropping his backpack on the floor and pouring himself a coffee. Leonard is a philosophy major at the university. He is twenty-two, very tall and skinny, still waiting to fill out into manhood or perhaps just missing his mother's home cooking.

'Another opening, another show,' he started singing, not quite in key.

I stacked everything into my in-basket. 'There should be crowds forming downstairs within the hour.'

'Let's hope so.' Graham laughed.

'I'm going to change,' I said, grabbing a garment bag off my coat rack. 'I'd like to see you guys ready when I come back. Maybe you can update Leonard on our news while I'm gone.'

I took my dress and make-up into the bathroom that was just outside my office. I closed the door, then opened it again and peeked into the hallway to make sure it was empty. I had been locked in there during my little adventure last month and I still don't feel totally safe yet. I stepped into one of the stalls and secured the door to ensure my privacy before I stripped off my standard uniform of jeans and sweater, and pulled a slip over my head. I let myself out and stood in front of the mirror to freshen my face, and then pulled my brand new dress out of the garment bag. Cam had done everything in his power to keep me from shopping while we were away, but it hadn't worked. I found this gem in a little Victorian shop in Nanaimo and grabbed it even though it was overpriced. It's all ivory lace and buttons, with a high collar and cuffs. It has the palest pink under-dress that makes it glisten. It hangs to just above my ankles and fits like it was made for me. I put on a pair of strappy sandals, taking advantage of the unseasonably warm October, and was pretty pleased with what I saw in the mirror. Except for the hair. I pulled a barrette out of my make-up bag and pulled my hair up into a ponytail but decided that wasn't right either. I twisted and coiled and snapped the barrette in. A few strands fell out in just the perfect places – another hair accident that had turned out quite successfully. I keep this great pair of pearl earrings and a necklace in my desk that completed my outfit perfectly. Not really the style for a show called *Rock and Roll* but I always like to be a little different. I gathered up my discarded clothes and headed back to my office.

Graham whistled as I came through the door. 'Great dress.'

'Thank you.' I did a little curtsy. A few others had joined Graham and Leonard and they were all in uniform and waiting for instructions. We don't really have a formal uniform; the ushers wear black pants, white shirts, black bow ties, and black cardigans. We provide the bow ties and cardigans and they provide the rest. Not a very formal look, but I like it. Better than the green polyester jackets they used to wear and the upkeep is much cheaper too.

'Are we ready for another show?' I asked.

'We're never ready.' Graham laughed. 'But, somehow, we always pull it off.'

By seven o'clock, I had my staff and volunteers in place and the bars were open. We were ready for business. I called security and opened the main doors. All of the fire doors, as well as the entrance doors on the main floors, are on a magnetic locking system, controlled through the security desk. Security love it because it means there isn't much we can do here without them knowing what's going on. There was a small line-up at the box office downstairs, and a few people were milling about in the lobbies. I headed into the Rodeo Lounge to refill my coffee and check up on things.

The Rodeo Lounge is our members-only lounge. Anyone who donates enough money to the Foothills Stage Network is allowed access to this private little room, with free drinks and plenty of FSN employees fawning over them, encouraging them to donate even more next year. Only the really big donors get into this room, everyone else just gets T-shirts or free tickets, which is good since we can never seem to give them away in our lobby market.

There was a plate of hors d'oeuvres sitting on top of the bar in the lounge, and I helped myself to a couple while the bartender had his back turned to pour my coffee. I took a sip and, seeing everything was under control here, set the cup down behind the bar. I usually just keep roaming around before the show, checking out all the staff positions and making sure our customers are happy. I knew I would be back to finish my coffee before it was cold.

I stopped to talk to two of the ushers sitting at the sales tables, and then headed for the house-right door, which led into the theatre. It was time to check in with the stage manager and see how things were going. In the theatre, there is very strict protocol about who does what and when, and sometimes to whom. The director or stage manager is in charge of the entire theatre until about half an hour before the play is scheduled to start. Usually the actors are all over the theatre warming up, some on stage, some in the seats, and some even doing chin-ups hanging off the first balcony, although I always pretend not to see them, so I don't have to write a report afterwards. About thirty-five minutes prior to the show, the stage manager starts shooing the actors backstage and into costume. When the stage is clear, the actors happily ensconced in their dressing rooms and the curtain down, the theatre becomes mine. From that point on, everything from the stage to the street is my responsibility, while the stage manager takes care of everything onstage and backstage. However, before he 'gives me the house', absolutely no one is allowed in the theatre proper. There would be actors wandering around in various stages of undress, making horrible noises to loosen their vocal cords or stretching into incredibly revealing yoga postures to limber up their bodies. Once, I even found one sitting in a box seat, drinking scotch from a bottle! It would never do for the audience to see them like this, and most of the actors don't even like the ushers to see them before the show. All the romance of the theatre is gone at this point. The curtains are raised, allowing full view of the backstage area, trapdoors are open where ghosts might disappear, and wires are hanging where other ghosts might fly across the stage. The technicians are very visible, still being dressed in their street clothes, not in the all-black required during a show. The language is always much more colourful at this point of the evening than it is once we actually let the audience in. So, I quietly tiptoe in about thirty-five minutes prior to the show and wait for the stage manager to clear them out. Then he turns to me, smiles and says, 'The house is yours.'

Every night, this still gives me a little chill. I have never really lost the excitement of live theatre. What would or wouldn't happen tonight? Would someone miss a cue, would some equipment fail, would we have a good audience? It is all just a question mark every night and that's why I love it so much.

The stage manager had told me the house was mine and the volunteer guarding the door smiled at me as I came out and let it close quietly behind me. I let myself into the hallway of the technical booth, ready to let the audience know the theatre was about to open. There are three booths back there: one for the stage manager, and one each for lighting and sound. There is ladder access through a trapdoor to a projection booth upstairs, which also connects with the director's booth. I pulled my notes out of my file folder and heard the door open behind me. I turned to see who was coming in, since I was the only one who should be in there at this point. It was Cam.

'When I asked Graham where you were, he told me to look for the most beautiful woman in the theatre and that would be you.'

'You're sweet,' I said, feeling my cheeks heat up in a blush.

'He wasn't kidding, either – you look gorgeous. Is this for opening night, for my benefit, or because your mother is due any minute?'

'It's for you,' I said. 'Did you even have to ask?'

'Katie, you are such a horrible liar. Does it have anything to do with the fact that Stephan Bouchard will be here?'

'Cam, you were with me when I bought this dress. I didn't even know he'd be here then.'

'Yo, Kate!' Scott yelled at me from one of the booths. 'You're not alone in here. Just thought you'd like to know.'

'Thanks, Scott.' I blushed even redder and lowered my voice to a whisper.

I heard the 'God mike' click on and the stage manager's voice came out across the auditorium sound system.

'Ladies and gentlemen, this is your thirty-minute call. Thirty minutes please. The house is opening.'

'I'll just be a second,' I told Cam as I pushed him out the door and closed it tightly behind me. I turned my lobby PA system on and took a deep breath. 'Good evening, ladies and gentlemen, and welcome to the Foothills Stage Network's production of *Rock and Roll*. We would like to remind all patrons that the use of cameras or recording equipment is strictly forbidden. We also ask that all cellular phones and pagers be turned off before entering the theatre. Ladies and gentlemen, the house is now open.'

I could hear the doors opening as the ushers welcomed the audience into the theatre auditorium. I turned my PA off and left the booth. Cam was waiting for me just outside the door with two cappuccinos in his hands.

'Here you go.' He handed one to me.

'Thanks.' I smiled and took the coffee. 'By the way, you are looking pretty hot yourself tonight. Is this for my benefit or because my mother is due any moment?'

'This,' Cam did a little turn, showing off his suit for me, 'is strictly for your mother's benefit. I intend to make a major impression here. You, I no longer have to impress.'

I looked over towards the ticket-takers, wondering why my mother hadn't arrived yet, when I saw Stephan coming up the stairs. How complicated was this night going to get?

'Cam, can we go over and chat in a civilized manner?' I asked.

'Yes, Katie, I think I can manage that,' he said, taking my hand possessively as we walked over to greet the new Maestro.

'Katie, you look beautiful,' he said as soon as he saw me. 'You have turned into a stunningly beautiful woman.' Stephan kissed me on both cheeks and then shook Cam's hand as I quickly reintroduced them.

'You look pretty sharp yourself,' I said, admiring his suit. 'Nice tux.'

'Oh, I have a million of these,' he said, brushing off my compliment. 'This is pretty much the required uniform in my line of work. When I have to wear it for a special occasion I feel like I'm going to work. When I have fun, I wear my jeans.'

'Just like me,' I agreed. 'Can I buy you a glass of wine?'

Stephan checked his watch. 'I am supposed to be backstage by seven fifty-five.'

'We have time,' I said. 'I'll take you back myself. Are you staying for the show tonight?'

'I seem to have this free ticket so I might as well. It will give me a chance to see how the acoustics are before the competition starts.'

We wandered over to the bar and I ordered a glass of wine for Stephan and a beer for Cam, who was happy to exchange his coffee for a beer at that moment. Frankly, I could have used a glass of wine myself, but I was still on duty. We moved away from the bar line-up and stood in the centre of the lobby making small talk. I saw Graham watching me with a sly smile on his face and suddenly felt very self-conscious. But not half as much as when I heard my name called out from halfway down the main stairs.

'Katherine,' the voice called from behind me.

I turned and saw a woman racing up the last stairs, pushing past the ticket-takers and waving frantically at me.

'Mother,' I greeted her, embarrassed, as she sped across the lobby to greet me. We hugged and then she stepped away and looked me up and down.

'Your dress is beautiful,' she said. 'You could get it shortened quite easily and I'm sure no one would notice.' She finally turned her attention away from my dress. 'What is that cast you're wearing all about? And why didn't I know that you had hurt yourself?'

'Nothing, Mom. I promise I'll tell you all about it later.'

'Including why you didn't call and tell me about it?'

I ignored her little jibe. 'You look great, Mom. I am so happy to see you. How are you?'

'I'm wonderful.' She smiled at me. 'Except that your little girl at the coat-check counter tried to charge me to check my luggage.'

'Did you tell her that you're my mother?' I asked. My mother feels like everyone at my theatre should know her and respect her. I think she thinks my position is much more important than it actually is.

'Only after she told me it would be five dollars for everything. She's not going to get many tips with that attitude.'

'Mom, I pay them to do that. We don't believe in being polite to customers around here.'

'Sarcasm does not become you, Katherine.' She finally noticed Stephan and Cam standing beside me. At the sight of Stephan her eyebrow raised into a pointed arch, her lips tightened, highlighting the fine lines that outlined them, and I felt like I should warn the lobby to duck and cover.

'What in the hell are you doing here?' she asked Stephan.

'Mrs Carpenter, it is a true pleasure to see you again.' He offered her his most winning smile, which made my knees go weak but didn't seem to do much for Mom.

'It's McInnes now,' Mom said icily and then turned back

to me. 'Katherine, please tell me you're not seeing this man again.'

'No, Mom, I'm not. I'm seeing this man.' I turned to Cam. 'Let me introduce you to my boyfriend. This is Cam. Cam, this is my mom, Agnes McInnes.'

'Ms McInnes, it's lovely to finally meet you.' He shook her hand and tried his best smile on her. It worked a little better than Stephan's had.

'Don't tell me you're a musician too,' she said.

'No, ma'am, I'm a building engineer.'

I thought I heard Stephan snicker but I ignored him.

'Good, a regular pay cheque. That's important, Katherine. And you can always trust a blue-collar man to be open and honest with you.'

Though she was talking to me, her gaze had turned back to Stephan. I realized I may have gotten over him, but Mom still hadn't.

'Mom, actually Cam and I are living together,' I said. 'I don't want you to be upset; it's not that I was keeping it a secret. We've just moved in together recently.'

'Darling, that's wonderful,' she said, surprising me with her reaction. 'Because I have a little surprise for you, too.'

'What's that?' I asked, hoping for a present but not some sort of life-altering announcement, which is usually what I get.

Graham had noticed I was busy and had gone ahead and given the ten-minute announcement for me.

Mom turned and grabbed the arm of a man who had been standing just behind her, pulling him into our little circle.

'I didn't know quite how I was going to tell you this,' Mom began, 'but your news just made it so much easier. This is Lawrence, and he and I are living together, too. Don't be angry with me, Katherine, but we've been living together for a while now, but I just didn't know how to tell you.'

I didn't know what to say but Cam jumped in for me, shaking hands and exchanging pleasantries with the man. I heard the five-minute announcement and was relieved that I had an excuse to get away from there and let the news sink in. I pulled some tickets from my pocket and handed them to Cam.

'I'll give you my house seats and you can all sit together.

Cam, would you mind helping Mom and Lawrence find their seats? Stephan, you and I better get backstage.'

I kissed Mom's cheek quickly and pulled Stephan after me, across the lobby, before anyone could say anything else.

'You have a most interesting life.' He laughed as I led him past the dressing rooms and into the wings stage-right.

'You just shut up,' I said, not very politely. 'I have had more than enough surprises for one day.'

It was getting pretty crowded in the wings, with Stephan, the VIPs from the Concert Hall and Foothills Stage Network, the two techies, and a couple of representatives from the piano competition. There were four ushers waiting at the door to escort all these people back to their seats as soon as the announcements had been made, and several actors were pushing past us all as 'places' was called.

I could hear a hush come over the audience as the house went to black and a spotlight hit the curtain. The assistant stage manager pushed our guests out onstage and the public relations coup began. It seemed to go on for ever as everyone had something to say, using up his or her fifteen minutes of fame. I heard a huge round of applause as it was announced that Stephan was taking the helm of the Symphony, beginning with the competition. I spent most of those minutes trying not to crack up as Scott and Trevor made faces, imitating the people on stage. The actors, safe from view on the backstage side of the curtain, were doing the wave, and I think one of them even mooned whoever was speaking. Actors sometimes don't have much respect for these little preshow announcements, as it throws off their schedule. Finally I heard them begin to leave the stage and I led the group back out to the awaiting ushers who in turn led them quickly towards their seats in the auditorium.

I followed everyone out into the main lobby and flopped down on to one of the sofas. Graham came over to me and opened his mouth to say something, but thought better of it when he saw the look in my eyes.

'How long until intermission?' he asked instead.

'Seventy-five glorious minutes.'

'Can I do anything for you?' he asked, trying to be solicitous.

'Get me a new life. This one is getting far too complicated for me.'

Intermission was crazy, so I didn't have time to talk to anyone then, and at the end of the show I was busy signing staff out. Cam told me Mom was exhausted from her trip so he had given her a key to the apartment and put her and Lawrence in a cab. I decided to enjoy myself as long as I could before I had to go home and deal with my mother again, so Sam, Ryan, Cam and I danced until two o'clock in the morning, when the last person was cleared out of the lobby. I left Sam to collect her own pots and pans along with her catering assistant while I changed back into my jeans and then we all joined the backstage party.

I think it was close to four thirty when we finally got home. Mom and Lawrence were asleep on the hide-a-bed in the living room, so Cam and I tiptoed upstairs and climbed quietly into bed. I was awake for a long time, listening to every little noise that came from the night, feeling uncomfortable about my mom sleeping with a stranger in my living room. When Cam got sick of my tossing and turning, he turned the radio on very softly and then pulled me close to him.

'I know what it's like,' he whispered into my ear. 'My parents are divorced too. I lived through both of them getting remarried. It's hard at first, Katie, but don't worry; it'll get easier after a while.'

I don't like the fact that Cam seems to be able to read my mind, but I really do love that man.

Wednesday October 22

I woke up to the smell of coffee wafting up from the kitchen. I smiled and thought how lucky I was to have Cam. The man can cook like nobody's business, cleans up after himself and almost always has coffee ready for me when I wake up. Which is why I was really surprised when I rolled over and found him still in bed beside me.

'Morning.' He smiled at me as he caught my cast that was about to flop down on his face. You'd think I would be used to that stupid thing by now, but I still kept forgetting I had it on.

'Sorry,' I said, rolling back to my side of the bed. 'I thought you were up already.'

'It's your mom and Larry,' he said. 'They've been up for about an hour.'

'I didn't hear a thing,' I said, trying to stretch the last of the sleep from my body.

'I heard her tell him to be quiet. I think she knows we got home late.'

'Mom's been here for these things before,' I explained. 'She knows the parties run late. That's why she took a cab from the theatre; she knew I'd want to be out all night long.'

'We should get up,' he said, throwing the covers back. 'Spend some time with them before we have to go to work.'

'Do we have to?' I whined, my voice growing from a whisper.

'Is that your dulcet tones I hear, Katherine?' Mom yelled up from the kitchen. 'It's about time you sleepy heads got out of bed. It's a glorious fall day and you're sleeping it away.'

'Good morning, Mom,' I said as I sat up and leaned over the ledge of the loft, looking down into the kitchen. 'Did you sleep well?'

'Like a log,' she said. 'And I love what you've done to your kitchen. I don't think I've ever seen this place so clean and organized.'

'You can thank Cam for that, Mom; he's taken over the kitchen and almost everything else.'

'I like him better all the time. Why don't you come down? I've poured some coffee for you both.'

'Coming,' I said, climbing over Cam. I pulled on a pair of sweat pants and threw Cam's robe to him.

'Where's Lawrence?' I asked as we all sat down around the table.

'He's gone out for a run,' Mom said. 'He'll be back soon.'

'So why haven't I heard about him before?' I asked, taking advantage of the man's absence to find out about him.

'I didn't know how to tell you, Kate. He's the first serious romance I've had since I divorced your father. I wasn't sure how you'd react.'

'You've had other romances?' I asked.

'Well, more like flings.'

'Mother!' I was shocked; I didn't even know she was dating. And the thought of my mother squiring a different man about town every night was making me more uncomfortable by the minute. My face must have revealed my feelings, because Mom quickly brought the situation back under control.

'You're getting off the topic. We're talking about Lawrence here.'

'Does Geoff know about him? About you two living together?' I enquired on behalf of my brother.

'No, I thought I'd wait and see how you reacted first, before I told him.'

I noticed Cam had opened the paper and was pretending to concentrate on the sports section.

'Are we making you uncomfortable?' I asked him, angry that he didn't seem to be concerned with any of this.

'Not at all.' He smiled. 'I just haven't heard anything that I feel I should comment on.'

'He's a very smart man,' my mother noted.

'How long have you been living together?' I asked, not letting her get off-topic.

'Only about six months.'

'Six months! Just when were you planning on telling me?'

'You hadn't told me about your new roommate,' she pointed out.

'We've only been living together two weeks,' I countered.

'Three weeks,' Cam threw in before getting up and pouring more coffee. 'More or less.'

'Mom, I can't believe you didn't tell me about this.'

'Kate, it's just that you tend to overreact to things. Especially when they involve me.'

'What are you talking about, overreacting?' I said, hearing my voice rise and then trying to rein it back down. 'I am not overreacting. I'm just surprised, that's all.'

'Well, sometimes you and I seem to set each other off. I actually wasn't even going to tell you this time because Lawrence was originally not going to be able to come. But then his schedule changed and here we are.' She sighed.

'Mom, you can tell me anything,' I said, trying to make peace. 'Unless it's about your sex life. That I never want to hear about, OK?'

'Let's forget this,' she said. 'I've told you and we're here now and I really want you to get to know him. He's a wonderful man.'

'I'm sure he is,' I said. 'How did you meet?'

'I think I'll save that story for when you're over this first shock, if you don't mind.'

'So do you two have any plans for today?' I asked.

'I thought we could visit with you for a while, especially now that I want to get to know Cam a little better. I certainly think your taste in men is improving, by the way. I realize your play has just started but we'll have some time together, won't we?'

'Well, that's where the other complication comes in. You heard them announce last night that the piano competition has been moved to my theatre. It starts on Friday.'

'That's why that horrible little French man is here?' she asked.

Cam snickered and then quickly tried to cover it up with a cough. I gave him a dirty look.

'Mom, I got over Stephan; I think it's time you did, too.'

Cam finally decided to jump in and change the subject.

'I've got some time off coming to me. I could take some next week – I'll be happy to take Katie's place. We can do some sightseeing, maybe go to Banff, and then we can stop in at the theatre and have dinner with her.'

'That sounds like a good idea,' Mom agreed. 'But, Kate, surely you can let your assistant take over a couple of your shifts and we can all do something together?'

'I'll have to see how things go,' I said. 'I hate to commit to anything when we've only just opened, especially when I have no idea what's going to happen with this piano competition.'

'I know you'll work something out,' Mom said. 'Now, where shall we all go for breakfast?'

'Are we going out?' Cam asked.

'We always do,' Mom said. 'Kate can't cook and I don't mind cooking one or two meals while I'm on vacation, but I won't do all the cooking for her.'

'Well, I can cook,' Cam said. 'I'll whip something up. It looks pretty nice out; we can eat on the balcony.'

'He cooks too?' Mom asked with that arched eyebrow again.

'Come on, Mom, help me wipe down the chairs on the balcony. Cam needs his space to create.'

I rinsed out a rag and Mom followed me out on to the balcony. I started wiping the chairs while she sat in the lounge chair and watched.

'I like him,' she finally said, breaking the silence.

'I'm glad.'

'I like him better than I've liked any of your other boyfriends.'

'Well, I do too.'

'But I'm surprised that you let him move in.'

'Why?'

'Because you usually don't let anyone this far into your life.'

'I guess Cam's just been more persistent than the rest.' I decided to take her comment for what it was – a comment, not an argument. It's so hard to get along with your parents as an adult. Every time Mom comes to town I seem to revert to a five-year-old.

'I'm glad he's here. I don't think you were meant to be alone.' She leaned back in the chair and watched me work.

'I'm fine when I'm alone,' I protested. 'I'm independent, capable of looking after myself, I've got lots of friends . . .'

'Kate, I wasn't attacking you,' she interrupted with a twinkle in her eye. 'Now, don't you go breaking up with him just because I said that.'

'What are you talking about?' I asked, preparing for a fight.

'You know how you are. Whatever I say, you have to go off and do the opposite just to prove me wrong.'

'That's not true.' I felt the ire rising again and tried once again to fight it back down. 'I never let other people influence what I do.'

'And you're just as stubborn as your father. Having the both of you in the house when you were growing up was like having two bulls at either end of a china shop. Sometimes your brother and I used to sneak out for a little peace and quiet.'

'I admit I have my moments,' I said. 'What about Lawrence?'

'Why don't we call him Larry, now that we all know each other? It's what he prefers. I just call him Lawrence in formal settings. And anyway, what about him?'

'Do you love him?'

'Very much. It's not doubt about our relationship that kept me from telling you about him, Kate; it was doubt about whether you were ready to hear about it. I knew it would be hard for you to see me with someone who isn't your father.'

'Mom, I'm thirty-three years old.'

'Don't remind me!' She laughed. 'So it doesn't upset you that I'm living with someone who isn't your father?'

'I wouldn't go that far,' I admitted. 'But I'll get used to it. Besides, you and Dad have been divorced for a long time; it's about time you got on with your life.'

'You're so cute when you're trying to sound all grown-up and mature. But good, then we'll all get used to each other and have a nice visit,' she said as I finished cleaning the last chair. 'Now tell me why you're wearing that cast on your arm.'

'There was a murder at the theatre during the last play. I

kind of got in the middle of it and had a little tussle with the killer.' I stopped the story quickly as I noticed the look of horror on her face. 'It's nothing serious. The cast is coming off this week.'

'Oh my God! Did they catch the killer?' she asked. 'Are you safe, Katherine?'

'I'm fine, Mom. He's in jail waiting for his trial date. And Cam took very good care of me through it all, so there's nothing to worry about.'

Mom didn't look totally convinced. 'Will your hand be all right?' she asked, still looking worried.

'Of course it will. Just a little break, nothing serious.'

'Will it affect your piano playing?' she asked.

'No, Mom, but it's not like I play seriously any more.'

'That's why I hate Stephan so much. He took your music from you. Among other things.'

'No he didn't. I made that choice on my own and it was a good decision for me at that time.'

'You played so beautifully.'

'So do a lot of other people, Mom. I wasn't anything special.'

'But it might have been different if that man hadn't come into your life.'

'Yes, it probably would have been different, but I'm not going to get all teary-eyed about what might have been. I am very happy with the way my life has turned out. There's no way to say if I would have been successful as a pianist.'

Cam came out on to the balcony carrying plates and silverware and Larry followed him with a bottle of wine and some glasses.

'Look who managed to find his way back,' Cam said.

'It's my faultless sense of direction.' Larry laughed, setting the glasses down and opening the wine. 'I also managed to find the nearest liquor store. It's a gift I have.'

'Wine for breakfast?' I asked.

'Kate, it's almost three in the afternoon,' Mom said. 'That's what happens when you party all night and sleep the day away.'

'With my job I've become a creature of the night,' I said.

Larry had opened the wine and filled all our glasses. 'I propose a toast. To the four most wonderful people in the city.'

'And the two best boyfriends,' Mom added.

We clinked our glasses and drank.

'This is nice,' I said, feeling the tangy Merlot warm my throat.

'That's what happens when you pay more than ten dollars a bottle, Katie.' Cam laughed.

'Hey,' I scolded him, throwing the rag at him and missing. The story of my life.

'Everything is ready,' Cam said, setting his glass down. 'Are you all ready to eat?'

'I'm starved,' Mom said.

'Katie, would you set the table?' he asked, stepping back inside.

I set everything up and Larry pulled the chairs around the table. Cam came back out, carrying a huge, steaming platter covered with waffles, fresh fruit, and sausages. He had a big pitcher of syrup in his other hand.

'I hope blueberry syrup is OK?' Cam asked.

'We don't have blueberry syrup,' I said. 'There's some table syrup in the pantry.'

'I know, Katie, but I really hate that fake maple syrup so I made up some fresh blueberry syrup.'

'You made syrup?' I asked. This was beyond my comprehension; I thought you could only do that in a factory. But I poured it generously over my waffles anyway.

Mom looked like she was about to burst, she was so pleased with Cam's abilities and the fact that I had finally caught such a man.

'How did you know that waffles were my favourite?' she asked.

'Lucky guess, Ms McInnes,' Cam said, blushing from the attention.

'Stop that Ms McInnes nonsense and call me Aggie.'

I took a bite and thought I had never tasted anything quite so good.

'You have outdone yourself,' I said, leaning over and kissing his cheek. 'I think I'll keep you around for a while.'

'If she won't,' Mom smiled, 'I will.'

The rest of the afternoon went well. We sat around the table, chatting and gradually getting to know each other. Turns out

Mom has done rather well for herself. Larry is a successful dentist with a thriving three-day-a-week practice, who loves to travel and also lavish time, money and attention on my mother. I almost found myself wishing I had someone like him until I realized that I do. Mom and Cam had gone into the kitchen to do the breakfast dishes and they didn't seem to be having any problems getting along, which was a big relief to me. Mom seemed to like how he was organizing the apartment and I think she secretly hoped he might be able to organize my life, too.

Cam and I got ready for work and explained the new locks to Mom and Larry, making sure they understood how important it is to me to have my place locked up and protected. I might act like the big tough girl around everyone, but it had really rattled me to be attacked in my own home. It had taken away the sense of safety that I used to have, knowing that when I closed and locked my apartment doors, I was safe from the world. Once I felt like everyone understood, I took the arm of the most handsome handyman around and we headed for the Plex, with Mom and Larry following close behind, also arm in arm. They had decided to drive in with us – Larry had heard about Cam's car and was anxious to see it for himself. I don't understand this fascination that men have with classic cars. I used to drive an old car and all it did was cost me money, which is also what Cam's car seems to do to him. But he doesn't seem to care. Cam has a thirty-two-year-old Hemi Barracuda that he loves more than me, and everyone we meet seems to think the Fish, as I refer to it, is the greatest thing ever. All I know is that if he spent that much money on me, we might never fight again.

Mom had planned to do a little shopping after we dropped them off and then take the C-Train back to the apartment later. I'm not sure how Larry felt about spending the afternoon shopping, but I could tell he was looking forward to spending some time with my mom. I was beginning to like him more and more, this guy who seemed so hung up on my mother.

Once at the Plex, I logged in at the security desk and was surprised at the huge pile of messages that were waiting for me. I walked down Tin Pan Alley – the backstage way into my theatre – and let myself in. The backstage area was dark and deserted so I kept on going up to my office. I was surprised to see the lights on and Graham working behind my desk.

'Should I be worried about you going after my job?' I asked.

'No, I thought you would want to spend the afternoon with your mom so I thought I would get a head start on things,' he said.

'What do you really want?'

For a moment he feigned innocence, but then gave it up when he saw the steely look in my eye.

'I need a night off so I can go out with Mandi,' he confessed.

'It's a deal.'

'I haven't even told you when yet,' he said.

'It's OK, I think I can survive one night without you here. You might have to leave me some notes on what I'm supposed to do.' I laughed. 'So what have you got done so far?'

'I worked out the lobby set-up. We have to take all our merchandise down and sell theirs during the day, and also set up a donation table and a display board. All of which will have to be taken down and our stuff set back up for the evening. I don't think it's going to be too bad, though – only about a half-hour of staff time once we get the hang of it. The thing that the competition people are most worried about is that our staff enforce their rules. They really want to be strict on the no cameras or recording devices . . .'

'That's nothing new.' I took my coat off, poured myself a coffee, and settled into one of the chairs.

'They want the adjudicators to have five empty rows between them and the rest of the audience so no one can distract them.'

'Or read the adjudication sheets over their shoulders? Still easy, we'll just put up some ropes and reserved signs. What else?'

'Strict closed-door policies during performances. Admittance to the auditorium only during the breaks. Also, no one backstage without a pass.'

'That's going to be harder to control here than at the Concert Hall.'

'I think we can just put an extra usher on house-right, by the backstage door, rather than having the regular usher try to control it.'

'Good thought,' I agreed. 'Anything else?'

'No, everything else seems pretty standard. I think all we have to do is make sure the staff know the rules and you can handle everything else.' He smiled at me. 'That is, after all, why you make the big bucks.'

'So you think this is going to be easy?' I asked.

'No, I think it *sounds* easy, but I think we are going to be dead by the time it's all over.' He shook his head. 'These are going to be long days.'

'No worse than any other festival,' I said. 'Just a little more prestigious. And probably a little more press too, but we're getting used to that! How are the staff sign-up sheets looking?'

'They are filling up nicely. Everyone wants to work the piano competition.'

'Why?' I asked. 'The hours are long, and the competition itself is going to be fairly boring.'

'For the celebrities, Kate. You haven't read the literature yet, have you?'

'No,' I admitted.

'If you had, you would know who is supposed to be here. Even you might get a little excited about some of them.'

'I doubt it. Seen one, seen them all.' I checked the clock and noticed we still had a bit of time before the ushers were due to arrive. 'Would you mind getting set up for tonight, if I sneak out of here for about a half-hour?'

'Didn't you just sneak in?'

'Graham,' I warned, 'didn't I just give you a night off?'

'Fine, fine. What's up?'

'It's a surprise,' I said. 'But I promise it's a good reason. All you have to do is the time sheets and count out the floats for the sales tables. I'll do last night's deposits later, OK?'

'Not a problem. See you later.' He waved at me, shooing me out of my office.

'Thanks, Graham,' I called over my shoulder as I let myself into the fire escape that leads to the street.

Calgary has been having a beautiful, warm and late autumn, something we don't always get, with warm days and long, cool evenings. The leaves were just beginning to turn and the colours of the trees were stunning. It was still warm enough outside that I didn't have to worry about carrying a jacket yet.

I wandered down the street, past Grounds Zero, waving at Gus through the window, and on down the block. I was pretty sure that by the time I walked back Gus would know where I had gone, whom I had talked to and what I was going to have for dinner. I shook my head as I pushed through the revolving door into the Palliser mall below the Calgary Tower. I don't know how Gus does it, but he really does seem to know everything about everyone.

I walked into the medical clinic in the mall, signed myself in and was led, almost immediately, into an examination room. The sign on the desk said that Dr Brock Benson was on duty and I could hardly wait to see him. Family doctors are more valuable than gold in this city. If you don't have one, you can spend years looking for one who will take you, and I have just never had the time to make that kind of a commitment. Besides, until just recently I was very healthy and not at all accident-prone. I have used this clinic several times, and Dr Benson is the reason I keep coming back. I don't know if he is a good doctor, but I do know he's great to look at while he treats you. He has jet-black eyes, long curly black hair that hangs to his very broad shoulders, and the greatest stomach muscles I have ever seen. Well, I haven't really *seen* them, just felt them once as he leaned against me while he peered into my ear.

The door to the exam room opened and Dr Benson appeared, dressed in black pants and shirt, black tie and his white lab coat. Luckily I was sitting on the table because I felt my knees quiver.

'Hi, Kate, I haven't seen you for a while,' he said as he rolled a stool over and sat in front of me. 'What's new with you?'

'A few stitches, a few bruises, and this,' I said as I held my cast up.

He took my arm and knocked on the cast. 'This looks well worn. How long have you had it on?'

'Too long. Please set me free, Brock, I have a really busy week and I just can't stand it a minute longer.'

'What did you do to it?' He opened my chart and made some notes.

'I broke it.' I smiled at him, trying to be charming.

'Funny, funny.' He smiled back at me. 'But I'm not taking it off unless you tell me all about it.'

'OK, you win,' I said. 'Did you read about the murder at the theatre last month?' I asked. He nodded, so I continued my story. 'Well, I got a little too close to the murderer and he pushed me around a bit. I got a bump on my head, some stitches on my lip and the busted arm.'

'Where did you get this put on?'

'At the Foothills Hospital emergency department.'

'And are you trying to get it off early or is it really time?'

'It's really time,' I lied, but only a little. 'Please?'

'What did you break? Do you remember what they told you?'

'A bone with a Latin name,' I said.

'OK, I'll take it off,' he finally agreed. 'But I'm walking you over to X-ray as soon as the cast is off, and if it isn't healed, I'm putting another one right back on. Agreed?'

'Fine.'

'Who took the stitches out of your lip?' he asked, peering at my face with that special scrutiny that only a doctor can muster.

'You really don't want to know,' I said.

'You're probably right. OK, hop down and follow me to the plaster room.'

'The plaster room?' I asked.

'Casts are a messy business so we keep all the casting materials in one room. Less mess to clean up at the end of the day,' he explained.

We walked down the hall and he opened the door to another treatment room.

'Sit on the stool and put your arm up on the table,' he instructed as he dug through the drawers on the other side of the room. I noticed a pair of rubber wellingtons in the corner but I didn't have the nerve to ask about them. He followed my gaze and smiled. 'It's for when I'm putting on a plaster cast. I've ruined too many nice pairs of shoes with the plaster dripping.'

I laughed at the thought of trying to take him seriously if he was wearing those.

'This isn't going to hurt,' he said, approaching me with what looked like a circular saw.

'I think I just changed my mind,' I said, pulling my arm back.

'Is this your first cast?' he asked.

'Yes.'

'Well, calm down. It looks like a saw but it just vibrates and separates the plaster. Pretty neat little gizmo. The worst you'll feel is a little heat. If it gets too hot, just let me know and we'll stop for a second while it cools down.'

I hesitantly put my arm back up on the table. He was right. The cast split open, right down the middle, and he gently slipped my arm out.

'How's it feel?' he asked.

'Weird,' was all I could manage as the nerve ends all tingled with their first exposure to fresh air in weeks.

'It will for a while. This poor arm has been sensory deprived and everything will seem strange at first. I want you to remember to take it very easy for the first few days. The muscles are going to be weak and you could easily overdo it. I'm also going to refer you to physiotherapy starting Friday.'

'I don't have time, Brock. How about in a couple of weeks?'

'How about I put a cast back on until you do have time?' he countered.

'OK, I'll do it on my lunch break or something. So, is that it?'

'Nope, we're going to go take a picture now.'

True to his word, he walked me over to the radiology office and waited around while the X-rays were developed. He then pronounced me cured and led me back into his office, where he scribbled some notes on a prescription pad.

'This is for physio. I wrote the address and phone number of the clinic at the bottom and I'm going to check up on you to make sure you've got an appointment.'

'Can I go now?' I asked, anxious to get back to the theatre.

'No, one last thing. Let me put some lotion on it.'

'It does look pretty disgusting,' I said, looking at the dry, cracked skin. 'Is this going to last long?'

'No, just put lots of lotion on it.' He led me over to the sink and washed my arm gently, patted it dry, and rubbed some lotion on it.

'Do you treat all your patients this well?' I asked.

'No, only the loud-mouth pushy ones. I figure they need a little extra tender loving care.'

'I don't know why I keep coming back here,' I said. 'There are plenty of other doctors in this city.'

'But none who are taking new patients.' He laughed. 'And none who would treat you as well as I do. Now get out of here. And take it easy on that arm.'

I wandered back down the street towards my theatre, feeling so much better already. I stopped in at Grounds Zero, bought two mochaccinos from Gus's part-time waitress and took them through the stage door. I stood by one of the security doors and waited for Nick to buzz me through.

'You're going the wrong way, Kate,' he called to me through the window.

'I'm going to see Cam,' I told him. 'Now buzz me through and get on your radio and tell him I'm on my way down, please.'

The door buzzed and I pulled it open, trying to balance the two take-out cups in my newly freed hand. Cam's office, or at least his desk, is in the lowest basement level of the Plex. I can get down two flights with my common area keys, but the lowest sections are strictly off-limits without an escort. That is where all the heating and air-conditioning systems are located, as well as the equipment storage. As I came down the stairs, Cam was waiting by the door to the last level I could access.

'What are you doing here?' he asked, relieving me of one of the coffee cups.

'I missed you and wanted a cigarette,' I said.

'I've noticed you don't smoke around your mother.'

'What can I say, I'm a wimp,' I admitted. 'If she doesn't see me smoking, we can both pretend I don't actually do it and she doesn't have to lecture me about it. It's the way I handle a lot of things with my mother.'

He let me through the door and we went down the last flight of stairs. His desk was a disaster area. I don't know how Cam can be so clean and organized at home and have such a messy desk. He sat down on the chair beside the desk and pulled another beside it for me. I ignored it and sat on his lap, giving him one of my best kisses.

'What was that for?' he asked. 'Not that I'm complaining.'

'I missed you and I feel like celebrating.' I held my arm up for his inspection. 'Look.'

'When did you get your cast off?'

'Just now. Graham had everything under control at the office, so I slipped over and saw Dr Brock Benson.'

'Oh, so you got your cast off and your turn-on for the day?' he asked. 'Is that what that kiss was about?'

'No.' I stayed on his lap but leaned over and grabbed my coffee cup. 'It was because I never got to do that this morning and I missed it.'

'So shouldn't you be at work now?' he asked.

'Yes, but I'm going to sit and finish my coffee with you first.'

He put his arm around my waist. 'Are you going to stay sitting on my lap?'

'I might. Why, are you uncomfortable?'

'No, but I might not let you go back to work. I know some very quiet and secluded places around here that only I can get into.'

'No way. We swore that we would never have sex in this building. Everyone who has ever tried has got caught.'

'How about we go parking on the way home?' he asked.

'Get those hormones under control. My mother is going to be here for two or three weeks; you'd better get used to this deprivation. Remember, our bedroom doesn't have a door or even a wall.'

'All right, I'll change the subject. How's your arm feel?'

'Not bad.' I stretched it out and moved my fingers around a bit. 'I like being able to use it again.' I ran my fingers through his hair. 'It seems to work OK,' I added.

'I can hardly wait to see what else it can do.' He laughed, wiggling his eyebrows at me.

'You are irascible.' I swatted his head and stood up. 'But I love you anyway.'

'I love you too.' He stood up with me. 'Are you leaving me now?'

'I have a feeling that if I don't leave now I'll end up naked.'

'That's not such a bad thing,' he said.

'But it's really bad timing.' I gave him another good kiss. 'That one was so you'll miss me this evening.'

'It's working,' he said. 'I'll come up to the theatre when I'm done here.'

'I'll have a beer waiting for you,' I promised. 'Going to walk me upstairs?'

'Sure. I can stop in at your office and check the temperature.'

'Why?' I asked.

'So I have an excuse to walk you up there. You were complaining about the heat, weren't you?'

'Last winter,' I said.

'Well then, it's about time I got around to checking it out. Let's go.'

Cam dropped me off at my office and headed out to make his rounds. Graham had everything ready and was dressed in his black pants, white shirt, black bow tie and black cardigan. The consummate usher. I pulled my long black skirt off the rack where I kept my theatre clothes, added a cream silk shirt and a hand-woven vest. I changed in the washroom outside my office, fixing my make-up and pulling my hair up into a loose knot on top of my head. I came back into the office, dumped my jeans on to a pile under my desk and started searching for shoes.

'Have you seen my black pumps?' I asked Graham, who was sitting in the window studying a script.

'Yes, Kate, I borrowed them last week to wear with my new black dress.'

'A simple no would suffice,' I said, finding them in my desk drawer. 'What are you reading?'

'A script. I have an audition for *Jack and the Beanstalk*.'

'Another theatre classic,' I joked. 'Want me to run lines with you?'

'Maybe later,' he said. 'This is just my first read-through.'

'This will be your second gig with the kids' theatre, right?'

'I haven't got it yet,' he protested, thinking I was bringing bad luck by saying it before it was true.

'Of course you'll get it. They don't get many people of your calibre who will work for free.'

'I would prefer it if you would call it volunteer work,' he said. 'It makes it sound more noble.'

I glanced at the clock; an hour to go. The ushers should

start arriving in about half an hour. The stage crew should be arriving about the same time. 'Have you done a walk-through yet?'

'Nope.' He didn't look up from his script. 'Want me to do it now?'

'No, you keep reading. I'll go,' I said as I slid on my shoes.

'Thanks,' he called down the hall after me.

I wandered through the first balcony, straightening the chairs in the box seats, checking for litter, and generally making sure everything was in good shape. I ran up to the second balcony and finished up there before going down to the orchestra level. I wandered through all the rows in the dimly lit theatre, but my attention was on the rehearsal piano sitting on the stage, which they hadn't moved since this morning's rehearsal. I hadn't played seriously in a very long time and I was suddenly anxious to see if my arm still worked. Normally, despite all my protests to Stephan, I try to play every day when no one is around and I'm very proud of how well I can still perform. Usually I only play in the privacy of my own home, as I've become very private about my music over the years. But I knew it would be at least two weeks before I was alone at home, and I really wanted to see what kind of shape my arm was in.

I checked around the theatre, trying to determine if I really was alone. I took the stairs down to the orchestra level, tiptoed up on to the stage and quietly pulled the bench out. I sat down and listened again, in case anyone had come in. I didn't hear a sound. I put my hands on the keys, played a chord, and then pulled back. I still seemed to be alone.

My fingers were stiff and my arm felt weak, but it remembered what to do. I lost myself in some obscure little classic that I remembered from years ago. It felt wonderful to play with two working hands, and I admit I got a bit of a thrill playing on a stage again. It had been a long time since I had been on a stage sitting behind a piano.

I finished the piece and rubbed the aching muscles in my right arm, when I heard clapping coming from stage-right. I stood up and looked across the stage, trying to see who had sneaked up on me. I saw Scott walking across the stage towards me.

'When did you get here?' I asked, embarrassed that anyone had heard me.

'Just after you sat down. I didn't say anything because I wanted to wait and hear what you were going to do. I have to admit, I was expecting something more like Chopsticks.'

'I'm sorry, I know I shouldn't be on the stage.' I quickly got up from the piano and pushed the bench back into position.

'Don't apologize,' he said. 'I had no idea you could play like that.'

'I had been hoping to keep it my little secret,' I said. 'I don't suppose it could stay *our* little secret?'

'Of course it can,' he assured me. 'But why the big secret? It's not like you're bad.'

'I just like to keep my music private,' I tried to explain. 'It's one of those long stories that I promise to tell you over several beers one night, OK?'

'OK,' he agreed. 'Now get off my stage so I can clear the piano. Unless you want to help me?'

'I think I'll pass on that one,' I said, taking the stairs off the edge of the stage and getting back to my side of the theatre. 'I'll see you later.'

Scott pushed the piano into the wings. I walked up the stairs towards the doors into the lobby and was surprised to see Stephan standing in the corner by the door, hiding in the shadows.

'You startled me,' I said, growing a little tired of finding men hiding in the shadows. 'What are you doing here?'

'I came to see you. Graham told me you were in the auditorium so I came to look for you. What a surprise to see you sitting on the stage at a piano. Especially after all that protesting you did about how your music was now a private thing only for you.'

'I just got my cast off,' I explained. 'I wanted to test my arm out.'

'I don't believe you,' he said. 'I think you want to be on the stage, whether you admit it to yourself or not.'

I was tired of the conversation and tried to push past him into the lobby, but Stephan grabbed me around the waist and pulled me back to him, holding me very close.

'Stephan, what are you doing?' I asked, putting my hands on his chest and trying to push away.

'Katherine, we could be such a good team, both musically and otherwise. Why won't you just admit that?'

'Stephan, you and I were an item a very long time ago. Right now I am very happy with Cam and I have no desire to rekindle an old relationship. Especially a bad relationship. You and I can be friends and we can work together, but that's it.'

'I understand,' he said but didn't let me go.

'Stephan, you've got a wife, a daughter – why can't you just be happy with that?'

'Because I want you,' he said. 'You know how I've always felt about you.'

'Well, you had me and you lost me,' I said quietly. 'End of story. Please, let me go.'

'May I at least hope you might change your mind?' Stephan asked.

'I can live with that,' I said as he finally released me and I stepped a safe distance away, my heart pounding in my chest.

'You still play beautifully,' he said.

'Thank you. I've got to get back to work. Can we discuss all this later?'

'Of course,' he agreed, stepping aside so I could get through the door. I pushed my way past him into the lobby and ran into Graham, who was standing just on the other side the door.

'What are you doing down here?' I asked.

'I heard what was going on over the speaker in your office,' he said. 'I was just coming down to make sure you were OK.'

I ruffled his hair. 'Thanks.'

'I mean, I know you can handle yourself,' he said. 'But I just wanted to make sure.'

'I appreciate it,' I said. 'Even if you are overprotective.'

'You play great,' he said, referring to my impromptu concert, which he must also have overheard. 'Why the big secret about it?'

'Doesn't matter,' I said. 'It doesn't seem to be much of a secret anymore.'

The evening went smoothly. I managed to get all my scheduling done for the first week of the competition, and Cam was finished his shift and in my office by ten. The show got out at eleven and we had the lobby cleared by eleven fifteen, which was some sort of theatre record, at least in my world.

Cam and I walked arm in arm to his car and he opened the door for me. I slid in, leaning over to unlock his door. Cam pulled the key out of his pocket and put it into the ignition. I reached over and put my hand on his, stopping him from starting the car.

'What's wrong?' he asked, turning toward me.

'I was just thinking how much I wish we were still away at the beach.'

'We've only been back a couple of days,' he said.

'I know, but you and I are supposed to be getting used to having each other around. This is supposed to be our honeymoon period – or at least our adjustment period – and I just wish we were alone.'

'We'll be alone soon,' he said. 'We had lots of time together last month.'

'Doesn't count,' I said. 'We had police sitting outside the apartment door the whole time. You know, I don't think we would have ever moved in together so quickly if we hadn't been forced into it.'

'Are you having regrets?' he asked.

'No, none at all. I'm surprised how much I love having you there. But now I'm greedy and I want you totally to myself all the time.'

He put his arm around me and pulled me close to him. 'Did you have a bad night?'

'No, actually it was a pretty good night. It's just all these people who want my time right now – Mom, Stephan, the theatre, the piano competition . . . I feel like I'm barely going to see you.'

'I'll hang around the theatre with you,' he promised.

'Where do you think we'll be in ten years?' I asked.

'Wow, where did that come from?'

'I don't know. I just feel this weird romantic feminine thing coming out of me that I never knew I had.'

'All right, I'll play the game. Ten years from now I'll be old and fat and you'll be young and gorgeous. We'll have thirteen kids running around the loft and a dog named Spot.'

'Thirteen kids in that tiny apartment? It's going to be pretty crowded.'

'Well, I'll build an addition or something,' he said. 'Where do you think we'll be in ten years?'

'Alone and in bed together,' I said. 'At least that's what I'm hoping for.'

'I think we have to work out some sort of a compromise here.' But he leaned over and kissed me anyway.

'Break it up in there!'

I jumped as someone pounded on the window and yelled at us. A flashlight beam pointed in from the other side. Trevor, Scott and Dwayne surrounded the car, peering in through the windows. I leaned over and rolled down my window.

'You're all just jealous,' I said.

'Get a room,' Scott shouted back.

Cam started up the car and I leaned out the window as he pulled out.

'We have a room, it's just that there are people sharing it with us right now.'

Cam honked the horn and waved as we pulled out on to the street.

'I told you we're never alone,' I said.

He laughed. 'Next time we go parking, we'll do it far away from this building.'

'I don't know; I'm convinced they'll find us wherever we go. Everyone else does.'

We finally gave up trying to be alone or intimate and drove home. I suddenly felt wide awake, getting my second wind as I always do at that time of night, and I realized I was starving as the elevator door opened and a wonderful aroma drifted toward me from one of the apartments.

'Who's cooking at this time of night?' I asked Cam.

'Usually it's us.'

'I'm starved. Maybe we should just go out and get something now. Cooking is out because Mom and Larry are probably asleep.'

'I really don't feel like going out, Katie,' Cam said. 'I'm tired and dirty and would like a shower. Let's just grab some cheese and crackers or something.'

'Or go introduce ourselves to whichever neighbours are making those wonderful smells.'

'You know what?' he asked as we got closer to our door.

'What?'

'I think those smells are coming from our place.'

'Are you sure?'

He slipped the key in the lock, turned it and threw the door open. 'I'm positive.'

I hurried in and peeked around the corner to find Mom and Larry both at the stove.

'Mom?'

'Kate, you're home,' Mom beamed, waving a wooden spoon around. 'What do you think?'

'What have you done?' I asked. Cam had already slipped off his jacket and was checking into all the pots on the stove.

'They have cooked us a feast,' Cam explained, dipping a spoon into a pot of something and tasting it.

'Yes we have,' Mom agreed.

'Mom, you're never awake when I get home.'

'I thought I best stay up if I ever wanted to see you this trip.' She laughed. 'Besides, Larry is such a good cook, I wanted to show him off. You're not the only one with a culinary wizard in your kitchen.'

I took off my coat and slipped it over the back of a chair. Cam scowled at me, picked it up and hung it in the closet.

'Well, this is a wonderful surprise, because I just happen to be starving. Let's eat.'

'Don't you even want to know what it is?' Larry asked.

'It's Thai,' I said, sniffing the air. 'You can't fool me; I can smell lemon grass at a hundred yards.'

'Good nose.' Larry smiled, ladling some soup into my bowl.

'It got that way from sticking it into everyone else's business,' Cam felt the need to point out.

We all had soup in front of us, and Larry brought out some vegetable rolls and dipping sauce and joined us at the table.

I took a mouthful of soup and thought I'd died and gone to heaven. 'Between you and Cam, I'm planning on eating very well this week.'

'Well, Katherine, there is something I should probably tell you,' Mom said.

'I hate it when you call me Katherine. It's always something bad.'

'It's not bad. It's just that some friends of ours called and they want to meet us in Banff for the week. They've already rented a condo, so we couldn't say no.' Mom smiled weakly.

'But we were just all getting to know each other.' I felt myself going into a whine, something Mom tended to bring out in me.

'Katherine, you have a very busy week ahead of you. We are just going to be in the way here. By the time we get back next week, things will be settled and you'll be organized and we'll have a much nicer visit.'

'You're right, Mom.'

'I'm what?' she asked.

'You're right.'

'I don't believe I've ever heard you say that before.'

'A sign of maturity, maybe?' I suggested.

'I never give up hope that eventually you'll grow up.' She smiled at me. 'So, we're going to leave tomorrow morning and we'll be back sometime next Monday.'

'OK. But, most importantly, are you going to leave us the leftovers?' I asked.

'Of course,' Larry put in.

'Not so fast—' Mom tried to cut him off.

'I think it's the least we could do to thank them for their hospitality,' he explained.

'We've only been here one day and she hasn't been very hospitable.' Mom turned to me. 'We'll leave you half the leftovers.'

'Cut it out, you two,' Cam jumped in. 'There's something neither of you thought of.'

We both turned expectantly to him.

'There aren't going to be any leftovers.'

Thursday October 23

The really nice thing about staying up until three in the morning talking to your mother is that you don't have to give her any excuses for sleeping in the next day. And she didn't have to give me any either. Not one of the four of us uttered a sound before two o'clock the next afternoon, and that was only when Cam and Larry snuck out for a run. Mom and I both crawled even further under the covers and didn't utter a peep until they came back. They seemed to feel refreshed, and decided it was time for all of us to be up and at 'em. I didn't argue too much because I did have to be at work in a couple of hours. And that couple of hours was up by the time I had waited for my turn in the shower.

Cam had the day off and he offered to give our guests a tour of the city. I think Larry cared less about seeing Calgary than he did about spending the afternoon driving around in the Fish. Cam asked him if he wanted to drive and Larry's face lit up. Mom looked a little bored by the whole car thing. My bet was she'd ask to be let off at the first shopping mall they passed. But at least I got a ride to work out of the deal. And because it was afternoon, Grounds Zero was open and I could start working on my daily caffeine intake.

So after all that I was actually a few minutes early and I decided to sit and visit with Gus for a few minutes. Gus is a very entertaining man; I love to hear him talking about his life. He had started working on the oil rigs as a young man, eventually moving into an administrative position and then a more executive position with the oil company, back in the days when you could work your way up without a college education and when you stayed with one company for your entire working life. When that company had offered an early retirement package, Gus had opened Grounds Zero. He was wise enough to know he wasn't ready for retirement yet. He loves people, he loves to be involved in everyone's business and he loves coffee. Plus, his grandkids lived a long way away, so we've become surrogates, people he can nag and cajole and watch out for. Mostly I think his wife is happiest of all that Gus isn't staying at home full-time, too.

'Afternoon, Kate,' he greeted me from behind the counter.

'Good afternoon to you, Gus. What's new today?' I asked as I slid on to one of the stools at the counter.

'Kate, I have just the thing for you. A mochaccino brownie.'

'You're selling mochaccino brownies now?' I asked, my mouth watering like Pavlov's dog at the mention of chocolate and coffee.

'Yes. My wife has been taking some baking classes and this is her latest creation.'

'It's bad enough that you're totally responsible for my caffeine addiction, but now you're going to be responsible for my weight gain too,' I said, reaching across the counter for a napkin in anticipation of the treat.

'You could just say no,' he pointed out.

'Not to brownies.' I lifted the lid off the cake dish and helped myself to one. 'I'll need a plate please. And a cappuccino.'

'Coming up.' He busied himself, grinding my beans fresh. It was nice to be his favourite customer. 'So, I hear the Symphony has a new conductor.'

'You're about as subtle as a ton of bricks, Gus. You're just dying to know what's going on, just like everyone else in this building.' I took a big bite of brownie so I wouldn't have to answer anything else right away.

'Kate, I'm way ahead of you.' He smiled. 'I know what's going on. I just wanted to know how you felt about it.'

'You're not catching me this time,' I said, taking a swallow of coffee to wash down the last of the brownie, wondering how I was going to avoid ordering one of these every day. 'I know that's how you get your information. You pretend you know everything, I start talking about it, and you soak it all up like a sponge.'

'Kate, if I had to wait for you to start talking to get anything—'

'Then you tell me, Gus. Tell me about the Maestro.'

He set my fresh coffee down in front of me and pulled a stool up for himself. 'Kate, I'm surprised at you. You don't trust me.' He snickered.

'You're right,' I agreed.

'And you're going to make me prove myself? After all we've been through together?'

'That's right. And guilt will not work on me,' I told him. 'See, you really don't know, do you?'

Gus smiled and took a sip of his coffee. 'I'm afraid you've got me.'

'Hah! I was right.' I smiled triumphantly, picking at the crumbs of brownie on my plate.

'All I know is that they hired this guy, Stephan Bouchard, as the new conductor. He's from France originally. But this isn't his first time in Calgary. He was a visiting professor at the university about ten or so years ago. I believe he worked with a bright young piano student named Katherine Carpenter. I also believe that she fell in love with him. Nasty thing, that, because he forgot to tell her he was married with a child. I think he taught there for about two years and then left. Took a job with some European orchestra and his career has been on the rise since then. His wife has also become famous. She's a lawyer, I think. Done some precedent-setting work with adoption, children's rights, that sort of thing, mostly in Third World countries where things like that are still a really big issue. Their daughter, Nicole, who was originally taught by you, is now a budding young pianist.' Gus paused and looked at me as he took a sip of coffee, his eyes twinkling mischievously. 'Now what makes this so interesting is that they are all back here now. He with the Symphony, the daughter to compete in the festival, the mother to cheer them on – and you. I also believe he has been around to see you several times and that Cam is not very comfortable about this whole situation. And lastly, I believe that you're a much better piano player than you've ever let on.'

'Is that everything?' I asked.

'No, I believe your mom, who hates Stephan for what he did to you, is going to Banff for a few days, even though she's really worried about leaving you alone here with him. Tell her the Rocky Heights Condos are nice but she really should have stayed at the Alpine Chalets. Far superior.'

I shook my head. 'You are truly amazing.'

'Yes, I am.' He chuckled, taking another sip of his coffee.

'How do you know this stuff?'

'If I told you, it wouldn't be a secret anymore, would it?'

'So can you predict the future, too? Can you tell me if Cam and I will live happily ever after with the Maestro Stephan Bouchard now living in Calgary?'

'That's something only you can answer,' he told me. 'Are you interested in Stephan – romantically, I mean?'

'Is that one of those polite euphemisms for asking me if I want to have an affair with him?' I asked.

'I'm way too much of a gentleman to ask that.'

'No, Gus, I'm not interested in him romantically. I was very young when I was involved with Stephan. All I saw was the package, the excitement. I didn't see the warts, such as the wife or daughter, for example. I'm much older and wiser now and I would never get involved with him again.'

'I'm glad to hear that. I think there's a lot more going on with that family than we know about.'

'What do you mean?' I asked.

'Just a feeling I have. But I'm working on it. If I find anything out, I'll let you know.'

I finished my coffee and handed the cup across the counter to him. 'Can I have a refill for the road?'

'Same thing?' he asked.

'Same thing. And another brownie. Make sure you give my compliments to the chef.'

'How do you sleep at night with all the caffeine in your system?' he asked, packaging everything up for me, eyes twinkling again.

I wandered slowly down the street and let myself into the front door of the theatre. I had been really good about signing in at the security desk recently, but the day was warm and sunny and I wanted to enjoy every last moment of it that I could. Plus, I could only follow the rules for so long; it's one of my failings. I climbed the stairs slowly to my office and heard singing. Graham was here already. I wandered into the office and plopped on to one of the chairs across from the desk.

'Morning, boss.'

'It's afternoon, Graham.'

'Well, when you work night and day, mornings and afternoons all sort of melt together.'

'We've barely begun. Just wait until the week progresses.'

'I'm not worried. I'm young. I can go days without sleep.'

'Don't be so cocky, Graham. You're going to age just like the rest of us.'

'But I have years to go before I have to worry about that. Whereas, you—'

'I believe you have a birthday coming up soon,' I said, cutting him off. 'Aren't you feeling any signs of your approaching mortality?'

'Kate, you can try all you want to depress me, but I'm only going to be nineteen, I'm dating a student nurse, and I have a good possibility of getting sex on a regular basis in the near future. Nothing you say could bring me down.'

'I just can't stand seeing someone happier than I am.' I sighed.

'So I've noticed.'

'Now tell me why you're here so early,' I said, taking the lid off my coffee and burning my tongue on the first sip. The heat was starting to seep through the Styrofoam and burn my fingers. I set the cup on the desk and decided I should let it cool awhile.

'I'm here to get things organized,' Graham explained.

'I know you don't believe it, but I *am* capable of organization. It's just that I like my desk to look this way.'

'That wasn't an insult,' he said. 'I just thought I'd try and help out a bit more. Your mom's in town and all these other things are happening in your life. I thought you'd appreciate not having to come in so early.'

'Speaking of that, have you seen Stephan today?' A part of me was hoping he had been here looking for me, while the sane part of me hoped no one had seen him.

'The Maestro left a note in your mail box,' Graham said as he picked up a piece of lavender-shaded notepaper and handed it to me. 'The paper is scented. I just thought I'd point that out to you.'

'You smelled it, but did you read it?' I asked.

'Yes. It says he is spending the day with his family but he will see you tomorrow.'

'Thank God.' I sighed, glad I didn't have to see him but happy he had been looking for me. I must be truly insane. 'One less thing to worry about today.'

'Is he bothering you?' Graham asked, concerned.

'Having him in town is bothering me. All sorts of old thoughts and feelings are being stirred around. I just need some time to get used to it all.'

'He's been coming around to see you a lot since he got here.'

'Graham, there is nothing going on,' I insisted.

'That's not what I said,' he protested.

'But it's what you meant. Now change the subject.'

'Nothing else I really want to talk about.' He smiled. 'Certainly nothing as interesting.'

'Figures.' I picked my coffee up and took another sip now that it was cooler. 'It's too quiet here today.'

'I thought you'd enjoy a little peace and quiet for a change.'

'It's never this quiet. It's like the calm just before the storm. It makes me nervous when it's like this.'

'You are paranoid,' Graham said, exasperated, shaking his head.

I stood up. 'I'm going to go check the theatre. I'll be back in a few minutes.'

I always like to check the theatre when I come in. I checked the bars for the inventory, the carpets to make sure the cleaners hadn't missed anything, and then I went inside, to the auditorium. I straightened the seats in the boxes, walked up and down the aisles to check for broken seats, stray programs – once I had even found a diamond earring. I usually get to talk to the backstage guys, sometimes the actors, and it just starts my night off right, knowing that everything is in its place and ready. But tonight it was even quiet in here. There was no one on stage, no music, and the lights were very dim. I was starting to feel very uncomfortable. Maybe Graham was right and I was getting paranoid. But the theatre was never quiet; there were always people around, exciting things happening, and noise everywhere.

I shook my head, trying to physically shake my feelings of unrest away, and wandered up to the balconies. When I found that everything was up to my usual standards, I headed back into my office and decided to change. Graham was still humming quietly, bent over the pile of schedules laid out on my desk. I grabbed a dress from the hook, a pair of pantyhose from my desk drawer and changed quickly. When I came back into the office, a few ushers had arrived and were chatting quietly.

I popped a CD into my office stereo and cranked up the volume. I couldn't stand the quiet any longer and wanted to get everyone going, inject a little energy into the room. But no sound came out; the batteries were dead.

The audience had been small and quiet – the keyword of my night – but the show went off without a hitch. I changed and was out and home early. Mom and Larry were already asleep, so Cam and I tiptoed upstairs and climbed into bed. Cam was asleep in minutes but it was way too early for me, even though I knew the alarm was going to go off really early the next morning. I tossed and turned and kept thinking about the quiet and the calm that always came before the storm. A couple of months ago, today would have seemed like a perfectly normal day. I guess that in the last couple of weeks I had just gotten used to having murder and mayhem happening all around me. Graham was right; I was getting paranoid. But it didn't help to know that; I still tossed and turned for another couple of hours worrying about the state of my mental health as well as the state of my theatre.

Friday October 24

The alarm went off and I jumped up, throwing myself over Cam to shut it off before it woke everyone in the house. Cam groaned and pushed me off him, cracking open one eye to look at the clock.

'It's five o'clock, Katie,' Cam said. 'Why do you want to be up this early?'

'It's the first day of the competition, Cam,' I whispered. 'Remember, my B.F.D.?'

'Your what?' he mumbled sleepily, trying to wrap me in his arms and pull the covers back over us, something that usually worked and kept me in bed for another hour or so.

'My big fucking deal!' I said, fighting to get away from him, quietly though.

'Oh, that,' he mumbled.

'I thought you were supposed to be a morning person,' I said as I crawled over him and pulled up the blinds. It was barely light out.

'I am a morning person,' Cam said as he pulled a pillow over his face. 'But this isn't morning. This is the end of the night. Morning won't be for another hour or so.'

'Well, I'll set the alarm for you and see you later.' I lifted the pillow and kissed him.

He pulled the pillow back over his face as I headed down to shower. I was dressed, out the door and, after a brisk walk in the chilly early-morning air, I was at the Plex by six. I got a few looks with my early appearance, but ignored them all and headed for my office. We didn't have to open until nine, and nothing would begin onstage until ten, but I wanted to make sure everything was perfect. This really was a B.F.D. for our theatre and I felt an enormous responsibility on my shoulders. Today, absolutely everything had to be in place and I wanted to make sure it was.

I got the coffee started before I did anything else. I did a quick preliminary inspection of the theatre while it brewed and found everything pretty much OK. I would do another more thorough inspection after a couple of cups of coffee, but for now I knew there wasn't anything big to deal with. Back in my office, I pulled out a bunch of time sheets and sat down with the checklist that I had prepared for this morning. I heard the door at the end of the corridor open and turned to find Graham bouncing down the hallway.

'What on earth are you doing here at six thirty in the morning?' I asked him.

'I could ask you the same thing,' he said, sitting down across from me and pulling an orange juice out of his backpack.

'I was here at six because I just wanted to make sure everything was ready,' I said.

'Face it, Kate, you're every bit as excited about this as I am. I bet you didn't even hit your snooze button once this morning.'

'OK, I admit it,' I said.

'Great. So are we just going to sit here or should we get started?'

'Let's get started,' I said, picking up my list and a pen. 'Let's start at the top and work our way down.'

I had my coffee while we went over our checklist. Then Graham and I spent an hour and a half checking every nook and cranny of the theatre, from the second balcony all the way down to the coat check. I was satisfied that everything was in place and we were ready for the competition to begin. The chairs were straight in the boxes, there were no errant programs littering the floors, all the lights were working, no doors were jammed and all the reserved signs and special seating arrangements were in place. Graham changed from his jeans into his uniform and I decided to do the same. I grabbed my black pants and jacket and a yellow tank top. I always felt very professional in this outfit, and I needed all the extra confidence I could get today. The ushers had started wandering in early as well. I guess the excitement was universal, at least in this building. We drank a pot of coffee and went over rules and assignments for the day. At nine o'clock I sent them to their positions and called security to unlock the doors. I felt the butterflies in my stomach, knowing there was no turning back now. This is what I love about my job.

I made my way down into the main lobby, slightly surprised to see so many people there. I noticed Stephan standing by the main bar, and he waved at me. I watched him pull away from the people he was standing with and make his way across the lobby towards me. I took a deep breath, steeling myself for our first encounter in a few days.

'You look lovely, Katie,' he said. 'Are you all ready for the circus?'

'Pretty much.' I smiled. 'Stephan, I wonder if you could you do me a big favour?'

'Anything,' he said.

'Could you please stop calling me Katie?'

'I understand.' He smiled, slightly condescendingly. 'Your blue-collar man is jealous? I'll try my best, I promise. Now, I want you to come backstage with me. Nicole is here. I've told her you work at the theatre and she wants to say hello.'

'Not before the big introduction,' I protested. 'She must have enough on her mind right now.' But he took my hand and started pulling me towards the house-right doors that lead backstage.

'She is fine,' he insisted. 'That child of mine is amazing; she never suffers from pre-show nervousness. Please, just come and say hello.'

'All right,' I agreed, following him, not that I had much choice without making a great big scene.

We made our way backstage, past all the competitors running in and out of the dressing rooms. Stephan deposited me in the green room and ran downstairs to get his daughter. The table was piled high with croissants and muffins, the counter was covered with juices, and I could smell a much better blend of coffee brewing than we normally use. Trevor and Scott were on the couch, dressed in their blacks, munching down as much food as they could get into their mouths. Technicians and free food are a dangerous combination.

'Hi, guys,' I said, grabbing a croissant for myself. 'Where's Dwayne?'

'He's hanging some lights,' Scott said. 'Last-minute changes.'

'You having fun yet?' I asked, grabbing a coffee.

'Only good thing about this is we get free breakfast every morning,' Trevor said, taking the coffee from me. 'Thanks.'

I poured myself another cup. 'How's it going?'

'It's not so bad,' Trevor said. 'Once we get it going, it should be pretty routine. And we won't have all these people running around here again until the closing performance. Normally it will just be one or two competitors hanging around.'

'Yeah, the first day is always the worst,' Scott agreed.

'Katherine?'

I heard my name and turned around. Stephan stood at the door with a beautiful young woman at his side. She was tiny, barely reaching his shoulders, and very petite, with long brown hair and Stephan's blue eyes. She looked timid, peering into the room shyly through her lowered eyelashes.

'Nicole?' I asked, not believing this was actually the grown-up version of the girl I once knew.

'Katherine? Kate?' She stepped into the room and took my hands in hers, a look of disbelief in her face as well. 'You look beautiful; you haven't changed at all.'

I pulled her to me and hugged her. 'I can't believe you're all grown-up. I suddenly feel so very old.'

'Imagine how I must feel,' Stephan said, joining us, his hand casually settling on Nicole's shoulder.

'And you're a concert pianist?' I said. 'I'm so proud of you.'

'Well, I'm hoping to be a concert pianist,' she said. 'This is just my first competition.'

'Colie, you played so beautifully when I knew you, I don't think you have a thing to worry about,' I promised her.

'We better get you downstairs and finish your make-up.' Stephan took her arm and I saw Nicole turn immediately to obey his command.

'Will I see you again?' I asked Nicole.

She looked up at her father and waited for him to answer.

'She'll be here for the entire two weeks,' Stephan said. 'I'm sure we'll all see lots of each other.'

'Good. Break a leg,' I said as her father led her back downstairs.

'That is one seriously cute chick,' Scott said, peering over my shoulder, watching her walk back to her dressing room. 'And one seriously overprotective father.'

'I'd be overprotective of my daughter with guys like you around, too.' I grabbed another croissant and headed back toward the lobby.

Graham was waiting for me at house-right, by the technical booth.

'You took long enough,' he scolded me.

'Calm down, Graham, there's still five minutes before it starts.' I stuffed the last bite of croissant into my mouth. 'Have you made any announcements yet?'

'No, I was waiting for you.'

'OK, well let's get this show on the road.' I slipped into the booth and turned the microphone on. 'Good morning, ladies and gentlemen, and welcome to the Centenary Theatre. This morning's opening performance of the Thompson-Mann Piano Competition will begin in five minutes. Please take your places in the theatre.'

Graham and I watched the people wander into the auditorium and find their seats. By the time I made my one-minute announcement the theatre was full, so I made my final announcement to the empty lobby and the ushers closed the doors. Graham walked over to the lobby television monitor and turned it on just as the house was going black.

'Will you be OK if I go inside and watch?' I asked him.

'Of course I will, Kate. Enjoy the show.'

I cracked open the door and slipped into the theatre. I stood just inside the auditorium until my eyes grew accustomed to the dark and then I quietly slipped into one of my house seats on the aisle. The house went totally black and suddenly the beating of the tympani split the silence. The crowd instantly grew still and then a spotlight came on, hitting the centre of the stage, where Stephan stood on a riser in front of the Symphony and facing the audience, holding his baton, awaiting the applause he knew would come. He had changed into his tuxedo and time seemed to reverse. Suddenly there I was, back in the concert hall at the university, sitting in the front row, adoringly looking up at Stephan as he stood in front of the orchestra. I felt that same excitement; a tingling that started in my toes and worked its way up my body. I was glad I was sitting so no one could see my knees shaking and I was really glad I was far enough away that Stephan couldn't see my reaction. He seemed to be staring straight at me, as he had all those years ago, tearing his way into my thoughts. But I have a small advantage that had been missing back then – I'm older, wiser and I know he is married. And yet my toes still tingled.

The audience rose to its feet and cheered, the orchestra applauded as well, and Stephan bowed, smiling that smile, again in my direction. He took one final gracious bow and then turned his back on the audience. He tapped his baton on his music stand, raised his arms, expecting obedience but the cheering didn't stop. He tried tapping his baton again, but neither the musicians nor the audience were ready to listen until he got his full due. Stephan set down his baton, turned back to the crowd and bowed again and again. The audience was still standing, showing no signs of stopping. Stephan finally let down his guard and flashed one of the brilliant smiles, the real and genuine article, the one that had hooked me so totally once upon a time. It seemed to work for this audience, too, as a wave of cheering and whooping suddenly accentuated the clapping. He bowed again, and then raised his arms to quieten the audience. Finally, reluctantly, they sat back down. Once again, he turned to the orchestra, picked up his baton, and this time they obeyed. The music began.

After the opening overture – and further resounding cheers – one of our local news personalities came out onstage and began the introductions. Endless rounds of organizers, directors from the board, and judges came out to take their bows. No one was as enthusiastic for this part as they had been at the beginning. Finally the stage was cleared and the competitors were introduced. There were fifty pianists from almost as many countries represented. Our stage looked very small and crowded, with the orchestra and now all these extra performers and dignitaries. Nicole was one of the last to be introduced and there was an extra loud cheer for her. I noticed Stephan watching her proudly as she took her place. Finally the stage was cleared, the host made a few closing remarks and the orchestra played once again. I decided to sneak out before it was over to beat the rest of the audience. I checked my watch and saw it was almost noon.

'How was it?' Graham asked as I pushed my way out the door and into the lobby.

'Great! Did you hear that cheering?'

'Yeah, was that all for your old boyfriend?'

'Enough, Graham. My past is going to stay my past, not public knowledge. We will refer to him as Mr Bouchard or the Maestro from this point forward. Understood?'

'Fine. So what's up now?' he asked.

'This should be over in about two minutes. Then all the competitors will be in the lobby for about an hour to meet the press. The competition starts at two o'clock.'

'So what are we supposed to do while all that's going on?' he asked.

'Hang around, eavesdrop on the interviews, the usual things,' I smiled. 'I'm going to go up and put some more coffee on. I'll be back down in a few minutes.'

'OK, boss.'

The auditorium doors flew open and the audience started to pour out. I hurried upstairs, trying to get out of the lobby before the people got out of the theatre. I closed the door to my office, giving myself some privacy, and put on a fresh pot of coffee. I sat in my chair and took a deep breath. I had to try and shake off this reaction I kept having to Stephan. It was very unnerving. He was in my past. I had thought I had dealt with him, but now I was starting to wonder if that was really true.

I heard some crashing and pounding coming over the speaker that hangs on my office wall. The sound system from the auditorium is hooked into my office so I can be up here working and still hear what's happening onstage. I walked over to turn the sound down, but hesitated when I heard an angry voice onstage.

'Stephan, I said I wanted to speak with you.' It was a woman's voice but I didn't recognize it.

'And I said I didn't want to talk to you right now,' he replied tersely.

'We have to talk. Nicole is about to go out and talk to the

press and you need to know what she is going to say.'

'I told her not to go. She doesn't need to do this. It will ruin her concentration.'

'She does need to do this,' the woman replied. 'She is going out to talk to the press if you won't talk with her.'

'I want you to stay away from Nicole. I know what she needs right now much better than you ever could.'

'I don't think you do, Stephan,' the voice said coldly.

'What are you talking about?'

'You need to listen to Nicole. She has been trying to talk to you for the last three months and you haven't listened. If you don't listen now, she is going out to tell the press everything she has been trying to discuss with you.'

'Would someone get this woman off my stage!' he screamed, in a rare moment of letting his anger show. 'She does not belong here!'

I clicked the speaker off and quickly finished with the coffee, then I went down to the main lobby, looking for Nicole. I had a feeling that something terrible was about to happen. I didn't know if I could stop it or not but I thought I should try to do something. I criss-crossed the lobby but didn't see her anywhere. Graham was standing by the main bar, flirting with one of the bartenders.

'Hey, boss.' He turned away from the bartender when he saw me approaching.

'Have you seen Nicole Bouchard?' I asked.

'Who's that?'

'Stephan's daughter, she's one of the competitors. Have you seen her?'

'Sorry, Kate, I don't know which one she is. I did see a group go into the Rodeo Lounge.'

I took off across the lobby to our private lounge. Graham must have sensed trouble because he followed close on my heels. I stopped at the open door, seeing Nicole sitting on the couch surrounded by a group of reporters. Nicole was speaking, reading a prepared statement, and my stomach turned over as I realized something terrible was happening and I was too late to stop it.

'I thank you all for coming and listening to what I have to say,' Nicole read aloud. 'I would appreciate you saving any questions until I have read my statement.'

She paused for a moment, trying to catch her breath and gather her thoughts. I saw her swallow hard, trying to get rid of the lump you could almost see in her throat.

'You all know that my father, Stephan Bouchard, is the newly appointed conductor of the Symphony. There is something you don't know about my father and it is something that I feel must come out. Child abuse and incest have been kept as dark secrets in our society, making the victims feel that they are the guilty party. That must not be allowed to continue. The victim must be allowed to heal and the guilty party brought to justice. My father has been sexually abusing me since I was five years old. I feel it is time for the world to know what kind of a monster he really is and for my family to stop pretending that this isn't happening. I intend to file a civil suit against my father and make him pay for his abuse.'

I couldn't believe what I was hearing. I looked beside me and saw Graham's mouth hanging open in shock as well.

'What the hell are you doing?' I shouted across the room, trying to have my voice heard over the cacophony of reporters all talking at once.

Graham put a restraining hand on my shoulder, trying to hold me back, but I pushed it off and walked across the room. Nicole looked up and saw me, and then averted her eyes as I came closer.

'I think I deserve an answer to my question,' I continued.

'Who are you?' one of the reporters shouted over the other voices.

'I am the house manager of this theatre,' I said, turning to face the crowd. 'This room is now closed. I want you all out of here.' I found myself trying to shout over the increasing noise. There were camera flashes going off and several people asking questions all at once. I suddenly felt like a movie star on a night out, albeit a bad night.

'You can't do that,' another reporter protested.

'Just watch me,' I threatened and then turned to my assistant. 'Graham, call security. Now are you all leaving on your own or am I going to have to throw you out?'

The room cleared slowly and with much protesting, so I posted Graham on the other side of the closed door to keep everyone a safe distance away. I turned back to Nicole and saw her still sitting on the couch, crying, with another woman sitting beside her.

'Who are you?' I asked the other woman, ready to throw her out myself if I had to.

'This is Aunt Joelle,' Nicole said, trying to wipe away her tears. 'She's also my therapist.'

Poor little Nicole, she looked so small and so very young, with tears dripping down her face and her mascara starting to puddle. She had always been a tiny little thing, with long, thick brown hair hanging down her back in curls and Stephan's distinctive blue eyes peeking out from under her bangs. She hadn't changed much over the years and still looked more like a child than a young woman, especially now, sitting here, dabbing at her nose with a tissue.

'I want to speak with Nicole alone,' I said, putting my arm around Nicole's shoulder.

'I don't think that's such a good idea,' the woman said and I recognized her voice as the one I had heard on my office speaker; the one who had been fighting with Stephan. 'Nicole is feeling very vulnerable right now.'

'My God, Nicole, do you realize what you have just done?' I asked, ignoring the other woman.

'She knows exactly what she has done. She needs to do this to start healing.' Joelle is a severe woman, with sharp angles in her bones, hair, and clothing. She seemed to be used to getting her own way and didn't seem to be afraid to use threats or intimidation to get there.

'Was this your idea?' I turned my attention from Nicole to her aunt.

'It is a sound therapeutic technique. She has been trying to confront her father but he would not listen. So she had to go public to be heard, to feel that her point is valid and justified, but mostly to stop feeling guilty.'

'I don't believe this. Nicole, you can't honestly tell me that your father abused you.'

'It's true, Kate,' she whispered. 'I've been remembering it over the past year. I had to do something; I couldn't live with the memories a minute longer.'

'Nicole, your father is never going to get over this. He loves you more than anything else in the world. Have you thought about what this will do to him professionally? His career may never recover.'

'What about me?' Nicole asked, the tears starting all over again. 'I, too, may never recover.'

'I knew you then, when this was supposed to be happening,' I told her. 'I knew your family. I can't believe this was going on. You were a very happy little girl and you idolized your father.'

'Stephan has always needed lots of women in his life,' Joelle jumped in. 'We all know his sexual reputation.'

'Yes, we do,' I agreed. 'But Stephan has always found plenty of grown women to meet his needs. He has never needed to use children to seek sexual fulfilment,' I almost spat at her.

'Perhaps he did,' she continued. 'You do not know everything that went on behind the closed doors of his home.'

'Neither do you,' I pointed out.

'But Nicole remembers.' Joelle looked very proud of herself.

'I hope you do, Nicole. I hope you really remember,' I said sadly. 'Because you have just destroyed three lives – yours, your father's, and your mother's. People never recover from this kind of accusation, you know. I pray this is the truth, because I don't think you, personally, will ever get over this.'

I gave Nicole a squeeze on the shoulder, got up and left the room, closing the door behind me. Both Graham and a security guard were standing outside the lounge.

'This room is still closed,' I ordered. 'No one goes in. If she wants to talk to the press, she can go out on the street to do it, but she won't say another word in my theatre. I'll be in my office if you need me.'

I climbed the stairs quickly, feeling the need to be alone with a locked door between me and what was happening in my lobby. I put my key into the door, opened it, and saw Cam fixing himself a coffee. He looked up and smiled at me, then noticed the look on my face.

'Katie, what's wrong?'

I flopped down on the window ledge and kicked my shoes off.

'Have you got a cigarette?' I asked.

He pulled out a cigarette and lit it for me, then poured me a coffee as I took a long drag. I felt my head start to spin from the cigarette, and I was calming down a little. Cam sat beside me, draped his arm around my shoulder and pulled me close to him. But he waited until I was ready to speak. I took one last drag off my cigarette before stabbing it out in the ashtray.

'I just happened upon a little press conference that Stephan's daughter was holding in the Rodeo Lounge,' I started. 'God, Cam, she just told everyone that her father has been sexually abusing her since she was a child.'

'What?' I knew he had heard me but he didn't believe what he'd just heard either.

'It's true. She must have had fifteen reporters in there and she just blurted it out.'

'Talk about timing.' He laughed, but I didn't reprimand him; he wasn't being cruel.

'It can't be true,' I said. 'She was a perfectly normal, happy child. She used to just adore her father.'

'These things can be very complicated, Katie. It could have been happening while you knew them.'

'No, there is no way that Stephan could have done that.'

'Katie, you have to be very careful,' Cam warned me. 'Make sure that you are not protecting the wrong person. I know you still have some feelings for Stephan but don't let those feelings cloud your judgment.'

'I know,' I said. 'I just don't believe it's true. God, Cam, I was sleeping with him. I mean, what does that make me, if he was leaving me and going to his eight-year-old daughter?'

'It would make you an innocent victim, like she might have been,' he said gently.

'It can't be true. I mean, he was a snake, and he lied to me about being married, but I just can't believe he was that kind of monster.'

'What did he have to say about this?' Cam asked.

'He doesn't know yet. Oh my God, I better go and tell him.' I started to put my shoes back on. 'Better he hears it from me than from some reporter.'

'Are you sure you want to get involved?' he asked.

'No, I don't want to get involved, but it's too late, I already am. Besides, Cam, would you rather have news like this come from someone you know or from a reporter as you're getting into your limo and leaving the theatre?'

'Well, I do hate it when those reporters bother me while I'm getting into my limo,' he joked.

I finished putting my shoes on and pulled away from him. 'Cam,' I warned.

'I guess you're right.' He put out his cigarette and set the ashtray on my desk.

'Will you come with me?' I asked hopefully.

'Do you think that's a good idea?' he asked.

'I don't know about Stephan, but I think I'll need a little emotional support.'

'OK, let's go.' He held out his hand for me and I took it.

'Let's take the fire escape,' I suggested. 'I don't want to run into any more reporters. I don't seem to be very good at handling them.'

We snuck down the fire escape and through the back hall to the stage-left entrance. There was crew everywhere, moving chairs, music stands, instruments, pianos, and trying to clear the stage for the first part of the competition. Trevor stood at the edge of the stage, supervising everything, and I walked over to him.

'Hi, Trevor.'

'Kate, we're a little busy right now.'

'It's important,' I promised. 'I need to find Stephan Bouchard. Have you seen him?'

'He's back there.' Trevor pointed to the back corner. 'Counting music stands or something. If you ask me, he's a little too involved here and is rapidly becoming the winner of butthead of the day. You could help us out a lot by getting him out of the way for a while.'

I turned around and saw Stephan in the far corner of the wings. I walked purposefully over and interrupted the conversation he was having with a stagehand.

'I need to talk to you, Stephan.'

'Katie, I'm busy, can we do this later?' he asked.

'No,' I insisted. 'I need to talk to you now.'

'Fine.' He turned back to the technician he had been talking to. 'If you'll excuse me for a minute . . .'

'This is private,' I said as I pulled him into the technical office, slamming the door behind us.

'Katie, what the hell is going on? This is a very bad time for me to be distracted.'

'It's a worse time than you think, Stephan. Do you know that Nicole was in the lobby talking to the press?'

'I know most of the competitors went out to the lobby to talk to the press,' he replied.

'Do you know what she had to say?' I asked.

'Why don't you tell me since it seems to be so important to you, Katie?'

'Stephan, she told them that you have been sexually abusing her.'

'Oh, that is very funny, Katie, thank you for wasting my time.' Stephan gave a sardonic laugh and put his hand on the doorknob to leave the room. He tried to pull the door open but I put my hand over his, stopping him.

'Stephan, I'm telling you the truth,' I said quietly.

He looked at me, waiting for the punchline to this terrible joke.

'She said that the truth had to come out. She was there with someone named Joelle, who said she was Nicole's therapist.'

'That meddling bitch!' He snarled, baring his teeth almost like a wild animal.

'You know her?' I asked.

'She's been after me to go into therapy with Nicole. Said there was something that we had to work out.'

'Well, she wasn't lying about that,' I said. 'Stephan, I wanted you to know about this from someone you knew, before you heard it from a reporter or something.'

'I should have heard it from my daughter.'

'I know you must be angry—'

'How would you know what I'm feeling? She's trying to destroy me.'

'Why would Nicole want to destroy you?' I asked.

'Not Nicole . . . Never mind, it is too long a story to go into right now.' He pulled my hand off his and opened the door.

'Stephan, please wait a minute,' I called after him. 'I want you to calm down before you go out there.'

'Where is Nicole?' he asked.

'This is neither the place nor the time to discuss this with her,' I said.

'That didn't stop her, did it? Now tell me where she is!'

I put my hand on his shoulder, trying to hold him back for a moment. He took my hand and squeezed it tightly.

'Where is she?' he asked, squeezing tighter.

'Katie is just trying to help here,' Cam intervened, putting his own hand on Stephan's shoulder, ready to pull him off me if need be. 'Let's not shoot the messenger.'

Stephan turned angrily towards Cam but restrained himself before he could do anything he might regret later.

'I'm sorry,' he said, releasing his grip on my hand.

He pushed past Cam and ran across the stage. I started to follow him but Cam grabbed my arm and held me back.

'No, Katie.'

'Please, Cam, let me go. I need to try and stop this.'

He hesitated for a moment and then let me go. I ran across the stage after the Maestro.

'Stephan!' I called after him. 'Don't do this!'

But Stephan ignored me and jumped off the stage, running through the auditorium and into the lobby. I turned to Cam, looking for guidance, but he just shrugged his shoulders, so I jumped off the stage and followed Stephan into the lobby.

'Nicole!' I heard him scream just as I pushed through the door into the lobby.

'Stephan, don't,' I whispered, more to myself than him.

'Nicole.' He ran across the lobby as Nicole made her way out of the Rodeo Lounge in answer to his call. He grabbed his daughter roughly by the arm. 'Come with me.'

'No,' she said. 'I'm staying right here.'

'You are going to come with me if I have to pick you up and carry you.' He started pulling her across the lobby toward the dressing rooms.

'Daddy, leave me alone,' she protested.

Graham came across the lobby to me. 'What the hell is going on?'

'Later,' I said. 'I'm closing the lobby. I'll make the announcement, you start getting these people out of here and I want the doors locked securely after the last one is out. No exceptions.'

'Yes, boss,' he said.

I made my way into the booth as Stephan dragged Nicole

physically across the lobby, flashbulbs popping. I turned on the PA. 'Ladies and gentlemen, the theatre lobby is now closed until the competition resumes at two o'clock. Please make your way to the nearest exit.'

I opened the door to the booth and saw Cam outside waiting for me.

'Well, that went really well.' I let out a half-hearted laugh.

He pulled me close to him and hugged me.

'That was what you call a no-win situation,' he said.

Graham and I sat in the lobby, enjoying the silence. I had sent everyone else to lunch but Graham had passed on that offer, preferring to stay and find out what had happened. I was lounging on the couch, watching the blank television monitor. Graham brought me a coffee, trying to lull me into a good mood so he could pump me for information, and sat down on the chair.

'So, how do you think the morning went?' he asked, the sarcasm showing even though he tried to keep a straight face.

'Gee, other than having one of our competitors use the competition as a forum to air her personal problems; our new conductor losing his cool totally in front of the press, the audience, and the board of directors; and me probably about to be fired for kicking the press out of the theatre on the opening day of the world famous piano competition? I guess it went pretty well,' I told him. 'I'm sure some people have had worse days at the theatre – Mrs Lincoln, for example?'

'If you get fired, can I have your job?' he asked.

'I'll give you a reference, but I'm not sure a reference from me will do you a lot of good right now.' I sat up and lit a cigarette, something I shouldn't be doing out in the open in the lobby, but since I thought I was already in a bunch of trouble, what was one more infraction?

'So what are we going to do to top that this afternoon?' Graham asked. 'You know the public, they always expect more.'

'Maybe we could burn the place down,' I suggested, only half kidding.

'Seriously,' Graham said. 'What is going to happen this afternoon?'

'I don't know. The directors for the competition are meeting right now to decide if Nicole should be allowed to compete. They are obviously worried about what effect her little press conference will have on the festival. I'm sure the Symphony's board of directors is meeting right now to discuss how this is going to affect them as well. I just hope the ink is dry on Stephan's contract. He might be the one person who's in more trouble than me right now.'

'Doesn't matter,' Graham said. 'Those contracts usually have some sort of morality clause. If they want, they can probably toss Stephan out on his *oreille*.'

'His what?'

'It's French for ear.'

'You need to work on your pronunciation a bit,' I scolded him.

'Well, it was in a book I read. I thought I was being clever.'

'Good try. Well, I guess we'll just wait here and see what happens next,' I said. 'If we don't hear from anyone by two o'clock we just open the doors and pretend like everything is normal.'

'So, Kate, have you noticed that this place is becoming more and more exciting? We never had stuff like this happen last year. I'm really beginning to enjoy working here.'

'Well, I'm not enjoying this quite so much.'

'Katie.'

I turned to see who was calling me, butting my cigarette out quickly. Stephan stood at the doors to the backstage area. He looked exhausted, dark circles ringing his eyes, the grey seemingly overpowering the black of his hair. He was still in his tuxedo pants but had no jacket on. His ruffled shirt was open at the neck and his bow tie hung, undone, around his neck.

'Graham . . .' I began.

'I know, go somewhere else, find something to do, and miss all the good stuff, like always.' But he got up and headed for the elevator. 'I'll get some lunch and see you in about a half-hour.'

'Thanks.'

Stephan crossed the lobby and sat in the chair that Graham had just vacated. He slouched down and ran his hands through his hair.

'I'm sorry for the way I acted,' he began. A good way to start, I decided.

'You don't have to apologize,' I told him, since it doesn't cost anything to be magnanimous. 'Can I get you a coffee or something?'

'I'd like a beer,' he said. 'Can you swing that?'

'I have the keys, I can do anything.' I walked to the beer fridge and pulled out a bottle of European beer. I had never seen Stephan drink a beer and I just couldn't imagine him chugging down a Bud Light. It just didn't fit his image. I opened the bottle and brought it over to him, joining him on the couch again.

'You carry this here?' he asked, reading the label.

'We're not total heathens, Stephan. We even have some red wine from France, if you can imagine that!'

'Sorry,' he said again. 'But you don't have to get sarcastic about it.'

'Are you all right?' I asked, realizing he had bigger things than me to worry about.

'No, Katie, I'm not all right. But I don't know *what* I am yet so don't expect any explanations on my emotional state.'

'Is there anything I can do?'

'You could turn back time to this morning, convince my daughter that I have never done those things to her and confiscate all the pictures the press took of me dragging her across the lobby.'

'That was a bad move,' I agreed.

'I was insane at the time, out of my mind,' he explained.

'I can understand that. What are you going to do now, Stephan?'

'I don't know. Go back to the hotel, wait for Carole to arrive, plan a way to kill that bitch Joelle.'

'Is she related to you? Nicole referred to her as Aunt but I don't remember you ever talking about her before.'

'No, she and I dated at university many years ago. She has been a friend of the family for a long time. Nicole asked if she could see her professionally, to work on her visualization and confidence. She was having some serious problems with stage fright. Well, Nicole got over that well enough, but then Joelle turned into some sort of crazy person, insisting that

Nicole's problems stemmed from me and Carole, that we had raised her in some sort of psychologically dysfunctional family. She just would not let up on us, prying into the most intimate areas of our life. Carole finally told her that Nicole would be finding a new therapist and Joelle backed off.' He took a big sip of his beer and let out an almost inaudible sigh. Stephan was not good at showing his emotions to others. 'I just don't know where all this has come from.'

'Did you talk to Nicole?'

'No, we were both too upset. She stormed out of the theatre and I sat in my dressing room and listened to some Wagner. Nothing like Wagner when you're angry.'

'I hate Wagner,' I said.

'But you are hardly ever angry.' He smiled at me. 'Almost always happy, my Katie.'

'That's right, you've missed the PMS years.' I laughed, trying to lighten his mood a little.

'I don't know what to do, Katie.' He ran his fingers through his hair again, almost pulling it from his head.

'Stephan, tell me the truth,' I insisted. 'Look me straight in the eyes and tell me if there is any truth to this at all. Did you ever do anything you shouldn't have, anything that might even be misconstrued as inappropriate?'

'Don't be ridiculous; I have no trouble attracting a woman if I want one, why should I turn to children?' He was incensed that I would even ask this, and there was hatred in his eyes as he turned to me.

'That's not an answer, it's an evasion,' I pushed him, hoping I could read the truth through those angry eyes.

He sat up straight, grabbed me by both shoulders and looked me directly in the eyes. 'I swear on all that is holy that none of this is true.'

'Well then say it!' I demanded of him.

'I have never touched my daughter in any inappropriate or sexual manner. *Mon Dieu*, it makes me sick even to say it out loud.'

'Then fight, Stephan, for Nicole's sake. You've got to make her believe that it isn't true. Do whatever you have to do to give her back her family.'

'And how do you propose I do that?' he asked.

'I don't know,' I admitted. 'You and Carole have to talk with her, work with her, maybe find a psychologist of your own. Don't give up. I'll be here and if there is anything I can do, I'll do it. Just don't let her be alone thinking you don't love her.'

He leaned over and kissed my cheek. '*Merci.*'

I sat on my favourite stool at Grounds Zero waiting for Gus to finish making my mochaccino and bring it over to me. I'd left a note on my desk letting Graham know where I was and telling him to go ahead and open up if I wasn't back by two o'clock. Gus brought my coffee over to me and poured one for himself.

'I hear you had a pretty exciting morning at the theatre,' Gus commented.

'I could do without these exciting mornings, Gus.'

'Oh, it keeps life interesting, Kate.' He took a sip of his coffee.

'Gus, I feel like I'm trapped in the middle of this again. Just like the murder. I don't know how this keeps happening to me. One minute I'm sitting at the theatre, the next minute hell is breaking loose all around me and everyone is turning to me to figure things out.'

'It's the friends you pick, Kate; all those exciting people. If you hung around with some senior citizens' bridge group, maybe your life would be a little quieter.'

'I don't play bridge.'

'Then you should either learn to play or get used to these adventures. Besides, Kate, you aren't really involved. It happened in your theatre, that's all.'

'Stephan Bouchard is my friend,' I admitted. 'I am involved, like it or not.'

'Yeah, I know all that, remember?' Gus said. 'But I've also heard that it was a long time ago.'

'It was. Try as I might, I can't seem to keep my private life private or my past in the past, can I?'

Gus chuckled. 'Well, Kate, I think there's a few people in housekeeping that haven't heard about it yet. But you have to be careful about getting involved.'

'Didn't we have a chat just like this about a month or so ago?' I asked.

'I believe we did, and I was right then, wasn't I?' he asked.

'More or less,' I admitted grudgingly.

'Then maybe you better listen to me this time. This is a different game than murder, but it's still a very dangerous one,' he warned.

'It's not dangerous, Gus, this is just about a mixed-up twenty-year-old. Nicole is mad at her dad for some reason and she's picked this way to get even. She's just too young to realize an accusation like this is not the way to do it.'

'I hope you're right.'

'But?'

'But I don't think you are,' he finished. 'I think there's a lot more to this than meets the eye.'

'Then you better keep your ears open and find out what's going on for me. I certainly haven't heard anything other than the obvious, including from Stephan or Nicole.'

'Don't worry, Kate, my ears are always open,' Gus promised.

'Are you hiding?' a voice behind me asked.

I turned, surprised to see Cam standing there.

'As a matter of fact, I am. What are you doing?' I asked, happy to see him.

'Looking for you. Luckily you're so predictable I didn't have to spend too much time looking.' He laughed, leaning over and kissing me on the cheek.

'It's time for me to get back to the theatre,' I said. 'Want to walk back with me?'

'Sure,' Cam agreed. 'Gus, can I just have a Colombian to go, please?'

Gus fixed a to-go cup for Cam and added it to my tab.

'See you tomorrow, Gus,' I said as we headed outside.

'Watch your back, Kate,' I heard him yell after me as the door closed.

'What's he mean by that?' Cam asked.

'Gus doesn't think I should get involved in any of this mess between Stephan and Nicole.'

'Gus is a smart man, Katie. Maybe you should listen to him.'

'Cam, I am involved already.'

'You are only involved if you let yourself be,' he explained.

'Just because it happened in the theatre you work at, doesn't mean it's your problem.'

'Cam, Stephan is a friend. I feel like I need to be there for him.'

'You haven't seen Stephan for, what, ten, fifteen years? What makes you think you owe him anything?'

'Because he didn't do it,' I stated simply.

'And just how do you know that?' he asked sceptically.

'He told me, Cam, and I believe him,' I said in my don't-argue-with-me voice. Cam ignored it.

'And you haven't seen him in years. Who knows how much he's changed in that time.'

'You're wrong. I believe him and I feel I have to help him.'

'God, you're insane. When did you decide to become the superhero?' he asked.

'That's not fair,' I protested.

'And should we talk about your instincts? A couple of weeks ago you were ready to have me thrown in jail,' he reminded me. 'Do you really think you're the best one to judge Stephan's character?'

'I was trying to keep you out of jail,' I protested lamely.

'You thought I was trying to kill you.'

'That's different.'

'How is that different?'

'It just is.' I probably wasn't going to win this argument, but I couldn't just give in.

'I told you I was innocent and you didn't believe me,' Cam said incredulously. 'And we've been dating for well over a year. This man you haven't seen for ten years tells you he's innocent and you're ready to jump right in and save him? I don't get it, Katie.'

'Maybe it's not logical, Cam, but I do believe him. And I don't know what all the excitement is about. I'm not getting involved in any of this; all I'm going to do is talk to Nicole.'

'Katie, don't talk to Nicole, she needs professional help.'

'I'm not going to counsel her, I'm just going to talk to her,' I explained. 'I did used to know her really well, you know?'

'Again, she was ten at the time, wasn't she?'

I just stared at him, standing at the entrance to the theatre, neither one of us reaching for the door because neither one of us was willing to back down.

'I suppose that nothing I can say or do is going to change your mind?' he finally said.

'No.'

'You really make me crazy, Katie.'

'I know I do. I'm like Jessica Rabbit, though. I'm not really bad, I'm just drawn that way.'

'So, what happens after you talk to Nicole?' he asked.

'I don't know. I'm kind of hoping she'll just decide she's made a mistake and apologize to everyone,' I admitted.

'Do I need to remind you that this is the real world?' Cam asked me, finally opening the door for me.

'No. I just hope I can make some sort of a difference here. This has just all gone so very wrong.' I walked through the door and we climbed the stairs to the main lobby.

'I know it has, Katie, but sometimes things just go wrong. That seems to be the way the world works.'

'There's always the Kate Carpenter Detective Agency,' I suggested.

'What?'

'Well, we did pretty well last time. We put a murderer behind bars.'

'Not before he almost dropped you off a forty-story tower. We're not playing that game again.' Cam's voice was firm this time.

'Cam . . .' I tried my half-whining semi-seductive voice.

'Nope, absolutely not. You talk to Nicole if you want, but you are not going back into the detective business again.'

'All right, all right. I won't push my luck. Now come on, we're making a scene,' I said, noticing the ushers had all turned around listening to us argue.

'I hope you appreciate how much I put up with,' he said as we walked across the lobby to my office.

'I bet your life was really boring before I came into it.' I laughed.

'Don't you keep saying how much you want a nice, boring normal life?'

'Maybe I don't really mean it. You should kiss me goodbye and let me get to work,' I suggested.

'I'll come back up to the theatre when I'm done,' Cam said. 'I think your mom wants to take us out for dinner tonight.'

'I thought she was enjoying all the home cooking,' I said.

'She loves my cooking,' Cam said, 'but she feels sorry for me. She thinks I'm doing all the cooking and cleaning and that I deserve a break. You know, a man's work is never done!'

'Oh, you are such a suck-up,' I said. 'She's going to like you better than she likes me if you keep this up.'

'That's the whole idea.' He smiled, giving me a quick kiss and heading off in the opposite direction.

I pushed through the door and ran up the last flight of stairs to my office. Graham was behind the desk, on the phone again, which he hurriedly hung up, when he saw me coming down the hall.

'Are you and Mandi becoming a big item?' I asked, knowing from the look on his face that's who he had been talking to.

'She's cute,' he said, as if that was explanation enough. And I guess that at eighteen years old, it probably was.

'Good, a foundation to build a lifetime on,' I teased him.

'You seem in much better humour,' he said.

'I am. A good fight with Cam always cheers me up.'

'I guess it's good to have a hobby,' Graham said. 'And speaking of foundations to build a lifetime on . . .'

'Stop right there; we're not talking about my personal life here, remember?'

'But my personal life is fair game?' Graham asked. 'That doesn't seem right.'

'I'm the boss, dude, I make the rules.'

'Well, boss, the doors are open, the public is inside, and if you turn up the speaker you will hear the first competitor playing their first selection.'

'Any problems?' I asked, not really wanting to know.

'Not one, but it's only been a few minutes.'

'Has anyone been looking for me?' I asked.

'Yes, actually. The head honcho of the piano competition is in the Rodeo Lounge, waiting to speak with you, and the Spaz was up here trying to find out what's happening. Apparently there was quite a mob of reporters at the stage door after we booted them out of the lobby.'

'No surprises there. I'll go talk to the festival person now, but I intend to spend the rest of the day trying to avoid the Spaz. And I expect your full cooperation in that endeavour.'

'Gotcha,' Graham agreed.

The Spaz is head of building services. He is a former cop who takes himself very seriously. During our murder investigation last month I was forced to spend way too much time with him and I hope never to repeat that mistake. He is officious, arrogant, chauvinistic, and full of self-importance – all qualities I hate in anyone but myself.

I left the office, went back downstairs and into the Rodeo Lounge. There were several members of the board in the lounge. When they saw me come in, they made their excuses and left me alone with the chairman – a middle-aged woman, famous for bringing this competition to the renown it now holds, and for the life of me I couldn't remember her name. I made a mental note to start carrying my clipboard with me this week. I was going to be awfully embarrassed if I had to make any introductions.

'Ms Carpenter?' she asked, glancing at her own clipboard. Nice to know I wasn't the only one with this problem.

'Kate,' I said, extending my hand to shake hers.

'Quite an exciting morning,' she commented, forgetting to introduce herself. I couldn't decide if she just assumed I knew who she was or if she was trying to get the psychological advantage in this meeting.

'Very,' I agreed, sitting down and assuming the small talk portion of our conversation was now over. And I was right. She straightened her jacket and turned slightly to face me.

'I wanted you to know that we're very pleased with the way you handled that little situation this morning with Nicole Bouchard.'

'Well, thank you,' I answered, my voice betraying my surprise. 'I wasn't sure what kind of response I was going to get for kicking the press out of the theatre.'

'Well, better removing them than having them photograph Maestro Bouchard fighting with his daughter.'

'Hopefully, we won't have to do that again.'

'We have met with Nicole Bouchard and she has assured us she will not use the competition as a forum to air her personal problems. We've decided to let her compete as long as she abides by her word. Should anything else happen, she will be disqualified immediately and escorted from the theatre.'

'I'm glad she's able to continue,' I commented.

'We'll be keeping a very close eye on her. We're not expecting the media to let up, though.'

'No, they usually don't,' I agreed.

'As long as you're prepared for the onslaught.'

'After last month, my staff are very experienced in handling the press.'

'The murder . . .'

'The murder,' I echoed. 'I don't think we'll ever live that down.'

'It must have been very exciting,' she said.

'Let me put it into perspective for you. It felt pretty much like you must have felt this morning when one of your competitors was accusing your host of sexually abusing her.'

'Enough said, Kate.' She laughed. 'I like the way you work. And I like that you're not seeking the fame. It can be addictive for some people.'

'Well, not me. I prefer the peace and quiet myself,' I assured her. 'But you know where to find me if you need me?'

'I just hope I won't need you for anything more than handing out programs.'

'Me too.' I laughed along with her.

There was a knock on the door and we both turned to see who was there. Nicole was standing there, looking very small, very young, and a lot less confident than she had this morning.

'I'm sorry to interrupt,' she said softly. 'I just wanted to talk to you for a minute, Kate, before I go back to my hotel.'

'That's OK, Nicole, I think I'm finished here.' I turned to the chairman to see if that was true.

'I'll see you later,' she said. Taylor, that was her name. Taylor St James.

'Colie, why don't we go up to my office? We can talk privately there.'

Nicole nodded and followed me up the stairs. This is why I never do aerobics at the gym; I get a great cardiovascular work-out just getting to my office. When we arrived, Graham was on the phone again. I hoped he would get over this girl soon; I liked him much better when he was single and more focused. He turns into an airhead when he's dating. He hung up the phone and looked up at me.

'I know, get out of here, find something else to do,' he said before I could ask it of him. 'I'm getting tired of this, Kate. I'm beginning to feel like a yo-yo.'

'See you later, Graham.' I ignored his comments and closed the door after him.

'Do you want a coffee or a juice?' I asked.

'No, I'm fine,' Colie said, sitting down in front of the desk. I poured myself a coffee and took a seat behind it. I felt I needed the authority of being behind the desk right now, to make her really listen to the wise words I was about to impart, as soon as I could think of any.

'So, pretty exciting morning,' I began.

'I'm sorry, Kate.'

'Colie, you don't have to apologize to me.'

'But I want you to know what I'm apologizing for. I'm very sorry I put you in the middle of my family's personal problems. I'm not sorry about what I did.'

'Colie, do you really understand what you did?' I asked. 'Do you have any idea what this has done to your father's reputation?'

'Kate, I didn't do this to ruin my father. I did this to make him face the truth.'

'Is it the truth?' I asked. 'Are you absolutely sure? Because once you say something like this out loud, Nicole, there's no turning back.'

'Aunt Joelle said it was the best thing to do,' she said.

'God, you answer questions just like your father – by avoiding them.'

'I trust Joelle; she's helped me through a lot recently.'

'Nicole, I think you should see somebody else. Get a second opinion.'

'Kate, I said I was sorry I got you involved in this, but I trust Joelle and I trust what she is telling me to do.'

'This isn't about me or about what you did this morning. It's about saving your family.'

'I think it's about saving me,' she said.

'Then getting another opinion won't hurt anything.'

'It'll hurt the trust I've built up in my relationship with Joelle,' Nicole said stubbornly.

'Has she told you not to see anyone else?' I asked.

'No, not really. I just think it's best for me not to.'

'Colie, you're going to tear your family apart, you're going to ruin your father's career, and you're not doing yours much good either.'

'None of that's important to me,' she interrupted. 'This is about my emotional state, about me being able to be a functioning adult, about being able to have a successful relationship with a man.'

'It should be about your family, Colie, because nothing else in your life is as important as them.'

She got up, seeing she wasn't winning me over to her side. 'I'm sorry I've bothered you.'

'Colie, please think about it,' I begged her.

'I knew you wouldn't believe me,' she said coldly. 'I knew you'd take his side.'

'I want the truth to come out just as much as you do, Nicole. Why are you so afraid?'

'I've got to go.' She almost ran for the door.

'Nicole, I want what's best for you,' I said. 'Whether you believe it or not.'

But she was already halfway down the corridor. Sometimes I really wish I was a drinker, because I'm pretty sure at moments like this a good stiff scotch would be just the thing. I lit a cigarette instead and then pulled out some paperwork.

The next time I looked up, it was five o'clock and Cam was standing in the doorway, watching me work.

'What are you still doing here?' he asked when I finally looked up at him.

'My job,' I said, hoping it was the right answer.

'I believe you have a physiotherapy appointment.'

'How the hell did you find out about that?' I put my pen down, looking for an escape but he had me trapped.

'Katie, we live together and the doctor left a message on the machine.'

'Well, I can't go today. I'll call and reschedule for tomorrow.' I picked up the phone.

Cam strode across the office, took the phone out of my

hand and set it back in its cradle. Then he picked up my bag, turned off the light and held his hand out for me.

'I'll walk you,' he said.

I stood up and took his hand. 'Just what I need, two mothers in town at the same time.'

'Since you have no intention of looking after yourself, I thought I'd take on the job,' he informed me.

I took his arm and let him lead me down the hall. 'Well, I have to admit that I'm definitely ready to get out of here for the day. But wouldn't you rather go to dinner?' I tried.

'We'll go to dinner after your appointment. I told your mom we'd meet her and Larry later.'

'OK.' I finally gave in. 'Where are we meeting them?'

'At Vaudeville's.'

'All right. Well, let's get this over with.'

The sun was still shining and there was a crispness to the air that signalled the wind was changing direction and would soon be coming from the north, bringing winter with it. I love the crisp last days of fall – the colours, the freshness in the air. I felt better before we were even at the end of the block.

'So, how'd the rest of your day go?' he asked as we walked.

'Not much better. I had Stephan crying on my shoulder in the lobby and Nicole crying on my shoulder in the office. Then I spent the rest of the afternoon suffering a major guilt attack that I could have doubts about what either of them said.'

'Don't you think this is something they should work out for themselves?' he asked.

'Probably,' I admitted. 'But I don't think they will.'

'Well, if you aren't going to stay out of it, what are you going to do now?'

'I thought I'd talk to this Joelle person. I just don't feel like she's on the up and up.'

'What makes you think that? Your extensive experience in psychotherapy?'

'I've never had therapy.'

'My point exactly,' he said, laughing.

'Anyways, I thought I'd assign Graham to dressing-room patrol tomorrow. Maybe he can get to know Nicole a little better.'

'And what am I going to do?'

'Why, Cam, are you volunteering to help out?'

'I figured I should volunteer before I was drafted.'

'That's the spirit.' I laughed. 'Here we are.'

Cam opened the door for me and I checked in with the receptionist. A few minutes later Adonis himself walked into the waiting room.

'Katherine Carpenter?' a melodic Irish voice asked.

I stood immediately and took his outstretched hand. 'Pleased to meet you.'

'I'm Sean,' he said. 'Would you like to follow me?'

'Anywhere,' I said before I could help myself.

An hour later I was infinitely more relaxed as I collected Cam from the waiting room.

'He wants to see me every day this week,' I explained as I set up my appointments.

'I bet he does,' Cam said. 'Is he joining us for dinner, too?'

'No, Cam, I thought I'd see him secretly behind your back.'

'Good, then I'll be much less jealous.'

'Come on, let's get out of here.' I took his arm and led him back outside.

The evening show was relatively peaceful compared to the afternoon. Cam and I made it home before midnight and I headed straight up to bed. We'd had a great dinner with Mom and Larry and packed them off to Banff in their luxurious rental car. I hoped Larry was planning to treat me that well at Christmas and told him so.

'There are some messages on the answering machine,' Cam called up to me.

'I don't care.' I already had my clothes off and was crawling gratefully between the sheets.

'You stay there, I'll turn the volume up.'

I heard the machine beep as he rewound it.

'Hi, Katherine, it's Mom. We've decided to head to Lake Louise instead. We'll still be back next week, try not to get too stressed out with this little festival that's going on.'

'Little festival,' I mumbled. 'Did you forget that it's being broadcast around the world, Mom?'

'I heard that, Katie,' Cam called.

There was another beep and the next message began.

'*Bonsoir*, Katie, I mean, Katherine. This is Stephan. I just wanted to apologize once again for the stir I caused today. I don't know what you said to Colie, but I want to thank you. She came to see us this evening and we're all going to a family counsellor after the competition is over. She has decided that Joelle may be too close to the family to be impartial. I am just happy to do anything to keep our family together and get that bitch out of our lives for good. Thank you again, *mon petit chou. À demain.*'

Cam shut the machine off and came upstairs.

'I guess I should apologize,' he said. 'It appears your meddling may have done some good this time. Once again we've wasted another day arguing.'

'A day arguing is never wasted,' I smiled at him, 'because we spend the night making up. Especially since Mom and Larry have gone . . .'

Saturday October 25

I felt lousy when the alarm rang in the morning. The thrill of the festival was wearing off quickly. Getting up at five in the morning was probably one of the major factors in my lack of enthusiasm. I was going to take the C-Train to work and I stopped to buy a double cappuccino at a push-cart stand that was just opening for the morning rush. It tasted about as bad as you would expect, but at least there was caffeine in it. I bought a newspaper from the box and got on the platform just as the train arrived. I stood in the back, only having a few stops to travel, and turned the paper over so I could scan the front page. And there it was. Not a picture of Stephan dragging Nicole through the lobby – I seemed to have prevented that one from happening – but an old file photo of him, going over a musical score with a young student from his time at the university. A young student who was looking up into his eyes, full of adoration. A young student that was undeniably me.

'Oh, shit,' I said aloud, seeing the people on the train turn to look at me suspiciously. Well, I guess those people in housekeeping that hadn't heard about me and Stephan would know now. And then I started laughing. It did nothing to ease the other passengers' minds about the state of my mental health, but it certainly made me feel better.

By the time I was at the Plex I felt even better, having released some of my tension with six blocks of laughter, and I headed straight up to my office. I was very surprised to find someone waiting outside my office at that time of the morning. The theatre didn't open for another two hours. But I was even more surprised when she turned around and I saw who it was.

'Hello?' I asked, not quite believing my eyes.

'Katherine?' she asked, obviously not sure it was me, either.

'Carole?'
'Yes, it is I.'
Stephan Bouchard's wife. Nicole's mother. What in the hell did she want to see me about? And why did I suddenly feel like a very guilty twenty-year-old who had just been caught with her husband, the famous conductor and infamous philanderer? My past and present seemed to be melting together right there in the hallway.
'How did you get in?' I asked, avoiding the important questions for a moment.
'One of the security guards let me in. With those people, you just have to show the right amount of authority and they'll do whatever you ask. And so here I am.'
I opened my office door, flipped on the light and let her in. She was a strange woman, Carole Bouchard. I had only met her a couple of times before, preferring to avoid socializing with the wife of the man I was sleeping with. But I had found that she behaved totally differently when Stephan was around. When he was watching, she was quiet, unassuming, shy and soft-spoken, deferring all the decisions to him. The one time I had met her without Stephan, I had barely recognized her. She was aggressive, arrogant, and had even seemed taller, larger than I had thought she was. That was one of the main reasons I had avoided her. The woman I had met that day did not seem the type who would tolerate her husband's mistress. She had scared me and I had run. That was the woman standing in my office right now and it was almost like being around my mother. I suddenly felt young and intimidated. But I was now ten years older, and if age hadn't brought wisdom, it had brought on the ability to bullshit with the best of them. Don't let them smell your fear, that's my motto.
'So what can I do for you?' I asked, sitting myself down behind my desk. Position of power, I thought once again, and I hadn't offered her a coffee or a seat, trying to let her know she wasn't invited for a long stay in my world. I had usurped her authority, I thought.
She sat down across from me, made herself very comfortable and stared me straight in the eyes. So much for my attempt at psychology.

'We have to get something clear,' she said to open the conversation.

'And what is that, Carole?'

'My family has been interfered with enough recently. I want you to leave them alone.'

'I don't think I have been interfering with your family,' I protested.

'I don't particularly care what you think. I am telling you what I expect from this point on,' she told me.

'I'm sorry, I don't quite understand where this hostility is coming from,' I said, truly perplexed.

'Is this some sort of stupid attempt at playing innocent?' She practically sneered at me. 'I know you and my husband have a history. Back then you were young, naive and you didn't know any better. Now you are older and should know enough to leave a married man alone. I know he has been sniffing around you, but I wish to make it perfectly clear that I do not intend to share him anymore, especially with the likes of you.'

She knew? I was shocked. All these years I had assumed that Carole never found out about me, about my relationship with Stephan. How could I have been so wrong? But, then, I seemed to have been so wrong about so many things back then. I shook myself back to reality and tried to remember what we had been talking about.

'I have no intention of having any sort of affair with Stephan,' I said quietly, after what I'm sure was too long a pause.

'Good. Next, you will leave my daughter alone. She has been affected enough by outside influences. All this nonsense about abuse. Now, we have begun to try to straighten all this out, but I do not need your advice about second opinions or which doctors to see.'

'I don't see how that's causing any harm . . .'

'I believe you're childless,' she said coldly.

'Yes, I am. However, that does not mean I don't have any common sense.'

'Well that is another argument entirely,' she said, dropping me an icy stare. 'The present discussion is about you staying out of my life and the life of my family. I have everything well in hand. Do you understand what I am asking of you?'

'Yes, I do. However, do you understand that I intend to do whatever I must to protect the reputation of my theatre and this festival?'

'Katherine, I can be a dangerous woman,' she said as she stood, indicating our meeting was nearing an end. 'Please don't try to threaten me. I will do whatever I have to do to protect my daughter – including walking all over you. If you think I can't have you removed from this theatre, you are sadly mistaken.'

With that, she strode off down the hall. I stood at my door, watching her leave, making sure she found her way out. And then I remembered I should breathe. I sat back down behind my desk, finally opened my coffee and took a sip, finding it cold.

'Shit!'

'I should think you could come up with a better expletive than that after that little encounter,' Graham popped his head around the corner.

'How long have you been here?'

'I caught most of it. I was hiding in the locker room, listening with all my might.'

'At least there would have been a witness if she grew fangs and drained all the blood from my body.'

'Kate, I think she did just that.' He smiled, hoping to lighten my mood. It didn't work.

'I would really like to know what I did to deserve that.' I shook my head and took another sip of coffee. Cold or not, I needed the caffeine in that espresso right then.

'From my experience reading all the great tragedies, I don't think that outburst had anything to do with recent happenings. I think you're paying for your past little dalliance with the Maestro. And from the amount of venom she spewed, I think you're the first other woman she ever actually got to confront. There was years of built-up hostility there.'

'You know, I try so hard to come to work and do a good job. I don't bring my personal problems in with me.' I sighed.

'But they sure do follow you here.' Graham laughed again, but still no response from me. 'Boy, this is a tough room.'

'Sorry, Graham. I promise I'll work on my mood.'

'Good. And I think while you're doing that, I'll go work somewhere else,' he said.

'That's probably your safest choice,' I admitted.

I heard the door at the end of the hall open again. It was going to be a busy morning.

'Quick, close the door before anyone sees I'm here,' I whispered to Graham.

'Too late,' he whispered back, and stood up. 'I'm out of here.'

I turned to see Joelle standing at my office door as Graham scurried quickly in the opposite direction.

'I'm sorry, but the theatre is not open yet,' I tried, in a valiant effort to stave off another confrontation.

'I need to speak to you,' she insisted angrily.

How much of this did I have to take in one day?

'I'm afraid I really don't have time right now.' I made one last attempt at avoiding this scene by trying to look very busy at my desk.

'I suggest you make some time.' She, too, sat without invitation and waited for my attention.

I put down the file that I had been pretending to work on and took a deep breath.

'What exactly can I do for you?' I finally asked, my frustration showing in my tone of voice.

'I want to let you know what kind of harm you have done to Nicole,' she stated bluntly.

'Boy, I have a lot of power. Today alone I have single-handedly destroyed marriages and families, and undone years of therapy. Am I correct in assuming this is the way you're headed?'

'You have no idea what I was trying to accomplish with Nicole yesterday.'

'No, I don't. But I do know what you were doing to the festival. And that's where I come into this whole little mess you've created.'

'Well, by coming in where you don't belong, and then talking to Nicole later, you have destroyed my relationship with her.'

'I doubt I could have accomplished that in one afternoon,' I tried to point out.

‘Nicole and her family have totally cut off all contact with me. They will not see me or take my telephone calls.’

‘Well, I can’t say I blame them, Joelle.’

‘It’s Dr Bergere,’ she pointed out. So that was the way it was going to be. Well, I don’t really need any new friends.

‘You could have picked a better time and an infinitely better forum for your little announcement. I can’t believe you could think that press conference would do anyone any good. And I really can’t believe you are surprised that the Bouchard family is angry.’

‘I just want you to know that whatever happens is on your shoulders,’ she told me. I had just about had enough of this, but she continued.

‘You interrupted a carefully laid-out plan. I have been working with Nicole for years and this was the culmination of that therapy. We have been working toward a confrontation with her father for months now and you destroyed it. I don’t know if Nicole will ever recover from this.’ I noticed tears in her eyes, which she rapidly blinked away.

‘I think Nicole will be just fine. She has a family that loves her and there are plenty of qualified doctors out there that can help them all begin to heal.’

‘You have no idea what you are talking about. No one cares about Nicole like I do. No one knows what is best for her like I do.’

‘Dr Bergere, I think you are losing some of your professional detachment here.’

‘I do not believe I have to take medical advice from a music major,’ she almost spat at me. Maybe this was some sort of French trait I had not known about.

‘And I do not believe I have to take any more of this from you.’ I stood, hoping she would take the hint. Thank God she did. She was much easier to manipulate than Nicole’s mother had been. And, strangely enough, she seemed much more emotional, too.

‘This is not the end of this,’ she promised as she stood up.

And then she made her exit, stage–right, so to speak. I was having a real problem getting the last word in today. I reached for my coffee but was diverted again by my phone ringing. I thought about ignoring it, but then thought better of it.

'Hello?'

'It's Graham.'

'Are you too scared to come see me in person?' I asked.

'Yes. But I'm really calling because I was just in the theatre. The Maestro is onstage and he's looking for you.'

'Thanks, Graham, I'm taking the fire escape and I'm out of here. I've had two rounds taken out of me by two members of the Bouchard family already this morning. I think that entitles me to a bit of a break, doesn't it?'

'Yeah, go, I'm good here. When can I expect you back?' he asked.

'I'm going to give everyone a chance to cool down. I'll be back in time for the start of the morning rounds of the competition.'

'OK, I'll handle things until I see you again.'

I grabbed my keys, locked the office and headed down the fire escape. I heard footsteps on the stairs below me and panicked for a minute. These were the stairs I was almost killed on last month. The circumstances suddenly seemed very familiar.

'Hello?' said a familiar voice.

'Cam, it's me.'

We met on the landing and I wrapped my arms tightly around him.

'What's up with you?' he asked.

'I am having a really lousy day. Can I hide out in your office for an hour or so?'

'Sure. I take it we're sneaking through the basement so no one sees you.'

'You take it correctly,' I agreed. 'Now, let's go. Graham just warned me that Stephan is looking for me.'

'I thought you wanted to get involved.'

'Well I do, sort of. But my self-esteem is a little trampled right now and I need some time to rebuild before I fight my next round.'

'Are you going to tell me about it?' he asked.

'Downstairs, in your office, when I have some coffee in one hand and a cigarette in the other.'

'Oh, that's why I was coming up. I'm out of coffee. Can I borrow some from your office?'

'Can't we get some from security?'

'Katie, it'll be fine. Stephan is your friend, remember?' I wasn't sure if he was trying to reassure me or if he was being sarcastic, but at this point he was my only form of escape so I didn't really care.

'All right,' I agreed and pushed open the door. 'After you.'

I actually had the key in my door and was just beginning to feel safe when I heard someone enter the corridor behind me. Please let it be Graham, I prayed.

'Katie!'

No such luck.

'Stephan.' I turned around and greeted him, my voice full of forced happiness, a fake smile plastered on my face.

'What the hell have you been up to today?' he demanded. Round three had begun.

'What are you talking about?' I answered his question with one of my own, but none of my psychological tactics were having much effect today.

'You have been talking with my wife, with Nicole and with Joelle. What right do you have to interfere with my family?'

'I would hardly say that any of these discussions were started by me. I—'

'You are my friend. Speaking with me, offering me advice, that is one thing. I would like to know exactly what you hoped to accomplish.'

'Stephan, you're too angry to discuss this right—' But he cut me off again.

'You're damned right I'm angry!' he continued. 'I can't believe that you have gone behind my back.'

'Stephan, I am trying to explain to you—'

'Why won't you answer me, Katie? Tell me what you are trying to do to my family.'

There was no arguing with Stephan right now; he was out of his mind with rage. Cam took a step towards Stephan, putting himself between us.

'Look, I don't think this is the time to discuss this. Why don't you go have a coffee, calm down, and we can talk this out later.'

'This has nothing to do with you,' Stephan sneered at him. 'Don't you have something you could go repair?'

Cam remained surprisingly calm. I, however, was now getting quite angry.

'Get out of my theatre,' I said, very calmly and quietly.

'Not until I have some answers from you.'

'No, Stephan, this discussion is over right now,' I said as I turned back to my office door and tried to open it.

Stephan reached out and grabbed my shoulder, pulling me back toward him. 'Don't you walk away from me!'

'I realize you're not used to a woman walking out on you, but I told you this conversation is over.' I tried to remain calm and in control, but my stomach was in knots and he was hurting my shoulder.

'Not until I say so,' he said coldly.

'That's enough,' Cam said, pulling Stephan's arm from my shoulder and shoving him back a safe distance from me.

'I told you to stay out of this,' Stephan said.

At that moment, I knew what was going to happen but could do nothing to stop it. I saw Stephan's hand curl into a fist as he drew back. Cam's arm shot out and blocked the punch. He struck back with one of his own. Stephan didn't even see it coming.

'I said that was enough,' Cam said calmly as he stood over Stephan, who was now looking up at us from the carpeted floor. His hand was gingerly exploring his bloody nose.

'Cam . . .' I was speechless.

'Get the coffee, Katie.' I wasn't about to argue.

I grabbed a couple of packages of coffee and some filters and followed him down the hallway. Stephan still lay on the floor, speechless.

Cam took the stairs two at a time and I had to run to keep up with him.

'Cam!' I called after him.

Nothing. We were in a hallway now. I was trotting several paces behind him.

'Cam!'

'I don't want a lecture,' was all he said.

'I wasn't planning on giving one,' I promised. 'Would you please just slow down?'

'I have to get back to my office.'

'I thought I was going with you.'

'You are.'
'Not if I have a heart attack and die in this corridor. Now wait up.'
Cam finally stopped and waited for me to catch up. 'He started it.'
'I know he started it. I saw the whole thing, remember?'
'I know.'
'What is the problem?' I asked.
'I'm upset.'
'I've noticed, Cam, now chill out. I've never had a man fight for my honour before. I'd like to enjoy it.' I laughed.
'You're not angry with me?' he asked, surprised.
'No. I didn't expect you to stand there and take his punch. I just didn't realize you were such a powerhouse.'
'I did some fighting in my youth . . . So you're really not mad?'
'Actually, it was kind of exciting. But that doesn't mean that I ever want it to happen again.'
'It will if anyone ever lays a hand on you again.'
'Cam, Stephan is very upset. His whole family is falling apart. His reputation and career could be in ruins. I didn't like his outburst but I can certainly understand it.'
Cam started walking again, but slower this time, allowing me to keep up with him.
'Is it true, what he said about you speaking with his wife and with that psychologist?'
'It is. But I didn't instigate it,' I protested. 'His wife was at my office when I got there this morning, and then the psychologist just appeared at my door with steam coming out of her ears.'
'I find that hard to believe.'
'But it's really true this time – ask Graham. He was there and he saw and heard everything. I had this whole stream of women in and out of my office this morning. Very threatening women.'
'So are you heeding their warnings?'
'Well, I did find something very interesting,' I told him, avoiding the question.
'I don't want to know.' He started walking faster again.
'I found it interesting that the mother was so cold and

calculating. The only emotional response I sensed from her was hatred.'

'Should I call you Counsellor Troi?' he asked. 'Sensing feelings. Can you tell me how this is going to end? Or when?'

'Cam, I know that *Star Trek* is only a television show and it's not real and that I'm not really an empath,' I said to humour him. 'Now, any more sarcastic comments or may I continue?'

'I couldn't stop you if I tried.'

'You're right about that. Now, the doctor was *amazingly* emotional. She acted much more like I would have thought a mother should act.'

He held open the door to his office for me. I tossed the coffee to him and sat in his chair, pretending I didn't really need to catch my breath. I didn't need the lecture about smoking or working out right now.

'Katie, everyone acts differently in crisis situations. I don't think you can really tell anything by the way they acted. Besides, I believe your history with Stephan may be colouring some of their emotions. And some of your responses to them.'

'Just make me some coffee and quit trying to be logical.'

'A little logic never hurt anyone.'

'No, but you're ruining all my theories. Do you have a cigarette?'

'Are you really trying to quit smoking?' he asked.

'Yes. I smoke half as much as I used to.'

I started rifling through his drawers and finally found a carton. I pulled it out and held it up proudly.

'This doesn't look like you're very serious about quitting,' I said, proud of my find.

'It's old,' he said. 'It's been in there for months.'

'Yeah, right.' I opened a pack and lit one.

'You're changing the subject,' he said, handing me a coffee.

'Oh, no, my virtuous one. You asked me if I was serious about quitting.'

'I believe we were discussing the fact that you are already developing theories about this situation. But theories aren't required, because this is over. The family has pulled together and is going to get help working through their problems.'

'But I still think those reactions were very strange.'

'Katie, quit thinking. It's dangerous for you.'

'Is that a compliment or an insult?' I asked.

'It was meant to be a conversation stopper. Could we change the subject to something a little more innocuous? It is still very early in the morning, you know?'

'Cam, I don't think there is such a thing as innocuous between us. We seem much better at thorny subjects where we have totally opposing views.'

'But we used to get to argue all day and make up all night.' He smiled, rolling my chair closer to his.

'Did you forget?' I asked.

'Forget what?'

'That my mother and Larry are in Banff? When we get home tonight, we will have the apartment all to ourselves.'

'All right!'

'But for now, I should get back up to the theatre and see if there's anyone else waiting to yell at me.'

'OK. Do you need an armed escort?' he asked.

'No, I'm sure Stephan has calmed down and I should be OK.'

'Well then, I'll pick you up later.'

'I'll be waiting,' I promised, leaning closer and kissing him. 'And I can hardly wait.'

'Me too.'

'Good. See you later.'

'Katie, I know you like to have the last word, however . . .' he said as I tried to open the door.

'What?'

'You can't get out of here without me and my keys.'

'You know, I just haven't been able to make a good exit all morning.'

'Don't worry, you're not losing your touch. Everybody has bad days.'

I stood at the bottom of the stairs. 'Well, nowhere to go but up.'

'Very funny.' He laughed. 'By the way, did you see the newspaper this morning?'

'Oh, I was wrong, I did just sink further down.'

'No, really, you looked cute. Gazing innocently up into the Maestro's eyes.'

'I was twenty-one, how come nobody will give me a break?'

'Well, actually I thought it was kind of exciting,' Cam said.

'Why?' I asked, dreading the answer.

'Well, I've never dated a cover girl before.' He laughed, following me up the stairs.

I took the fire escape back up to my office, hiding out in case Stephan was still around and still angry. I remembered his temper and I was afraid that he might not have calmed down yet. I was also afraid that someone else might be looking for me. But at least my mood was a little brighter than a couple of hours ago.

I heard Graham singing 'Matchmaker, Matchmaker' as I walked down the hallway.

'Let me guess, you just got off the phone with Mandi?'

'Yes I did,' he admitted, a slight blush in his cheeks.

'There's just one thing I have to know.'

'What's that?'

'Does she dot the "i" in her name with a heart?'

'No, Kate, she doesn't. She dots it with a happy face.'

'Oh, God, it's worse than I thought.' I laughed at him. 'Anything happening around here?'

'No, it's been quiet since you left.'

'Let's just hope it stays that way.'

'Your mother called. She said they're having a wonderful time and she hopes everything is going well here.'

'Was she mad that I wasn't around?' I asked.

'She didn't seem to be. I thought she was here for a couple of weeks,' he said.

'She is. She and her beau are off to Banff for the week. We did get a little busy around here. And it seems she's become a globetrotter since she started dating Larry.'

'Must run in the family.'

'A cheap hotel in Long Beach does not compare with a first-class condo in Banff,' I answered.

'From my point of view, a night in a cheap motel in Lethbridge would be a treat.' He laughed.

'Well if you got a real job instead of trying to be an actor you could afford to take a vacation once in a while.'

'You'll regret your sarcasm when I'm a world-famous actor.'

'I hope I live to see that day.'

'Well, I see your mood has changed. Are you ready to do some work?'

'Do I have to?'

'Well, I've managed to do almost everything. I guess we can't avoid the paperwork any longer.'

'OK. Get out of my way. And you better put some coffee on; I think I'm going to need it,' I said, settling at my desk. 'I'd like to actually see some of the competition this afternoon.'

I did manage to avoid any more confrontations and we got through both the competition and the evening performance. The changeover was getting much smoother as we all had more practice with it. After work I met Cam at the stage door. He had the car running outside, warmed up and waiting. There was hardly any traffic and we were home in no time. I pushed the elevator button and wrapped my arms around his waist.

'All I want to do is climb into bed, put a movie on, and cuddle up really close to you,' I said.

'That sounds like a really great idea,' he agreed.

'And tomorrow morning we don't have to get up and look after our company or wait in line for a shower.'

'Maybe we could even shower together,' he suggested.

'That's a definite possibility.'

'This is sounding better and better.' He smiled at me.

The elevator reached our floor and the door opened. He took my hand and we walked down the hall toward the apartment. Cam opened the door for me and I was surprised to find the lights on.

'You go first,' I said, pushing Cam through the door to check for intruders.

'I thought you were one of those independent women who didn't need a man,' he whispered.

'I lied.'

And then Sam poked her head around the corner.

'Hi guys, it's about time you got home.'

'Sam?' I hoped I didn't sound too disappointed to see her. I should have held off on giving her the new keys for another week or so. But I guess I'd never thought we would suddenly be so jealously guarding our privacy.

‘I’ve been working all day on this new recipe. I had to come over and test it out. I hope you don’t mind, but I put Bonnie upstairs on your bed. She fell asleep about an hour ago but made me promise to wake her up when Auntie Kate and Uncle Cam got home.’

‘No, I don’t mind,’ I lied. So much for going to bed and watching a movie. Or going to bed and doing anything for that matter.

‘Where’s your mom?’ Ryan asked as we joined them in the kitchen.

‘She and Larry went to Banff for a week,’ Cam explained.

‘Uh-oh.’ Sam giggled. ‘I think we just crashed their first night alone.’

‘It’s OK,’ I promised. ‘We’re getting used to it. But this dinner better be good.’

‘Well, have a seat and we’ll find out,’ Sam instructed.

The aroma of her curry began to melt my frustration and I did what I was told, dropping my coat over the chair and sitting at the table in the kitchen. Ryan and Cam joined me, while Sam dished out the meal.

Sam and I have been friends for longer than either of us would care to admit. We’ve shared elementary school teachers, we’ve shared broken hearts, and we’ve shared practical jokes. The first time we separated at all was for university. I studied music in Calgary but she chose to leave town and go to the Culinary Arts Institute in New York. I took that personally and didn’t speak to her for the entire time she was away. Not only was it incredibly lonely for both of us, but I missed a wonderful opportunity to tour New York and the Hudson Valley. And she had not been there for my whole little episode with Stephan. When she came home, and we were both older and wiser, we finally mended the tears in our friendship. We often wondered if I would ever have had an affair with Stephan if I still had Sam in my life. Probably not. I think I was lonely and reaching out to anyone who would have me, and Stephan took advantage of that.

Of course, Sam handled her own heartbreak in ways that would take many chapters in a book to explain. Since she came home, we’ve both realized how important our friendship is to us, and it has helped us endure many of life’s ups and downs. When Sam met Ryan, I knew that handsome firefighter was the one for her, but I was worried that her getting married would make my role in her life a smaller one. But she had worked hard to keep us all balanced. And when she had Bonnie, she had us both in the delivery room, something I still haven't fully recovered from. That little girl was the perfect way to gently break me into the idea of children. I love her dearly but can give her right back to her mother at any time. Cam has rounded out our circle nicely, getting along with Ryan and Sam almost better than I do sometimes, and worshipping their little daughter.

Sam brought the final plate over and set it at her place and then joined us at the table. The plates were piled high with steamed jasmine rice and a beef curry full of carrots, onions, garlic, nuts and raisins. My mouth was watering now as I greedily picked up my fork and tested it out as requested. The explosion of flavours in my mouth was almost overwhelming and I closed my eyes as the aromas of the spices filtered through my nostrils.

'Sam, no matter what else I have ever said about you, you are a culinary genius,' I told her, picking up my wine glass and raising it to her.

Cam and Ryan both agreed, nodding in unison as their mouths were full.

'I wanted to do this for a wedding I'm catering next week. They wanted an all-ethnic buffet and I just didn't even know where to start.'

'Well, you've got a winner here,' Cam told her, finally able to stop eating for a minute.

'I honestly agree,' I promised her. 'When I first saw you appear around the corner, I was disappointed we weren't alone, but now I'm willing to build a second bedroom so you can live here!'

'Kate, you're just too easy,' Sam told me. 'All it takes is good food and you'll do anything for anybody.'

'Well, there is one other way to influence her,' Cam said, laughing.

'So, anyone see the newspaper this morning?' Ryan asked.

'Oh, please,' I begged, knowing I couldn't change the course of this conversation no matter how hard I tried.

'Yeah, there was this famous conductor and a young student who looked a lot like you, Kate,' Ryan continued, his eyes twinkling.

'Yes, Ryan, that was me. From years ago when I was a mere baby attending university. I believe the man in the picture was one of my professors, but I don't recall his name,' I joked.

'Oh, I think I remember him,' Sam said, and then she guiltily looked at Cam, realizing she might be giving away my secrets. 'He taught orchestral performance, didn't he? And then moved to France?'

'It's OK, Sam, he knows pretty much everything.'

Sam sighed. 'Thank goodness.'

'Yeah, Stephan has been plaguing my existence for the last few days. And today I was honoured by a visit from his wife, who tore a strip off one side of me, and some sort of auntie, who tore a strip off the other side. That was after little Nicole had a go at me yesterday. It's been quite a fun week in my world.'

'What's it like, having him around?' Sam asked, and then looked at Cam again. 'Or maybe just forget I asked that. We can talk next week some time.'

'He's a total jerk, if you ask me,' Cam said. 'I've had to pull him off Katie a couple of times.'

'Really?' Sam asked, dying to know all the details, but realizing I couldn't get into all of it in front of Cam.

'They're all a little emotional right now,' I explained, trying to play it down. 'Did you read the newspaper article or did you just look at the pictures?'

'We read the article,' Ryan said.

'Then you know about Nicole's little press conference and how she's accused her father of molesting her?'

'I thought he was bad news,' Sam said.

'There is no way he did that. He would have to have been molesting her while we were having an affair. I just can't believe that is possible.'

'But if he did it, he should be thrown in jail and they should throw away the key,' Sam said, and I didn't see any disagreement from anyone in the room.

'Don't we still have the whole innocent-until-proven-guilty thing in this country?' I asked.

‘I just think we’ll never all agree on this and we should talk about something else,’ Cam said, seeing the exasperation growing in my eyes.

‘I love you,’ I told him, happy that he was letting this go, knowing how I felt about it all. I pushed my plate away, after cleaning up the extra sauce with some nan bread. ‘And I think I’m going to go up and check on Bonnie.’

I tiptoed up the stairs to the bedroom. Bonnie was lying peacefully on the bed, sleeping soundly. She had pushed the covers off, and I sat down beside her and leaned over to pull them up again. I thought I’d just lie down there with her for a minute or two and then I’d go help with cleaning up downstairs. I don’t remember anything else after that.

Sunday October 26

The alarm rang for the fifth time, its foghorn-like blast cutting through the silence in the bedroom, and for the fifth time I pushed the snooze button. Rolling over, I tucked my head under the pillow and was almost asleep again when I suddenly found myself on the floor looking up at Cam who was looking down at me.

'I'd like to sleep in today,' he snarled, 'and hearing the alarm ring every nine minutes is not helping.'

'Who's not a morning person today?' I asked as I picked myself up off the floor.

'Who got to go to bed early while I stayed up and entertained your friends and cleaned up the kitchen?'

'You could have woken me up. I didn't fall asleep on purpose; it was an accident.'

'Go to work, Katie.'

I trudged downstairs and climbed into a very cold shower, which didn't help my mood at all. I had taken my last cold shower, I swore, and the building super was going to hear from me today.

The thing I hate most about these early morning shows is that Gus doesn't open his coffee shop until nine. Theatre is a late-night business so he doesn't miss out on much by sleeping in. But a double espresso would sure help me get going and the guy at the outdoor stand by the C-Train wasn't there this morning.

I signed in at security and headed down Tin Pan Alley toward the back door of the theatre. I stopped at the green room. The technicians were a step ahead of me and already had their coffee on so I swiped some.

'That's twenty-five cents, Kate,' Trevor scolded.

'Put it on my tab.'

'If you ever pay your tab we can all retire,' Scott joked.

'It's too early to take this kind of abuse,' I said, admitting defeat. 'I'll be in my office if you have anything nice to say to me.'

'Be careful on the stage, we haven't been out there yet this morning. It's probably still a mess from last night.'

I pushed my way through the doors and out on to the stage. Trevor was right, the set was half down, with wires and props scattered everywhere. I shook my head, glad I didn't have to attend to this clean-up, and turned to jump down off the stage. I froze in my tracks, not believing what I saw. I knew I should scream, but I couldn't seem to catch my breath. As a matter of fact, I was pretty sure I was about to faint. I took a deep breath, closed my eyes and prayed I was imagining things.

'Scott! Trevor!' I finally screamed.

I heard a glass crash and a moment later they raced through the door and on to the edge of the stage.

'God, Kate, don't do that. I thought you'd killed yourself,' Trevor said.

I turned and looked at them. They must have seen something in my eyes, because they both ran the rest of the way, toward me.

'What's the matter?' Scott asked as he grabbed my arm, catching me before I fell.

I turned and pointed up to the second balcony. A body was swinging slowly, like a pendulum, suspended by a thick rope from the railing of the second balcony. It was hanging almost perfectly between the first and second balconies.

'Holy shit!' Scott whispered.

'Kate, call security and call the police.' Trevor took charge of the situation. 'Come on, Scott, let's get up there and see if there's anything we can do.'

They both jumped off the stage and ran for the door. I stood, hypnotized by the gentle swaying of the body.

'Move, Kate! Call them now!' Trevor commanded before they headed through the door.

Trevor's tone broke me out of my fugue and I ran into the green room and grabbed the phone.

The supervisor answered the phone on the second ring. 'Security desk, this is Nick speaking.'

'Nick, it's Kate. I need you to call the police.'

'What's up, Kate?' he asked in his usual jovial tone.

'You're never going to believe it.' I felt a giggle beginning but I stifled it quickly.

'Try me.'

'Nick, I just found a body in the theatre.'

'Very funny, Kate. What do you really need?' he asked.

'Nick, I'm serious.'

'You found another dead body in the theatre?' His voice filled with disbelief.

'Don't make me say it again. Are you calling the police?' I asked.

'You're telling me the truth?' Nick asked once again.

'I swear on my mother's grave.'

'Your mother is alive,' he pointed out.

'Nick, quit fucking arguing with me and just call the police! Come down here yourself if you don't believe me.'

'OK, I'm calling the police. I'll be there in a couple of minutes. Where is it?'

'Somewhere between the first and second balconies. I'm onstage though, and Scott and Trevor have gone up to see if there's anything they can do to save her . . . And Nick?'

'If you say April Fool's, you're a dead woman.'

'Can you page Cam for me?' I asked, feeling my bravado fading as my knees started to shake.

'Right away.' Nick hung up the phone.

I made my way back out on to the stage. Trevor and Scott sat on the edge of the second balcony, watching as the body still swayed slowly to an invisible tempo.

'It's too late,' Trevor said when he saw me back on the stage.

'The police are on their way,' I confirmed.

The door opened again and I turned to see Nick rush out on to the stage. His face turned pale and he involuntarily crossed himself.

'Oh my God! Are you going to cut her down?' he called up to Trevor.

'It's too late,' Trevor said. 'She's been dead for a while.

We better leave everything until the police get here.'

Nick turned his back and sat down.

'I'll get you some water,' I offered, looking for any excuse to leave the area.

I stood in the green room, running the cold water longer than I had to. I pulled a glass out of the cupboard and filled it, then ran a paper towel under the tap and held it to my forehead.

'Katie?' I heard a voice in the hallway.

'I'm in here, Cam,' I called.

He ran through the green room door, shirt tails flying.

'You broke a few speed limits to get here this fast.' I laughed.

'What the hell is going on?' He wasn't laughing with me; his face was all worried. 'They gave me a nine-one-one page and then put your name after it. I thought something horrible had happened.'

I tossed the paper towel in the garbage, picked up the glass of water and took Cam's hand. 'It has. Follow me.'

I led him out on to the stage and pointed up to the second balcony.

'Jesus Christ.'

'Here's some water, Nick,' I said, handing the security guard the glass.

He took it gratefully, drank some and then held the glass to his forehead, as I had just done. I noticed a little colour returning to his cheeks.

'What happened?' Cam asked.

'I don't know. I found her when I was on the way up to my office.'

'Who is it?'

I was surprised Cam was the first one to ask. 'Nicole's therapist, Joelle Bergere.'

Cam laughed. 'I knew it. Two deaths in this theatre in the last couple of months and you know both the victims. This is why I keep telling you to stay out of other people's business.'

I turned to him, ready to let him have it. I opened my mouth and all that came out was a giggle.

'You're right.' I giggled again, not able to stop myself. 'I'm beginning to feel like I'm stuck in a novel. A really bad novel.'

He came over and wrapped his arms around me, leading me off the stage and into the green room. He closed the door behind us and my giggles turned to tears. I hate that he knows me so well, almost as much as I hate turning into a sobbing hysterical woman.

Cam held me, not saying a word, until I calmed down.

'You'd think I'd be getting used to this,' I half-laughed and half-cried.

'I'd like to think we'll never get used to it. I'd also like to think that we'll never have to get used to it. One death in this place was enough for a lifetime.'

I pulled away from Cam and grabbed a Kleenex, trying to repair my make-up in the mirror. I had mascara halfway down my cheeks. Finally I gave up, wet the dishcloth hanging over the faucet and washed my face.

'Let's just go home right now and pretend Scott and Trevor found her,' I suggested.

'You found her, Katie; you have to be here for the police.'

'It was just a thought.'

'And what about Stephan's message on our answering machine the other night? Was this who he was talking about?'

I felt a knot of fear in my stomach. 'Yes, it was. But he couldn't have . . .'

'Let's leave it for the police to figure out.'

'Fine by me,' I admitted. 'The instant I saw the body, I knew I was tired of playing cops and robbers.'

'That makes me very happy.' He smiled.

I threw the dishrag into the sink and poured us both a coffee.

'Thanks,' he said, taking a sip. 'Are you OK?'

'I'm fine. I think it was just shock.' I moved closer to him and wrapped my arms around his waist. 'Thanks for coming. Guess you didn't get to sleep in after all.'

'I knew I would never have a boring life with you, Katie. I just never expected it to be quite this exciting.'

'I'm glad I'm not letting you down.'

There was a knock at the door. I looked up at Cam and gave him a quick kiss. 'Our public awaits.'

He pulled away from me and opened the door.

'Cam, Katie, didn't think I'd be running into you guys so soon.'

'Ken, I thought you worked homicide, not suicide?' I smiled at the young police detective.

'When I heard there was another body found here, I had to come check it out. I didn't think it was fair to put another detective up against you guys.'

'Are you drinking coffee yet?' I asked, remembering how health-conscious he was. Ken Lincoln had just turned detective and the investigation last month had been his first homicide. We had gotten to know him quite well as he tried valiantly to protect me against the bad guys.

When the detective first walked into my theatre, he looked much younger than I had expected a homicide detective to be. I had an image of someone in his forties, slightly out of shape, with a bit of a beer belly from all those nights sitting in the pub with his buddies discussing their cases, maybe balding, and with a definite aroma of stale cigarettes and coffee. He should have been wearing a rumpled raincoat, like Columbo, and should be divorced due to the pressure his wife had suffered from being married to a cop. However, the detective I got was young, slim, with thick black hair covering his head and barely any grey, let alone a bald spot. He walked with a bounce in his step and certainly didn't look like he suffered from overwork or long hours of sitting at a desk. He also dressed much better than I had ever expected from a cop. I guess years of watching police shows on TV have ruined my perception.

And now here he was again, in his impeccable Armani suit and polished loafers. You might have thought he was on the take from the way he dressed, until you saw he wore a Timex watch and drove a ten-year-old car. He just likes to dress well.

'No, thanks,' he said in response to my offer of coffee. 'How about you telling me what's going on?'

'I was cutting through the theatre on the way to my office and I found her hanging there. I swear that's it, Ken; I know nothing else about this.'

'Do you know who it is?' he asked me, raising an eyebrow.

He caught me on that one. 'OK,' I admitted. 'I met her once. Her name was Dr Joelle Bergere. She was a psychologist, I think, or a therapist of some sort.'

'How did you know her?' he asked.

'She was a friend of Stephan Bouchard – he's the new conductor of the Symphony. And I knew him years ago.'

'Is he the same Stephan Bouchard that made the front page

yesterday?' Ken asked, eyebrows still raised. 'And was that you in the picture with him?'

'Yes, it was me. And yes, he's the same one.'

'And did the fact that she's a psychologist have anything to do with yesterday's headlines?'

'Apparently,' I admitted reluctantly, afraid I was incriminating Stephan with every word. 'She has been counselling Nicole Bouchard for quite a while.'

'And how did Stephan feel about her?' Ken asked, hitting the proverbial nail on the head. No wonder he'd made detective so young.

'You should ask him about that,' I answered defensively.

'I think we have a tape on our answering machine that you might want to hear,' Cam jumped in.

Damn him. 'I was getting to that.'

'I'll send someone by for that later today,' Ken said. 'Is there anything else? No, forget I said that. From my previous experience there's probably a lot more. We'll get into that later. And you can tell me how you seem to know so much about all these people, especially since you said you didn't know anything else about this. Would you mind showing me where the body is?'

'I'll take him out,' Cam offered.

'We'll all go,' I said, sounding braver than I felt.

Cam took my hand and we led Ken out on to the stage. Once again I pointed up to the balcony and Ken turned to look. Scott and Trevor had been joined by two police officers, waiting patiently for instructions from Ken. As I watched Ken I thought I noticed his face pale a little at the sight, but he covered well. I guess he hadn't hardened himself to the sight of a body yet either. I wondered how many investigations it would take before he could.

'Is the coroner on his way?' Ken called up to his men.

'Yes, sir,' one of the officers called back.

'OK, seal the place off until the lab guys get here,' he instructed, and then turned back to me. 'How do I get up there?'

'Through those doors in the back and up the stairs to your left,' I answered.

Ken turned to Nick. 'You'll bring the people from the coroner's office here as soon as they arrive?'

'Security's waiting at the stage door for them,' Nick assured him.

'I hate to be indelicate, Ken,' I said, returning to reality, 'but what's going to happen to the piano competition today?'

'I don't know, Kate,' he said.

'This competition is a big deal and in about a half-hour I'm going to have the committee hounding me to get you guys out of the theatre so they can get on with the festival.'

'Kate, this is an official investigation. You should remember – we've done this before, quite recently, I believe.'

'Don't tell me,' I said. 'I know how this works, all too well. What do you want me to tell them?'

'Nothing. I'm not letting anyone in this theatre until we're finished. They can stay out in the halls and grumble all they want. But no one gets in until I'm finished.'

'Easy for you to say,' I said. 'What am I supposed to do? Hide in my office?'

'Kate, we'll be as fast as we can. I swear I will do everything in my power to get this over with as quickly as possible.'

'OK, OK. Nick, is security ready to intercept the officials?' I asked, pretty sure that this would be a little more than my ushers could deal with.

'We've got all the entrances covered,' Nick said. 'We'll keep everyone out until the police give us the all clear.'

Ken started towards the door.

'Am I free to go?' I asked.

'It depends on how far you're going,' Ken said.

'My office, OK?'

'I'll see you and Cam there before I leave,' he said, leaving the auditorium to make his way up to the second balcony.

I turned back to Cam. 'Well, shall we?'

'Not that I have much choice,' he replied. 'Lead the way.'

I hopped off the stage and cut through the house-right doors. Cam had his keys out and opened the fire-escape door. He led the way up, knowing I still felt uneasy after being pushed down the same stairs, and he reached for my hand. He was such a sweet man, considering what I put him through. The phone was ringing as I opened my office door. I ran in and answered it.

'Kate Carpenter.'

The line was dead. I had missed the call, but the message light was flashing. I dialled in my code and was greeted by a pre-recorded message.

'You have ten messages waiting.'

I hung up. 'Ten messages already?'

'I'll make the coffee,' Cam said.

'Please tell me you brought cigarettes with you.'

'You're quitting, Katie,' he said as he disappeared into the bathroom to get some water.

'I'm starting again,' I shouted after him. 'I think this is as good an excuse as any.'

I picked up the phone again, dialled in my code and listened to my messages. News travels faster than the speed of light around this place. I scribbled messages down, deciding I wasn't going to return most of them. I knew I'd see all these people soon enough. Cam came back into the room and tossed a pack of cigarettes on to the desk.

'I love you,' I said, taking one out. 'Do you have a light?'

'Will you still love me if I don't?'

'No.'

'Well then, you're lucky, I have a light.' He leaned over and lit my cigarette. 'I love you too.'

'Good.' I finished with the last message and hung up the phone.

'Aren't you going to return your calls?' he asked, sitting on the edge of the desk.

'Later. How does news travel so fast in this building?' I asked. 'Every department head left a message asking me what is going on. God, I don't know what's going on yet but everyone else seems to.'

'There are going to be reporters here,' Cam felt the need to point out. I don't know if he was trying to comfort me or scare me.

'I don't want to deal with reporters,' I whined.

Cam crossed to the window. 'I was right, come look.'

I reluctantly joined him. 'Both TV stations?' I asked.

'And both papers.' He pointed to the news vans parked across the street. 'And there's the first radio truck pulling in.'

'There's a leak in this building.'

'That's what happens when the TV stations start paying for

news tips,' he explained. 'And they listen to the police scanners, you know.'

'I have a headache,' I said, leaning against him.

He put his arm around me. 'It'll be OK. This is a suicide and it'll be over as soon as the body is removed.'

'Promise me?' I asked.

'Promise.'

'Now tell me how you know that.'

'Because I know everything, remember?'

'I don't recall ever admitting to that,' I protested.

'But I live with the hope that someday you might.'

I tried to pull away from him but he wouldn't let me go. 'I've got to get changed, Cam.'

'Just stay here for a minute,' he said, holding me tight.

I melted into his arms and felt the tension of the morning start to drain away. I actually started to feel better. I also started to feel something else and, impulsively, I turned to Cam and kissed him.

'What's that for?'

'Don't talk,' I said as I kissed him again.

I reached out, without letting go of him, and pulled the blinds closed.

'Katie . . .'

'I told you not to talk.'

'Are you sure?' he asked.

'Very.'

'I thought you didn't want to do it here.'

'That was before my adrenaline started pumping . . . something about finding that body downstairs.'

'What if somebody comes in?'

'Wedge a doorstop in the door,' I told him as I pulled his shirt over his head. I started unbuttoning my blouse while he did as I'd said.

'Are you really sure?' he asked again, wrapping his arms around my waist and pulling me close to him.

'You remember when we saw *City Slickers*?' I asked.

'Uh-uh.'

'You remember my favourite line in the movie?' I asked, my breathing becoming heavy as I struggled with removing more clothes.

'No.'

'When Billy Crystal explained the basic difference between men and women when it comes to sex . . .'

'Still don't remember,' he said.

'He said when it comes to having sex, women need a reason and men just need a place,' I explained.

'So . . .'

'I've got a reason and you've got a place. Now stop talking.'

'I never knew you understood men so well.' He laughed as we kissed again.

Cam undid my bra and slid it off. I unzipped his jeans and they dropped to his knees. I was amazed at how exciting it was, knowing we could get caught any second. I almost fell on to the desk and pulled him on top of me. He was trying to unbutton my jeans when there was a pounding at the door. Cam stopped kissing me and I tried quickly to gather my wits.

'Yes.' My voice cracked and I cleared my throat and tried again. 'Yes.'

'They need you downstairs, Kate.'

It was Graham.

'I'm just changing. I'll be down in five.'

'I'll let them know you're on your way,' Graham said as I heard him head back down the corridor.

Neither Cam nor I moved until we heard the door at the end of the hall close. When I knew we were safe, I broke into a fit of giggles.

'Bad idea,' Cam said.

'Really bad idea,' I agreed, getting off the desk and trying to find my bra.

'Here,' Cam called as he untangled it from the blinds and tossed it to me.

I dressed in record time and pulled my hair back into a ponytail. I checked Cam to make sure everything was on right side out and headed for the lobby.

Graham was sitting at the bottom of the stairs waiting for me.

'What took you two so long?' he asked.

'Sorry, I couldn't find my pantyhose,' I tried.

'Oh, God.' Graham stood up and turned away from me, then turned back again. 'Oh, God, don't tell me.'

'What?' I asked, thinking a good defence would throw him off the track.

'Look, what you two do in the privacy of your own home is one thing, but this is work.'

'What are you talking about?' I asked, knowing that the sheepish look on Cam's face was giving us away.

'For my sake, just wash the desk, OK?' Graham headed for the bar, disgusted with both of us. 'I'm going to start the inventory. Detective Lincoln is on stage and wants to see you.'

'Thanks, Graham,' I called after him.

'You want me to come with you?' Cam asked.

'Are you in a hurry to go anywhere else?'

'Not now.'

'Then come along.'

I took his hand and we walked back into the theatre. I glanced up to the balcony and noticed the body was gone. That was a definite improvement.

'Ken?' I called.

'Be there in a minute,' he answered from the stage.

'So how do you think Graham knew?' I asked, turning back to Cam.

'Graham knows everything,' Cam said. 'He's a scary person.'

'It was you. The look on your face.'

'I've never had anyone walk in on me in the middle of . . .'

'Never?' I asked, unbelievingly.

'Never.'

'Well, he didn't really walk in on us.'

'Close enough, Katie. At least as close as I ever want to experience.'

'That's too bad.' I smiled. 'I was kind of enjoying the adventure.'

'Well, you'll always have the memories,' he said. 'Because we are never going to do that again.'

'We'll see.'

'Kate?'

I turned and found Ken standing right behind me. I felt myself blush, hoping he hadn't overheard too much of our conversation.

'So, what's up?' I asked, trying to force normal colour into my cheeks.

'Due to mounting pressure from your superiors and mine, we've finished here in record time. It appears the chief of police is a big supporter of this competition. So the theatre is yours.'

'With time to spare.' I winked at Cam.

'Thanks for your cooperation,' Ken said as he turned to go.

'Did you find anything?' I asked.

'You'll have to read about this one in the papers,' Ken said, still heading for the exit. 'My lips are sealed. But I'll probably be back to talk to you about this sometime later today or tomorrow.'

'But, Ken, don't we have some sort of right to know how the investigation is going?'

He finally stopped and turned around. 'Kate, last time you got lucky. You lived. You are not getting involved with this investigation in any way, shape or form, and the easiest way for me to avoid that happening is if I say goodbye and walk out this door right now.'

'I think I resent that.'

'I'd rather have you pissed off with me than the police chief.' He laughed as he turned and started down the stairs. 'I'll call you if I need anything else.'

'Just don't bother calling me next time you want free theatre tickets,' I shouted after him.

'OK – but we're still on for dinner on the seventh, right?' he asked.

'We'll see you guys then,' I agreed, losing another battle.

'Well, I guess you were told,' Cam said.

'You know I don't like it when people tell me what to do,' I said.

'Get used to it, Katie. You can't fight City Hall.'

'We'll see.'

Graham pushed his way through the doors into the theatre.

'Do I have to knock or are you two decent?' he asked.

'Give it a rest,' I said, giving him my best dirty look.

'So do we have a show?' Graham asked.

'We have a show. Let's do a good inspection of the theatre and make sure they didn't forget anything. I hate it when the audience has to remove the crime scene tape to get to their seats.'

'Do you guys want some help?' Cam asked.

'Sure, why don't you take the second balcony, Graham you take the first balcony and I'll take down here.'

'OK, boss,' Graham said, heading up the stairs.

'A thorough inspection,' I called after him. 'I don't want any of our patrons finding anything out of the ordinary, because I'm sure everyone will be looking for something!'

'Yes, boss!'

Cam headed upstairs and I started walking up and down the rows, checking behind the seats and straightening chairs in the box seats. Something caught my eye when I was about halfway down. I leaned in behind the seat and pulled out a small journal. I opened it and flipped through the pages. I couldn't find a name anywhere, so I dropped it in my jacket pocket and finished my inspection.

I hid in my office for the rest of the day and had Graham heading off the reporters. It worked well for us, because they thought Graham was just an usher and they pretty much ignored him; it was me they were after. Considering the way it had started, I managed to end the day quietly enough. Cam met me at security and we drove home in silence, both exhausted.

When Cam let us into the apartment I dropped my coat and bag in the hallway and headed straight upstairs. Cam flipped on the lights and bent over to pick up my coat.

'Here, let me get this for you,' he said sarcastically.

I ignored him and crashed on the bed.

'You're wrinkling your suit,' he called up the stairs.

'I don't care.'

'I'm not pressing it for you.'

'I suddenly care.'

I stood up and pulled a hanger out of the closet. I took my jacket off and checked the pockets. I felt something in one of them and pulled out the journal I had found earlier and then forgotten. I hung my jacket up and sat on the bed, leafing through it again. I heard Cam bounding up the stairs and he threw himself at me. The journal flew out of my hand and I fell backwards with Cam on top of me.

'Is this your idea of foreplay?' I asked, trying to catch the wind that he had knocked out of me.

'Was it good for you?' he asked jokingly.

'You're wrinkling my suit,' I felt the need to point out.

'Your mom is not here and I have been waiting all day to finish what we started this morning.'

'I'm kind of tired,' I teased.

'I'll iron your suit.'

'OK, do with me what you will . . .'

Monday October 27

I sat straight up in bed, my nightmare still fresh in my brain. Where was I? I felt the panic rise and then I realized I was in my room, I was safe, and I wasn't dropping off a forty-foot tower. I reached out in the dark and felt Cam lying beside me.

'Katie?' he asked, sleep heavy in his voice.

'Uh-huh,' I said with that post-nightmare terror in my voice.

'Are you OK?' His arm reached up and rubbed my back.

'I'm OK,' I lied. I rarely lie to him. He always knows. But I have to try to maintain my independent woman status, even when I'm filled with terror.

I heard the covers rustle as he turned toward me.

'Come here.'

He didn't have to ask me twice.

'What did you dream about?' he asked, enveloping me in his arms.

'I don't remember.'

'Really?'

'Really,' I promised.

'You want to talk or go back to sleep?'

'Sleep,' I said, feeling sorry for him, knowing he probably had to be at work as early as I did.

He kissed my forehead. 'Goodnight.'

'Night.'

I cuddled really close to him. I listened as his breathing slowed and I knew he was asleep again. It took me a lot longer.

I sat at my desk staring out the window. It was still dark outside and I was already at work. Something was wrong with this picture. I just can't get used to working days. I turned my stare to the coffee pot, willing the last of the water to drip through so I could finally pour myself a cup. I heard the door open at the end of the hall.

'Hello, Graham,' I called.

'It's Leonard.'

'Leonard?' I asked, surprised. 'What are you doing here this early?'

Leonard dropped his duffel bag and plopped his tall frame into the chair across the desk from me. He stretched his legs out and they came halfway under my desk. Leonard is another of my regular ushers. A university philosophy major, I feel pretty sure I'll have him for the next eight years, right through his doctorate.

'I'm here to talk to you about the party. It's tough to talk to you without Graham being around.'

'The party?' I asked, not comprehending exactly what he was talking about. And then it slowly dawned on me. 'Graham's birthday party?'

'That would be the party I'm talking about,' Leonard confirmed.

'Shit.'

'I take it that means you forgot.'

'Well I didn't forget exactly. I just sort of got sidetracked.' Thank God, the coffee was done. I poured two cups, one cup for myself and one for Leonard.

'Kate, it's a week from tomorrow.'

'I know.'

'You said you'd take care of it,' he reminded me. 'I was just wondering if you needed some help, because none of us have heard anything from you about it.'

'I know. God, I'm so sorry. I will take care of it all,' I promised.

'Do you have any ideas or do you need some help?' he asked. 'We really don't mind; we just want Graham to have a good party. Especially now with all this going on.'

'No, I can do this. I don't suppose you have any idea of who we should invite?'

'Well, actually, I did come up with a list.'

'OK. Here's what we'll do. We'll hold it in the loading dock next week after the show. I'll keep him busy during act two and you guys can decorate and then when he leaves, we'll all be there to surprise him. I'll get my friend Sam to do the food. She'll do it for cost because she owes me big time.'

'That was easy,' Leonard commented.

'It's what I do best. Organize last-minute emergencies and make everyone believe I spend weeks planning things. But that's our little secret, OK?'

'OK.'

'There are two things I'll need help with. You'll have to take care of inviting people because, like you said, Graham is always right beside me.'

'I can do that,' Leonard assured me.

'And the other thing is the decorations. I don't have any time to go shopping. Can you do some balloons and banners and things like that?'

'It might do you some good to take a break and go shopping.'

'Don't you start with the nagging,' I warned. 'I get enough of that from everyone else I know.'

'All right. I'll buy the decorations.'

'Just let me know when you're going and I'll give you some cash.'

'We could all chip in, Kate.'

'I know. But I want to do this for him.'

The door at the end of the hall opened again.

'Good morning, Graham,' we both called in unison.

Graham practically bounded into the office. He was getting really good at getting around with his brace. He sat down beside Leonard and pulled some orange juice out of his backpack.

'Leonard, I'm not used to seeing you here this early. Are you after my job or bucking for a raise?' Graham asked.

'Trust me, it wasn't on purpose. I set my alarm for the wrong time.'

Graham twisted the cap off his juice bottle and tossed it into the garbage. 'Two points!' he cheered.

'Well, since you're all here bright and early, let's take advantage of it and get some work done,' I suggested.

'Only under protest,' Leonard joked.

'Protest noted. How about if you guys get the lobby set up. And you should probably load up a couple of extra cases of ice cream into the freezers. That seems to be selling really well with the piano crowd.'

'Did you notice the reporters outside?' Graham asked.

'No,' I said, getting up and walking over to the window. He was right; there were two news vans parked outside.

'They're lined up outside the door already. Are you going to let them in?' he asked.

'I don't have much choice. The festival is open to the public. As long as they have tickets they can come in. But no pictures, no tape recorders and no questions.'

'And I still don't get to talk to them?' Graham asked. 'How am I ever going to get my picture in the paper if you won't let me talk to the reporters?'

'Sorry, dude, you're going to have to find some other way to get famous.'

'Can I at least say my "no comments" with attitude? Maybe someone will notice me.'

'No. And if there's anyone famous here, you can practice acting normal in front of them as well.'

'Aw, Kate, you're ruining my day before it's even started.'

'I know it will be a stretch, Graham, but with your talent I know you can carry it off.'

'Come on, Leonard, Kate hasn't had enough coffee yet. I usually try and make myself scarce until she's on her third or fourth cup.'

'Funny, Graham. Do a nice job on the lobby.'

'We will.'

They took off down the hall and I checked the time. Eight o'clock. I had an hour until we had to open the theatre. I searched my drawer and found a cigarette. I lit it just as the phone rang.

'Kate Carpenter,' I said.

'Ms Carpenter, I'm with the *Calgary Sun*—'

'I'm sorry, I have no comment. You'll have to speak with a Foothills Stage Network representative.'

'I just wanted to know—'

'Sorry. Please call back and ask the receptionist for the publicity department.'

I hung up the phone and it started ringing again. The switchboard opens at eight. I was beginning to think it was going to be another long day.

'Kate Carpenter.'

'Hi, I'm calling from the—'

'I'm sorry, I have no comments to make. You'll have to speak to our publicity department or the police.'

'May I just ask a question about—'

'No.' I hung up the phone. I was a little short-tempered this morning. I would have to watch it or I'd be hearing from the publicity department. But then the phone rang again.

'I have absolutely no comments to make, so please quit calling.'

'Katie?'

'Oh, hi, Cam,' I said sheepishly.

'I was going to ask how your morning was going but I guess I can figure that one out on my own.'

'It's not so bad. I'm just a little grumpy.'

'You should go to bed earlier when you have to get up so early.'

'I really hope you're not leading into a lecture here,' I warned him.

'No, not me, I would never lecture you.' Cam laughed. 'I know much better than that.'

'Good.'

'I'll be in about three,' he continued. 'Do you need anything from home?'

'I thought you had to work this morning,' I said.

'No, I traded shifts with Mike last week, but I gotta get going, I've got some errands to run. Anything I can bring?'

'Nope, just you.'

'Great. I'll take my lunch break early and drive you to your physio appointment and then we'll grab a bite to eat.'

'Cam, I don't really have time for physio today.'

'You know that Graham is perfectly capable of taking care of things for an hour or two. Besides, the festival is down at three and your show isn't up tonight; it's Monday. You have lots of free time.'

'Well, I wanted to get home early, do some laundry, get to bed at a decent time . . .'

'Katie . . .' His voice had that parental tone so I gave up.

'OK, OK, but you don't have to escort me. I can find the place on my own.'

‘I’m sure you can find it on your own. However, I’ll feel much more secure that you actually went if I take you. I know when it comes to taking care of yourself you can be a little neglectful.’

‘OK. But you’re paying for dinner.’ I knew I wasn’t going to win this one.

‘It’s a deal. Do you want me to meet you at the theatre?’

‘No, I’ll meet you at the stage door,’ I promised. ‘Now tell me why you’re up this early when you don’t have to be at work until four?’

‘I was worried about you,’ he told me.

‘Why?’

‘You had a bad dream last night.’

‘I know. It was nothing.’

‘It wasn’t nothing. And I just wanted to make sure you were OK.’

‘I am. Really. I don’t even remember what I was dreaming about. I think it was just the delayed shock from finding the body yesterday. But I’m OK now.’

‘Promise?’

‘I do.’

‘OK. I’ll see you later.’

‘Cam?’

‘Uh-huh?’

‘I love you.’

‘I love you too, Katie. Don’t work too hard today.’

‘I never do. See you at three.’ I hung up the phone and it started ringing again as soon as I put it down. I forwarded it to voicemail.

The ushers slowly wandered in and got into uniform. Nine o’clock came way too fast. Although I was tempted to hide in my office and do paperwork, I realized I was going to have to face the crowds at some point. I leafed through the program and found that Nicole Bouchard was scheduled to play in the afternoon, so I would probably have a safe and quiet morning. I put on some lipstick and headed downstairs. My worries proved unfounded as a small, quiet audience wandered through the theatre to find their places. Graham and Leonard had all the reporters in the lower lobby by the coat check, explaining to them why they couldn’t come in without tickets and how the theatre was not against free speech, it was just against free admission.

The afternoon proved much less peaceful. We closed for lunch at twelve and by twelve thirty there was a line-up going out of the building. I felt my stress level growing as the line grew longer.

'Kate, telephone,' Graham called to me from across the lobby.

'Who is it?'

'Security.'

I crossed the lobby and picked up the phone. 'Kate speaking.'

'Hi, Kate, it's Nick.'

'Hi, Nick. What's up?'

'I should be asking you that,' he said. 'Have you seen the crowd outside your theatre?'

'Yes, I have.'

'I didn't realize classical piano competitions were so popular.'

'Nicole Bouchard is playing this afternoon,' I explained. 'I guess everyone wants to see her.'

'I wish you had warned us about this,' Nick said. 'Well, I have someone here claiming to be the girl's mother. She's asking to be let in backstage so she doesn't have to face the press.'

'So why are you asking me? Can't the Maestro just take her back with him?'

'She's alone. I haven't seen Maestro Bouchard yet today,' Nick explained.

I felt a slightly evil shudder surge through me. 'So if I say no, you make her line up with the crowds outside?'

'Are you going to do that to her?' Nick asked.

'She's not exactly my favourite person right now.' I thought about this. It was very tempting to throw her to the dogs outside. I looked around to see if I could see any officials from the piano festival around and pass the decision off on them. The rules did state that no one was allowed in during the lunch break, I reasoned. But, tempting as it was, I just couldn't bring myself to do it. 'Send her down, Nick. I'll have Graham meet her at the back door.'

'That decision took an awfully long time,' Nick teased me.

‘Just remember never to cross me. I have the potential to be a real bitch.’ I hung up the phone and sent Graham down to meet the woman and seat her in the theatre. I decided now might be a good time to sneak up to my office for a while. I wasn’t up to facing her again.

At two o’clock the theatre was full, standing room only. The audience sat in hushed silence, awaiting Nicole’s appearance on stage. I sat in one of the reserved boxes in the first balcony, surveying my kingdom and awaiting her appearance as anxiously as the rest. I noticed that a large percentage of my staff was in the theatre too, rather than at their allocated posts. I then heard the almost inaudible click as a microphone was turned on.

‘Ladies and gentlemen, competitor number fifteen, Nicole Bouchard.’

Nicole’s tiny figure appeared stage-right, and she slowly crossed to the piano. She had on a simple black dress and a string of pearls that made her look like she was playing dress-up in her mother’s clothes. The piano bench scraped slightly as she adjusted her position. Her fingers were poised over the keys as she turned to face the panel of adjudicators, awaiting their signal to begin. The bell rang out across the silent hall and Nicole turned her eyes back to the piano. I found myself edging forward in my seat, awaiting the first note. I saw something glisten on her cheek. Was that a tear? My heart poured out to her, realizing the pressure she must be under. The bell rang again, and I saw her give an involuntary shudder, and then she played her opening chord.

‘Come on, Nicole, you can do it,’ I whispered under my breath.

And she kept playing, flawlessly, each note filled with the emotion that was boiling inside her. There were tears running freely down her cheeks now, but she kept playing, without hesitation or error, through to the last chord. The audience sat in an embarrassed silence, as Nicole didn’t move from the piano bench when she was finished, but sat there as if she didn’t remember what to do next. And then Stephan came out on to the stage and walked slowly across to where his daughter sat. He took her hand, helped her up and wrapped his arm around her waist, slowly leading her off the stage. I looked down into the audience and saw Carole Bouchard, sitting as still and quiet as the rest of the audience. She made no move to go to her daughter. There was a quick, uncomfortable smattering of applause and then silence again.

'Ladies and gentlemen, there will be a fifteen-minute intermission until the next competitor. Thank you.'

I stood up to go back to my office, but decided to go backstage instead. I ran into Scott standing outside the green-room door.

'Have you seen Stephan?' I asked.

'He and his daughter walked offstage and straight into a waiting limo.'

'So, what's the buzz back here?' I asked.

'Everyone's pretty quiet right now.'

'I'm not surprised. That was a pretty emotional moment.'

'Katherine.'

I heard my name and turned to see who was calling. Carole Bouchard was storming down the hall, wearing a perfect ice-blue suit, anger flaring in her eyes. And I had done so well to avoid her up to this point.

'Take me to my family,' she demanded.

'They've left.' I smiled politely at her.

'What do you mean?'

'Stephan and Nicole have left. He had a limo waiting outside and they have gone. I guess you should try the hotel.'

'How dare he?'

'I'm sorry, did you miss your ride?' I asked. 'I could call you a taxi.'

She didn't deign to answer, but spun around and beat a hasty retreat.

'Nice lady,' Scott said sarcastically.

'Yeah, and I seem to bring out the best in her.'

During the next competitor's performance, I decided to stay in my office and try to call Sam about Graham's party.

'Hey, Kate,' she greeted me over the phone. 'You guys are on the news again.'

'I don't even want to talk about it.'

'Rough day?' she joked.

'It's just that no matter what I do, I seem to be getting

dragged into this. And I think I told Cam I didn't want to get involved.'

'But you know them all. You're like some sort of sick psychological focal point for this family.'

'Well, I'm tired of it. Nobody's being nice to me anymore.'

'I don't put up with whining from my five-year-old; I'm not about to sit here and listen to it from you,' she admonished me.

'OK, OK. Are you doing anything next Tuesday?'

'Tell me why first. There's a big difference between telling me you have free tickets to Jann Arden and asking me to cater something for a hundred people.'

'Don't you trust me?' I asked, pretending to sound hurt.

'Not in the least. Now tell me what you want and how this affects me.'

'It's Graham's birthday. I promised I'd take care of the party. And then I sort of lost track of time.'

'Did you tell them you would bake?' She laughed.

'Sam, there is no one left in the building who has any sort of illusions about my culinary abilities. I told them you'd do it.'

'So you better hope I'm free next Tuesday.'

'And are you?' I asked.

'Let me check my book.' I heard papers rustling in the background. 'I have a luncheon, but I think I can manage a birthday party if you don't want anything too fancy.'

'No. Just a cake and some chips and dips. Stuff like that.'

'Kate, the day I bring a bag of chips to an affair that I'm catering is the day I turn in my license.'

'Well, just don't go to a lot of trouble.'

'Do you have a budget?' she asked.

'I'll just give you my credit card number and worry about it later.'

'And what kind of cake?'

'Chocolate. Are there really other kinds of cake?'

'I knew that was a stupid question,' she said. 'I don't suppose you're organized enough to tell me how many people will be coming?'

'Anywhere between fifty and a hundred.'

'Well that narrows it down. Is this one of those last-minute things you're trying to throw together?'

‘No, I’ve been thinking about this for months,’ I said. ‘I was just trying to find a better caterer for a change. But they were all booked already. ’

‘Yeah, yeah. Well, don’t worry, I’ll make you look good.’

‘You’re the best, Sam.’

‘So how is the festival going?’

‘I told you I didn’t want to talk about it,’ I insisted.

‘But you always say that. It’s this game we play where I pretend I have to drag the information out of you.’

I heard the door at the end of the corridor open and saw Cam coming down the hall.

‘Shit.’

‘What?’ Sam asked.

‘I lost track of time. Cam’s here to make sure I go to my physio appointment.’

‘Saved by the bell!’ Sam laughed. ‘But it’s a good thing someone’s looking after you.’

‘Oh, don’t you start. I was perfectly capable of looking after myself before Cam came into my life.’

‘Capable, maybe, but you don’t always make the best choices.’

‘I swear I’m going to find a new friend who’s not so patronizing.’

‘Just let me know when,’ Sam said. ‘I’m dying to meet the person who can put up with you.’

‘A little respect or I’m going to cut off your supply of free theatre tickets,’ I threatened.

‘Katie,’ Cam whispered, pointing to his watch.

‘Gotta go,’ I told Sam. ‘We’re going to be late.’

‘Well, call me if anything else exciting happens.’

‘I promise I’ll try and call you later tonight. Bye.’

I hung up the phone. Cam was holding out my bag for me, which I took from him.

‘Hello, dear, how was your morning?’ I asked.

‘We can talk in the car,’ he said. ‘We’re going to be late. I’ve been waiting at the stage door for fifteen minutes.’

‘I’m sorry. I got a little distracted.’

‘Apology accepted, but only if you get moving.’

‘Only if I get a kiss.’

He pecked my cheek. ‘Can we get going now?’

'That wasn't a kiss.'

Cam sighed, but pulled me toward him, bent me over backward, and kissed me like he had never kissed me before.

'Now?' he asked.

'I'll follow you anywhere.'

Cam dropped me off at home after dinner and went back to the Plex to finish his shift. I did a load of laundry, moved some dust around on the furniture and ran the vacuum cleaner, although it looked like Cam had done that fairly recently. When I was tired of playing homemaker, I carried the clean laundry upstairs, put it away and sat on the bed to call Sam and update her on the day.

'Hello?' she said.

'Hi, it's me. I have a few hours until Cam gets home; have you got time for girl talk?'

'I've got Ryan upstairs reading a bedtime story to Bonnie, and then I have to do some prep work for tomorrow. Other than that, go!'

'So, what do you want to hear about, the dead body?' I asked, knowing that was pretty much the main topic on everyone else's mind.

'Actually, I was hoping we could talk about Stephan.'

'Oh, that,' I said.

'Yeah, well, "oh, that" is a pretty big deal, Kate. What was it like when you first saw him there, in your theatre? I mean, my God, talk about a blast from the past!'

'It was weird. It was like time stopped and I had been moved back ten years. And I felt like that little girl again, too, all weak and wimpy and totally under his power. I mean, I would never go back to him, but he really has some sort of a weird hold over me. Every time he touches me—'

'Touches you?' she asked.

'Well, there were a couple of embraces, mostly in greeting, and then once when he kissed me—'

'He kissed you!' she exclaimed. 'I hope you slapped his face.'

'I think I forgot that part of it,' I admitted. 'And then there was the time when he thought he could maybe win me back. He thinks Cam is just a lowly blue-collar worker and not good enough for me.'

'Kate?' Sam asked. 'Is this Kate Carpenter I'm talking to? Been my friend since kindergarten? What is happening with you? I mean, I can maybe understand letting this happen once, but three or four times? Anything up with you and Cam?'

'No, I totally love Cam and have no desire to get together with Stephan in this lifetime – or any other lifetime for that matter. Like I said, though, he's got some sort of strange power over me, a spark . . . I guess that's the spark that he used to fan into a flame.' I laughed.

'Well, at least you're honest about it.'

'Only with you,' I warned her. 'None of this gets back to Cam. I've told him it's in my past and I'm totally over it. And I think he's chosen to believe that.'

'So is this what you were like when he was around the first time?' Sam asked.

'It was terrible. I seemed to lose my free will. Even when I found out he was married and had a family, there was a part of me that still wanted to be with him no matter what. Luckily my mom took me in and got me through it.'

'So, is he that good-looking?' she asked. 'I mean, in the papers he's cute and all, but drop-dead gorgeous?'

'Beyond drop-dead gorgeous,' I said. 'And famous and powerful and it's a pretty heady combination.'

'And a murderer,' Sam said.

I was silent for a moment.

'Kate, you're not going to defend him, are you?' she asked.

'Well, no, I guess not. I mean, he left a message on our machine saying he wanted her dead. I just can't believe the man I knew could do any of this.'

'People change,' she said. 'You're not the person you were ten years ago.'

'I know.'

'And it's interesting how you feel he was so honourable and you should protect him. You do remember that he was cheating on his wife with you and not telling you he was married?'

'I know, my mom kept saying that, too. I just always felt I had to defend him and I don't know why. I told you, it's that strange hold he has on me.'

'Well, just be careful. Don't be getting yourself into any

trouble over him. If he's so rich and famous and powerful he can look after himself.'

'Yeah, I guess I have to think about this a little.'

'And you have a great man right now.'

'Really, Sam, I would not take Stephan back; I just feel like I owe him something.'

'You don't.'

'See, my logical and sane brain understands that, but my totally screwed-up heart doesn't seem to understand it at all.'

'I know it's hard,' Sam said. 'Look, Ryan's coming down now. I've got to go; he's going to help me with the prep for tomorrow.'

'All right, I'll probably talk to you tomorrow,' I said.

'OK, keep that chin up and that heart in check,' Sam warned me.

'Night, sweetie,' I said, hanging up the phone.

I went to bed early, hoping to catch up on some of the sleep I'd been missing out on. I had been lying down for an hour, and although I was very relaxed, I wasn't even close to sleep. Ten thirty is four hours earlier than I usually go to bed and my body was not about to adapt to this new schedule that easily.

A little while later, I heard the front door open. The lights went on and off downstairs before Cam tiptoed upstairs. I pretended I was asleep, and watched him undress through half-closed eyes. He climbed quietly into bed, trying not to disturb me. I am never this polite when he's sleeping. He reached out and brushed a stray hair from my face.

'You're not asleep, are you?' he asked.

'No.'

'Why didn't you say anything?'

'You were being so polite, trying not to wake me up. I thought it was cute.'

He kissed me. 'I'm glad you're not asleep,' he said.

'Me too.'

Tuesday October 28

I sat at my desk, staring out the window at the still, dark world. I broke my trance, poured a coffee and decided to walk through the theatre. The auditorium was dark. I reached out and hit the switch for the cleaning lights. Slowly the dimmer control kicked in, the lights came on and I was surprised to see someone sitting in the middle of the theatre. She didn't move as the lights came up, so I walked down the aisle to where she sat.

'Carole?' I asked.

'Hello, Katherine.'

'What are you doing here? The theatre's not open yet.'

'I told you I was very good at bullying those little security people. When I get arrogant enough, I can get almost anything I want. And I wanted to be here alone for a while.'

'Why here?' I asked, hoping to get an answer even though I knew Carole wasn't particularly fond of sharing things with me. But she actually turned toward me and I noticed her eyes were wet. She held a damp hankie in her hand.

'When Stephan and I were first married, I used to spend hours in the theatre while he rehearsed. I would sit with my law books and study while the orchestra played. And then later, before he started . . . well, later, I would write briefs in the theatre. I have written some of my best closing arguments as some of the most famous orchestras in the world rehearsed. Those were wonderful times.' She sighed. 'Times when we were young and in love and wanted to be with each other all the time. Times before my career took me to one end of the world, and his took him to the other end. You know, when you are in my field of law, you usually end up in a dirty Third World country, or a camp with no toilets and running water. Stephan's career took him to the greatest cities of the world, where he stayed in the finest hotels, ate the finest food and drank the finest wine. Is it surprising that he might want someone there with him to share it with?'

'And now?' I prompted.

'And now, when I need solace, where do I go? Well, here I am, in the theatre again, hoping some of that magic from the past will return. But there is no music; Stephan is not standing onstage, stealing hidden glimpses at me. But I am also not the young beautiful thing he married, am I? We're both hardened and jaded by the lives we've led.'

'Are you all right?' I asked, worried by this sudden flow of emotion and information, something I had never seen come from this woman before. 'Can I call someone for you?'

'Who, Stephan?' she asked, suddenly laughing harshly through her tears. 'I'm not even sure he would come. It has been a difficult marriage, you know? But I suppose you do know. You and all those other little girls he has tutored over the past twenty years. I knew what he was like, but I thought I could marry him, change him. At first he only wanted to be around me, you know, and I thought that part of him had changed. I was a silly young girl.'

She reached over and picked up a glass that had been sitting on the floor beside her. I realized why she was being so forthcoming as she took another sip of wine.

'Let me call you a cab and get you back to the hotel,' I offered.

'Yes, he is a difficult man, and life has been far more difficult than I ever imagined. Married to him, raising his child. I was so young and foolish then. And now, I can't even find what I came here to find,' she said, totally ignoring my suggestion.

Spare me from philosophical drunks at eight in the morning, I thought. But I tried to speak much more gently.

'Come on, Carole,' I said as I took the glass from her and pulled her up. 'Let's get you into a taxi.'

'But I haven't found what I'm looking for,' she protested.

'I don't think you'll find it here. You need to go back to your family now.'

'Perhaps it's because there isn't any music playing,' she commented as I steered her out into the hall and toward the security desk. 'There was always the most beautiful music playing, you know? It was the soundtrack to my life. Does your life have a soundtrack, Katherine?'

'No, my life doesn't have a soundtrack,' I said to humour her.

She had started humming a requiem, suitable for her present state of mind. We made it to the security desk and I sat Carole down on the bench by the front door.

'Morning, Kate,' Nick greeted me.

'Nick, will you call a taxi and make sure Mrs Bouchard gets in it and back to her hotel?'

'You on clean-up duty this morning?' he joked.

'It appears that way. Can you call a cab?'

'I'll take care of her for you.'

'Thanks, Nick.' I smiled at him and then turned back to Carole. 'All right, Carole, Nick is going to be here to look after you until your taxi arrives. If you need anything you just ask him, OK?'

'I may have misjudged you, Katherine.' She smiled sweetly at me, fresh tears streaking her cheeks.

I smiled at her attempt at a compliment.

'But probably not.' She turned away from me and went back to her requiem.

The smile dropped off my face and I turned away, realizing there was no point arguing with her when she was drunk.

On the way back to my office I stopped to retrieve Carole's glass and half-empty bottle of wine. I set them on my desk, poured more coffee and sat down to try to find a cigarette. I lucked out and found a whole pack in the bottom drawer of my filing cabinet. I lit one, took a sip of coffee and sat back down just as Graham came in.

'Isn't it a little early to be hitting the bottle?' he asked.

'It's not mine.'

'And are you going to tell me whose it is?' he asked.

'No.'

'I'll just find out later,' he promised. 'You know there are no secrets in this building.'

'All right already.' I blew smoke in his direction. He coughed and waved his hands, trying to clear the air. 'I found Carole Bouchard in the theatre this morning and she had this with her.'

'Wow! A definite slide in the downward direction.'

'Graham, as much as I don't like Carole Bouchard, I can understand why she would be a little upset right now,' I said. 'We should probably try and show a little understanding.'

'She didn't seem very upset in the theatre yesterday, while Nicole was performing.'

'Like Cam keeps telling me, everybody reacts differently. She's a lawyer; maybe she's used to keeping a cool and calm demeanour in public. Plus, I would imagine that being married to Stephan would teach you that as well.'

'And then getting caught in a theatre half-corked the next day? Sounds a little suspicious to me.'

'You're right,' I said. 'But I don't think her behaviour has anything to do with what is going on here. I think she is having trouble on the home front.'

'Kate, why are you showing such restraint?' Graham asked. 'There has been a murder—'

'Suicide,' I corrected him.

'A death,' he compromised, 'in our theatre. The place is practically brimming over with suspects who all hated the dead woman – and each other – and there is all this strange behaviour going on. Are you not in the least bit curious? Don't you want to get to the bottom of this?'

'Graham, do you remember that the last time I tried to "get to the bottom of this" I just about got killed?' I asked.

'It didn't stop you then.'

'Well, it's going to stop me now. Besides, I promised Cam I would behave.'

The phone rang. For a moment I hesitated, deciding whether I really wanted to answer it or not, since the onslaught from the press hadn't stopped yet. Then I realized it might be Cam checking up on me and picked up the phone.

'Kate Carpenter.'

'Hi, Kate, it's Ken Lincoln calling.'

Detective Lincoln? I didn't think I'd be hearing from him again after he was so adamant about keeping me out of the investigation.

'Ken, what's up?' I asked, trying to keep the sudden excitement I felt from showing in my voice.

'I have some news for you,' he continued.

'I thought you weren't going to share anything with me.'

'Well, it's probably going to be in the papers today and I thought you should be prepared.'

'What is it?' Now my curiosity was really aroused.

'The body we cut down from your balcony – it wasn't a suicide.'

'What?'

'There are some suspicious findings in the autopsy, which I do not intend to divulge to you, so don't even ask.'

'OK, I won't ask,' I promised.

'Somebody worked very hard to make this look like a suicide, but it was definitely murder.'

'Oh my God!' What else was there to say?

'Kate, I want you to be very careful,' Ken warned me.

'What do you mean?'

'Kate, once again there is a murderer on the loose in your theatre. You seem to know most of the people involved and I don't want you getting caught in the middle of this. I don't want you to put yourself in danger.'

'I promise I'll stay out of it,' I assured him.

'OK. Now I told you about it just so you'd know before the newspapers come out. I don't want you saying anything to anyone. I've got to talk to a lot of people today and I don't want anyone forewarned.'

'I should tell my staff,' I argued.

'You can tell Graham and that's it. And, Kate, please do not call Maestro Bouchard and tell him,' Ken instructed me. 'I want you to understand how serious I am about this. Do you understand what obstruction of justice is?'

'Yes, it's bad, right?' I tried a little levity but he wasn't buying it.

'It's serious and it's what I should have charged you with last time. But if you tell anyone involved before I have had a chance to question them, I will put you in jail, do you understand?'

He was serious, so I decided I should become serious also. 'Absolutely, Ken, my lips are sealed until you tell me otherwise.'

'I really do mean it; I don't care if we're supposed to have dinner together or if you give me theatre tickets, I will charge you and put you in jail.'

'OK, Ken, I honestly understand the gravity of the situation and I will not say anything to anybody. Can I ask you if Stephan is under investigation?' I asked.

'That is none of your business. I just want you to remember what I've said.'

Boy, Ken was getting much more assertive in this detective role.

'I understand, Ken,' I vowed. 'I won't do anything until I hear from you again.'

'Great.' He sounded relieved that I hadn't put up a fight. 'I'll probably see you around the theatre today or tomorrow.'

'OK, I'll talk to you later.'

I hung up the phone and turned to see Graham hovering over me expectantly.

'Well?' he prodded.

'This is to be kept totally confidential,' I warned him. 'Or my butt's in jail.'

'OK. What?'

'It wasn't a suicide.'

'A murder?' he asked, his eyebrows rising.

'A murder,' I confirmed.

'Another one?'

'Hard to believe, isn't it?'

'Not with the kind of people you know,' he joked. 'So what now?'

'Nothing. We keep this quiet. Ken is starting an investigation and wants us out of it.'

'You can't tell me you still don't want to get involved,' he said.

'Well . . . no.'

'You hesitated.'

'I did not.'

'You did too. You had to stop and think and then you remembered that Cam made you promise not to get involved.'

'OK, maybe I did. But we're not getting involved. However, there is supposed to be something in the newspapers, so it's probably going to be like a zoo in here.'

'Do you think the PR department is doing this?' Graham asked.

'Doing what?'

'Killing people in the theatre. One murder each show and we're almost guaranteed a sell-out.'
'Graham, that's sick. But possible.'
'So, do we start checking into this?' he asked again.
'No,' I insisted, sounding much surer than I felt.

We had made it through the morning and Graham and I were just sitting on the sofa in the lobby, flipping a coin to see who would go pick up a couple of sandwiches for lunch. I had lost but was trying to figure out a really good reason as to why he should go instead, when I saw Ken Lincoln climbing the stairs.
'Ken,' I called, waving him over to us.
'Kate, Graham,' he greeted us, sitting on the arm of the chair across from us. 'Working hard as always, I see.'
'Finally taking a break,' I corrected him. 'You always miss out on the hard work.'
'Yeah, I understand how watching theatre performances all day can be very exhausting.' He laughed.
'So, did you just come here to rattle my chain, or was there something I can do for you?' I asked.
'I did want to ask you some questions,' he admitted.
'Guess I'm going to get the sandwiches after all,' Graham groaned, standing up and holding out his hand for money.
'Thanks, Graham,' I said, handing him a twenty-dollar bill. 'I expect change back from that.'
'So, how was it today?' Ken asked. 'Are the reporters still everywhere?'
'I don't know if it's getting better or if we're just getting used to it.'
'Can we take a walk?' he asked.
'Sure, where do you want to go?'
'I thought you could show me around inside the theatre,' he asked.
'Sure.' I got up and squeezed my sore feet back into my shoes. We crossed to the house-right doors and I opened them for him. 'Anything special you wanted to see?'
'I'm just interested in the set-up. And how you guys are running two events in here at once.'
I walked over to one of the box seats and leaned against

the rail. Ken stood beside me and watched as I pointed things out to him.

'Well, the five adjudicators are over there, and they have five empty rows behind them, so that no one can see what they're recording on the adjudication sheets. Basically, the contestant comes onstage, gets ready and then turns and waits for the head judge to indicate that the panel is ready. They ring the bell, we close the door, the contestant plays their selection, takes a bow and then we do the same thing all over again.'

'From nine to five?' he asked.

'Well, that's the intent. But it's more like from nine to whenever they finish. We've had a couple of early days and a couple of days where one audience is leaving just as the other is trying to get in.'

'And then for the evening show?' Ken asked.

'Well, a whole bunch of strong young men move the piano off the stage and the big doors in the back, which open into the shop, are opened and the set is rolled in and reassembled for the night's performance. We're only able to do this because it's a fairly easy set to assemble and disassemble.'

'And then at the end of the night?'

'Well, the first night, the guys stayed and did the set-up for morning, but after that they started coming in early to do it. As long as we have the piano set up at eight thirty for the piano tuner, it's all fine. So the stage is usually a mess all night long.'

'Can you take me up to the balcony where we found her?' he asked.

'Sure,' I said, leaving the box and leading him back into the lobby and up the stairs.

'And I'd like to go down all the fire escapes from up there too, just to see all the different ways in and out.'

'Ken, if you tell me what you're looking for, I might be able to help you out a little more,' I offered.

'Nice try, Kate.' He smiled. 'Now just show me the exits, please.'

By the time we were done, the lunch break was long over and I was eating my cold BLT in the back of the main floor bar, while selling ice-cream sandwiches.

* * *

The day had been long, busy, and hard work. The press had been everywhere. The newspapers' announcement that the suicide was actually a murder had sent everyone into a frenzy. Detective Lincoln had been in and out of the theatre and the administration offices most of the afternoon. He had talked to everyone about everything. I kept trying to get close enough to eavesdrop, but Ken was getting used to my tricks.

I hadn't seen Cam all day and had only spoken to him once when he called to make sure I went to my physiotherapy appointment. I wasn't going to go, but after promising him, thought better of it. I was finished before Cam, so Scott dropped me off at the apartment and I put the kettle on to boil, turned on some lights and went upstairs to get undressed. I tossed my clothes over the chair and ran downstairs when the kettle started whistling. I made a pot of tea and took a cup back upstairs to bed with me. I turned on the radio and grabbed a book I had been struggling to get through for months, but felt my eyes growing heavier by the moment.

'Katie, are you home?'

I jumped at the sound of his voice. I must have fallen asleep, the book having landed on the bed beside me. I should have read it when I was trying to fall asleep last night, I thought.

'I'm up here,' I called groggily to Cam.

'Been home long?' he asked.

'I don't know. I fell asleep. What time is it?'

'It's after midnight.'

'I guess I've been home a while then,' I said.

'Can I bring you anything up?' he asked from the kitchen.

'I'll have another cup of tea please,' I said, straightening the bed and moving over a bit to make some room for him.

Cam climbed up the stairs with a cup of tea in one hand and a beer in the other. He handed me the tea and kissed me.

'How was your day?' he asked.

'Same old stuff.'

'You're such a bad liar.' He smiled at me.

'What do you mean?'

'I read the paper today. Turns out there was a murder in the theatre.'

'Oh, that.'

'Yeah, that,' he said. 'So are you going to talk about it?'

'You told me not to get involved. I'm just trying to behave.'

'Do you mean to say that you and Graham weren't going around asking questions today?' Cam asked, his voice full of disbelief.

'No. He wanted to, but I promised you I was going to stay out of it, remember?'

'I remember, I just didn't believe you.'

'Besides,' I admitted, 'Ken threatened to throw me in jail for obstruction of justice if I opened my mouth once today.'

'Now I see.' He smiled, climbing into bed beside me. 'So I should just call the cops on you and then you'll listen to me.'

'Something like that.'

'Katie, the bed's wet,' Cam said, throwing the covers back and running his hand over the stained sheets.

'Oh, sorry, I jumped when you came home. I must have spilled some of my tea.'

'You go get some sheets, I'll strip the bed,' he said.

'But my half is dry.'

'Katie . . .'

'OK, I'm going, I'm going.'

I shook the sleep out of my head, then went downstairs to get the bedding out of the linen closet and brought it back up to Cam. He had the bed pulled out and was standing in the cramped space between the bed and the wall. I shook the sheet out and tossed it across to him. He leaned over and tucked it into the side of the bed.

'What's this?' he asked.

'What?'

He pulled a little journal out from under the bed. 'This.'

'Oh, that. I forgot about that. I found it in the theatre the other night.'

'What's it doing behind the bed?'

'Well, I was trying to read it that night, when you jumped me. And I mean literally when you jumped me. It went flying and it must have fallen behind the bed.'

'Whose is it?' he asked as we continued with the bed.

'I don't know; I was just starting to go through it when you interrupted me.'

He pulled the comforter on the bed, climbed out from behind it, and pushed it back against the wall.

'We need more space,' he said. 'Or less furniture.'

I got back into bed and grabbed the journal.

'I'll just take these down to the laundry hamper,' he said sarcastically, gathering up the dirty sheets as I tucked myself in.

'OK.'

'Can I get Your Majesty anything else while I'm downstairs?'

'I'm fine,' I called to him. I opened the journal and started reading through it.

'Katie, don't you get involved in that journal. I have other plans for you tonight.'

'No, I won't,' I lied, turning the page.

He came back upstairs and climbed in beside me. He propped some pillows behind his back and pulled me over to him.

'I told you I didn't feel like reading tonight,' he insisted.

'Oh my God!'

'What?' he asked, letting me go, thinking he had hurt me.

'This is about Stephan,' I said.

'I don't believe it.' He rolled his eyes and tried to pull the journal out of my hands.

'Cam, stop.' I pulled back.

'Katie, don't do this. Close that book and promise me you'll give it to Ken in the morning.'

'Listen to this.'

'Katie, please. You promised you were going to be good.'

'Cam, please, just listen to the first few pages.'

'Is there anything I can say to make you put that book down?' he asked.

'Nothing,' I said firmly.

He grabbed his beer and lit a cigarette. 'OK, go ahead.'

I turned back to the first page of the journal and started reading.

It's spring and almost time for school break. Such a bittersweet time, for I'll get to go home to see my family but I'll be separated from him for almost a month. We haven't been separated that long since we started seeing each other and I'll miss him so. Plus I don't trust all those other girls. He is handsome, talented and headed for greatness – all the girls want him, but he's mine. I just don't trust them to leave him alone while I am gone. He'll be here, practicing, and they'll be throwing themselves at him. I can't blame him; he's only a man. But I am so afraid. I want to spend the rest of my life with him. I told my mother I didn't want to come home, to leave him, but she said I was just being a silly young girl and a month apart would only make our relationship stronger, if he really loves me. She is too old and just doesn't understand. But she is paying my tuition and she will stop if I don't come home for the holiday. I know she thinks I'm too young for a serious relationship, but if only she met him, I know she would see how right this is. How much I love him and he loves me. But what am I to do? I cried, I screamed, I pouted, I stopped talking to her, I even tried talking to Father, but she still insists I come home. So I must leave my beloved Stephan in three more days. I don't know how I'll ever survive it!

'It sounds like a teenage girl's daydreams,' Cam said.

'Well, that would be about right. A young college girl in love with Stephan would sound a lot like that, especially if she had never been away from home and had overprotective parents. He was probably her first love.'

'You sound like you speak from experience,' Cam said, only half-jokingly.

'OK, I was young and stupid once too,' I admitted. 'I pity you when I find someone from your college years.'

'So what is all this supposed to prove?' he asked, referring back to the journal.

'I don't know. It's just interesting that I found this in the theatre the day that Joelle Bergere was killed. Do you think it belongs to her? That she was in love with Stephan?'

'I think you need to give it to Detective Lincoln tomorrow and not worry about it.'

'I will give it to Ken, that I promise you. But doesn't this interest you at all? Not even a little bit?' I asked.

'I'll tell you what interests me,' he said.

'Yes?'

'It interests me that you speak and read French and I never knew it.'

'Oh, that's another story from my time with Stephan. I totally dedicated myself to learning French. I took classes and insisted that he and I only speak French when we were together. It just seemed so romantic at the time. I guess some of it stuck.'

'Some of it?'

'All right, a lot of it. It came in handy when I was a secretary. Bilingual jobs pay a lot more than regular secretarial jobs.'

'So why do you never speak French?' he asked.

'Because you wouldn't understand what I was saying,' I explained. 'Although that could have some benefits.'

'So have you read enough for tonight?' he asked hopefully.

'Just a little bit more. I don't have to read it aloud,' I offered.

'No, if you're going to read it, you might as well share. I'm not going to get any sleep until you're finished.'

'I thought you were in the mood for something else?' I asked.

'My mood is fading quickly,' he said.

'Oh, well then, I guess I better read faster.'

'Good guess.'

> *I have been home for almost a month now. Stephan has written me every day but letters are not the same as being with him. And he does not express himself as well on paper as he does when we speak. He tells me of his music, of the parties he goes to, of studying for exams, and of how his concerto is coming along. He tells me he loves me and misses me and begs me to come back to him quickly. But I know he is never lonely. He is the most popular boy on campus and there are always people around him. How jealous I am of those people. The ones whose parents are not so unreasonable as to insist they come home, who can stay in the city and do as they wish, see who they wish. I feel like I am being treated like such a child. But it is all going to stop when I return to school. I have a plan. I am going to bring Stephan home to meet my parents, and then I know they will approve. And once they approve, we will be free to openly declare our love for each other. I know Stephan has been keeping it quiet*

to protect me and protect my reputation, but it is time for us to let the world know how we feel about each other. And I have decided that I will sleep with him. That way, he will know how serious I really am and that I really love him. I can hardly wait to get back!

'OK, enough,' Cam said, ripping the journal from my hands and setting it on the bedside table. 'I really don't need to listen to how some eighteen-year-old has decided to give it up for her boyfriend.'

'But, Cam, this has the makings of a great heart-breaking romance.'

'Is this a woman thing?' he asked. 'One of those things that men just don't get?'

'It's because men don't have hearts.'

'What do you mean by that?'

'I mean you don't understand true romance. You can be romantic, but you don't really understand romance.'

'An eighteen-year-old girl pining over an eighteen-year-old guy and planning to lose her virginity is romantic?' he asked.

'It's not the facts. When you just look at the facts, it's boring. It's the underlying meaning. Look at this poor girl; she's planning on making love for the very first time – declaring her undying love to the world. It's moving.'

'I was right,' he said.

'About what?'

'It is one of those things that men just don't understand.'

'Well, maybe.'

'Or it's one of those things you women just make into a big deal to make us think we don't understand. You're probably going to meet with all the other women and laugh at me tomorrow.'

'I thought I was the paranoid one.'

'Can I turn off the light now?' he asked.

'You're not going to let me read anymore?' I asked, hopeful he would give me the journal back.

'No. Enough is enough. Tomorrow you give the journal to the police and we are finished with this.'

'OK.' I curled up under the covers, my back toward him.

Cam switched off the light and settled in himself.

'What's this?' he asked.

'What's what?'

'Is there a specific reason why your back is toward me?'

'No.'

He curled up close to me and started rubbing my back. 'Are you mad at me?' he asked.

'No.'

'Then why are you being monosyllabic?'

'Because you didn't think I was going to give that book to Ken.'

'That's not true,' he protested. 'I just wanted to make sure you did.'

'I'm not a child.'

'Katie, I'm just worried about you. I don't want anything to happen to you.'

'Can I read more of the journal?' I asked.

'No, it's time to sleep.'

'We can't go to sleep mad,' I said.

'I'm not mad.'

'OK, I'm not really mad either,' I gave in. 'But you have to promise me that you won't ask me once whether I gave the book to Ken or not.'

'OK, I won't,' he promised.

'And you have to promise not to remind me to go to my physiotherapy appointment.'

'You are asking a lot.' He laughed.

'Those are my terms.'

'OK, I promise I won't ask you about physio either. Anything else?'

'No, Cam, I think that's enough for one night. Now we can go to sleep.'

'We're not mad anymore?' he asked.

'No, we're not mad anymore.'

'Good, because I'm not sleepy anymore.'

Wednesday October 29

I woke up before the alarm went off, reached over and turned it off so it wouldn't wake Cam. I've really been trying to adapt to living with someone and considering their feelings, something you have to work at after so many years of living alone. I tiptoed downstairs, had a quick shower and crept back upstairs to get dressed. I pulled on my jeans and a sweatshirt and grabbed the journal off the nightstand. I put it in my pocket and turned for the stairs.

'Katie,' Cam called sleepily from bed.

I walked back over and leaned down beside him. 'It's early, Cam,' I whispered, running my fingers through his rumpled hair. 'Go back to sleep.'

'Did you reset the alarm?' he mumbled.

'Yes, I did. I'll see you later.'

'How come you're up so early?' he asked.

'The festival, you dope. Did you forget?'

'I guess.' He sounded like he was practically asleep again. 'See you later.'

I let myself out quietly and grabbed the first C-Train to the Plex without even stopping for a coffee. I was leaving earlier than normal and I really hoped Cam hadn't noticed because I didn't want to explain why. I was a woman on a mission.

I was in the admin tower by six o'clock. The only other people in the building were security. It wasn't unusual for me to be there, but I preferred that no one witnessed what I was doing. I punched my code into the photocopier, laid the journal on the glass and pressed the start button. I was going to turn the journal over to Detective Lincoln, just like I had promised Cam, but I wanted to finish reading it. I had it collated and stapled in no time, turned off the photocopier and the lights and headed back down to my office. I sealed the original journal in an envelope and wrote Ken's name on it. I put the photocopy in a file folder, labelled it inventory, and filed it. I only felt a little bit guilty. Then I lay my head on the desk and closed my eyes. Graham would wake me when he got in.

'Kate.' I felt someone gently shaking my shoulder. 'Time to wake up.'

'Five more minutes, Mom,' I pleaded.

'I know you're tired when you mistake me for your mom.'

I cracked open one eye and saw Graham staring back at me.

'Oh, it's you.'

'Well, good morning to you, too.'

I reluctantly pulled myself into a sitting position. 'I'll pay you a million dollars to pour me a cup of coffee,' I whined.

'I want to see the cash,' Graham teased as he poured it anyway.

I pulled my cigarettes out of the desk and lit one, taking the coffee gratefully from Graham.

'Have I told you recently what a healthy way that is to start your morning?' Graham asked. 'I mean, have you ever considered maybe a glass of orange juice or some fruit?'

'My body would go into shock.'

'So, as much as I really don't want to know the answer, why are you sleeping in your office?'

'I got in early to try to get caught up, but I guess I got in too early. I should have stayed in bed for another hour instead.'

'Thank God,' Graham said.

'What?'

'I thought you and Cam had a fight.'

'No, nothing more than our usual.'

'Good. So you'll just be in your normal grumpy mood, not a thoroughly disgusting one?'

'Depending on how much you piss me off today.'

'Point taken. I'll save my mindless banter and sarcasm for later in the day after you've fed your habits and addictions more thoroughly.'

'Just as long as we understand each other.'

Graham pulled a bottle of orange juice out of his backpack, opened it and tossed the cap into the garbage can.

'Two points,' he cheered. 'Now you remember what day it is today?'

'Yes, Graham, I may be tired but I still know it's Wednesday.'

'No, not that. Do you know what I'm doing tonight?'

'Oh, that's right. You're hoping that little nurse is going to give you a physical.'

'You are so crass.'

'So how long are you here today before you have to go home and scrape the mould out from between your toes?'

'I'd like to leave now,' he said.

'Take a reality pill, Graham.'

'OK, I told Mandi that I'd pick her up at seven, so I'd like to be out of here by five. It's not easy to make myself this beautiful, you know.'

'Just don't go overboard with that cheap cologne I gave you for Christmas,' I warned him.

'I bought myself some good stuff for an occasion such as this. I was tired of the jokes I was getting every time I wore that other stuff.'

'I promise I'll do better next Christmas. I can ask Cam for advice this year.'

'And I promise I won't buy you another cookbook. I'll buy you take-out menus instead.'

'So where are you taking Mandi tonight?'

'No way. I am not telling anybody, especially you. I have enough pressure on me; I don't even want to think about you guys crashing my date.'

'I would never do such a thing,' I protested.

'I don't believe you for a minute,' he said. 'You've been teasing me about Mandi since the day you first met her, when I was in the hospital. I'll tell you all about it tomorrow. And that's the best you're going to get out of me.'

'I remember when you actually used to have some respect for me.'

'That was before I got to know you.'

'Well, since you've already lost your respect for me, why don't you go stock the beer fridges for me? It was a busy night last night.'

'I suppose I can do that. But just tell me this, are you going to give me all the shitty jobs today just because I'm taking the night off?'

'It's tempting, but I'll try to restrain myself,' I promised. 'Now, get out of here and let me go back to sleep.'

I was sitting in the lobby, working on my fourth or fifth cup of coffee and watching the competition on the lobby monitor. The day was going smoothly enough but I was getting concerned that I hadn't seen Stephan for a couple of days. Graham was fretting that he hadn't been able to corner any celebrities. But otherwise, it almost seemed like a normal day. And just when I thought all was well with the world, I heard my name called from across the theatre. I turned and saw Ken Lincoln striding towards me.

'Ken, I wondered when you'd be getting around to me,' I greeted him. 'You rounding up the usual suspects or whatever it is you do?'

'Something like that. I was hoping you could take me backstage, actually.'

'I'm going to assume you've cleared this with the festival brass?' I asked.

'I certainly have.'

'OK,' I said as I stood up. 'But I wonder if I could have a few minutes of your time first.'

'Don't tell me, you've been investigating the murder,' he said, his eyebrow rising as he got ready to read me the riot act.

'No, I haven't. You don't have to bring the handcuffs out. But I do have something to give you that I found in the theatre.'

'What?' he asked, his interest piqued.

'Maybe we should wait until we're in my office,' I suggested. 'This might be important and you might not want anyone to hear about it. I know how you like to be so secretive with these clues.'

'Well, you've got my attention, lead on.'

I took him up to my office and closed the door. I sat behind the desk and handed him the envelope with the journal in it. He took the envelope and ripped it open, flipping through the journal.

'And what is this?' he asked.

'I found it tucked in behind one of the seats in the theatre the day of the murder.'

'And you've been holding on to it since then?' he asked, anger flaring in his voice.

'Calm down. I wasn't hindering the investigation or hiding evidence or anything. I took it home to see if I could figure out whom it belonged to and started to read it, but it fell behind the bed. Cam just found it last night.'

'And I can check with him?' he asked.

'You used to be way more trusting of me. But, yes, you can check with him,' I promised.

'I was way more trusting because I didn't know you very well – did you ever think of that?' he asked, his face dead serious but his eyes twinkling.

'Is that your best cop impression?' I asked.

'Kate, you make it so hard to be serious. But I would think that after almost getting killed, more than once, you might start to believe this stuff is a little bit dangerous.'

'Reading a journal?' I asked.

'Reading a murderer's journal.' He flipped it open. 'It's in French.'

'I read French. If you flip through a couple of pages, you'll notice Stephan's name. That's why I thought it might have been important.'

'I'll have to get this translated.'

'I could do it for you,' I offered.

'Nice try, Kate, but we have people in the department that can do it.'

'I thought I'd try,' I smiled.

'You mean to tell me you haven't read the whole diary?'

'No, I haven't.'

'Boy, you are showing some restraint,' he said. 'So, do you want to tell me how you know all these people?'

'Not really,' I admitted. 'But apparently you and two people in housekeeping are the only ones that don't know all about it yet.'

'Well, fill me in then, before I have to go and learn about it on the streets.'

'OK, once upon a time, there was this very naive girl named

Katherine, and she went to university to learn how to play the piano, and this very handsome professor named Stephan taught her many, many things, not all to do with the piano. And it was all a lot of fun until Katherine found out about the wife and daughter, and then Katherine spent the summer crying, like only a scorned young girl can do.'

'Do you tell this story to young children at bedtime?' he asked.

'No, but I should. Teach them to ask handsome French men if they are married before they go and sleep with them,' I said. 'Anyway, I had to finish my degree so I made a certain amount of peace with Stephan; I assumed that his wife didn't know about us and I even taught piano lessons to his daughter, Nicole.'

'Very civilized,' Ken said.

'It was more about not throwing away three years of college,' I told him.

'And what about our victim?'

'Well, I just met her this week. I had never heard Stephan or Nicole talk about her before, when we were young. Apparently she was an old friend of the family though.'

'OK, well that clears some things up then.' He smiled at me. 'Now I've got some people waiting backstage for me.'

'You're not going to tell me anything, are you?' I asked.

'No, I'm not.'

'This is really making me crazy.'

'Well, I think it's a much safer way for you to live.' He stood up, ending the interview. 'Shall we?'

'OK, I give up.'

Ken must have snuck out the stage door because I didn't see him again. I had hoped I could walk him out and find out whom he had talked to, but he was obviously avoiding me – and my questions. Graham was out the door at five on the nose and that was when I remembered I had forgotten my physio appointment. Cam had better keep his promise not to ask me about it because if he found out, I was in for an evening of 'I told you so's'.

I managed to run the show just fine that evening, without Graham, but I certainly noticed that I did a lot more running around than I was used to. I would have to remember to be nicer to him for the next couple of days. When the patrons and staff had finally cleared out, I took the photocopy of the journal and put it into my backpack. I locked up my office and headed for home. The competition was starting late next day due to a scheduling conflict and I could actually sleep in. One week down, one week to go!

'Hello?' I called as I opened the apartment door.

'I'm in the bath,' Cam answered.

'I'm going up to bed,' I called through the door.

'Don't you want to come and join me?' he asked.

'That's a very tempting offer. Just let me dump my stuff upstairs.'

'I'll run some more hot water for you,' he promised.

I took my backpack upstairs and put it in the back of the closet. Out of sight, out of Cam's mind. I undressed, put on my robe and wandered back down to the bathroom.

'It's nice and steamy in here,' I said as I hung my robe on the door.

'Come on in, the water's fine.'

I climbed in and lay back against him. He wrapped his arms around me.

'How was your day?' he asked.

'Long.'

'Tomorrow's a sleep-in day. You can recharge.'

'I know. I've been waiting all week for a late start. Do you have to go in tomorrow?'

'No. I'm off unless somebody calls.'

'Are you going jogging in the morning?' I asked.

'No. I think I'm due for a good sleep-in too.'

'Good. I've missed our mornings together. I've forgotten how much I hated working a day job.'

'And your mom's not due back for how many more days?' he asked.

'A few. Long enough that we can get caught up,' I promised.

Thursday October 30

It was so nice to wake up on my own, without an alarm clanging at me through my dreams. The bed was warm, the sun was up, and Cam was lying beside me, his arms wrapped around me. I thought about turning to look at the clock and see what time it was, but decided I didn't care enough to expend that amount of energy. Nor did I want to ruin the mood, since being alone like this seemed to be becoming a thing of our past. I snuggled closer to Cam and closed my eyes again.

'Morning,' he whispered.

'Not yet,' I begged. 'Give me a couple more hours before I have to face the world or leave you.'

'OK.'

Boy, he was easy.

'But answer one question for me,' I said.

'Sure.' His voice reverberated softly in my ear, the hair on my neck quivered as he exhaled sleepily and I burrowed deeper into his embrace.

'How did I get to bed last night?' I asked.

'You don't remember?'

'No.'

'What do you remember?' he asked.

'I remember getting out of the bathtub, lying on the couch and putting in a movie. That's it.'

'You fell asleep before the previews were over.' He laughed softly. 'I carried you up here.'

'That was nice of you.'

'I'm a nice guy.'

'Yes, you are. And I promise to reward you for that. But later.'

'It's a deal.'

With the sun shining on me through the crack in the drapes and the warmth of Cam's body next to me, it didn't take me long to fall back asleep.

I woke up again and felt totally rested. Cam was propped up in bed beside me, reading. He had two cups of coffee on the bedside table and handed one to me as I rolled over.

'When did you do this?' I asked, sitting up a bit and taking the steaming liquid from him.

'I snuck out about twenty minutes ago. You didn't seem to notice.'

'Oh, honey, I would have eventually,' I teased. 'Thanks for the coffee though.'

'You're welcome.'

'Have you been awake long?'

'Not too long. You know that I can't sleep in as long as you can.'

'No one can sleep as long as I can.' I laughed. 'What're you reading?'

'I thought I'd try this book you've been reading,' he said, holding up the book that I had been struggling with for months. It's always a mistake to read something only to make people think you're smart.

'Good luck. All it's done for me is put me to sleep every time I've sat down with it.'

'Actually, I'm kind of getting into it. I think the secret is reading it in the daytime, not at night when you're tired.'

'I always knew you were smarter than me,' I told him.

'Well, you were only a music major,' he joked.

'So is there anything special you want to do today?' I asked, sipping my coffee.

'I thought you'd probably want to stay in bed and read,' Cam said.

'Cam, it's a beautiful day out, and we haven't really had a lot of quality time together recently, have we? What makes you think I want to lie in bed and read?'

'Katie, I thought you were really anxious to read that journal.'

He looked nonchalant, but I knew he was trying to trap me as he sat there and innocently turned the page in his book, not even making eye contact. But I was beginning to know Cam better than he thought.

'I told you I was going to give it to the police and I did. And as I recall, you weren't going to ask me about it,' I felt the need to point out, proud of myself.

'Oh, yeah, and I forgot to tell you that the physiotherapy clinic left a message on the answering machine about you missing your appointment yesterday.' He just smiled as he turned another page.

'Oops.'

'I promised I wouldn't say anything and I won't,' Cam said. 'You were right; I'll try to be less patronizing.'

'Thanks.'

'But I still thought you were curious about the journal,' he tried one more time.

'I told you I gave it to the police,' I insisted. Ha, I was going to finally win one with him.

'What about the copy you have in your backpack?'

Shit.

'What?' I tried innocently.

'Are you telling me you didn't make a copy of it?' he asked.

'Did you go through my backpack?' I asked, thinking the best defence was always a good offence.

'No.'

'Then how did you know?' I asked again.

'I didn't know for sure,' he smiled at me. 'But I was pretty sure. Now I know.'

'I hate you sometimes.' I swatted at him.

'Face it, Katie, you are just too predictable. But remember what curiosity did to the cat.'

'But cats have nine lives, so I'm safe for a while.'

'So are you going to read it?' he asked.

'Are you going to be mad at me?'

'No, I've thought this through,' he explained. 'I don't mind if you read the journal, but I still don't want you getting involved. No questioning people, chasing down suspects, or trying to help the police in any way.'

'I can live with that,' I said as I jumped out of bed and got my backpack from the closet.

'You know, the fact that you actually put your pack away

was a pretty good hint, too.' He laughed. 'You never put anything away.'

'I'll remember that next time I'm trying to hide something from you.'

'Will you get me some more coffee while you're up?' he asked, handing me his mug.

I grabbed my mug too. 'I suppose it's the least I could do since you have it waiting for me most mornings.'

I ran downstairs and back up in record time. I climbed over Cam, lit a cigarette and opened the photocopied pages to where I had left off.

'Do you want me to read out loud?' I asked.

'No, I think I had more than enough the other night. Just let me know if you find anything interesting.'

'Trust me, I will.'

He turned back to the book and I dove into the journal.

> *I am on the train now, heading back for the city and the university. Stephan wrote and told me he cannot meet me at the station because he has a rehearsal. I understand. Besides, I will see him soon enough. Perhaps Mother was right; absence has certainly made my heart grow fonder. Tonight I have a wonderful dinner planned. I will cook for him and then we will have a wonderful night, catching up on everything that has happened while I have been away. I never thought I could feel this way about a man. I have always been so sure that I would have a wonderful career; I thought I knew what I wanted to do, and now I could just throw it all away and follow him to the ends of the earth if that is where he leads me. It won't matter that I don't have my career; I will have his love and that will be more than enough for me forever. Who could want more than the love of an amazing man like him?*

Cam was right, this was a little on the sophomoric side. But I knew there had to be something in the journal that would explain the Bouchard family's situation. The fact that I found it right at the time of the murder just made it fate; I was meant to find the answers to this.

Well, I have done it. I spent the night with Stephan and I told him how much I love him. It was everything I dreamed it would be and more. He is more handsome and exciting than I ever knew. It was the most glorious night ever. And then afterward, as he lay dozing in my arms, I told him he was my first – that I had been saving myself for the man I would spend my life with. He seemed so touched and moved by this that he held me tightly all night long while we slept. In the morning we said a tender goodbye and he promised to call me later. I know this is the right thing to do and the right man to do it with; I know this will bring us closer together. I am more in love with him than I was yesterday, something I never thought possible. Now I must start planning a visit with my parents so they can meet him. Perhaps we can rent a car and drive out one weekend. I'll talk to him tonight and see what he thinks and then I'll call Mother and tell her that I'm bringing the man I'm going to marry home to meet them. Madame Bouchard – that will be me! But I must stop writing now. I have so much to do today. I must clean the apartment, shop for dinner tonight. And Stephan has left some laundry for me. I told him I didn't mind. I want him to know what a wonderful wife I will make. I will wash and press his clothes, cook for him, and provide him with a wonderful safe haven to come home to. He will know I am the right woman for him.

'This girl's in trouble,' I said.

'What do you mean?'

'She's slept with him and now he's got her doing his laundry and cooking for him.'

'And there's something wrong with that?' he asked.

'It's classic. He doesn't love her; he's just using her for whatever he needs at the time.'

'Something about this sounds vaguely familiar, though,' Cam said.

'You know something about this?' I sat up, excited.

'It sounds like your arrangement with me. I cook, I do your laundry and you sleep with me. Does this mean you're just using me and when you're done with me you're just going to toss me out?'

'That's different.'

'How?'

'I'm a woman. It means something totally different when it's the woman doing it.'

'Different how?'

'It just means I'm smarter than most women. You think we actually like cleaning and cooking? I was just smart enough to find a man who would do that for me.'

'I think I found you,' he pointed out.

'Is that so? I seem to recall asking you out for coffee.'

'Doesn't count; you didn't know Patti and I were separated. You thought it was just coffee.'

'You were planning something different at that point?' I asked.

'Hey, I was just separated. I was supposed to immediately go into the rebound relationship that I kept hearing about. I figured you were it.'

'So you were on the prowl?' I asked.

'Hey, I just bought my first pair of button-fly jeans. I was hot and I knew it.'

'You were something, all right. I'm not sure if hot is the way I would describe it.'

'You thought I was hot,' he pointed out. 'I don't recall having to talk you into anything back then.'

'I told you before; I have never slept with anyone else the first night I went out with them. Besides, we worked in the same building, I knew some things about you, I asked some people about you. It wasn't like you were a one-night stand from a bar or something.'

'You thought I was hot,' he pressed me. 'Just admit it.'

'Get over yourself.'

'If you didn't think so, what am I still doing here?'

'This brings me back to the original point. You cook, clean and do my laundry for me.'

'And that's it?' he asked.

'And I think you're pretty hot,' I finally admitted. 'Especially in your button-fly jeans.'

'I knew it.'

‘Just don’t let it go to your head,’ I said, trying to turn back to the journal, but Cam tried to pull it from my grasp.

‘Why don’t you put that down for a while?’ he asked, wiggling his eyebrows in that obviously suggestive way of his.

‘I want to read this. I think there might be something in here that will help me understand things.’

‘Remember how you’re not going to get involved?’ he asked.

‘I’m just reading it.’

‘And planning how you can figure out this murder before the police do.’

‘I am not. You may think you know me well, but you don’t know everything.’

‘I know I can make you put down that journal.’

‘And how can you do that?’

‘By doing this.’ He moved very close to me and I felt his teeth nip at my ear lobe, along with the ensuing shudder that ran down the back of my neck and sent those butterflies loose in my stomach.

‘OK, so you’re right again,’ I said, tossing the journal on to the floor.

I finally tore myself reluctantly from bed at four o’clock. I really should have been at the theatre by five, but when Cam joined me in the shower I decided I could be a little late for once. I dressed, slapped on some make-up and pulled my hair into a ponytail. Cam didn’t say anything to me as I put the journal into my backpack and threw it over my shoulder. Maybe he was serious about not nagging me about it. I wish I had been more sincere in my promise not to get involved.

In my office, I put the coffee on and sat on the window ledge, staring at the traffic, while the coffee dripped through the filter. I saw a motorcycle pull up by the front door of the theatre. The passenger got off, pulled off his helmet, and I realized it was Graham. He secured his helmet on the back of the bike and then the driver pulled off her helmet. It was Mandi! He leaned over and kissed her, then she put her helmet back on and he waved to her as she sped off down the street. He stood there, watching her leave, and stayed there until she was out of sight. God, he was going to be insufferable today.

I poured myself a coffee, lit a cigarette and tried to steel myself for his relentless good humour.

Soon Graham practically floated into the office, poured himself a coffee and sat across the desk from me. He took a sip and made a face, but forced himself to take another sip.

'Coffee?' I asked, incredulous at his choice.

'Rough night,' was all he said.

'Most people find a little sugar helps the taste if you're not used to drinking coffee,' I explained.

'It's bad enough I'm putting this shit into my system; I'm not going to compound my error by adding refined sugar to it.'

'And you're missing your leg brace?' I asked.

'Mandi cured me.' He smiled, his eyes going all dreamy as he remembered something from the night before.

'So how was your date?'

'Astounding.'

'That's all I get? I want details.'

'I am a gentleman, and gentlemen don't give details. Suffice to say I am madly in love. With a whole lot of lust thrown in. But I totally respect her; let me assure you of that. Anyone who can do what she can do . . .'

'Graham, I just don't get this. This woman dots her "i"s with happy faces; she doesn't strike me as your type.'

'Well, Kate, you were already taken. What was I to do?' He smiled at me.

'So what did you guys do last night?'

'Oh, look at the time,' he said, standing up. 'I better go stock the beer fridges or something.'

'Graham!' I called after him as he started down the corridor.

'Sorry, Kate,' he called back.

'If you don't tell me what happened last night, I won't tell you my secret.'

'You don't have any secrets I want to know,' he said, but he had stopped his retreat.

'It's about the murder,' I teased, dangling the bait to see if he would take it.

Graham came back into the office, poured himself another coffee, and sat back down across from me.

'Maybe I do have time for another coffee,' he said. 'I'm sure the second cup can't be worse than the first.'

'That's better. You go first.'

'No, You go first. I don't trust you, Kate.'

'I'll give you this much. I have a journal that I found in the theatre. I think it belongs to the dead woman.'

'No way!' He sat up straighter and suddenly looked very interested in what I had to say.

'Really,' I promised. 'Now tell me about your date.'

'I want to know about this journal,' he insisted.

'Nope, you next.'

'OK, but there's not much to tell. We were going to go out for dinner, then a movie, and then I thought dancing might be fun. When I picked her up, she was cooking dinner, had romantic music on, and we didn't leave her place until four o'clock this afternoon.'

'A woman who knows what she wants.' I laughed.

'And a woman with impeccable taste in men,' he agreed. 'But now, show me this journal.'

I reached down to pick up my backpack, but hesitated when I heard the door at the end of the hallway open. Graham and I both turned and saw several of the ushers heading for the locker room.

'Later,' I said, tucking my backpack under my desk.

'Aw, Kate, I told you I didn't trust you.'

'Hey it's not my fault they all showed up to work on time. I've never actually insisted they do that, you know.'

'Well, you unlocked the door so they could get in,' he pointed out.

'Whatever. Just don't you tell anyone about this journal or you'll never see it.'

'OK, but when do I get to see it?' he asked.

'Tomorrow. As soon as the competition gets started, we can read it.'

'Why don't you just let me take it home tonight?' he asked.

'Do you read French?'

'No.'

'That's why; it's written in French,' I explained. 'I'll read it to you tomorrow. I promise. Besides, aren't you going to be seeing Mandi tonight?'

'I don't know yet. I have to call her later.'

'Trust me,' I promised, giving him a little insider

information. 'You'll be seeing her tonight.'

'Oh, like you're an expert on relationships.'

My phone started ringing and I realized I hadn't even checked my messages yet.

'Kate Carpenter,' I said, picking up the phone and leaving Graham hanging.

'Hi, Kate, it's Sam.'

'Hi, Sam.'

'So you don't answer your phone at home, you don't check your messages at work – do we have to get a pager for you?'

'I was home all morning. Cam must have turned the ringer off on the phone.'

'Oh, a romantic morning.' I still can't understand why all my friends feel such a need to get so involved with the intimate details of my life. And Cam thought I was a busybody. Then I looked across at Graham, blushing as he got that dreamy look in his eyes again, and I realized I probably was just as bad as the rest of them.

'So I'm just signing the staff in, Sam, is it quick or should I call you back later?'

'I just wanted to know if you guys want to grab a bite after the show tonight.'

'No way. Mom is due back sometime tomorrow and this is our last night alone.'

'So I shouldn't come over and make dinner for you?' she asked.

'If you show up tonight, I swear I'll not only take your key away but I'll have you arrested for trespassing,' I promised. 'And I know just the detective to do it, too.'

'OK, I get the hint. What about tomorrow night? I'm anxious to meet this man your mom brought home to meet her daughter. He looked pretty interesting when I saw him at the theatre.'

'He's a nice man. You can come over tomorrow night, but I don't know what time they are supposed to be back in town.'

'Do you want me to cook?' Sam asked.

'I'm sick of home-cooked food,' I said, not believing I would ever hear those words coming out of my mouth. 'I think we should order pizza.'

'I know this great new place that's just opened up.'

'No, Sam, not designer pizza. I want cheese, pepperoni, salami, mushrooms, peppers and onions.'

'Not even a little basil?' she asked.

'And not a single sprig of rosemary either. You know I crave real food every once in a while.'

'That's not real food; it's a bunch of chemicals bundled together to look like some sort of meat by-product to the unsuspecting public.'

'But it tastes good.'

'OK, I give up. Give me a call tomorrow and let me know what time.'

'All right.'

'And don't stay up all night with Cam. Try and get some sleep.'

'I promise I'll be in bed by ten thirty tonight.'

Cam is always treating me and surprising me with things, so on the way home I stopped at the deli and the liquor store and I came home with wine, grapes, chocolate and a movie we had both been dying to see. The apartment was quiet, but there was a light on in the bedroom. I tiptoed upstairs to show Cam what I had brought home with me. He was sound asleep, snoring softly, the book he had been reading lying open on his chest. I picked the book up, set it on the nightstand and pulled the covers up around him. I was disappointed but didn't have the heart to wake him. I turned back for the stairs to put the wine in the fridge for another night.

'Oh, what the hell,' I thought, turning back and diving for the bed.

We had drunk the wine, eaten the grapes and chocolate and ignored the movie. We lay in the darkened bedroom, a couple of candles flickering in the corner.

'I told you,' he said.

'Told me what?'

'That you thought I was hot,' he snickered in my ear.

'Yeah, I guess it's hard to hide, huh?'

'Do you remember that first night?' he asked. 'It's funny, it's been going through my mind a lot since we talked about it last night.'

'Are you getting all nostalgic about us?' I asked. 'That's so sweet.'

'Well, I don't think you ever had anyone treat you like I did.' He laughed again.

'You were very direct,' I admitted.

'I thought you were going to swallow your tongue when I asked you if you liked the view of my bottom.'

'That's not exactly how I remember it.'

'Yeah, you remember it how you want,' he said. 'That's the way it happened.'

'I don't think so.'

'Tell me how it happened then,' he said.

I fluffed my pillow, got comfortable and then shivered as I remembered that freezing day when I had first seen Cam.

I had raced up the stairs and into the warm building. It was freezing outside and all I could think about was getting warm where the wind wasn't blowing a wind chill of minus 35. I hate working on nights like that. I hate just leaving my apartment on nights like that. I stood inside the door for a minute, just letting the warmth permeate my frozen cheeks. I unwrapped the scarf from my neck and pulled off my hat, trying to shake some life back into my flattened hair. That's when I turned around and saw Cam. Or at least the backside of him. I'm not usually attracted to that part of the anatomy – I like eyes and a nice smile – but this was a very nice butt, in jeans that were not too tight but fit well enough to let anyone know what might linger underneath. The butt of a dancer or a runner, I thought. I followed the muscled legs down to the leather hiking boots on his feet before I thought to look up and see what the rest of the body might be like. Sandy-brown hair hung to the collar of a white Oxford shirt. He was the man of my dreams, but I had no idea who he was or how to approach him so that he didn't walk out of my life, never to be seen again. Cam handed his walkie-talkie across the pass-through window to the security guard and I realized he must work in the building. So why hadn't I seen him before? And where could I find him again? I remember wondering.

I finally decided inaction was doing me no good whatsoever and stepped up to the security window, standing shoulder to shoulder with the new love of my life. I smiled at Steve, the security guard, and asked him something innocuous, probably about the weather, just to start a conversation. He smiled back at me, made some small talk of his own and then turned back to Cam and finished signing in his walkie-talkie and keys.

I had screwed up my courage and turned tentatively toward him, standing right there beside me, our shoulders almost touching, and I smiled and said hello.

'I think you actually said hi,' Cam told me now.

'Yeah, I'm known for my profound greetings.' I laughed.

And then Cam had turned to me and asked if I enjoyed the view. Man, I was so shocked that I was speechless. I finally managed to ask him what he meant. Cam had smiled and pointed to the mirror hanging above the security desk, where he had been watching me watch him, and then he asked me again if I had enjoyed the view.

I turned to him and apologized, begging his forgiveness, feeling like the stupidest woman on the planet. I felt so humiliated. I mean, I don't usually perv on guys like that to begin with, but I never thought he'd have been able to see me looking him up and down and up and down and up and down again! So I had just kept stammering my apologies – my version of how to make a good impression.

And then Cam had said he guessed he should be flattered by it. And as my face turned a thousand shades of red he just said goodnight and left. For I minute, I was pretty sure I would never see him again. Or at least I thought he'd probably never want to see me again. And then I realized I had really liked what I'd seen, so I turned back to Steve and asked him who that man was. He wasn't a big help. All he could tell me was his name was Cam something-or-other and that he was the new maintenance guy.

I was so busy trying to wrap my scarf around my face, to cover up my blushes, that I didn't notice the twinkle in Steve's eyes as he tossed my keys across the desk to me – keys that Graham had left there for me earlier. I turned away to head for the theatre, trying to think of some plan to make up for that embarrassing first meeting. Steve called down the hall after me so I turned back to the security desk, thinking I had forgotten something. And then Steve said those words that changed my life for ever. He said he'd told Cam about my wrap party that night and Cam had said he would probably be there.

I broke out into this stupid big grin, thanked Steve several times, and promised him free theatre tickets for ever, I think. Luckily, he moved to Winnipeg and I haven't had to come through with that promise. And then I skipped off down Tin Pan Alley to my office.

'Wow, the real version,' Cam marveled, snapping me back to the present.

'Only for you, mister. If I tell this to anyone else, the tale will change drastically to make you the sex-starved one who pursued me.'

'Do you remember that party?' Cam asked me.

'Uh, not really,' I admitted. 'I do remember much later in the evening though, waking up with you here and wondering what the hell I'd gotten myself into. I used to dislike men who stayed all night. I knew you were going to be a challenge.'

'And have I been?'

'Probably not as much of a challenge to me as I've been to you,' I admitted. 'But I wouldn't trade it for the world.'

'Me either,' he said, getting up to blow out the candles and then crawling quickly back under the warm covers with me. 'Did you enjoy the view?'

'Very much.' I laughed.

Friday October 31

The alarm rang and I shut it off right away, dreading the day ahead. Not the piano festival, not the murder, not getting up at this hour, not even Halloween. It was my birthday. I lay there for a minute, dreading what would happen next.

'Morning,' Cam said sleepily.

I waited.

'Katie, did you fall back asleep?' he asked, shaking me a little.

'No, I'm awake.'

Nothing. He hadn't found out. I hate my birthday. Not the growing older part – well, that's not my favourite, of course – but the celebration part. Everyone always wants to surprise me. I hate the feeling you get before you open a door, wondering if there are thirty people waiting behind it to shout surprise at you. I hate people feeling like they have to give me presents, the sincere greetings and the false ones. I always feel so uncomfortable by just one day's outpouring of warmth. I want the people who love me to treat me that way 365 days in the year, not just for one day – and I do the same for them. So, several years ago, I had made all my friends cease and desist with birthday parties, mentions, card exchanges and anything vaguely related to a birthday celebration. I now refuse to tell any new people in my life when my birthday is. And I've successfully managed to avoid the topic with Cam this long into our relationship. Now I was worried that he had done some digging around and might have found out at work. But it looked like I was safe for another year. I kissed him on the forehead, got showered and dressed and headed for work, feeling slightly less full of dread. One down, one to go.

At the Plex I opened my office door slowly, expecting it to

be filled with balloons and confetti. I was safe; it was just the office, as messy as I had left it yesterday. I had been worried about Graham finally finding out, too. He had gone through a phase a couple of years ago, doing everything he could to figure it out. I actually had to leave my wallet at home after I found him rifling through my purse one night, looking for my driver's license. We had several words about that one, but he still didn't give up. However, I had stayed one step ahead of him and it was still my little secret. Eventually Graham had let it go, realizing how serious I was about keeping it to myself. Relieved, I put the coffee on and settled down to begin the day.

Later my staff arrived, looking as tired as I felt. The theatre is a night-time business and none of us are used to working days. I managed to get everyone into position and I heard the first of the day's competitors playing while I sat in my office and decided to have a cigarette. I poured myself a fresh coffee and pulled the journal out of my backpack. When I heard someone coming down the hall, I quickly covered the journal with my newspaper and leaned back in my chair, trying to look innocent.

'What's up, Graham?' I asked as he sat down.

'All is right with the theatre world, so I have come to see this mysterious journal.'

'Are you sure there's no one around?' I asked.

'Positive. Leonard is watching things downstairs and I told him where he could find me,' Graham said. 'I also told him I had a rough night last night, so he better not need me unless it was life or death. You are not getting out of showing me this journal.'

'OK, OK. I've read the first couple of entries already, and I'm not reading those again because they were kind of boring. But, basically, this belonged to a young girl in her first year of university who was madly in love with Stephan.'

'So who does it belong to?' he asked.

'I don't know. I flipped through the whole thing and I couldn't find a name anywhere. I think this young girl thought that if her mom found it she would have plausible deniability.'

'So do you think it was Dr Bergere's journal?' he asked.

'Sounds like it. She had it awfully bad for him back then.

She goes on and on about how her parents just don't understand, how this is her one true love and how she's planning on marrying Stephan and spending the rest of her life with him. You know, all that young girl, dreamboat kind of stuff.'

'So how is this helping you solve the murder?' he asked.

'I'm not trying to solve the murder, remember? I'm just curious. But you have to admit, if Dr Bergere was madly in love with Stephan, it puts a whole new slant on the dynamics of her relationship with his family. And it's probably pretty unethical that she was counselling Nicole, too.'

'You don't think she was still in love with him, do you?' he asked.

'I don't know. I haven't found out how it ends yet.' I laughed. 'But if she was, she certainly shouldn't have been Nicole's therapist, and I might even begin to wonder about this story about child abuse, wouldn't you?'

'It definitely makes it much more suspicious,' he agreed. 'So how much of this do you think the Maestro's wife and daughter know?'

'I don't know. It was a long time ago. I'm not sure if he'd even met Carole yet. Maybe she went to the same university, or maybe she met him some time after he broke up with this girl.'

'And do you think Stephan loved Dr Bergere?'

'It's hard to tell. This journal is just filled with adolescent drivel. She's convinced the world is wonderful, like any teenager in love. Who knows how he really felt.'

'So read on,' he instructed me.

I pulled the journal out from under the newspaper and flipped to where I had left off.

'You were going to read this without me,' Graham protested.

'No, I was just getting ready to come and get you,' I mumbled quickly, hoping to cover up my lapse.

'As always, I don't believe you, but go ahead.'

> *Life is so wonderful; I can't believe my good fortune. Stephan has been over every night for two weeks. I have cooked for him and he is allowing me to do all his laundry. I even snuck over to his apartment and cleaned it for him. He told me I did a wonderful job, but he wasn't*

pleased I was in his apartment without his knowledge. He told me to let him know next time I wanted to do that and he would be there, then he could take me out for dinner after I was finished. I think he was afraid I might mess up his papers. He has music everywhere in his apartment. I think he likes to compose whenever the mood strikes him; there was even some in the bathroom.

I told Stephan I want him to meet my parents, but he says he is too busy right now. When he said that, I cried and he was so sweet. He wrapped his arms around me and assured me he wanted to meet my parents, too, but now was not a good time. I dried my eyes and told him I understood, but I will keep trying to arrange it. After all, how can he ask my father for permission to marry me if he hasn't even met my father yet? I think Mother is getting curious about him, too. I think she hoped we would drift apart while I was home for the holidays, but since we haven't I know she wants to meet him. She still tells me I am too young for a serious relationship every time I speak with her. Sometimes even I wonder if all this is worth it, trying to please both Stephan and my parents. But I know, the moment I see him, that he is worth it. I would give my very soul if I could be with him for the rest of my life.

'I need more coffee,' I said, setting the pages down and rubbing my eyes. I hadn't used my French in a long time and this was hard on my tired brain.

'I'll pour.' He brought the pot over and filled my cup.

'So what do you think so far?' I asked.

'I think you were right,' he said. 'She's pretty pathetic. Please tell me I never sounded like that when I was that age.'

'Graham, you still sound like that. You sounded like that this morning.' I laughed.

'Kate, if I can't talk about the journal, you can't talk about my love life.'

'Fine,' I agreed. 'But I think it's pretty standard for a girl that age to talk like that, especially if it's her first big love. That is such a dramatic moment in a girl's life. Or should I say melodramatic?'

'Do you know this from experience?'

'Graham, I was never like that. I was born very mature.'

'I'd love to see your diary from when you were that age.'

'I've burned them all. No one will ever know what I was thinking back then.'

'That's too bad; it could be a real eye-opener,' he said and winked. 'And maybe we'd finally all understand you.'

'So do you want me to keep going?' I arched one eyebrow, so he'd know I meant business.

'Can you find something exciting in there?'

'You mean you're not finding this exciting?' I asked.

'I was hoping for something a little deeper, maybe more meaningful or more in the way of a direct clue or something.'

I flipped through some pages. 'Here, I think this part starts to get a little better now.'

> *I think there is another woman. I don't know what to do. I feel liking driving to Paris and throwing myself off the Eiffel Tower. That way I would be in all the newspapers and he would know that he was responsible. He would know what he is doing to my heart. I don't know why he is doing this; I have done everything for him that a woman could possibly do. I have been with him every night; I cook for him, clean for him, take care of his clothes – what more can I possibly do? I thought this is what a man wants, a woman to take care of him. And I have taken care of him in every way a woman possibly can. I tried to talk to my mother, but she just told me I was young and should start dating lots of other boys. She just doesn't understand. I don't want to date other boys; I've found the man I want to marry, who is my soulmate, my other half, the man who completes me. I just have to learn how to please him. But how can I please him when I hardly ever see him anymore?*
>
> *And now I have to meet with my professors. No one understands. I am going through the biggest crisis of my life, trying to convince Stephan that I am the one for him, and my professors want to meet with me. I know my grades have fallen and I'm afraid I am going to be put on probation. But I don't even care about that. I am*

only meeting with them to honour my mother, who insisted I go and straighten everything out. She even wants me to get counselling, or come home and go to the local college. It is all so very difficult to deal with. Everything seems to be falling apart right now.

'Stephan's coming,' Graham warned me after a quick glance down the hall, and I slid the journal back under the newspaper.

'Kate?' Stephan stopped at the door, waiting to be invited in.

'Stephan, come on in. Graham, we can finish this later.'

'I'll just go check in with everyone and see how things are going,' Graham said as he stood and offered Stephan his seat.

'May I have some coffee?' Stephan asked.

'I don't think it's quite up to your standards,' I apologized. 'But do help yourself if you're feeling adventurous.'

'Have you got a cigarette?' he asked.

'I've never seen you smoke,' I commented as I handed him one and reached over with my lighter. He cupped my hand with his and lit his cigarette, and didn't let go afterwards. I pulled my hand gently from his and quickly turned to put my lighter away so he wouldn't see the blush that had risen in my cheeks.

'How are you?' I asked.

'Not well.' He sighed, dropping into the chair and taking a big sip of coffee. 'You drink this every day, huh?'

I nodded, smiling apologetically.

'Katie, this was supposed to be a happy time – a prestigious new position, my daughter in the festival, I just don't understand what's happening.'

'Life, Stephan. That's what's happening.'

'Katie, the police have been around questioning me.'

'I know. I know the detective, Ken Lincoln, and he told me he would be talking to you.'

'They think I killed her.'

'Oh, Stephan, I don't know what to say.'

'Why would they think that, Katie? How could they think I could do such a horrible thing?' he asked. He looked so broken, suddenly so old.

'I don't know, Stephan. I don't know what the police are thinking or what kind of evidence they have. You have to have faith that they will find the real killer.'

'Katie, I need your help,' he pleaded.

'Stephan, I don't know what I can do,' I said, although I suddenly wanted to stop bullets for him. He was doing it to me again. I wondered if Stephan even knew what he was doing or if this was subconscious after years of getting women to do whatever he wanted.

'You can't let them arrest me. I can't leave Nicole right now; she needs her family with her. If they were to arrest me, I'm afraid that would finish her. I don't think she could take it.' He looked so beaten. I had never seen him like this.

'I just don't know if there's anything I can do,' I said again, feeling like I was letting him down.

'Katie, you know the police, you know the people in this building and you know me. You know I didn't do it – I couldn't do it.'

'I believe you, Stephan.' I wondered if he only used his powers for good or if I was getting dragged down a path where I was offering to protect a child molester and murderer.

'Katie, I have no one else.'

'I'll do everything I can,' I promised – what else could I say? – and then I came around the desk and hugged him.

I was feeling a little emotional after my chat with Stephan, so I left Graham in charge and wandered down to Grounds Zero. It was partly the fresh air I craved and partly a really good cup of coffee, probably with an extra shot of espresso. Gus was behind the counter, as always, and came over to meet me as I sat on my usual stool at the counter. I felt another stab of birthday dread. Gus actually knows when my birthday is and it has taken many, many arguments to get him to start ignoring it. But every year at this time I am afraid he might revert. Gus isn't a man easily talked into an opposing viewpoint.

'Well, good morning, Kate. How are you and what can I get you today?' he asked.

'A murderer.'

'Kate, you're not getting mixed up with all this again, are you?' he chastised me.

'I don't know what to do, Gus. Stephan was just in my office and he looked so pathetic. He's scared they're going to arrest him but he's even more scared he's going to lose his daughter, lose his family.'

'They won't arrest him unless they have evidence against him,' Gus assured me.

'But he didn't do it.'

'Kate, I want you to think really clearly for a minute. Clear the picture of that handsome man with those big blue eyes out of your head and tell me how you know for sure that he's an innocent man.'

'I just know him and I know he couldn't do it.'

'Kate, maybe the Stephan you used to know wasn't capable of murder, but how many years has it been since you've seen him? What could have happened to him in those years? Do you really know what kind of man he is these days?'

'Quit asking reasonable questions and pour me a coffee,' I said irritably. If I couldn't win an argument, I could at least change the subject.

'It's head over heart, Kate. What your heart thinks is good and kind but it's not always right. If you lead with your head, you might stand a better chance of staying out of these messes.'

'Very deep. You're working on that coffee, right?' I asked.

'You know, for such a professed cynic, you're a big softy. Someone gives you a sad look and off you go defending them,' he said as he put a cup in front of me. 'There's your coffee.'

'I am not a softy. I just believe in defending the underdog. Besides, I didn't come here for a lecture; I can go home for that.'

'Cam primed me for this,' Gus said, a big smile on his face. 'Since neither one of us was getting through to you by ourselves, we decided a tag-team approach might have a better chance of succeeding.'

'It sounds like it.'

'No, it's true. He told me any time you came in here talking crazy I was supposed to rein you back in and call him immediately.'

'Good joke. The only problem is I half believe it's true.'

The door opened and I turned to see who was coming in. It was Cam.

'Shit, it must be true,' I said.

'Hey, Katie, what are you doing here?' he asked, grabbing the stool beside me.

'Ducking out on my responsibilities. I felt the need for some fresh air and a bit of a break.'

'Let me guess—'

'Don't even bother. It's just that the theatre is getting smaller and smaller every day. There is nowhere left to hide.'

'Who're you hiding from today?' he asked.

'Her conscience,' Gus butted in.

'See, I'm not even safe here anymore,' I complained.

'Have you heard from your mom yet?' Cam asked.

And then it all clicked together. Mom had come to visit so I wouldn't be alone on my birthday. And it just happened to be nice timing to introduce me to Larry. What was I going to do when they came back tonight?

'Not yet,' I said, hopefully calmly. I would have to deal with that later; I had enough to deal with right now.

'Any idea when they're supposed to get back?' he asked.

'Who knows? They might have made plans to go to Tahiti by now.' I was only half-joking about that.

'Jealous of the travelling she's doing, Kate?' Gus asked.

'You kidding? Anything that keeps her from a three-week visit with me is a bonus.'

'It is a little crowded in the apartment,' Cam agreed. 'But you know, I was thinking that we could maybe do some renovations.'

'Like what?'

'To start with I could knock out the half wall in the bedroom. That way when we're alone it'll be wide open and look really big.'

'And when we have company?' I asked.

'I'll hang shutters so we can close them for privacy.'

'I don't know, it sounds like a big messy job.'

'I keep hoping the building will go condo,' Cam said.

'Why, so we have to move?'

'No. I like the loft as much as you do. But if we could buy up our place and the place next door, then knock out the wall, we could have a really great place with two bedrooms.'

'God, am I living with Tim "the Tool Man" Taylor?' I asked.

'Just think of all the space we'd have.'

'I suppose you want the appliances to have more power, too?'

'No, this is just a space thing, I swear. I mean, we could double the size of the living room, the kitchen, the bedroom . . .'

'Well, the building is not going condo,' I said.

'There's talk of it.'

'And just how do you know that?' I asked.

'I was helping the landlord with the air conditioning a couple of days ago. He was telling me about it.'

'Did you get paid?'

'No, but a significant discount will be shown in my share of this month's rent.' He laughed.

'I can't afford for the building to go condo,' I said, suddenly worried. Great, one more thing to worry about.

'I'm sorry I said anything. Look, don't worry about it. If it happens we can dip into my savings for the down payment. I'm never going to let you lose your home.'

'Thanks.' I smiled at him, some of the worry abating. So this is what the whole love thing is about – that warm feeling in your heart that said you would never be alone and you would always be looked after.

'Thanks for what?' he asked.

'You successfully got my mind off my other troubles and gave me something brand new to worry about,' I joked as I stood up. 'But I think I better be getting back to work.'

'Oh, Sam left a message on the machine. She wants to know how many people are coming to Graham's birthday party.'

'It's OK, I talked to her already.'

'But what about Graham's party?' he asked.

'What about it?' I asked.

'Were you going to invite me?'

'Oh, I guess I forgot about you. Are you free on Tuesday night? Because if so, I can provide you with a really hot date and pretty much guarantee you a good time.'

'I think I can fit it into my schedule. Who's the girl?'

I kissed him. 'That will be a surprise for later! And we're trying to keep the party a surprise. That's why I didn't tell you.'

'See you later,' he called after me as I started back for the theatre.

I tried to get back to the journal all afternoon and most of the evening without any success. At the end of the evening, I put it back into my backpack and vowed to finish it at home. I didn't care what anyone said about getting involved; I had to know what happened in the end. Scott dropped me off at home and I could hardly wait to get upstairs. I had the perfect plan in my head, which involved Mom and Larry already in bed or about to be, Cam still being at work and a quick call to Sam to cancel pizza night. Then I would get into my pyjamas and curl up with a cup of tea and the journal.

I turned the key in the door and walked into a full-fledged party.

'Katie,' Cam greeted me with a kiss. 'You forgot to tell me you had invited Sam and Ryan over tonight.'

'It doesn't matter,' my mom piped up. 'Sam always comes with good food. They brought some of her new dips to sample.'

'Hi, Mom.' I gave her a hug. The good thing about being so stressed about the whole birthday thing was that I really didn't care that Mom hadn't asked me how I was. There were a couple of bottles of wine open on the coffee table and bowls of dips and vegetables everywhere. This didn't look like it was going to be an early night.

Cam slid my backpack off and helped me off with my coat. 'Are you going to join us?' he asked.

I looked longingly at my backpack, sitting on the floor in the corner. I'd get to it tomorrow, I promised myself. I had to get to it tomorrow; time was running out.

'Sure, I'll join you,' I said, sitting down on the floor in front of the coffee table and pouring myself a glass of wine. 'But when I'm tired and bitchy tomorrow, you guys will have no one to blame but yourselves.'

'We'll live with it,' Sam promised.

'So I thought we agreed on high-fat, totally non-nutritional pizza when you guys came over. Now, I'm not a caterer, but I believe these are vegetables. And if I recall correctly they are supposed to be good for you.'

'I'm testing these for your party on Tuesday,' Sam explained. 'What do you think?'

'I think they're great. Can I afford them?'

'You can afford almost anything. You gave me your credit card number, remember?'

'Actually, I gave you Cam's credit card number. Which is

probably better, because he has a higher limit than I do.'

'Great, then I'll double the order,' Sam said.

'Is there a party on Tuesday?' Mom asked. 'We'll have to stay for that, Larry.'

'It's just for Graham's birthday,' I explained.

'Well, we can stay and meet all your little friends,' Mom teased me. 'We were going to leave sometime on the weekend, but a couple more days won't make a difference.'

'The more the merrier,' I agreed. A few more days. Why not? Nothing else was going smoothly either.

We finally cleared the place and got Mom and Larry settled, then Cam went up to bed and I stayed downstairs to load the dishwasher. Just as I was finishing up, Mom came into the kitchen and gave me a big hug.

'Happy birthday,' she whispered, so only I could hear. And then she kissed me on the cheek and trundled back off to bed.

I grabbed my backpack on the way upstairs and pulled the journal out before climbing into bed. Cam reached over and turned out the light.

'Hey, I was reading,' I protested as I reached over him and turned it back on.

'It's late, Katie. I'd like to try to get some sleep.'

'Cam, I haven't been able to read this all day.' I felt my voice rising, and then pulled it back down to a whisper when I remembered we had company downstairs once again.

'Tomorrow, please?' he asked.

'Fine.' I thought I had given him a 'fine' that definitely meant it wasn't, but he ignored me and turned off the light and we both settled under the covers.

'You know, those shutters might not be such a bad idea,' I said.

'What?'

'The renovations you were talking about this afternoon.'

'I don't suppose we could talk about this tomorrow?' he asked.

'Sure. Goodnight.'

He curled up further under the covers and all was quiet.

'How long do you think it would take to do it?' I asked.

'Goodnight, Katie,' three voices called out, one from beside me joined by Mom and Larry downstairs. I took the hint.

Saturday November 1

I sat behind my desk, a coffee beside me and a cigarette burning in the ashtray, but I didn't have the strength to pick either of them up. I plopped my head down and wished the file folder I had landed on was a pillow. Graham picked that exact moment to appear at the door.

'I am finding it very hard to work in an environment with an energy level this low,' was his greeting this morning.

'I'm sorry,' I mumbled, not picking my head up off the desk, 'but you try working the equivalent of two full-time jobs and having company at home as well. I'm surviving on, like, no sleep here. And I would never say this except in my weakened state, so you can't hold it against me later, but I'm not as young as I used to be, you know.'

'I'm working just as hard as you and you don't see me complaining.'

I opened my eyes and saw him grinning at me.

'You're fifteen years younger than I am and getting sex on a regular basis. You won't need sleep for at least another month. But boy am I going to be there to gloat when you crash and burn.'

'It'll never happen,' he promised. 'I treat my body like a temple. I rarely drink coffee, I don't smoke, I hardly drink liquor and I eat only fresh fruits and vegetables and organic, free-range proteins. This body will never give out on me.'

'That's what I thought at your age and look at me now.'

'Yeah, look at you now. Pick that head up off your desk and get some energy going here or I'm going home.'

I sat up. Graham took a good look at the circles under my eyes and refilled my coffee for me. 'I think you need more of this,' he said handing me my cup.

'Do I look that bad?' I asked.

'I'm sure that once you put some make-up on, it'll be fine.'

'I do have make-up on,' I whined.

'Oh. Well, it's not that bad.' He sat down and rummaged in his backpack for a bottle of orange juice. 'Are we going to get back to that journal today?'

'We've got to try. After Stephan's visit yesterday, I feel like I have to try to find some answers. He was in rough shape.'

'Oh, don't fall for that load of crap.'

'What do you mean?' It's funny how even the hint of an argument can perk me right up.

'It's just so typical.'

'I'm not following you.'

'Stephan is this really handsome, famous man. He is used to getting exactly what he wants, either with his looks, his talent, or his reputation. And that's exactly what he's doing with you.'

'You're not telling me anything I don't already know.' I sighed.

'But he's not getting what he wants right now. He's the golden boy and this was supposed to be another one of those golden moments in his life, but it's not turning out that way. He's about to lose his family and his job, all very publicly. So he stumbles upon you. Good old reliable, gullible Katie. And she knows the detective. So what's it going to take to get her on the team?'

'Graham, I know there's a point here somewhere and I'm certain you are going to get to it really, really soon.'

'Well, he can't use his looks, or fame or money in this situation, so now he's using the final option. He came in here and made you feel sorry for him. He looked like a sad, broken, pathetic man and you fell for it hook, line and sinker.'

'I beg your pardon?'

'Look, Kate, I'm as curious about this journal as you are, but he has just manipulated you big time. You're ready to mount your white steed and charge into battle for him.'

'That's not true,' I said, trying to defend myself.

'Who's the one that's been going around swearing he couldn't have done it?'

'Me, but—'

'Kate, listen to yourself. Has Ken Lincoln told you anything at all about this case or his investigation?'

'No.'

'Well then, all you have is a journal written about twenty years ago, by a lovesick little girl, which you are convinced will clear Stephan of whatever evidence the police have on him.'

'I thought you were on my side,' I said, more anger showing in my voice than I had planned. Had Graham hit a nerve? I guess I was a little more sensitive about this than I'd realized.

'I am now and always will be on your side. I just don't want you to fall for his act, at least not all the way. Let's read through this journal objectively and see what we find.'

This time, I took a deep breath before I spoke. 'That's a fair request. But you can't just ask me to forget the Stephan I knew.'

'Is that the man who didn't tell you he was married, or had a family? Do you think he's as honourable now as he was then?'

'I didn't ask if he was married,' I admitted.

'Moot point.'

'OK, I'll give you the fact that Stephan may not be the most honourable man who ever walked the face of the earth, if you'll give me the fact that he is far from a murderer.'

'I can't say that. Think of it from my perspective and what I've seen of him.'

'Why can't you just take my word for it? Don't you trust me?'

'I trust you. I don't trust him and what he's done to you. He's done nothing but manipulate you since he first walked in the theatre.'

'Well, I haven't exactly discouraged it,' I admitted. 'He's a very charming man.'

'That would be the point I've just been trying to make. So, why don't we both decide to be impartial and I'll watch your back if you'll watch mine?' he asked.

'I'll do my best,' I promised. I supposed I should find Cam and apologize to him. I realized I had been enjoying the attention I received from Stephan, and Cam had been putting up with it – and with me.

* * *

It was another one of those days when everyone wanted something and I was needed in five places at once – straightening out seating mix-ups, taking away tape recorders from anxious relatives who wanted to record their son's performance, fielding the press, getting change, restocking ice cream . . . It's not a glamorous life but a busy one. It was three o'clock in the afternoon before Graham and I managed to get a minute to read the journal. I sat on the sofa in the empty lobby and he sat beside me. Even though the lobby was empty, I read softly in case anyone should walk by and overhear us as the poor girl took us from the heights of teenage love to almost suicidal despair.

I have been put on probation. The meeting with my professors did not go well, and if I do not pull up my marks by next semester, I will be asked to leave the university. Stephan was supposed to come over and see me after the meeting but he never showed up. Three days later I finally got in touch with him. He said he had a great inspiration and had been holed-up in his apartment for days writing a great concerto for some sort of examination or concert. I don't know what it is for and I don't care. I needed him and he wasn't there for me. I told him I was going to kill myself, told him I was taking pills as soon as I hung up the phone. And then I hung up the phone and waited. And then he came to see me, to apologize for not being there when I had really needed him. He tried to explain how his music overtook him, how he lost track of minutes, hours – even days when he was writing. I nodded and pretended I understood, but how can I? Those minutes and hours and days with his music keep him away from me. Right now, I hate his music. I know it will be what takes us to the top of the world, he as a famous maestro and me as his beloved wife, but I want it to take the appropriate place, behind me. I have to be the most important thing in his life. I have to figure out how to make that happen.

When he saw how full of despair I was, how I was beyond all consolation, he told me that I had to learn to put up with this until he graduated. He has to make his reputation and then we can plan our future. We will be financially secure, able to go anywhere we want in the world, able to have anything we want. Couldn't I see how this would all be worth it? he asked me. And I did begin to see. I began to see the grand house we would live in, the limousines we would ride in. I saw my passport with stamps from every country filling every page. And I saw myself on his arm, wearing designer gowns and diamond tiaras. He had said we would plan our future together. We would be married and spend our lives together – isn't that what he had said? I knew then I had to learn to be patient with him. If he needed days to be alone and write, I would give him those days. I will have to structure my time, my life around him. I will be there for him whenever he needs me, and the rest of the time I will study. That way I can get off probation and stay in university. For if I am asked to withdraw and get sent home, I know that will be the end for us. It is going to be hard but I know my whole future depends on it. I can do it.

'I'm going for supper,' Graham said.

'But there's still tons of pages to go. I thought you wanted to hear this?'

'Kate, there's nothing in there. Dr Bergere had a crush on the Maestro when she was young. End of conversation. They both grew up, worked it out, and remained lifelong friends.'

'They didn't sound much like friends when they were arguing onstage last week,' I pointed out.

'Everyone argues. You should know that better than anyone. Besides, she was trying to tell him something he didn't want to hear. Most people get angry when that happens. You should know about that, too!'

'Aw, come on. Let's just read for a few more minutes.'

'No way; I want to get something to eat before the show tonight. You go ahead and give me the *Reader's Digest* condensed version later.'

'You're taking all the fun out of this,' I called after him as he walked across the lobby.

'You should take a break, too,' he called over his shoulder. 'All work and no play . . .'

'Yeah, yeah, yeah.' I turned back to the journal.

It has been hard work, but I'm off probation. I made a wonderful dinner to celebrate, but Stephan had to cancel. He did come over later and we had a wonderful night together. I just wished that once he would stay for the whole night. But he had to practice, he had to write, he had to study. His whole life depends on the reputation he is making now, and I am beginning to realize this.

Sometimes I wonder why I am working so hard. I could quit school, be a waitress, help support Stephan and not have to study. I am never going to use my degree anyway. I am going to be the wife of a great Maestro! But somehow, I don't think Stephan will want to marry a waitress. He will need a wife by his side who equals his reputation, not one who has to hide her background.

And he still hasn't met my parents. Every time I speak with them, Mother asks if I am dating lots of boys. They never ask about Stephan. They have found out that he is a musician and I'm afraid that didn't do much to raise him in their esteem. They want me to make a good marriage and have a successful career. They are so old-fashioned. Don't they know it is the eighties? I don't have to marry well; I can marry whoever I want! I will be responsible for making my own life great. And since they haven't met Stephan, they can't see the spark that I see. That spark that was going to grow into the blazing bonfire that would be his career. Sometimes, when I'm feeling particularly angry with them, I imagine being at the premiere of another of Stephan's great concertos. All the press from all the papers in the entire world will be there and so will my parents. And with the cameras flashing, as my mother reaches out to hug me, I will ignore her. Walk right past her as if she was some sort of street urchin. They will be humiliated in front of the entire world and I will save all the clippings from all the papers and laugh at them. Yes, it's worth all the effort I'm putting into it. That one moment will make it all worthwhile.

A hand touched my shoulder and I jumped, letting out a little scream and tossing the journal halfway across the lobby.

'I didn't mean to scare you,' Cam said, stifling a giggle.

'Don't you ever do that to me again,' I said, trying to catch my breath.

'Must be some good reading to have you that involved,' he commented, sitting on the couch beside me.

'I was reading the journal.'

'That would have been my guess,' he said.

'No lectures,' I warned him as I got up and gathered up the loose pages.

'No lectures. You can read all you want, as long as you're not—'

'Getting involved,' I finished for him.

'I've said that once or twice before?' he asked.

'Once or twice. You and everyone else in my life. As a matter of fact, Graham and I started out our day with just that discussion,' I told him.

'Was he for or against?'

'He was pretty much on your side this time.'

'I knew I always liked that boy.' Cam smiled. 'We have to get him a real nice birthday present.'

'I'll get him the same thing I'm getting you. A thesaurus so you can find other ways of telling me not to get involved.'

'I know lots of others ways,' Cam said. 'You just don't listen to any of them.'

'So what are you doing here?' I asked.

'I thought I'd come by and see if you wanted to grab a bite to eat.'

I glanced at my watch and decided I had the time, even though I didn't want to be taken away from the journal. But I did want to mention to Cam that I appreciated the patience he had been showing me as I wound my way through this complicated piece of my past.

'I'll go if you let me read for a half-hour in bed tonight?' I asked.

'Just a half-hour?'

'I promise, one half-hour and then it's lights out.'

'And you won't argue?'

'Yeah, right. I thought you knew me better than that. Of

course I'll argue. And I'll probably whine, too. But I'll let you win the argument.'

'OK, it's a deal.' He stood up and held his hand out for me. I took it and stood up.

'Where are we going?' I asked.

'My office.'

'What have you got in mind for dinner? Me?' I said jokingly.

'No, I brought something from home. I was going to save you for dessert.'

'No way,' I protested. 'Remember the last time we tried something like that?'

'Hey, you're the one that said it was exciting.' Cam winked, helping me up of the sofa. 'I brought a doorstop and a bottle of wine. We won't get caught, but if we do, we won't care.'

'I'll eat dinner, but we're going to have to talk about the rest of this,' I said as he led me down the fire escape.

Graham and I met back in my office after dinner. He had the same blush on his cheeks that I felt beginning on mine. We immediately turned away from each other and began discussing the ticket sales for our show, without making eye contact once. It wasn't the most exciting conversation in the world, but it was the most innocuous subject I could come up with on the spur of the moment.

Cam picked me up after the show and we drove home in silence, both too tired to talk. Silence is never a problem with us, though. Cam is the first man in my life with whom I feel comfortable in silence. There was a note on the door from Mom and Larry, saying they'd got tired of waiting for us to get home and had gone out for dinner. I breathed a sigh of relief, knowing that I could actually get back to the journal. We changed quickly, got into bed, and Cam didn't argue about turning out the light and going to sleep. He did pull the blankets over his head in silent protest. I turned away from him and opened the journal.

> *I know I am a stupid, jealous young girl, but I can't help myself. I know Stephan is seeing other women and I don't know what to do about it. I have given him everything I have to give, I have done everything he has asked of me,*

but it does not seem to be enough. I cry, I scream, I beg and I plead, but he will not admit that there is someone else. If he would only tell me the truth, I could forgive him. But he insists it is his music. Always his damned music!

I have tried to surprise him, showing up at his apartment unannounced, bringing his laundry back, or surprising him with dinner, but he won't even let me in. He screams at me about how he must not be interrupted when he is creating. I believe he is creating something altogether different than the concerto he keeps telling me about. I see the waitresses in town, and how they smile at him. The same way I smiled after our first time together. I feel nauseous when I think about him being with them when I am at home, waiting for him. I know it will be different when we are married, but I am so afraid that maybe he will like one of them better than me, despite everything I have done for him, everything I have given him. But there has to be something else I can do to win him, to ensure he is mine forever. And I will think of it, before it is too late. I have invested too much time in this relationship to give up on it . . .

'Katie?' a voice whispered in my ear.

'Hmmm.' My eyes must have accidentally closed because I had to force them open to see who was talking to me.

'Katie, it's late, give me the journal.'

I felt something tug out of my hand and then I rolled over and curled up under the warmth of the covers.

'You fell asleep,' Cam's voice whispered again. But I ignored him; I was too tired to form a word, let alone a full sentence to answer him.

Sunday November 2

I never heard the alarm go off or Cam get out of bed, but both things must have happened, because Cam was standing over me, gently shaking my shoulder and calling my name.

'Good morning,' I said, trying to smile and be polite despite the fact that it was not my favourite time of day. 'I didn't hear you get up.'

'I think you were tired. You fell asleep reading last night.'

'I meant to fall asleep.'

'You did not. You still had the journal clutched in your hand and the cutest little line of drool running down your chin.'

'Now I know you're lying. I do not drool, just as I do not snore and I don't know how many times I have to tell you these things.' I sat up in bed and suddenly realized it was light out. 'What time is it?'

'It's eight thirty.'

'What? You let me sleep in?' I jumped up, feeling suddenly panicked.

'Don't worry, I called Graham and told him you'd be late.'

'Why? Why did you do that?'

'For one thing, I thought you could use the sleep,' Cam said, sounding vaguely patronizing. 'And for the other, you have a physiotherapy appointment at nine this morning.'

'You went behind my back and made an appointment? Without even consulting me?'

'Calm down, I did not make the appointment for you.'

'Then who did, my fairy godmother?'

'Well, you're close. They called when you missed your appointment yesterday and your mother took the call. Apparently she and your physiotherapist had a great conversation and it turns out that they take Sunday appointments so she booked you in and promised them I would get you there on time.'

'I'm sorry,' I said. 'But you have to admit, it sounds like something you would do.'

'Apology accepted. Now you had better get up and get dressed. I don't want your mother coming after me for not getting you there.'

'You're right about that. You'll lead a much happier life if my mother is not angry with you.'

'Well, at least now I know where you get it from. And you certainly come by it honestly.'

'Katherine,' Mom called from downstairs, 'quit arguing and get down here and dressed. You are not missing another appointment.'

'You know,' I whispered to Cam, 'that idea you had about the shutters is beginning to sound better and better.'

'Oh yeah?' He looked pleased with himself.

'When can you start?'

I tried reading the journal on the way to physio, but Cam was in a playful mood and kept flipping the pages at me. He thought he was pretty funny but I was not amused. I tried reading again during physio, but Sean was in the mood to discuss why I had not been doing my exercises, how I was never going to get my strength and mobility back if I didn't keep up the stretching and weight program he had me on. I was even less amused. I gave up trying to read on our drive to the Plex, and decided I had better head straight for the theatre to see how Graham was doing.

He was bubbling over – again.

'I got news!' he said, beaming.

'We're getting raises?'

'Better than that!'

'OK, since you obviously don't want to tell me how the festival is going, tell me your news.'

'We're finally getting a celebrity.'

'This is your news?'

'This is great news. Don't you even want to know who?'

'No.'

'Richard Carpenter.'

'Richard Carpenter is good news?' I asked sarcastically.

'Well, granted, I had hoped for a big director, someone who could discover me and cast me in some huge big-budget feature. But you have to admit that Richard Carpenter is a great musician. He'll be here for the closing night ceremonies.'

'I'm obviously going to have to tie you down that night. And you remember the rules?' I asked.

'What rules would you be talking about?'

'The rules about not auditioning for honoured guests.'

'You're not going to hold me to that?' he asked.

'I certainly am.'

'I'll sing for him while I show him to his seat.'

'Nothing of the sort. If you even open your mouth, you're toast.'

'I'll come up with some sort of a plan,' he promised.

'That's what I'm afraid of. So how about this morning? Is everything going smoothly?'

'Like a top. It's been the quietest day we've had since this thing started. It seems almost surreal.'

'Good,' I said, thinking it would give me a chance to get back to my reading. 'I'm going to Grounds Zero to have breakfast. I'll be back in an hour or so.'

'Not a problem. But try having some fruit for breakfast instead of a brownie.'

'I'll have orange-flavoured coffee. Will that fill my vitamin requirements for the day?'

'Just add a little cream to your coffee to fill your dairy requirements and you'll be set, having covered none of the major food groups.'

I sat at a booth in Gus's restaurant, ordered a brownie, a coffee, and then half a grapefruit out of guilt. Gus brought over my order and lingered at the table. Once again, I reluctantly pulled myself away from the journal and looked up at Gus.

'What are you reading?' he asked.

'Oh, just some notes from upstairs,' I lied.

'Oh?'

'You sound like you don't believe me.'

'I just worry about you, Kate.'

'So why does my reading notes from the producer make you worry about me.'

'Something I overheard yesterday.'

'What did you overhear?' I asked.

'That somebody was looking for a journal they had lost.'

'What?'

'I couldn't see who it was. There were two people leaving just as I was taking an order on the phone. But I heard them talking about a journal that they thought they had lost in the theatre. I thought you might have found something like that. Maybe that's what you were reading.'

'No, I haven't found anything like that.' I hate lying but I've been doing more and more of it these days.

'Maybe the cleaners found it,' he thought out loud, trying to bait me into telling him more than I wanted to.

'I'll check into that,' I promised. 'Too bad you didn't see who it was. Maybe they wrote their name in it, though.'

'That writing looks like a woman's hand,' he said.

'His secretary wrote it, Gus. You know, I think you're getting way too suspicious in your old age.'

'Maybe, maybe not.'

'Did you see anything? Hair colour, what they were wearing? Anything that would help us find the people that were talking about the journal?'

'Why are you interested?' he asked. 'If you haven't found anything like that?'

'I don't know. I guess Detective Lincoln might want to know who it was. It might tie in with his investigation in some way.'

'Oh.' When Gus answered that way, it spoke volumes. And all those volumes said he didn't believe a word I'd just said. Damn, I hate him when he's like this.

'Well, I couldn't see who it was,' he continued. 'There were people going out and people coming in. I just perked up when I heard the name of your theatre mentioned.'

'Well, I'll make sure I mention it to Ken when I see him next time,' I promised.

'You make sure you do that. And you make sure you keep yourself safe.'

'I will.'

Gus turned and walked away from the table and I finally turned back to the journal.

I finally know what I am going to do. I know the one way that I can win Stephan and he will have to forsake all the other girls for me. I'm so excited I can't even think about it without smiling. I feel like breaking into song all the time. And it is so simple I don't know why I didn't think of it before now. I can't even write about it – I'm scared that someone may see – but at the same time, I am almost bursting to tell someone. I don't trust my girlfriends, though, and I certainly can't talk to my mother about this. Stephan is definitely out of the question. I know he would never approve of what I am thinking, but years from now, looking back on his past and the life I have made for him, he will know I have made the right decision for us. We will grow old together and someday, when the time is right, I will tell him how I planned our lives out for us, when I was a young girl and everyone said I didn't know what was best. I will show them all that I did know what was best.

But how long will it take? I will be loving and caring and patient. I can't let anything come between us until I have a chance to make this work. I will do exactly what Stephan wants me to, when he wants me to. And I won't show my jealousy anymore. I don't have to be jealous anyway, because I know now that he will be mine and only mine. There is no other way!

'What is she planning?' I wondered aloud, taking a break to sip my coffee and trying to put myself in the mind of this young girl. This was beginning to get really interesting, and somehow, I didn't sense that Stephan and Joelle were about to have the pleasant break-up that Graham had predicted. I knew that any woman who invested that much time, energy and emotion into a relationship, as she apparently had with Stephan, would not get over him easily. But was this starting to point to Stephan – a crime of passion, perhaps? I had to finish this; my wandering mind was taking me in directions I didn't want to go. I flipped the page, lit a cigarette and turned back to the journal.

'Katie!'

I turned toward the door and saw Cam standing, half in and half out of the restaurant, waving frantically to me.

'What's going on?' I called over to him.

'It's your mom.'

Suddenly not caring at all about the journal and filled with utter panic, I stubbed out my cigarette, grabbed the journal and my bag and ran with Cam to the parking lot.

We had been sitting in the emergency room for over an hour. The nurses had assured us that my mom was back there, she was alive, and that the doctor would be out to tell me the rest as soon as he possibly could. I had called Graham to let him know where I was, and then sat back down beside Cam to wait.

It was another two hours before Larry and a doctor walked back out into the waiting room to find us. I rushed over to meet them and Cam wasn't far behind me.

'What's happened?' I asked frantically. 'What's wrong with Mom?'

'It's my fault,' Larry apologized. 'I insisted we do it. She told me she didn't have much luck with horses but I really wanted to go riding and I talked her into it.'

'You went horse-back riding?' I asked. Visions of Mom being thrown or dragged or a combination of the two started racing through my head.

'I'm sorry. I should have listened to her. She wasn't exactly a natural rider. Even on an old trail horse . . .'

I gave up on Larry and turned to the doctor. 'So what happened?' I asked her.

'It's just a slight fracture.'

'Of what? Her spine, her skull?'

'Her wrist,' the doctor said.

'Her wrist?' I repeated. 'That's it?'

'She slipped on some manure in the barn,' Larry said. 'Snapped like a twig.'

'Is she going to be OK?' Cam asked.

'She's in the casting room right now. That and a little Demerol and she'll be right as rain,' the doctor joked. 'You can take her home as soon as they're finished with the cast.'

‘I just hope you got pictures,’ I said to Larry, feeling my mood lighten considerably as we started down the hall to collect my mother.

When we got home, I phoned Graham again and he assured me that he was just fine and I could stay at home and look after my mother for the evening. I felt guilty for leaving him there, but took a secret pleasure from an evening at home. I hoped the Demerol would kick in and Mom would pass out early, leaving me with the last few pages of the journal. Not a chance. Sam and Ryan showed up, bringing more food. We all sat around the coffee table with more wine, spread out dinner when we’d gone through most of the wine, and ate heartily. Mom looked like the Queen of the May, tucked into bed, pillows propping her up every which way and high as a kite on painkillers. Poor Sam was still trying to get a final body count for Graham’s party, which was only a few days away. She tried to explain that she really needed to know how many people she was supposed to feed in order to cater this affair properly. I promised I would take care of it first thing tomorrow, and then we avoided the topic for the rest of the night.

When everyone had said his or her goodbyes and we finally got Mom to quit giggling and go to sleep, I climbed into bed with the journal.

‘Katie, you’re not going to start that again tonight, are you?’ Cam asked.

‘Just one page,’ I promised.

‘I’m just going to have a quick shower,’ he said. ‘But when I get back . . .’

‘I’ll only read until you come back up.’

‘No arguments tonight, I’m exhausted.’

I didn’t answer. I was too busy trying to find where I had left off in the journal.

> *I’ve done it! I’m so excited. It’s been on my mind so much, I can’t believe the day is actually here. I’m nervous, I’m excited, and I’m counting the days now until our life together can really begin.*

I know this is the right thing. I still haven't told anyone, but I know I have made the right decision. I even stopped by a shop yesterday and tried on wedding gowns. It was the most glorious day. I cried when I saw myself in the mirror. The dress was so beautiful and I couldn't help but picture my wedding day. I just wish my mother had been with me. But she still doesn't understand how much I love Stephan. Soon she'll know. The whole world will know. Life is so wonderful again.

And I had another meeting with my professor and he was proud to tell me that I have made the honour roll. That's how I know this is the right decision, because suddenly everything in my life is going right again. All my efforts, my hard work, my dedication is beginning to pay off.

And Stephan finally finished his concerto. It was brilliant. I sat in the back row of the theatre and cheered when he came onstage after the performance to take his bows. It was our first performance together. I will remember this moment forever. I bought a beautiful box and cut all the clippings from the newspapers and put them inside. This will be the box where I keep all the important memories from our life together. I showed it to Stephan, when he came over to see me two days later, and he was very proud that I had all his clippings. I washed his ruffled shirt, the one he had worn with the tuxedo the night his concerto debuted, and I found myself dreaming of the day he would have a closet full of these and I would have a closet full of gowns to match. After all, a woman of my standing could not be seen in the same gown twice. I would wear them once, and then donate them to charity auctions. All women would love to wear the dress that the great Maestro's wife had been seen in.

Now I just need God on my side. I cannot do this without Him. And I have no idea how long it will take Him to jump in and help me with this. I have been going to mass every morning and praying for this to work. I have lit candles, made offers to every saint that might have any influence, and prayed harder than I have ever prayed in my entire life. Mother would be very proud of my new-found dedication to God. But how long will it take? More unanswered questions. I can't talk to Mother; I can't take books out from the library in case someone sees – and Stephan might see them when he comes to visit. What excuse could I ever come up with to explain away an apartment full of medical textbooks? He would definitely be suspicious of that. No, I have to be patient and figure this one out for myself. I have also heard that if you are nervous or anxious it can make a difference and slow things down. I don't know if that is true or not, but I'm not going to take any chances. I am meditating every night, taking vitamins, sleeping well, exercising – doing everything I can do to make it work. Now it is just a matter of time.

But how much time? See, I am being impatient again. I have to work on patience; it is definitely one of my weaknesses. But I stopped taking my birth-control pills two months ago. How long is it going to be until I am pregnant?

'Foolish girl,' I said out loud. 'Trying to catch a man that way never works.'

I heard Cam climbing the stairs and, as much as I really didn't want to, I set the journal on the nightstand and held the covers up for him.

'You'll never believe what I just read,' I said when he had switched the light off and was settled under the covers.

He cuddled up to me, still warm from the shower, his breath soft on my neck.

'Katie, I love you, but could we talk about this tomorrow? I'm exhausted.'

'Of course,' I said, slightly disappointed. But I kissed him on the forehead and whispered goodnight. After all, it wouldn't be fair if I always got my own way, would it?

Monday November 3

I'm pregnant! It is a glorious day. I lit candles, went to two masses and called Mother and Father and told them how much I love them. My life is about to begin. I can hardly wait to tell Stephan. I know he will be upset at first, but it is for the best and I know he will see that very soon. I will make his life wonderful, and he, the baby and I will be the happiest family there ever was.

'This is crazy,' I said. 'I can't believe she did this. I wonder what happened to the baby.'

'Katie, if you don't put that down and get up, you're going to be late,' Cam admonished me. He was sitting on the chair, pulling on his socks. The alarm had gone off way too early, just as it had every other morning this week, and Cam had gone downstairs to start the coffee. I decided I had a few minutes and picked up the journal. And now Cam was dressed and on his second cup of coffee. I looked at the clock and realized I had been reading far longer than I thought I had. I tossed the journal aside and ran for the shower.

'So she got pregnant, on purpose, and thought that would make Stephan fall in love with her and marry him?' Graham asked me.

We sat in my office, the day's festival activities underway, music playing softly over the office speakers. I had the journal in my backpack and could hardly wait to get back to it, to find out how he reacted when she told him her big news.

'That's where I left off,' I confirmed.

'That's insane. How could she think that trapping him like that would give her this happily-ever-after life she was dreaming of?'

'Do you know what I think?' I said.
'I can't even begin to imagine.'
'I think that she's crazy.'
'Oh, give me a break.'
'No, really, Graham. This goes beyond a teenage girl fantasy. She's obsessed.'
'Well, this definitely puts a whole new slant on things. But you're not really helping Stephan here, are you? She's crazy, stalks him throughout the years and then he finally kills her.'
'Not necessarily.' I didn't want to hear him say out loud what I had been thinking.
'It just seems to point to a crime of passion. They've got this whole strange past, maybe even a child, and his wife probably doesn't even know about it. Stephan might have killed her to shut her up, protect his reputation.'
'Maybe,' I finally admitted. 'But it's too late to turn back. We're on to something, and I guess if he is guilty and I can prove it, then I have to do it.'
'Have you talked to Detective Lincoln about this yet?' Graham asked the other question I had been avoiding.
'No. He's got the original journal and is having it translated, so he knows as much as I do. But I thought I'd try to finish it tonight and then I'll talk to him tomorrow and see what he has to say about it.'
'You mean you'll tell him what you think about it,' Graham said, eyebrows raised.
'Something like that.'
'And what if Stephan is guilty?'
'I don't know. I still can't believe that he could kill anyone. But you're right – this is getting pretty twisted. There's a lot more going on here than I ever thought could be possible. And if there is a child somewhere . . . who knows? Maybe with Nicole getting all this attention right now, Dr Bergere felt Stephan should start paying attention to his "other" family But I haven't got to the end yet; I don't even know if there *is* another family.'
'So what are you going to do?' Graham asked.
'Finish the journal. I can't make any decisions until I finish.'
'And then?'
'I don't know. I guess that first I have to see what happens

in the end. If it points to Stephan, I feel like I have to talk to him. I think I owe him that much.'

'Kate, if you think it points to the Maestro, the only one you should talk to is Detective Lincoln. What if he did kill Dr Bergere and you tip him off?'

'I don't know,' I said, pulling at my hair. 'This is giving me a headache. Let me get through the last few pages and then we'll talk.'

'I just feel like nothing good is going to come of this.'

'Something good already has.'

'What?'

'My French has improved.'

Oh, my God. I was right. There is another woman. He came to tell me tonight. Thank God I decided to go ahead with my plan, because there is nothing he can do about it now. He has to marry me.

I don't care if he has been engaged to her for three years, that their families had planned this since they were children, or that he is in love with her. He doesn't know what love is. He will when I tell him my news.

And yet I didn't tell him. That was supposed to be why he came over last night. I cooked a romantic dinner, bought a new dress, and I was going to tell him after dessert. But then he dropped his little bombshell on me. Told me about this girl, this tramp that he is going to marry. I am so upset that I couldn't tell him. But I am going to go to his place tomorrow. I know he doesn't like me to surprise him by showing up unannounced, but this is too important and he must know. Besides, I am not going to walk down the aisle in a maternity wedding dress. We must start planning our wedding quickly, while I still have my figure, so I can't put off telling him any longer.

Then he will know who he really loves and who he will really marry – the one that has taken care of him for all this time. It is me and I am about to get my pay-off.

The phone started ringing and pulled me away from the

journal. I was getting really frustrated by the fact that the world seemed to be against me finishing this thing.

'Kate Carpenter,' I answered.

'Kate, it's Sam.'

Oh shit, I hadn't called her. She really was going to kill me. Or worse, not cater the party.

'I'm warming up the oven,' she continued. 'Getting ready to bake a cake, but I have no idea how many people this cake has to feed.'

'Sarcasm doesn't become you,' I told her. 'But I deserve it. I don't know how many people you have to feed either. Can I call you back in ten minutes?'

'Do you absolutely positively promise that you're going to call me back within an hour?'

'I said ten minutes,' I repeated.

'But I know you better than that. Call me within the hour or you won't have a birthday cake tomorrow, OK?'

'OK, I'll talk to you soon.'

I hung up the phone and took off in search of Leonard.

Ten minutes turned into hours. I talked to Leonard, talked to Sam, talked to Leonard again and I got roped into going shopping for decorations with him. By the time I got back, Mom had called and I got roped into running some errands for her as well. When I got back to the theatre, the catering department was waiting for me to go over the arrangements for the closing-night party of the festival, and by the time I got finished, the ushers had arrived for the evening shift. It might be a dark day for our theatre, but the festival had some catching up to do and they were taking advantage of having the theatre all to themselves.

I was just changing into my jeans, ready to go home for the night, when my phone rang. I picked it up and answered gruffly, hoping it would be a short conversation.

'Hi, Kate, it's Ken Lincoln. Am I calling at a bad time?' he asked.

'No. The festival is over for today; I was just on my way out.'

'I'm just calling to let you know I'm going to be stopping by the theatre tomorrow; are you going to be around?'

'I'll be here all day.'

'Great, well I'll see you then.'
'Why are you coming by tomorrow, Ken?' I asked.
'You know, Kate, I was also going to thank you for being so cooperative and staying out of this investigation. Don't disappoint me now when it's so close to the end.'
'Are you going to make an arrest?' I asked.
'That is information that I have no intention of sharing.'
'You are, aren't you?'
'Kate . . .'
'Did you read that journal I found yet?' I asked.
'I've read some of it. They're still finishing the translation. I promise I'll tell you more tomorrow, when it's over, but not until then.'
'Ken, don't arrest the wrong person.'
'Are you telling me not to arrest Stephan Bouchard?'
'No, I'm just asking you to be very sure. There are some people involved here that I care about.'
'Kate, I wouldn't do anything unless I was very sure about it. Now, we'll talk tomorrow. For now I would like you to continue to be good and stay out of it. Just one more day to go, OK?'
'I'll do my best.' It was a pretty noncommittal answer; I wouldn't feel too bad if I couldn't keep my word.
'I suppose that's the best I can expect from you. Bye.'
'See you tomorrow.'
I checked my watch and realized Cam had been waiting for almost fifteen minutes. I locked up and ran to the stage door. I was going to read that journal tonight, no matter what.

I lay in bed with a cup of tea and Cam snoring softly beside me. My eyes were heavy with sleep and I didn't know how long I was going to be able to stay awake, despite my determination to finish reading the journal. I took another sip of tea and quietly flipped the pages until I found where I had left off, careful not to disturb Cam.

> *The doctors told me I should remember that night. I should talk about it, write about it, anything to try and resolve what had happened in my mind and to let them help me. They were all a bunch of pompous and arrogant assholes that could never understand what I had gone through. But they*

are in total control of me while I am here. So I have started to write in this journal again to try and keep them happy . . . and to let them know exactly how I feel about them.

That night, when I drove to Stephan's house, the rain was pounding down harder than I had ever seen before. Thunder and lightning were crashing directly overhead, making the ground shake. I had borrowed my friend's car, so that the rain wouldn't ruin my new dress. I had parked the car in the space nearest the front door of his apartment building and turned off the lights and ignition. I covered my freshly styled hair with a sweater and made a mad dash for the door, but I was still soaked by the time I let myself in. I couldn't believe how easy it had been to get a key to Stephan's apartment, and how he had never guessed that I had it.

I looked down at my dripping clothes and laughed. It didn't matter. I was on my way to see my soon-to-be fiancé. How glorious that sounded, especially after last night, when I was afraid it might all be over. And in another month he would be my husband. My entire body ached with the thought of it, walking down the aisle in a beautiful white gown. A perfect wedding night in a beautiful hotel in Paris. I could hardly wait to get to Stephan's apartment and see him. And give him the good news. I dropped my hand protectively over my stomach and smiled. I was going to have a husband and a family. Maybe a little sooner than I had planned, in all the years I had dreamt about my wedding, but it didn't matter; he would be thrilled. And I would have to drop out of college, but being married to a famous composer and conductor, I wouldn't need a college degree. I could just stay home and raise a house full of children.

The elevator finally arrived at Stephan's floor, and I got out and ran down the hall with all the exuberance I could manage. After all I was expecting, I couldn't overexert myself. I let myself in and was surprised to see the apartment was dark. I quietly called Stephan's name, but he didn't answer. I thought he must be out.

I pushed my way into the bedroom, dropped my dripping coat on to the rack, and turned on the light. In that moment, my life changed for ever. Stephan was home. He was in bed, naked, with someone other than me.

He stood up and came over to me, muttering all sorts of apologies, but I turned and ran out the door, passing by the elevator and running down the stairwell. I thought I was going to be sick.

I didn't notice the rain as I got back in the car. I didn't stop to turn on the lights or fasten my seatbelt. I sped out of the parking space and into traffic. The cars I cut off blasted their horns at me but I ignored them. I couldn't see or hear anything except for the sight of him in the bed. I didn't see the red light, or the other car veering to try to avoid me. And I didn't see the windshield, even though I knew I went through it. And then I didn't see anything for a long time, until I woke in this hospital bed.

And they told me I would be fine, with months of therapy, but that I had lost the baby and any chance to have other babies. I cried for days, wondering how it could all have gone so wrong, wondering where Stephan was, and what would happen to me.

My parents came to see me, but when they found out I had been pregnant, all I could see was the disappointment in their eyes. I couldn't stand it and asked them to leave me alone. I wanted everyone to leave me alone. What I really wanted was to die. I wished for it, and even though it was a mortal sin, I prayed for it. But I didn't die. Instead, I suffered. But something, some part of me did die. It was my heart.

I looked at the clock and shuddered when I saw how late it was. I still had a few more pages to go, but I couldn't stay awake any longer. I was really sad after reading about the end of the girl's hopes and dreams. I turned off the light and cuddled close to Cam. He pulled me even closer to him and wrapped his arms around me. I started to feel a little better.

Tuesday November 4

The alarm rang and I pulled the pillow over my head to try and block out the sound. Cam finally reached over and shut it off.

'I don't want to get up,' I moaned. I didn't mind the occasional early-morning show, but I was going into two straight weeks now of this early morning nonsense, and my body was protesting in a serious way.

'It's the last day, Katie. All you have left are the closing ceremonies. And then you can sleep in again.'

'You mean I can sleep in tomorrow?'

'Yes, you can.' He smiled down at me.

'Bless you,' I said, climbing on top of him and kissing him. I dragged myself downstairs and into the shower. I turned on just the cold water and with an involuntary shudder I climbed in. I knew I was in rough shape when it didn't help.

Later, Cam dropped me off at the stage door and I kissed him goodbye.

'What time should I come by tonight?' he asked.

'The party is due to start as soon as we clear the lobby. But if you come early you can help decorate.'

'I'll come early. You look like you need all the help you can get today.'

'You don't know the half of it.' I smiled weakly at him and headed into the theatre.

Graham took one look at me, asked me how long I'd been up reading "that stupid journal" and sent me to the Rodeo Lounge for a quick nap. Sometimes, I love Graham. I think it is definitely to my benefit that he grew up with all those sisters. Normally I would have argued with him just for fun, but not today. When he woke me up at noon I felt a little guilty but I was in much better shape to face the day and pull off his surprise party.

I found a few minutes of quiet time in the afternoon and pulled the last pages of the journal out of my pants pocket.

> *I missed the afternoons I used to spend in the concert hall. I would sneak in, sometimes, and sit in the back row, doing my homework while Stephan rehearsed the orchestra. Those had been such quiet, happy times for both of us. I had dreamed of doing that my whole life, sitting in the back row and watching him rehearse. I would sit there and prepare my legal briefs to St Saens; I would bring our children in for the Mozart rehearsals, and at Christmas we would all sit quietly in the background and imagine the Sugar Plum Fairy dancing across the stage as he rehearsed the Nutcracker Suite. But now I don't know if I'll ever walk into another concert hall again.*

Oh my God! I realized this wasn't Joelle Bergere's journal at all – it was Carole Bouchard's. I was lost and confused. How had this woman – who had done everything in her power to trick and trap Stephan into a marriage he didn't want – ended up being his wife? And what about Nicole? The journal had said that she could never have another child. I looked up from the sofa and stared across the lobby to see Carole standing at the far end, staring back at me. She turned and left as soon as she saw me looking back at her. But in that one moment, I knew she had done it. I knew she had killed Joelle Bergere. Even worse, her look had said she knew that I knew. I nervously checked my watch and wondered when Detective Lincoln was going to be here. I really had to see him. I figured I was safe as long as I stayed in the theatre, surrounded by people, until he arrived. She wouldn't try anything with all these people around. Actually, she probably wouldn't try anything at all. I was beginning to think of life as a detective movie, but these things just don't really happen in real life.

Luckily I was pretty distracted for the rest of the day by the excitement of the upcoming party. I couldn't believe that Graham hadn't caught on to the surprise yet. All day long I found ushers in small groups, whispering about the plans or what they had bought him for his birthday. I had a small panic attack when we realized that nobody had invited Mandi, but I managed to get in touch with her at the hospital and she was now on the guest list. I was a little concerned that I still hadn't seen Detective Lincoln yet, but I forgot all about that as soon as the intermission for our evening show was over. That was my cue to get Graham out of the way so we could start decorating and sneak everything down to the loading dock. I called him into my office and he sat in the chair across from my desk, looking at me sadly.

'What is wrong with you?' I asked.

'I'm just really disappointed that you didn't remember what day it is today.'

'What do you mean?'

'It's my birthday,' he said. 'And no one except Mandi has remembered.'

'Graham, I'm so sorry. It's just been so crazy here that it totally slipped my mind. I'll tell you what, I'll buy you a drink after work.' I guess all my practice with lying was paying off, because he seemed to fall for this.

'Well, I'll be free,' he said dejectedly. 'Mandi got called into work for an extra shift, so I don't even get to see her tonight.'

'I know I'll be a poor substitute for Mandi, but I'll try to show you a good time.'

'Yeah, whatever.'

'I'll tell you what I'll do for you, just to round off your night. I'll send you up to the admin tower. There's been some changes to the policy manual and I need you to photocopy fifty of them for me.'

'Oh, Kate, that'll take the rest of the night. Can't I do it tomorrow?' he whined.

'Sorry, I need it for first thing tomorrow morning. Besides, you can be just as depressed standing at the photocopier as you can moping around here in the lobby. And you won't scare as many patrons up there as you will down here.'

'Fine,' he said, picking up the pile of originals I handed him. 'You know where to find me if you need me.'

I walked him to the elevator, and then the rest of us broke into action.

By the time Graham was back, the show was out, the lobby

was dark, and everyone was hiding in the loading dock, waiting to surprise him. His mood hadn't improved much, but I knew it would soon.

'Thanks, dude,' I said, taking the pile of useless papers he handed me. 'Now let's go get you a drink.'

'Kate, I really don't feel like going out tonight.'

'Come on, Graham. It'll be fun. And if you don't let me take you out, I'll feel guilty for the rest of my life.'

'And this affects me how?'

'If I feel guilty, I'll probably make the rest of your life miserable, too,' I informed him.

'OK, you win. But just one drink and then I'm going home to be alone and depressed.'

'Fine. Let's go. Cam's parked out by the stage door waiting for us.'

'Whatever.'

I got up and took his hand and started pulling him down the hall after me. 'Your boundless enthusiasm is overwhelming me,' I told him sarcastically. 'I hope you can work on that soon.'

'Why?' he asked. 'Everyone forgot my birthday. It doesn't matter how I feel.'

'It's going to,' I promised as I pulled him down the hall and we turned into the loading dock. Then the lights came on and close to a hundred people jumped up and yelled surprise. The look on his face was worth every minute of stress this party had caused me. And were those tears I saw on his cheeks? I guess he was suitably impressed.

It didn't take long for Graham's mood to improve, and a few people had obviously started partying before we arrived, so things were hopping in no time. Soon he was swaying on the makeshift dance floor with Mandi in one arm and a drink in the other. Everything was going better than I had hoped – until the fire alarm went off.

Cam was standing beside me when the bells started ringing. I turned to look at him, but he had no answers.

'It's a second stage alarm,' he told me.

'No kidding,' I said. We were drilled on fire safety and escape routes regularly. 'There weren't any memos that I missed about testing the alarms, were there?'

'No. Fire alarm tests are always on the second Wednesday of every month.'

'We've got to evacuate,' I said, my worst nightmare coming true. At least I didn't have a theatre filled with eight hundred people to try and keep calm, and despite being a little tipsy, most of party guests were quite adept at fire safety in this building. I ran over to the stereo and shut off the music.

'This is the real thing, guys,' I hollered over the noise of the party. 'Would everyone please follow Leonard through the fire escape.'

Leonard had seemed like the most sober one in the room, which is why I picked him, but for a minute no one moved. Then slowly people started heading towards the door that Leonard was holding open. As the bells continued to ring, the crowd started to move faster. Graham came over to me.

'Where do you want me, boss?'

'You know the drill; just like in the theatre, you're the last one out the fire escape and I'm the last one out after doing a final check of the theatre. Report to the fire captain in the staging area and I'll see you there.'

Graham ran off for the stairs, to make sure everyone made it out.

'I'll come with you,' Cam said, starting to follow me.

'No way, Cam, this is my job. You follow everyone else out like you're supposed to and I'll see you downstairs in a couple of minutes.'

'No, I'm staying with you,' he protested.

'Cam, this is my job. Please let me do it. And I need someone to look after Mom. Please go down to the staging area and then I'll know she's OK and I'll have one less thing to worry about.'

He stood as if to argue, but then thought better of it and headed for the fire escape to catch up with Mom and Larry.

I raced down the hall to the theatre, which we had left open so everyone could use the bathrooms and get their stuff out of the locker room. I checked the washrooms on the balcony level, calling out to anyone who might be around, poked my head inside the theatre to make sure it was empty, then I headed down the stairs. I noticed the light shining through the crack under my office door and thought I heard a sound come from inside. I was certain I had turned off the light when

Graham and I left the office. I had a bad feeling, but I had to check to see if someone was in there.

I put the key quietly into my office door and turned it slowly. I didn't hear anything. It must have been my overactive imagination again. I pushed open the door and edged slowly around it. Then I looked up and saw her. Carole Bouchard was sitting behind my desk. I grabbed for the slowly closing door, thinking I was pretty sure I could outrun her, but stopped immediately as she slowly brought a small pistol up from her lap.

'I don't think you should leave just now,' she said.

'What's this about?' I asked, hoping if I pretended I didn't know what was going on, she might just let me go. I didn't release the door, hoping I still might have a chance to escape.

'You're smarter than that, Katherine. I believe you know what I'm looking for.' She smiled. 'Now, why don't you just let that door close so we can have a little private conversation. I'm pretty sure everyone else has left the building by now, no?'

I reached into my pocket for the journal pages she had seen me reading in the lobby.

'Slowly,' she warned me, waving the gun to reinforce her point.

I slowly drew the paper from my pocket and handed it to her.

'The police have the original,' I informed her.

'It doesn't matter. They won't put it together. You were the only one who knew enough about my family to come up with the answer.'

'You should have just burned the diary,' I said. 'Then none of this would have been necessary.'

'I should have, but couldn't. There's too much sentiment, too many memories . . . I could not make myself get rid of it. But now that I have these pages from you, there is no need to worry. No one will ever figure out the connection.'

'But I know,' I said without thinking. Stupid, stupid, stupid! I chastised myself. I never know when to just shut up.

'And that knowledge is going to die with you.' She smiled. 'Then Stephan will be sentenced for the murder of that bitch Bergere and spend the rest of his life in jail. Nicole and I will be left alone, to live our lives as we should.'

'I don't understand.' And this time I really meant it.

'You read the diary, I thought you had put it all together.'

'But Joelle is dead. I thought that's what you wanted. Why do you want Stephan to go to jail? Unless . . .'

'Yes, Katherine?'

'Joelle was pregnant too.' It slowly dawned on me. 'You were both seeing Stephan and you both got pregnant at around the same time.'

'Very good, my dear. Now you're beginning to see.'

'So you walked in on Stephan and Joelle. And you got upset, took off out into that storm and you were in a car accident? You're the one who lost the baby?'

'Yes, that was me.'

'And Nicole?' I asked.

'She is Joelle's daughter.'

'My God.'

'God had very little to do with it. If there were a God, would I have lost my child while Joelle got to keep hers? If there were a God, would I have been stuck with Stephan for all these years, knowing I was raising that woman's child? I was just a loving, innocent child myself. I believed Stephan loved me, that we would have a beautiful life together. But instead, it was all a lie and this is the life I got.'

'But you did get to marry Stephan,' I pointed out. 'It seems to me that is what you wanted. Why are you so bitter toward him?'

'Stephan didn't marry me because he loved me. He married me because I was lying in a hospital bed near death. He married me because he thought the car accident was his fault and he felt guilty. Imagine, all these years all he has felt for me is pity,' she said softly. 'You see, that night Joelle had told him that she was pregnant. Imagine, two modern girls in the early eighties, birth control everywhere, and we both turn up pregnant by the same man at the same time.'

'The odds are definitely against it,' I agreed. What exactly are you supposed to say to a psychopath who is holding a gun on you?

'Of course, I had been trying to get pregnant so Stephan and I would be engaged and married. Joelle was already engaged to him and she had just been careless. She never thought it would be a big deal if she got pregnant; they had already decided they wanted a large family as soon as possible. And she was trying to climb out of her lower class and into Stephan's high-society lifestyle. She wasn't like me. She came from a poor family. But her parents and his parents were great friends and they thought joining the two families in marriage was just fine. I knew what Joelle was thinking, though. For a girl like her, a good marriage was the only way she could have pulled herself up. She had already told Stephan that night she was pregnant, and he – as the honourable man he was – at least pretended to be happy and said he was going to marry her immediately. He was going to tell me the next day. But then I walked in on them and I ran off before either of them could stop me, had that horrible accident, and the next time I saw Stephan was a week later, in the hospital. He cried and apologized and promised me that he would always look after me.'

Carole stopped and sighed. Her eyes were full of tears, which she blinked quickly away.

'At that time, they didn't know if I would live, and then they wondered if I would ever walk again. Stephan was guilt-ridden and I decided to take full advantage of that. I could still have the future I had dreamed of, and I was not letting him back out of his promise. I knew I would need to be taken care of if I didn't fully recover, and if I did recover, I intended to take advantage of his money and fame.

'But then, after we were married and I was recovering, he told me that Joelle had delivered his baby. A little girl. They had named her Nicole. Stephan informed me that he had promised Joelle he would raise the baby and that his little girl would want for nothing. Which meant I would be raising Joelle's child. Even that I could have lived with, but Joelle never left us alone. She was always there, on the fringes of our lives, reminding me of that time. Reminding me that Nicole was not my child and that I would never have my own child. I have wanted to kill her since the day Nicole first came into our home. I knew I had to kill her when Nicole started therapy with her. I knew Joelle was going to do something to let the secret out and break up our family. And when she started in on this sexual abuse nonsense . . . Stephan may have been a monster to me, but Nicole was his perfect little princess. He never did anything to harm her. Joelle had ruined my life, but I was not about to let her ruin Nicole's.'

'So you killed Joelle and you plan to make sure Stephan is locked up for that. But what about Nicole?' I asked.

'Nicole is like I was; she is an innocent in all this. I am going to take her away and let her have a normal life. Everyone who could upset my plan will be gone.'

'Carole, why don't you just tell the police this story? I'm sure they'll understand why you did this.' It was a long shot, but I had to give it a try. And where were the police anyway? I wondered. The fire alarms were still ringing and no one had noticed I still wasn't out of the building.

She laughed. 'You do think I'm a fool. No, this story won't be complete for me until Stephan is in jail. Now, before that can happen, we must deal with you.'

'If you shoot me, the police will know it wasn't Stephan. They'll suspect you.'

'But I'm not going to shoot you. You're going to have a horrible accident. There are cables all over the stage and I'm afraid you're going to trip over a very high-voltage wire. It will be tragic. It's quite helpful that you've had a few drinks tonight.'

'What if I won't go with you?'

'Then I will shoot you. I'll be out of the country before they even begin to suspect me. What is it you say in English? In for a penny in for a pound.'

I stood at the door watching her mouth curl into a smile and realized it was the first time I had seen a real smile on that face. Carole really was a psychopath, created over years of self-inflicted suffering, and I knew I was in trouble. Time seemed to be slowing down. I wasn't scared and I certainly hadn't given up yet; I was just thinking. Fast. I needed a weapon, something to defend myself with. But this was my office and I knew there wasn't anything I could use as any sort of a weapon. I didn't even have a ruler. And what could I use to defend myself against a gun? I could try running, but I didn't think that even with the adrenaline rush I had going I could outrun a bullet. I needed to try and buy some time until somebody noticed I was missing and came after me.

I looked slowly over at the coffee pot and she followed my gaze.

'That's a good idea.' She smiled slowly. 'Pour yourself a cup of coffee. A little liquid always helps conduct electricity so much more efficiently.'

I poured some into a large take-out cup, snapped on a lid and wrapped a couple of napkins around it to protect my fingers from the heat. Where the hell were the firemen? I thought, suddenly realizing the fire alarm was still ringing. Wasn't anyone even wondering where I was? The coffee was piping hot. Two napkins wrapped around the Styrofoam cup and I could still feel the heat of it burning through to my fingers. I hoped that this could buy me some time.

'Let's go,' she instructed, waving the gun, and then noticed me staring down at the coffee cup, trying to formulate a plan. 'Bring that along with you. It will make such a good story. You were onstage, spilled your coffee and . . . *zap*. You'll make all the papers.'

Not with the headlines you're planning, I thought, feeling a little more secure now that I had the beginnings of a plan formulating in my mind.

I slowly put my keys in my pocket, opened the door and started down the hall. I didn't turn to see if she was following me – I didn't have to. She was so close I felt her hot breath on my neck. Less subtly I felt the gun poking into the small of my back. I quickly led her through the lobby and into the theatre. We climbed the stairs on to the stage and I turned to face her, wondering what she was going to do next.

'Over there,' she said, waving the gun to her left.

I looked over and saw a mass of cables and wires leading into a power bar and felt a shudder run down my spine.

'Perfect.' She smiled again. 'Now give me your coffee.'

Gladly, bitch, I thought, smiling inwardly as even more adrenaline rushed into my system.

I looked down at the cup again and slowly pulled the lid off. I held it out toward her, but not quite close enough for her to reach. She took a cautious step in my direction, and then another. One more step, I prayed silently, just one more step and, God, I promise I'll go to church every Sunday for the rest of my life and I'll even be nicer to my mother.

Then she took that step.

I saw my arm begin to move before I even heard my brain

give the order. I saw the steam rise from the cup and a couple of drops of liquid spill over the edge of the cup as Newton's Third Law of Motion began to take effect. I looked up at Carole's face and realized she knew what was about to happen. Suddenly time jumped from slow motion to fast forward and I knew she was trying to decide whether to jump out of the way of the scalding liquid or to pull the trigger. My arm jerked up and I heard her scream. Contact! But I heard something else, too. A sort of loud popping or banging noise. And then I felt a searing pain in my arm as I realized she had pulled the trigger.

My hand came up and cupped the wound on my arm. I felt blood trickling through my fingers. I was torn between a gagging feeling in the back of my throat and the weakness in my knees, which was beginning to spread through my whole body.

I heard a loud, high-pitched, continuous screaming and I ordered myself to stop. But the noise didn't go away and I realized it was Carole, her hands clawing at her suit jacket, trying to pull it off as the scalding hot coffee soaked through and burned her chest. I had been aiming for her face. But then I suppose she had been aiming for my head, too.

'Don't faint!' I ordered myself. Did I say that out loud? She was going to get off a second shot if I didn't get it together. I took a deep breath, my first in what felt like hours, felt a tiny bit of strength return to my legs and headed for the door as fast as I could. I stopped for a second at the door that led from the stage and crashed my fist into the fire alarm. I didn't know where the initial alarm had come from, but I was hoping the fire chief would notice a new one flashing on the main panel and send someone down to investigate it. I wanted someone to know where I was, preferably the entire City of Calgary Fire Department and maybe they could even bring half the police department with them. I was definitely in the mood to be rescued now; this was not the time for that independent woman crap I'm always trying to carry off.

I pushed through the next door and was outside the green room. There was a phone in there, should I try to call security? But Carole had stopped screaming. I didn't hear any noise coming from the theatre, which meant she could be right behind that door, right behind me, gun in hand. With that thought in my mind, running suddenly sounded like my best option. I pushed through the theatre doors and into Tin Pan Alley. The security desk was getting closer by the second. I crashed another fire alarm, just to make sure they knew something was going on down here, and then another one just outside the Heritage Theatre for good measure. I was halfway down the hall, feeling dizzy and sick to my stomach. The security desk was still ahead of me and the theatre behind when I heard a door crash open. I could hear feet pounding on the concrete floor, coming from ahead of me, the safety of the security desk, and knew someone had finally figured out I was down here and needed help.

But the theatre door was still behind me and I knew Carole was there. I turned my head as I kept trying to move forward while my body just wanted to sit down and sleep for a little while. I saw her bringing the gun up to take aim. I looked in front of me and saw the security desk was still around the corner. I was too far away; I wasn't going to make it.

'Carole, don't do it,' I begged her. 'You'll never get away with it now.'

'It doesn't matter,' she sneered at me, bringing the gun level with my face. 'This isn't about that any more. There is so much more between us.'

At that moment Ken and two police officers rounded the corner at a gallop.

'She's got a gun!' I screamed at them.

'Get down!' someone ordered, and I didn't waste any time obeying. My body had wanted to fall down for the last several minutes anyway.

'Drop the gun!' someone else yelled. 'Now!'

I have never played baseball in my life, but I did a great imitation of diving and sliding for home base that would have won a World Series game. I heard gunshots and instinctively pulled my arms over my head, trying to protect myself, waiting to feel another bullet penetrate me, praying it would just be another flesh wound. The next thing I knew, someone was pulling at my arms that were still wrapped around my head. I felt the terror that had been welling up inside me trying to break free and I let it. I started screaming.

'Kate, it's Ken. It's OK.' I felt his strong arms trying to hold mine down.

But it wasn't OK; someone had been chasing me with a gun. I kept screaming until I heard the one voice that could bring me back.

'Katie, it's Cam.' His familiar touch replaced Ken's grip on my arms. 'Come on, hon.'

I stopped screaming and opened my eyes a little; wanting to make sure it really was him.

'Are you OK?' he asked. I can't even begin to describe the look on his face, but I knew that after the immediate crisis was over I was in for a lecture to end all lectures.

'I'm bleeding,' I pointed out.

'I know. Come on, let's get you up.'

I felt Cam's strong arms on one side of me and Ken's on the other, slowly pulling me up to my feet.

'What the hell is going on here?' Ken asked.

I wobbled on my feet and fell into Cam. He wrapped an arm around my waist and held me securely.

'I promise I can explain it all,' I assured Ken. 'But I really need a cigarette first. And maybe to sit down.'

'Or maybe an ambulance,' Cam suggested.

'I believe there's one waiting at the stage door,' Ken said. 'Can you walk?'

'I think so. What about . . .' I began and started to turn to look behind me. There were two police officers standing over the inert body of Carole. No one was moving very quickly, and I assumed the worst.

'Don't look,' Cam said, pulling me forward.

'Cam?'

'Let's go,' he said again.

It was very crowded by the stage door. There was an ambulance waiting, and thousands of firemen, or so it seemed, and more police were pulling up by the minute, and every security guard in the building was milling about. As we pushed through, the crowd parted. No one knew what had happened yet, but I think the bloodstain on my shirtsleeve kept them silent for the moment.

On the steps to the stage door, I felt my legs give out and Cam sat me down on the top step. Ken called to the paramedics and one came running over with a stretcher, accompanied by a fireman.

'I don't need that,' I insisted. 'Just let me sit for a second.'

'Katie . . .'

'Cam, I'm having a really bad day,' I warned him. 'This is not a good time to push it.'

'OK, you can sit, but just for a minute.'

'Can I have a cigarette, please?'

He gave me a dirty look but pulled one out and lit it for me. I took a deep drag and immediately started to feel better. Was the Surgeon General really sure that smoking is so bad for you?

The fireman took his helmet off and looked down at me. 'Kate?' he asked.

I looked up and saw Ryan, my best friend's husband, looking down at me.

'What is going on here?' he asked.

'Don't tell Sam,' I begged him.

'How about if someone tells me what's going on?' Ken asked, but the friendliness was leaving his voice as his frustration grew.

I took another drag and then reached into my pocket for the journal pages, meaning to give them to Ken. And then I remembered Carole had taken them from me.

'Carole has some photocopied journal pages on her and I think they will explain most of it,' I said. 'Just so you know who's who, Carole's the one in the car accident. It was her journal.'

'So you found another murderer?' Ken asked. 'And once again almost got yourself killed. If you weren't bleeding, I'd throw you in my car right now and haul your ass to jail.'

'Don't want to ruin the upholstery?' I asked.

'Not for the likes of you,' he said sternly, but his eyes were soft and I laughed.

'OK, OK. I guess I did get a little bit mixed up in all this. But I swear I wasn't doing anything; I just read the journal. I guess she just saw me with it and thought I would figure it out,' I tried. 'Ouch!'

'Sorry.'

The paramedic had come from the ambulance with his medical bag to where we were sitting on the steps and was snipping away at my shirt sleeve.

'That's a good shirt,' I complained.

'Was a good shirt, Kate,' Ryan replied. 'Now behave yourself and let him do his job,'

'This is the price you pay for meddling,' Ken said. 'Didn't you just get a cast off one of those arms?'

'Is it bad?' I asked him, not really wanting to know the answer to my question.

'Looks like it's just a flesh wound,' the paramedic replied, pulling out a roll of gauze and wrapping it around my arm.

'Ouch!' I whined again.

'Quit complaining,' Cam said, 'It could have been much worse.'

'Are you pushing your luck again?' I asked, giving him another dirty look.

'God, you are cranky when you get shot,' he joked.

I looked at him and laughed, despite myself. I fell against him, still laughing, feeling almost hysterical.

'I do love you,' I said.

'Me too.'

'Still?'

'So far. But you're really pushing it, Katie. Love, honour and cherish is one thing. This whole guns and knives thing isn't what I signed up for.'

'But you still love me?' I asked again.

'Yeah, sure.'

'Good.'

'So now that you're secure about that, will you please let us take you to the hospital?' Ken asked. 'I'd like to get you checked out so I know it's safe to interrogate you ruthlessly.'

'OK, but I'm walking to the ambulance,' I insisted.

'Is she always like this?' the paramedic asked Ryan. Everyone laughed.

'A little respect for the patient?' I asked, trying to stand and then subtly grabbing Cam's arm so no one saw how shaky I really was. No one except Cam, who stood up and then picked me up.

'If you're trying to impress me . . .'

'Yes?' he said.

'It's working.'

And then I finally did it. For the first time in my life, I fainted.

Friday November 7

It seemed strange to be sitting in a different theatre, because I'm so used to being in mine. But at least I had enough pull to get pretty good seats. Cam and I sat in the Concert Hall, dressed in our finery. I had on the black dress, the pearls, the black hose and pumps. My grown-up look, I like to call it. Cam almost took my breath away when I saw him come down in his new slate-coloured suit and black turtleneck. Cam was a real anomaly in my life; he didn't fit a type. I had always dated types before and I had thought he was going to be the handyman, the blue-collar guy. But Cam fits into any world I choose to bring him into. I had started to walk towards him with that look in my eyes when he first came down the stairs, but he simply turned me around, handed me my shawl and pointed me towards the door.

'We'll be late,' he'd said.

We had driven through the quiet city, parked underground – just like the real theatre patrons do – and had a drink at the bar, staffed by a bartender that I actually didn't know. And now we sat in the Concert Hall. Somehow, the powers that be had moved mountains and managed to get it mostly back into one piece in time for the closing ceremonies. So it was going to be their theatre in the papers, not mine. Graham had been pouting severely about that until I managed to get a private box for him and Mandi. It was our birthday present to him since I had sort of ruined his birthday party. And now he sat up there quite happily, pointing out all the stars to his date. But it seemed right, in some way. This was the Concert Hall and the winner of the competition should have their debut performance in this place, not cramped on my little stage that was designed for live theatre rather than a full orchestra. But I also felt it was right that we were here. We needed to see this through to the end, and this, finally, was the end.

I noticed my shawl had slid down and I pulled it up over the bandage on my arm, not wanting to draw attention to it or myself. Cam noticed and took my free hand in his and gave it a squeeze.

'Is it sore?' he asked.

'Not really. I'm a pretty tough chick, you know?'

'Apparently.' He kissed me on the cheek and I felt a blush grow on my face.

Before I could say anything, the house lights dimmed and the musicians on stage grew silent. The concertmaster got up, walked over to the grand piano sitting in the middle of the stage, and struck a note. The violins began tuning and, after a moment, another note was struck and another as the rest of the orchestra joined in. Then the concertmaster sat down and there was silence. I saw the door open stage-right and the Maestro walked out in full regalia – tux, tails, baton. His blue eyes sparkled in the light under the shock of white hair. The audience was on its feet. Maestro Ferentino had been the founding conductor of the FSO and the patrons and the city loved him. I glanced over to my right and saw Stephan lead the standing ovation, a huge smile on his face. I don't think I'd seen Stephan with a real smile like that since I was twenty-one years old and I'd said something young and stupid. My naive remarks had always made him laugh back then and I was pleased to see him happy again. I've never hated Stephan, though I know that both Cam and my mother really want me to. As a matter of fact, I can't even work out what I feel for him any more; the events of the past few weeks were still swirling in my brain and I hadn't finished sorting them all out yet. But it felt right that he was sitting several rows away and I was here with Cam.

Maestro Ferentino had endured the ovation for as long as he could, and then finally got the crowd settled down and he turned and led the orchestra through their first number. Then he left the stage and returned with the winner of the festival on his arm. He stepped back and let her take her bows as the crowd cheered.

Somehow, the story would have ended well if it had been Nicole standing up there. And, according to Stephan, it would have been. But the morning after Carole was killed, Nicole had withdrawn from the festival. She had told them that there would be no way she would be able to keep up the concert schedule that would be demanded of her for the next year, with the loss of her mother and the circumstances surrounding that loss. Nicole had announced she was going to take a year off, spend time with her father and then see if anyone still wanted to hear her perform. So the brilliant young girl from Romania took her place behind the Bosendorfer grand and began her public life.

We had been invited backstage for a champagne celebration after the concert. I wasn't sure if I wanted to go or not, but now here we were, drinking champagne with the rich and famous. Stephan saw me before I saw him, so I forced a smile for him as he pulled me to him and kissed me on both cheeks.

'Ouch,' I said, as he grazed my wound.

'Oh, I am sorry, I forgot about that,' he said solicitously. 'Are you all right?'

'I'm fine,' I assured him, even though that subtle throb had just begun again. And not a painkiller in site.

'Katie – I mean Kate – what did you think of the concert?' he asked.

'You know I love Maestro Ferentino, but that was your orchestra, that was your rehearsal. I know he just got into town this morning. How did you feel about watching someone else conduct your brilliant performance?'

'It's funny,' he said, pausing to take a sip of his champagne, 'I thought it would be horrible. I wasn't even going to sit in the audience, but I knew that wouldn't look good, would it? But I felt quite detached. I know where I am really meant to be right now, and that is with my daughter, helping her heal from all that we have done to her.'

'I'm glad,' I said and meant it. 'How is Nicole doing?'

'Colie is very sad and very confused. We kept a lot of secrets from her and we manipulated her life and I am incredibly sorry for that. We all did it in the name of love, but that doesn't mean it was for the best, does it?'

'I suppose not.'

'So, we will go home, to Paris. We have an apartment there

that Colie has always loved, and we will see doctors, and we will talk endlessly and we will make music and we will see what comes out of it in the end. But I love my daughter and I will not give up on her or walk away from this. I am going to be there no matter what it takes.'

I couldn't help myself. I knew it might tick Cam off, but I hugged Stephan.

'I'm so sorry for the both of you,' I told him. 'But I am so happy to hear you say this. I know you will both be just fine.'

'*Merci, ma chérie*,' he whispered in my ear and then gently separated himself from me. 'Now I must go and say my good-byes, we are flying back in three hours and I must get back to Colie.'

'Well, you've got my email address; maybe Colie will write me when she's feeling up to it?'

'We'll always be in touch,' he said. 'I promise you that.'

Stephan shook Cam's hand and held it for a minute. 'You have an amazing woman there,' he said. 'Take good care of her.'

'I always do.' Cam smiled back at him.

'I guess that's true,' Stephan said, backing off. After all, he hadn't been there when I'd been shot. What else could he say to Cam?

'Katie, I hope you will find it in your heart to forgive me for what I have put you through. I never meant to put you in harm's way,' he promised. 'I was so desperate I didn't know what I was doing.'

'Stephan, it's OK,' I said. 'It's in the past, just like everything else to do with us. We'll start fresh from here.'

He smiled a bittersweet smile and then crossed the wings, went through the door and was gone.

Cam's arm came around my shoulder and pulled me close to him. 'You OK?' he asked, handing me his handkerchief.

'Uh-uh,' I lied, dabbing at my eyes.

'Is it hard to see him leave?' he asked. 'Even now?'

'Oh, God no!' I laughed, realizing what Cam had been thinking. 'The one good thing about this is I realized how I am *so* over Stephan. He is really a total jerk. I just hope he doesn't waste this opportunity to become a nice human being. It's Nicole. I'm just so sad for that little girl.'

Cam squeezed me tight and led me out of the concert hall. 'We can cancel dinner if you want,' he told me.

'No, I'm fine,' I said, taking a deep breath and trying to make myself mentally move on.

He walked me down the hall to Vaudeville's and the hostess led us to our table. We could tell our guests were there, as their coats were draped over the back of their chairs and there were drinks at the places, but they were nowhere in sight.

'The mannequins?' I suggested.

Cam pulled out my chair and then sat down beside me. We scanned the restaurant's various levels, and there they were, checking out the costumes on the mannequins. Vaudeville's is decorated with costumes from various plays that had graced the theatres here throughout the years. And many people spend their first time here wandering past the displays, reading about the costumes, and some even have their pictures taken with a costume from their favourite play. Eventually they saw us and made their way back down to the table.

'Kate.' Rebecca smiled, giving me a hug.

'Ouch.' I had to stop doing that.

She pulled away and inspected my arm where the shawl had fallen down again. 'What's this?'

'It's where Carole shot—'

'An accident at work,' Ken Lincoln interrupted, pulling out a chair for his wife.

'Wow, you really don't tell her anything about your work, do you?' I asked.

'And that surprises you?' Cam asked me. 'When was the last time you told me the whole story?'

'All right, we're not getting into this game,' Rebecca said firmly. 'Because every time we do, my husband steers it to you guys and then I end up never finding out what happened. So, Kate, what happened to your arm?'

I looked over at Detective Lincoln with a questioning glance, then ignored his warning look and turned to Rebecca. 'I got shot,' I said. 'By the wife of my college professor, who I had an affair with back in my university days.'

'Wow, I've heard of people waiting to get revenge, but that's an awfully long time.'

‘Well, it’s never that straightforward,’ I continued. ‘Seems she had just killed her husband’s first fiancée.’

Her mouth dropped. ‘Was my husband involved in this at all?’

I didn’t even look at Ken this time. ‘Well, I haven’t seen much of him, but he’s been around. I’m pretty sure he saved my life, but I’m a little foggy on those particular details, I’m afraid.’

Rebecca swatted Ken hard on his shoulder. ‘You know, I do understand you wanting to protect me from things, but you don’t have to keep *everything* a secret.’ She turned back to me. ‘So, let’s hear the story then.’

‘I don’t suppose you’d like to tell us about the closing performance of the festival?’ Ken asked. ‘I’d really love to hear what you thought about that.’

‘Hey, Ken, the night’s young.’ I smiled at him. ‘Lots of time for all sorts of stories.’

The waitress walked by and the detective stopped her, holding up his glass.

‘I’ll have another Scotch,’ he said. ‘And make this one a double, please.’

I laughed and then began the condensed version of the story for Rebecca. And I decided that I was happy this would be the last time I would have to tell the story of Stephan and me for a long, long time. I smiled over at Cam as he patiently listened once again, and I realized I had a much better story in the works right now.

Epilogue

The good thing about being shot is that it gets you a few days off work, even if it is only a flesh wound. The bad thing about being shot is that your mother wants to stay with you even longer to take care of you, despite the fact that she herself is injured and probably needs someone to take care of *her*. To my great relief, Cam, Larry and I managed to talk her out of staying. I think the only reason she finally agreed was because she knew Cam was here and she trusted he would take good care of me.

We got them into a cab for the airport and I breathed a sigh of relief when it pulled away from the curb. We were finally alone again and I was ready to take another go at starting our lives together.

Cam held my hand as we walked slowly back up to the apartment. He settled me on the couch with a cup of tea, put a movie in and sat down beside me. We were just cuddled up comfortably when the phone rang. I started to get up to answer it, but a dirty look from Cam and I sat right back down. He went into the kitchen and came back out with a hammer in his hand. He calmly unplugged the phone and set it on the floor, then proceeded to demolish it with the hammer. When he was sure it wouldn't ring again, he set the hammer down and joined me on the couch, a smug look on his face. I was really glad the ringer was off on the phone upstairs, or he might have gone after that one next.

'Feel better now?' I asked.

'Much.'

I guessed no one would be bothering us for the next couple of days, and I can't say I really minded. We cuddled back up, intent on the movie, when there was a knock on the door.

Cam stood up to answer it, picking the hammer up on his way.

‘Cam!’ I called after him and chased him to the door. Looks like we weren’t going to be alone after all. I wrestled the hammer from his hand and he kissed me. Another frantic knock brought our attention back to the interruption and Cam undid the locks, opening the door a crack.

‘Oh my God, I can’t believe it’s you!’